Chicana Sexuality and Gender

A book in the series

LATIN AMERICA OTHERWISE:

LANGUAGES, EMPIRES, NATIONS

Series editors:

Walter D. Mignolo, *Duke University*

Irene Silverblatt, *Duke University*

Sonia Saldívar-Hull, *University of Texas, San Antonio*

Latin America Otherwise: Languages, Empires, Nations is a critical series. It aims to explore the emergence and consequences of concepts used to define "Latin America" while at the same time exploring the broad interplay of political, economic, and cultural practices that have shaped Latin American worlds. Latin America, at the crossroads of competing imperial designs and local responses, has been construed as a geocultural and geopolitical entity since the nineteenth century. This series provides a starting point to redefine Latin America as a configuration of political, linguistic, cultural, and economic intersections that demands a continuous reappraisal of the role of the Americas in history, and of the ongoing process of globalization and the relocation of people and cultures that have characterized Latin America's experience. *Latin America Otherwise: Languages, Empires, Nations* is a forum that confronts established geocultural constructions, rethinks area studies and disciplinary boundaries, assesses convictions of the academy and of public policy, and correspondingly demands that the practices through which we produce knowledge and understanding about and from Latin America be subject to rigorous and critical scrutiny.

Beginning in the precolonial indigenous past, cultural symbols such as the Aztec mother earth goddesses have exerted a profound impact on the way women of Mexican descent have understood their sexuality and have imagined their roles within society and the family. Later history added other icons to the Aztec goddesses—namely, La Malinche, La Llorona, and the La Virgen de Guadalupe. Through legends, myths, and stories told to children and shared within communities and families, each of these figures has influenced generations of individuals in the construction of their gender identities. This present work examines the way different groups of Chicana and U.S. Mexicana women have made use of these cultural symbols to negotiate, contest, and transform the forces that have confined or demeaned them. The women reimagine (or "transcode," to use Stuart Hall's term) the negative elements attached to these figures and assign them new meanings as part of a struggle for self-empowerment and to defeat racial stereotypes and discrimination.

In studying these cultural refigurings, *Chicana Sexuality and Gender: Cultural Refiguring in Literature, Oral History, and Art* focuses on two distinct groups: Chicana writers and artists, who constitute a professional intellectual class, and other working-class and semiprofessional women whose oral narratives of their own lives collected by the author are analyzed along with the writing and visual representations of the professional intellectuals. To accomplish this Blake employs Michel Foucault's concept of residual countermemory. Following George Lipsitz's use of countermemory, Blake positions the narratives of these women as "the local, the immediate, and the personal" that builds out toward the total story, even though the total may never be fully known. Such narratives, Debra Blake argues, check the impulse to valorize a single unifying story and reveal the buried histories not written into the dominant discourse. She demonstrates how for both groups this cultural refiguring arises from the interrelated processes of revising history and recovering memory. In brief, the women follow the example of "the woman of discord" by disrupting the dominant discourses that have constructed these icons.

This meticulous interdisciplinary study reaffirms the importance of recognizing the diversity within a single culture, and accepting that so-called unitary symbols inspire diverse practices.

Debra J. Blake

✿ CHICANA SEXUALITY AND GENDER

Cultural Refiguring in Literature, Oral History, and Art

DUKE UNIVERSITY PRESS *Durham and London 2008*

© 2008 DUKE UNIVERSITY PRESS

Printed in the United States of America
on acid-free paper ∞

Designed by C. H. Westmoreland
Typeset in Scala with Meta display
by Keystone Typesetting, Inc.

Library of Congress Cataloging-in-Publication Data
appear on the last printed page of this book.

FOR GLORIA E. ANZALDÚA,

A BRILLIANT SCHOLAR OF INCOMPARABLE HUMILITY

FOR ALL THE WOMEN

WHO HAVE BEEN ABUSED OR VIOLATED

FOR MY FOREMOTHERS,

HELEN, PAULINE, AND GERMAINE

✣ CONTENTS

✿ ACKNOWLEDGMENTS

I thank my parents, Germaine and Willard, for supporting me through trying times. I remember my grandmothers, Pauline, who inspired me through her persistence and dignity in poverty, and Helen, who inspired me through laughter, dancing, and a tremendous will to live. Special thanks are due Barbara Eckstein at the University of Iowa for her unending support of my project and for encouraging me to conduct interviews with nonacademic women; Nancy "Rusty" Barceló for mentoring me in Chicana issues and encouraging me to attend NACCS; and Ralph Cintrón for guiding me to U.S. Mexicanas in Iowa.

Many people in Iowa City provided a combination of personal and professional support that sustained me. I can't thank them enough. Martha Patterson remains my greatest supporter and adviser. Carmen Ábrego provided friendship y buena comida. Radhika Parameswaran and Kevin Newsom gave me wonderful Indian meals and relaxing conversation. The members of the Women against Racism Committee, Radhika, Anne Donadey, Jodi Byrd, Junko Kabayashi, and Marcia Morris, provided insight and advice. My Iowa City "family," Katy Stavreva, Doug Anderson, Kai Lin Wu, Lauren Smith, Jenny Cooley, and Gloria Medina Sancho, at various times and locations supported a living space that was "home," that was fun, and where women's issues and theoretical and social concerns were always a topic of discussion.

Numerous others aided my research efforts. I thank Edmundo Cavazos for his generosity in driving me to meet the women I interviewed in Iowa and for sharing his pozole español recipe; Bryce Milligan in San Antonio for arranging interviews for me in that city during the 1995 Hijas del

Quinto Sol Conference; Randa Kutob for suggesting the interviews with the mensajeras in Tucson; Héctor Contreras and Joanne O'Hare for providing living spaces during my research trips to Tucson. This book would not be what it is today without the support and encouragement of Gloria Anzaldúa, Denise Chávez, Tey Diana Rebolledo, Ana Castillo, Marta Sánchez, Patricia Preciado Martin, Cecilia Portal, José Limón, Yolanda López, and Ester Hernández, among others. I am truly grateful to every one. More recently, I am indebted to María Herrera-Sobek, Norma Cantú, Elvia Nieble, James Wojtaszek, and Sherry Quan Lee, who fortified me with kindness and love. Abrazos.

I appreciate the help of the staff at the Cemanahuac Educational Community in Cuernavaca, Mexico, and especially Marie-Josée "Caniche" Mata, who shared her knowledge of Mesoamerican goddesses and the codices with me. I want to acknowledge the aid and friendship of Blanca Gutiérrez Galindo, who introduced me to Coyolxauhqui and the Templo Mayor Museum; Joe Rubio, who toured the ruins of Cholula with me and helped me understand the places and politics of San Antonio; and Dal Liddle, who diligently transcribed the interviews. The following reference librarians provided significant information and deserve many thanks: Nancy Brown at the Center for Southwest Research, Zimmerman Library, University of New Mexico; Teresa Márquez at the University of New Mexico Libraries; Christine Marin at the Special Collections Library, Arizona State University; and Margo Gutierrez at the Benson Latin American Collection, University of Texas, Austin.

I greatly appreciate the contributions of the women who shared their lives with me in oral history interviews; your lives and words have touched mine deeply. I heartily thank Virginia Urias, Evelyn Gonzales, Irma Vásquez, and all of the Tucson Mensajeras de Salud; Ventura Loya, Cindy Siqueiros, and Minerva Godoy in Iowa; and Mary Ozuna, Aurora Harada, and Vicki Rivera Reyes in San Antonio.

Various organizations funded my research, writing, and travel. The McKnight Foundation and the University of Minnesota provided summer stipends and conference funding. The American Association of University Women Educational Foundation and the University of Iowa Graduate College provided year-long fellowships. The University of Iowa Department of English provided financial support for travel to conduct archival research and interviews, and Associate Dean James Jacobson and Professor Kathleen Diffley found additional funding for travel and interview transcriptions. The U.S. Department of Education, National Resource Center Foreign Language and Area Studies Fellowship, and the University of Iowa Center for Studies Abroad supported two summers of study in Mexico.

I want to thank Reynolds Smith at Duke University Press for believing in this project through the long haul, and the readers and editorial board members who provided stimulating and beneficial reviews of the manuscript.

An excerpt from chapter 2 was published in *Perspectivas transatlánticas en la literatura chicana: Ensayos y creatividad*, ed. María Herrera-Sobek, Francisco Lomelí, and Juan Antonio Perles Rochel (Málaga, Spain: Servicio de Publicaciones de la Universidad de Málaga, 2002); and sections of chapter 5 were published in the article "Reading Dynamics of Power through Mexican-Origin Women's Oral Histories," *Frontiers: A Journal of Women's Studies* 14.3 (1998): 24–41.

✦ INTRODUCTION

In an interview in 1994, Gloria Anzaldúa noted that one goal of her writing was to "look at who constructs knowledges, realities, and information and how they control people's identities through that construction."[1] Anzaldúa's understanding of how external forces shape and influence perceptions of Chicanas and U.S. Mexicanas speaks to the power of representation. Her efforts to expose circumscribing images and false histories, along with those of other Chicana writers and artists, constitute one element in the struggle for individual and community definition. Another important element entails the agency of self-representation, what Cherríe Moraga calls *"the right to passion,"* the right of every Chicana and Mexicana to define herself and "love herself as both female and mestiza."[2]

The process by which women recover passion and come to power often involves recognizing the power of others to circumscribe women's lives through physical force and socially regulating ideas. The oral, written, and visual texts discussed in this book eloquently testify to struggles for self-empowerment and to an awareness of oppressive conditions affecting Chicanas and U.S. Mexicanas. The narratives depict women impassioned to speak up and act out against forces that create and maintain limiting gender roles, control and violate female sexuality and bodies, and perpetuate racist stereotypes and discrimination. At the same time, the narratives portray everyday, ordinary human beings, Chicanas and U.S. Mexicanas who maintain and negotiate, as well as contest, the forces that attempt to confine them. This book emphasizes how the storytellers themselves make meaning of their worlds and the complexities, contradictions, and varied experiences that characterize their existences.[3] Their narratives reveal how Chicanas and U.S. Mexicanas are influenced by and choose to act within, among, or against competing ideologies.

Chicana Sexuality and Gender is the first full-length study of Chicana literature to analyze oral histories as narrative representations along with fictional writings and visual artists' representations. When I began this study I intended it to focus on the writings of the Chicana feminist authors Anzaldúa, Ana Castillo, Sandra Cisneros, Moraga, and Alma Villanueva. The more I thought about their quite radical representations of Chicanas, the more I wondered how their nonacademic contemporaries, women of Mexican origin or descent living in the United States, would represent themselves. At first, I began looking for existing oral accounts by working- and middle-class women to understand a range of perspectives. However, I found few published or archived sources, and they did not explore contemporary issues of identity, spirituality, sexuality, race, or intimate partner relationships, including violence against women, which are common themes in Chicana writings.[4] The lack of existing narratives led me to gather oral histories by nine women: Minerva Godoy, Ventura Loya, and Cindy Siqueiros from Muscatine, Iowa; Vicki Rivera Reyes, Aurora Harada, and Mary Ozuna from San Antonio, Texas; and Evelyn Gonzales, Virginia Urias, and Irma Vásquez from Tucson, Arizona.[5] In relating personal experiences of struggle and accomplishment, their narratives alter dominant representations of how U.S. Mexicanas act and think. Their oral histories describe individual challenges to and revisions of traditional norms through the representations of their own life actions in the late-twentieth-century United States.

The oral histories I gathered represent the perspectives of five working-class and four semiprofessional women. I define "working class" as individuals who work or whose spouses or partners work at manual, unskilled, or clerical labor. In this study, the five working-class women include two women of retirement age, who completed high school or the equivalent, did not work outside the home or only for brief periods, and whose husbands are or were manual laborers. Also included are two divorced women, one who worked as a migrant farm worker and factory laborer, received her GED certificate later in life, and now lives on government disability payments. The other divorced woman began attending engineering college in Mexico but quit school after one year when she married and began raising children. She now lives with her daughter. The fifth woman, who supported herself first as a factory laborer and then as a

bookkeeper, is single and retired. Four additional women can be identified as "semiprofessional" by their schooling and the types of jobs in
which they are employed. Three women in their twenties have taken
community college or university courses working toward a B.A. degree.
They work fulltime in semiprofessional positions in nursing, insurance,
and social work. Their husbands work as unskilled laborers. One woman,
a single parent in her thirties, has completed a B.A. degree in secondary
education and an M.A. degree in special education. At the time of the
interviews, she was unable to find full-time employment as a teacher and
worked part time in secretarial positions and as a substitute teacher. The
latter was the only one of the nine women who had heard of or read a work
by a Chicana or Chicano author. Sandra Cisneros lived on the same street
she did and had given her a copy of *The House on Mango Street*.

Throughout the book, I use the term "U.S. Mexicanas" when speaking
of the nine working-class and semiprofessional women as a group. In
their historias, five of the women preferred to call themselves "Mexican"
or "Mexicana." The four others identified as "Mexican American," "Mexican with American and Mexican ideas," "Hispanic," and "American with
Hispanic background." The latter two, who use the official Census Bureau
term, are affiliated with U.S. government or education agencies that use
"Hispanic" as the official term for all Latin Americans and Spaniards
without distinguishing between the two. For both women, Mexico is their
national, cultural, and ancestral referent. One woman uses "Mexican
American" interchangeably with "Hispanic," and the other, of Mexican
and Dutch with some indigenous ancestry, spoke at length about her
pride in Mexican heritage and traditions. Several of the women remarked
that they identify themselves with more than one national, racial, ethnic,
or social cultural community, revealing palimpsestic or "nested identities."[6] "U.S. Mexicana" designates the women's status as U.S. citizens by
birth or naturalization, *and* their national, social cultural, and ethnic affiliation as women of Mexican origin or descent. Five of the women were
born in the United States and are second- or third-generation children of
Mexican immigrants. At the time I gathered their oral histories, the four
women born in Mexico had lived in the United States from ten to forty
years and are naturalized citizens. In referring to the women as U.S.
Mexicanas, I hope to remain sensitive to their expressed affiliation with
Mexico and Mexican heritage, while clarifying for readers their U.S. residency, which has influenced their thinking about rights and opportuni-

ties, especially for women. Notably, none of them identifies as Chicana. Several expressed discomfort with what some construe as the term's negative associations with "low class" or "wetback" status.

In contrast, the writers and artists whose works I discuss identify as Chicana, a term recovered in the Chicano/a civil rights movement of the 1960s and 1970s, which signals a political and historical awareness of racism, colonialism, and classism. Simultaneously, the term recognizes pride in indigenous and mestiza heritage. Chicana, as differentiated from Chicano, also reflects a strong feminist and lesbian of color sensibility, including identification with Third World feminist struggles. I also characterize the Chicana writers and visual artists whose works I discuss as "professional intellectuals." For the purposes of this study, professional intellectuals are individuals who have attained advanced degrees and are engaged in cultural change activities of an intellectual nature such as literary, theoretical, or artistic work, which constitutes a primary element of the profession by which they earn a living. Specifically, I chose the term "professional," because other terms frequently used such as "organic" or "public" did not fully represent the complexities of social class locations the Chicana authors and artists represent.[7] For example, many of the Chicana writers and visual artists who were born and raised in working-class locations write or create art with that experience in mind. Nonetheless, as professional intellectuals they are affiliated in some way with academia, for example, through the adoption of their literary works as standard texts for college courses, or as professors, speakers, or artists in residence at colleges and universities. Because of their current status as highly educated, middle-class Chicanas, their writings also portray well-researched historical ideas and theoretical perspectives.

Due to the historical lack of access to educational opportunities that Chicano/as and Mexicano/as have had in the United States, published scholarly analyses and fictional writings by them understandably emphasize *writing* as the desirable means of expressing subjectivity. This issue is heightened for Chicanas and U.S. Mexicanas because of the traditional lack of encouragement women receive to attend college and pursue writing careers. Writing is a self-produced form of expression, a narrative generated by the author herself and representing her own vision of self and the world. In contrast, most oral histories are initiated by an individual or organization outside the narrator's everyday world. Consequently, oral histories are mediated by interactions between the narrator and the interviewer (who often exist in different life circumstances) and by transferal of the spoken word to written, even translated, form. Thus, a published oral history is dually or collaboratively authored, and in the case of collected oral histories, multiply voiced, rather than self-produced.[8] Yet, few working-class or semiprofessional U.S. Mexicanas are writers and their voices and experiences are rarely heard in public discourse. Collected oral histories and life stories provide a venue by which working-class and semiprofessional women can reflect on their lives and creatively represent their worldview in a manner similar to Chicana writings.

In the following chapters, I look at the ways the Chicana professional intellectuals and the U.S. Mexicana working-class and semiprofessional women culturally refigure confining and demeaning constructions of female gender roles and racial, ethnic, and sexual identities. I use "cultural refiguring" to imply agency, a conscious choice to think and act for oneself or in the interests of a community. Cultural refiguring identifies deficiencies and destructive images, ideas, symbols, and practices directed toward women and disenfranchised peoples. It attempts to replace denigratory concepts with constructive and affirmative understandings, representations, or actions that view women as complex, multifaceted human beings. Cultural refiguring encompasses theories advocating social change, visual and symbolic revisions of stereotypes, *and* everyday acts of women's resistance that occur on a regular basis but often go unheralded and unnoticed.[9] This study focuses on narrative retellings, yet I read the oral and written texts as working through and beyond narrative boundaries to impact the material existence of women's everyday experiences. For example, the Tucson, Arizona, women's oral histories tell of their efforts to renegotiate embodied conceptions of female physical health and sexual pleasure through volunteer work encouraging lower-income women and men to use condoms for prevention of sexual disease. Their efforts work toward greater freedom and pleasure for women, who benefit from condoms as a birth control method, as well as a disease prevention device. Similarly, the professional intellectuals' essays and fictional stories raise awareness of how institutions and ideologies, such as the Catholic Church and Chicano nationalism, contribute to female sexual repression and inadequate gender role options. The writings provide alternative ways of thinking about female subjectivity and racial and ethnic identity by focusing on female pleasure, creativity, intellect, and indigenous identity. The refiguring efforts in the oral and written narratives provide alternative understandings of cultural norms and of the histories and collective memories that inform them. They work toward improving the quality and conditions of women's lives and increasing opportunities for self-fulfillment.

The oral and written narratives reveal that Chicanas and U.S. Mexicanas engage a wide range of actions and ideas that promote cultural refiguring such as publishing creative writing, theorizing new visions of being, facilitating women-centered support groups, participating in volunteer educational work or political activism, and performing individual acts of resistance to domination and control. Inevitably, differences in class, education, and social status among the working-class, semiprofessional, and professional intellectual women produce change efforts that are specific to each woman's particular economic and educational location. My special concern lies in examining the diverse strategies that emerge from these differences to better understand the many dimensions of Chicana and U.S. Mexicana experience. The project of this book is to read the diverse representational strategies among academic-affiliated and nonacademic-affiliated women and consider how their ideas and actions expand lifestyle choices and promote the health and well-being of women of Mexican origin or descent. Rather than considering the ideas in opposition to one another, I consider each woman's representational strategy as existing along a continuum of Chicana feminist thinking.

One of the most potent means by which the women in this study address regulatory forces occurs when they wield the power of representation to define what it means to be Chicana or U.S. Mexicana through reimaginings of culturally significant female histories, stories, and symbols. In particular, they draw strength and inspiration from creating their own visions of Mexican female cultural symbols such as La Virgen de Guadalupe, La Malinche, La Llorona, and Mexica goddesses. The significance of these reimagined female images resides not only in how they expose the ways in which Chicanas and U.S. Mexicanas have been demeaned, devalued, violated, and misrepresented but in how the women characterize themselves—and by association all Chicanas and U.S. Mexicanas—as active, sexual, philosophical, and creative women. Nowhere are these elements more evident than in the fictional and autobiographical literary works of the five Chicana feminist professional intellectuals.

Recurring themes in their writings expose how Spanish Catholic religious teachings and Mexican and white, male-dominated cultural concepts contribute to violence against women. They also reveal how sexual repression, guilt, or the shaming of sexually active women limits female development and how the idealization of wife and mother as the culturally mandated roles for women confines them. The writers refute narrow views of women by creating fictional characters or writing about themselves as women who boldly and painfully confront and reject cultural prescriptions. They embrace indigenous symbols, such as Mexica goddesses and La Malinche, reconceiving them as powerful female figures, symbols of artistic inspiration, sexual expression, and indigenous and mestiza identity. While the refigurings of Mexican female cultural symbols serve an important purpose in the authors' or characters' life stories, they do not transform the world. Instead, the Chicana feminist writings I discuss reveal the complicated struggles of women who live with oppression while striving for or imagining self-determination and social change. As the writers and their fictional characters testify, stepping outside the bounds of accepted behavior always comes with a psychological and emotional price, often ostracization from family and community. Feminist refigurings of Mexican female cultural symbols do not replace traditional patriarchal representations or erase the sexist, heterosexist, or racist ideologies that sometimes accompany the symbols. Rather, the Chicana writers' refigurings must be understood as competing with well-established Mexican Catholic religious and cultural representations and entrenched ideologies of gender roles for women.

The working-class and semiprofessional women's oral representations of themselves and Mexican female cultural symbols are not as boldly feminist or revisionist as the professional intellectuals' writings. However, their thoughts and actions reflect the influence of second-wave U.S. feminist thought that circulates widely regarding choices, rights, and opportunities for women. Although I did not ask, I suspect they would not call themselves feminists, given the cultural and societal stigmas attached to this term. Their self-representations are influenced by well-known Mexican cultural and religious beliefs, especially La Virgen de Guadalupe, which contrasts with the Chicana authors' and artists.' Furthermore, the U.S. Mexicanas' refigurings are enacted through volunteer work they perform in their communities or in their daily responses to oppressive living, working, or relationship conditions. In other words, the cultural refiguring they employ involves interpersonal actions rather than intellectual or imaginative thinking. In saying this, I am *not* implying that the active or practical response is better than the creative or theoretical. Instead, in this study, I attempt to show a range of responses and strategies used by Chicanas and U.S. Mexicanas to address harmful power dynamics.

Regarding the oral histories I gathered, the small sampling of women is not intended to represent the views of all or even many U.S. Mexicanas, and the inferences I draw are intended to apply only to these specific oral histories. In addition, the social-class distinctions I use reveal that some voices are not represented in this study, including those of recent or undocumented Mexican immigrant women and the growing number of professional women such as lawyers, doctors, and business owners or executives. A much larger and qualitatively different study is necessary to encompass the diversity of experience among women of Mexican origin or descent living in the United States.

Some explanation of the language, terminology, and spelling I use in this study is necessary. I chose not to italicize Spanish terms or phrases, except when they appear italicized in quotations or titles by other writers. This decision represents bilingualism as a common language practice of many Chicanas and U.S. Mexicanas, and as resistance to assimilation. Accent marks are used in individuals' names according to their preferences.

In chapter 3 and elsewhere, I use the Spanish term "las historias" in its dual meaning of both histories *and* stories to contribute to an understanding of the oral narratives as historical and fictional accounts. This term complicates any hard and fast distinctions between history as fact and story as fiction. The oral narratives provide a little-known history of contemporary U.S. Mexicanas' experiences. They also produce stories from the perspective of working-class and semiprofessional women, similar to literary depictions by Chicana writers that interweave personal and familial experiences. When referencing La Llorona (the Wailing Woman), I delete the article "La" when English articles appear in the same phrase. While this usage may seem odd, it eliminates the double articles that would otherwise result. Examples include "the Llorona legend" or "a Llorona moment," which translate as "the Wailing Woman legend" and "a Wailing Woman moment." I also capitalize the articles in the names of the Mexican female cultural symbols I discuss to indicate their iconic status, for example as in "La Malinche," "La Llorona," or "La Virgen."

Finally, I have chosen to use the more generic yet preferable term "indigenous," rather than "Aztec," when referring to the peoples and cultures of the central Mexican plateau region. In the seventeenth and eighteenth centuries, Spanish and European historians, anthropologists, and archaeologists began using the term "Aztec," conflating distinct indigenous peoples of the central plateau region who shared similar cultural symbols and practices, including the language Nahuatl. However, "Aztec" is not a Nahuatl word, nor was it used by Nahuatl speakers in referring to themselves. European scholars invented "Aztec" from the word "Aztlan," which refers to the originary place of the "Mexica" (pronounced mě-shē-kǎ) or "Tenochca" people, a specific indigenous group that came to power in the region. Widespread use of "Aztec" has propagated misinformation and misunderstandings about the diverse indigenous peoples of the central plateau region. For example, when scholarly (or popular) writings reference the "Aztec empire" or the "Aztec people," a unified cultural group is implied that mistakenly applies the practices of the dominant Mexicas to the whole. It is important to recognize that the diverse peoples living in the central Mexican plateau region identified themselves by distinct city-state or ethnic descriptors, such as the Tlaxcalans or Cholulans, and each group maintained its own specific practices and beliefs. They did not identify themselves as "Aztecs" or with the dominant Mexicas.[10] As the ruling cultural group at the time of the Spanish conquest, the Mexicas had subjugated neighboring city-states requiring them to pay heavy tributes. A number of indigenous peoples resented and resisted the Mexica wars of expansion and sided with the Spaniards, which led to the defeat of the Mexica capital, Tenochtitlan.

For these reasons, I avoid the use of "Aztec" and use "Mexica" to indicate the militaristic ruling elite. In particular, I distinguish the complex of mother earth goddesses and gods that the Mexicas appropriated from other peoples and refashioned over time to justify their continuous wars. This usage refers narrowly to the pantheon of deities common to the central Mexican plateau region, including those from early Teotihuacan and the Toltecas, the latter whom the Mexicas emulated to gain status. For example, the Mexica war/sun god Huitzilopochtli is considered a manifestation of the earlier, benevolent sun god Quetzalcoatl, revered at Teotihuacan and by the Toltecas. The wartime appropriation of gods and goddesses by the dominant Mexicas is a major refiguring emphasis of Chicana writings and visual art. I use the term "Mexica" in order to distinguish a particular indigenous group and its practices as specifically as possible and "indigenous peoples" to make transparent the diversity of ethnic groups and the differences hidden in the invented term "Aztec." Nonetheless, even umbrella terms such as "indigenous" are problematic, and there is no ideal term that encompasses the diverse peoples of ancient Mexico or the contemporary Americas.

Chicana Sexuality and Gender is organized around four Mexican female cultural symbols—La Malinche, La Llorona, La Virgen de Guadalupe, and Mexica goddesses—with a chapter devoted to the relevance of each in inspiring resistances and refigurings. These four cultural symbols form an axis around which much of Chicana and U.S. Mexicana thought revolves. The first chapter examines how representations of the four figures have been used by dominant forces from the sixteenth to the twenty-first century to regulate women, and how Chicana writers have been influenced by the articulations of their transformative foremother, the historical figure of Malintzin Tenepal, commonly known as La Malinche. In addition, chapter 1 analyzes how Chicana artists have represented the four Mexican female cultural symbols in the late twentieth and early twenty-first centuries. The works of nine Chicana artists are included in this study to show how visual refigurings of the symbols express elements of Chicana and U.S. Mexicana lived experiences and beliefs. Chapter 2 examines the significance of indigenous Mexican mother earth goddesses used in fictional and autobiographical writings by the professional intellectuals and compares their representations of spirituality to mainstream feminist religious and cultural thought. Chapter 3 discusses the relevance of La Virgen de Guadalupe in the lives of the working-class and semi-professional women from a semiotic perspective and shows how their refigurings of women's roles and sexuality are based in practical or action-oriented strategies. Chapter 4 examines both groups' shared experiences with the legend of La Llorona, the Wailing Woman, and its continuing relevance in Chicana cultural thought. All the fictional and oral history narratives regarding La Llorona reveal cultural anxieties about women's roles and sexuality, which are addressed in recent twenty-first-century refigurings of the Weeping Woman. In chapter 5, I examine the power dynamics that exist among Chicana authors, myself as an author, and the authors of the oral histories. The first section of the chapter considers the historical reception of written and oral narratives from a literary studies perspective and suggests that oral histories be "read" as literary representations and incorporated into the "canon." A second section analyzes how the differences in status and location between a white female researcher and the U.S. Mexicanas influenced the content of the oral histories and their eventual representation in this book. The final section discusses how differences in status and location between the Chicana authors and the U.S. Mexicana oral historians relate to the cultural symbols they identify with and the types of refiguring strategies they implement or portray.

chapter one

 THE POWER OF REPRESENTATION

History, Memory, and the Cultural Refiguring of

La Malinche's Lineage

> History is a theory machine.
> And theories are memory machines. RICHARD TERDIMAN

In an essay in *Massacre of the Dreamers: Essays on Xicanisma* connecting
the construction of patriarchal religious ideologies to the subordination
of female sexuality, Ana Castillo writes that "there remains much in arch-
eology about the Mexica goddess left open to interpretation. Again, as
women and as indigenous people, we must reconstruct our history with
what is left unsaid and not what has been recorded by those who have
imposed their authority on us." Castillo's statements indicate several significant concepts that resonate in many Chicana feminist writings: (1) the
precolonial indigenous past has meaning in the present whether understood through history, memory, or both; (2) the manner in which the past
has been represented by others fails to speak to or for Chicana or U.S.
Mexicana experiences and desires and often excludes them altogether;
and (3) the past must be re-membered and refigured by Chicanas and U.S.
Mexicanas from their own perspectives and experiences. In this chapter I
consider how four Mexican female cultural symbols—La Malinche, La
Llorona, La Virgen de Guadalupe, and the Mexica mother earth goddesses
—have been represented by multiple discourses from the sixteenth to the

twenty-first centuries. An examination of these discourses exposes the official histories that serve the interests of the dominant power and contribute to stereotypical renderings of Chicana and U.S. Mexicana experience. In addition, I consider how memory serves as a counterdiscourse to provide alternate and complex understandings of their lives.

The dominant discourses influencing the representations of the four cultural symbols include the Mexica (the ruling indigenous group in Central Mexico prior to the arrival of the Spanish conquerors), Spanish European, African Arab (Moor), Catholic, Mexican, and "American."[1] In response to these discourses, Chicanas and U.S. Mexicanas have fashioned counterdiscourses produced from their own personal histories and cultural memories. The interacting processes of recovering memory and rewriting history are displayed strikingly in Chicana artists' visual representations of all four symbols. Their artworks appropriate recognized elements of earlier visual depictions in order to maintain a cultural connection. At the same time, they replace negative elements of the representations by unearthing submerged cultural memories of the figures as powerful, active forces. Stuart Hall calls this practice "trans-coding," the reappropriation of existing meanings and assignment of new meanings.[2] Chicana and U.S. Mexicana cultural refiguring participates in transcoding by confronting the elisions and denigrations of women in history through a dual remembering process of reclaiming female-oriented symbols and preserving cultural memories. Furthermore, Mexica history shows that rebellious women played a role in making history long before the conquest, setting a symbolic genealogical precedent for the feminist expressions this study examines.

A common truism states that history is written by the victors. What is not commonly acknowledged is that dominant powers often revise their own histories to justify or represent a new era or ideology, as did the Mexica peoples before and after the conquest. In contrast to the Western conception of history as a factual progression of events, the Mexica conceived of history as dynamic, nonlinear, and cyclical, and as engaging cosmological narratives and event narratives equally. In *The Aztec Kings: The Construction of Rulership in Mexica History*, Susan Gillespie writes that the Mexica subscribed to a cyclical view wherein "history belonged to the past and also to the future. It explained that which had happened as well as that which would be." Like many cultures, the Mexica "actively manipulated 'history'—their understanding of the past—to explicate their sociopolitical situation."[3] Gillespie's elucidation of Mexica historical conceptions focuses on transgressive women as the dynamic elements of change. These women were individual members of royal families, generations apart, whose repeating presence in Mexica royal and divine genealogies was structurally preordained by the Mexica chroniclers. In the genealogies, these key women are all aspects of the mother earth goddess, whose transgressions sometimes resulted in and signified both death and rebirth. "They function in the histories to generate the next temporal cycle, an act that often requires their sacrificial death. Thus they are linked to a well-known event in the Mexica past, the sacrifice of the 'woman of discord.'"[4]

What Gillespie describes as a prophetic conception of history and genealogy yields multiple understandings. While the rulership of the Mexica was held almost exclusively by men, women's birth lines generated successive nobility and, at one point, a woman actually served as ruler. The Mexica queens—with the exception of the one woman ruler—appear in these narratives to have had little agency because their perceived discord and their sacrifice were repeated in order to generate the succeeding cycle.[5] However, if women are rendered as tools of the ruling male elite in these accounts, as evidenced by their construction as the woman of discord and by the need to sacrifice them, they also are conceived as powerful figures that ennoble dynasties, inaugurate eras, and generally possess, as does the mother earth goddess, life-giving and life-taking powers. The dynamic reproduction cycle they represent signifies repetition, disruption, and re-creation of history, genealogy, and the human life cycle. "With the commencement of each cycle, a woman endowed the succeeding kings with the right to rule, a woman who thereby merged with her counterparts before and after her, to whom she was structurally identical. She was one woman and many women at once, a means of achieving union but representative of opposition, a source of power yet also of chaos, a threat to the orderly progression of the world but absolutely necessary to its maintenance; in short, a woman of discord."[6]

Gillespie proposes that two female figures continue the woman of discord structure during the conquest and into the colonial and postcolonial periods. She argues that Malintzin Tenepal (La Malinche) and La Virgen de Guadalupe function as the structural equivalents to the goddesses and queens through actual and symbolic roles in disrupting and unifying the Spanish and indigenous cultures. Malintzin Tenepal, interpreter for Hernán Cortés, bore a child by him in 1522, which symbolized unification of the Spanish and indigenous peoples. Similarly, La Virgen de Guadalupe (Mother Mary) brings together the Spanish Catholic and indigenous Mexican religions through the church built in her honor, which is thought to have been built on the site of the temple of the goddess Tonantzin (Our Mother).[7] Although Gillespie does not include La Llorona (the Wailing Woman) in her analysis, La Llorona also functions as both a disruptive and unifying figure. Her actions and narrative weeping disrupt patriarchal and colonial authority. She unites the past and present representing the Mexica mother earth goddess who wandered the streets of Tenochtitlan warning her children of the invading Spaniards. La Llorona's weeping also represents La Malinche's betrayal by Cortés; and the Chicanas and U.S. Mexicanas whose partners are unfaithful or who are deceived by government and religious institutions. In rupturing silence and inaction, La Llorona functions as a successor in the lineage of the woman of discord.

The Mexica envisioned the ritual of the woman of discord as a crucial component of their origin history and rise to dominance in ancient Mexico. However, the Chicana and U.S. Mexicana oral, written, and artistic refigurings of the four cultural symbols can be read as late-twentieth- and early-twenty-first-century disruptions of national, patriarchal, and colonial rule. They portray the survival of indigenous peoples and the intermixing of diverse races and cultures in mestiza/o peoples. Similar to the Mexica scribes, the Chicana writers and U.S. Mexicana oral historians in this study record their histories of struggle, mediation, and resistance from their own perspectives. In disrupting and unifying two or more cultures through their self-representations, they also incarnate the woman of discord. Their refashionings follow the genealogy of Gillespie's "Aztec queens," the Mexica goddesses, La Malinche, La Llorona, and La Virgen de Guadalupe in causing rupture, chaos, and change. Like the woman of discord, their narratives herald a new era of women of color power that has altered the historical record and recovered lost memories of resilient female symbols. They bring together the transcultural, multiracial aspects of Mexican, American, and indigenous mestizaje forming a history of Chicana and U.S. Mexicana pride and self-determination. In addition, they function symbolically to generate the next temporal cycle, an indigenous mestiza postmodern existence.

Narratives about the past are often used as ideological persuasion by the dominant power to support its interests. At the same time, they are a mode of discourse that can serve nondominant peoples as an effective instrument of struggle, specifically as a means by which to deconstruct subjugating ideologies and reconstruct a new vision.[8] The Chicana and U.S. Mexicana written and oral narratives recuperate ancient myths, legends, and histories to formulate stories that represent their contemporary view of themselves and the roles of women. Through scholarly research, the professional intellectuals recover La Malinche and the goddesses, symbolically resculpting them in the image of late-twentieth-century Chicana feminists. The working-class and semiprofessional women use the symbols closest to them; some refigure La Virgen de Guadalupe to portray their own spirit and ingenuity and others use La Llorona as a model for resistance and self-defense.

In each instance of rewritten history Gillespie documents, the role of discourse used as an adjunct to force is instructive. Despite their conquests of neighboring ethnic city-states, the Mexica could not compel the transformation of consciousness necessary to unify conqueror and conquered through force alone.[9] The discourses of the woman of discord were necessary not only to historically justify the Mexica conquests and internecine conflicts but to convince the conquered of their place in the new order. The discourses of unification grew less convincing as the Mexica tribute tolls forced on conquered city-states increased, leading a number of city-states to side with Cortés shortly after his arrival in 1519. Similarly, the force wielded by the Spaniards, although more deadly than anything previously witnessed by indigenous peoples, did not convince them to give up their culture and religion. Many were killed for refusing to convert or submit to Spanish control. Spanish Catholic priests soon followed, attempting to convert by Catholic discourse what had not been accomplished through force. Nor was the discourse of conversion completely successful. Contrary to popular belief, neither the story nor the symbol of La Virgen de Guadalupe was embraced by the indigenous peoples.[10] Only in the late seventeenth century did criollos, Spaniards born in "New Spain" who felt politically marginalized by the ruling peninsulars, eagerly adopt Guadalupe devotion, popularizing a discourse of the criollos as the "new chosen people."[11]

When Mexico achieved independence from Spain in 1821, supporters of a democratic nation began forging national discourses that vanquished the colonial past and everything associated with it. La Virgen de Guadalupe was part of the new discourse; Malintzin Tenepal was not. Sandra Messinger Cypess writes that La Malinche, a respected figure prior to Independence, became a scapegoat in Mexican republican narratives. Cypess examines fictional narratives that associate La Malinche with Spain and regard her as an undesirable role model for post-Independence Mexico. She notes the historical novel *Xicoténcatl*, published anonymously in 1826, is the first narrative to negatively characterize La Malinche as a betrayer of her people. The novel was well known in Mexico and served as a source of inspiration for a number of works about the conquest.[12] The supplanting of La Malinche with La Virgen de Guadalupe as the mother of the new nation reinforced a dominant Catholic and criollo discourse significantly altering, although not completely eliminating, the status and regard for La Malinche and indigenous goddesses. In these examples, then, force and discourse combine to subjugate indigenous identity and female power and desire. Not until the mid-twentieth century would Mexican and Chicana writers recognize La Malinche's unifying qualities and restore her significance as indigenous and corporeal woman. Guadalupe would not be recovered by the Chicana professional intellectuals until the late twentieth century.

The narratives of the working-class and semiprofessional women indicate that the patriarchal discourse associated with Guadalupe as a Mexican Catholic female ideal, and the colonial and patriarchal violence of the conquest, are still very much a part of their lives. The discourses of struggle and resistance that the working-class and semiprofessional women create and enact, along with those of the professional intellectuals, must be added to the historical record. A cultural genealogy of resistance and refiguring can be traced beginning with the precolonial narratives of Mexica goddesses and queens, including La Malinche, La Llorona, and Guadalupe, and extending to the contemporary narratives and visual images that represent the experiences of Chicana and U.S. Mexicana women. This genealogy encompasses women of discord from the fifteenth to the twenty-first century who have struggled against poverty, enslavement, violence, exploitative working conditions, and limiting gender roles and sexualities. It includes historical figures who are known to have resisted and refigured such as Malintzin Tenepal, Sor Juana Inés de la Cruz, Doña Josefa Ortiz de Domínguez, Teresa Urrea, La Adelita, Emma Tenayuca, and Dolores Huerta, as well as many women who have struggled alone or unacknowledged.[13] The genealogy of the woman of discord is a continual and dynamic process that rewrites history to reflect contemporary concerns. Past resistances serve as present and future inspirations. The new discourses of Chicanas and U.S. Mexicanas address the "sacrifice" of the woman of discord by opposing and rewriting the subjugation of and violence against women, gays and lesbians, and people of color.

Indeed, the Chicana professional intellectuals and the U.S. Mexicana working-class and semiprofessional women continue the lineage of discord by disrupting long-held cultural conceptions of women's roles and sexualities and by unifying woman-centered visions with indigenous cultural practices and symbols. The cycle of contestation and reproduction that I examine in the writings and oral histories has been noted by Norma Alarcón in describing the history of the term "Chicano" as a microcosm of the history of the Chicana/o civil rights movement, a history of identity undergoing revision even as it is recorded.[14] For example, as late as 1995 the National Association of Chicano Studies changed its name to the National Association of Chicana and Chicano Studies to recognize women's existence and contributions. Nancy "Rusty" Barceló, one of the organization's leaders, noted that the name may need to be even more inclusive in the future to recognize the participation of a broad spectrum of U.S. Latinas and Latinos.

A part of this on-going struggle concerns Chicanas who actively participated and intervened in the transformation of Chicano history during the civil rights movement, yet whose contributions remain unrecognized. For example, the TV and video series *Chicano! The History of the Mexican American Civil Rights Movement,* which aired on PBS in April and May 1996, elides Chicanas' contributions and uses only the male-gendered ending in the title term "Chicano," despite long-standing criticism of this usage by many Chicanas. At a screening of the first part of the series at the National Association for Chicana and Chicano Studies Annual Conference in Chicago in March 1996, one of the female producers took the podium to apologize for the slighting of women's roles and contributions in the series, promising that the next production would be titled "Chicana." However, a separation of histories misses the point of an all-encompassing perspective. Since then, no series about Chicana contributions has been produced nor has the original series been rewritten.[15] The elision of women's contributions continues into the twenty-first century. For example, the art exhibition "Chicano Visions: American Painters on the Verge," on a five-year national tour, continued the exclusionary use of the male-gendered term in its title. The original tour collection, comprising primarily Chicano (male) works collected by the actor Cheech Marin, did not include works by Chicana artists. After protests by Chicana feminists, the exhibition was expanded to include six Chicana artists. When the exhibition came to Minneapolis, the arrangement at the Weisman Art Museum, University of Minnesota, placed works by Patssi Valdez and Diane Gamboa in a room apart from the main collection.[16] While this placement may have resulted from the design of the Weisman's gallery space, it effectively marginalized the works of the female artists. The predominance of male-oriented themes, including the sexual objectification of women in a number of the paintings, is mitigated somewhat by Tere Romo's examination of the "mestiza aesthetic" produced by Chicana artists' works. In her article "Mestiza Aesthetics and Chicana Painterly Visions," published in the exhibition catalogue, Romo discusses the marginalization of Chicanas within the art movement and how they differentiate their art from that of the male artists through subversive refigurings of domestic space and gender roles.[17] A September 30, 2004 panel discussion sponsored by the Weisman Art Museum and titled "Chicano Art: Past, Present, Future" featured a number of the exhibition artists, including Ester Hernández and Diane Gamboa. Nonetheless, the exhibition, which began its tour in 2002, retained a male-dominant perspective.[18] Recalling Alarcón's discussion, the history and future of the identity "Chicano" continues to need revisioning.

The oral and written narratives discussed in this study not only acknowledge and contest the official histories and dominant representations; they also inscribe a more complete history and memory. The narratives relate the actions of women empowering themselves through the creation of a woman of color and transcultural consciousness. As oral histories and autobiographies, they create subject discourses from within rather than being defined from without. They respond to multiple locations of erasure and marginalization from the sacrifice and devaluation of goddesses/ women in preconquest and colonial history and memory, to the degradation and erasure of indigenous and mestiza/o peoples in United States histories, to the patriarchal and racial imperialism of the Catholic Church, to male-dominant representations of Mexican national and Chicana/o civil rights histories, and to the white, middle-class perspectives of the women's and gay/lesbian history movements. These women of discord record historical, racial, gender, and sexual subjects in the dual sense of beings and narratives, which function as counterdiscourses that both contest dominant narratives and contribute to a broader understanding of history. In testifying to Chicana and U.S. Mexicana female experience, they overwrite the official histories and in so doing create new discursive subjectivities. My project configures history as both integral to an understanding of Chicana and U.S. Mexicana experiences and incomplete in that the total story of their contributions and struggles has not been written or told but must constantly be recounted to account for pluralities of experiences. From this perspective each Chicana and U.S. Mexicana story deserves attention in order to assess a collective experience.

COUNTERMEMORY, COLLECTIVE MEMORY, AND CULTURE

I have argued for a concept of history emphasizing multiple perspectives that include oppositional discourses. This definition of history coexists with Western official histories that favor broad understandings emphasizing overarching patterns and generally supporting dominant rule. Official histories exist primarily as secular, intellectual, and political exercises that retain enormous authority to legitimate or educate even as they are continually challenged. The February 1997 suspensions of two Chicana high school teachers in Vaughn, New Mexico, for teaching alternative historical perspectives serve as a potent reminder of the power that backs legitimized histories and the threat that counterhistories pose. Nadine and Patsy Córdova were suspended with pay for their refusal to stop teaching from the textbook *500 años del pueblo chicano/500 Years of Chicano History in Pictures* and other multicultural texts.[19] In an ironic twist, high school administrators deemed their teaching "racist,"[20] and they were fired for "insubordination" in July 1997. The sisters filed lawsuits against the Vaughn High School Board of Education and won $500,000 in out-of-court settlements, but the tensions in the small town had already forced them to remove their children from the school system and find jobs elsewhere.

Coinciding with and aiding the counterhistory movement, recent interdisciplinary scholarship, especially in anthropology, sociology, psychology, and art, has converged upon the significance of memory as history's counterpart.[21] Although they are different kinds of discourses, history and memory are nonetheless interdependent systems, drawing on and influencing each other, sometimes in contention, always shifting and exchanging. Memory is a way of making sense of the present and of moving into the future. Without memory there would be no such thing as history, and without history memory is insufficient.[22] Yet memory is subjective; it picks and chooses, exaggerates and diminishes, and is "subject to repression and therefore to slips, lapses, or silences" as Henry Rousso reminds us. "Memory is a structuring of forgetfulness" resulting in histories that appear universal but are full of gaps. Eventually countermemory calls attention to what has been forgotten, underwritten, or concealed from public view; "the return of the repressed" is a collective remembering that forces a reckoning with injustice and tyranny.[23]

In *Time Passages: Collective Memory and American Popular Culture*, George Lipsitz refocuses Michel Foucault's concept of residual countermemory, positioning it as "the local, the immediate, and the personal" that builds out toward the total story, even though the totality may never be fully known.[24] Countermemory checks the impulse to elevate a singular or unifying story, remembering instead the particular and the specific. Countermemory also reveals the buried histories not written into dominant discourses and forces reconsideration of the dominant perspective by providing new interpretations of the past. In particular, countermemory details localized experiences of oppression and in making them widely available provides alternative readings of dominant histories once accepted as the "truth." Aided by popular memory, representations found in the oral accounts people give of past events and social practices, countermemory creates a "dialectics of difference" that serves both unifying and oppositional functions.[25] Chicana/o popular memory, exhibited in folklore and music such as corridos (ballads), unifies the Chicana/o community through the portrayal of communal experiences such as a common history of oppression and resistance. It opposes dominant white narratives that participate in intentional amnesia for the purposes of erasing or devaluing cultures and peoples. Yet popular memory is largely male-identified; consequently the countermemory of the professional intellectuals' writings and the working-class and semiprofessional women's oral histories challenges popular memory's bias toward male heroes such as Gregorio Cortéz, Jacinto Treviño, and César Chávez, and its undervaluation of women.[26] Examples of this devaluation can be found in the constructions of La Malinche as the Mexican Eve for sleeping with the conqueror, or las soldaderas, the legendary female soldiers who fought during the Mexican Revolution and became configured as "loose women" because they consorted with male soldiers. The countermemories expressed in the women's oral and written narratives encompass experiences of gendered relations and sexuality codes that differ from Chicano (male) versions, even as they share overlapping historical, racial, and cultural experiences.

Countermemory combines both linear history and orally transmitted popular history to reconstitute history, the veracity of which is proved, Lipsitz asserts, through the rigor of collective memory and desire: "For these narratives to succeed they must resonate with the experiences and feelings of their audiences. For them to succeed completely, they must address the part of audience memory in touch with real historical oppressions and memories."[27] The visual and literary portrayals that accompanied the Chicana/o civil rights movement make this point. During the initial stages of the movement, images and writings such as murals portraying indigenous warriors and the nationalist document "El Plan Espiritual de Aztlán" conveying largely male- and heterosexual-oriented ideals succeeded with many Chicanas. However, some Chicanas rejected the male-only orientation of Chicano nationalism, recognizing how the discourse reflected their real-life subordination to men. They focused artistic energy on creating images and writings depicting female interests and desires. Thus, the early representations of the Chicana/o civil rights movement succeeded only partially in conveying Chicana history and memory. Chicana artists and writers countered with characterizations that relied on similar nationalistic symbols, such as La Virgen de Guadalupe and Mexica goddesses, but refigured them to convey a woman of color consciousness.

Not only is memory an important source of history; it is also crucial in defining identity, whether individual or collective.[28] Collective identities reproduce and are nourished by recognizable cultural identifiers and received traditions manifested in images, gestures, rituals, and festivals rather than in texts. Among peoples of Mexican descent or origin living in the United States, historical narratives and cultural practices often are maintained through oral traditions and reinforced by visual representations including objects and images in the home. For example, cultural symbols such as La Virgen de Guadalupe and the Mexica mother earth goddesses are reproduced in diverse locations and activities such as archaeological or pilgrimage sites and museums, ritual performances such as the all night prayer vigil on the eve of the feast day of La Virgen de Guadalupe, yard sculptures and jewelry, and body scarification such as tattoos, especially prevalent among young Chicanos and Chicanas within gang and prison cultures.

Likewise, the reproduction of images (symbolic and material) of all four female cultural symbols plays an important role in the identification of self and culture for the working-class, semiprofessional, and professional intellectual women in this study. But a significant difference marks their representations from those noted above. Chicana and U.S. Mexicana narratives and visual images do not merely reproduce the officially recognized (Church) image as is commonly done, for example, with La Virgen de Guadalupe. Rather, the artists, authors, and oral historians alter images and narrative representations to coincide with their perspective of themselves and how they exist within the culture. In writings, paintings, and even in the workings of the tongue, they reproduce cultural memory while adapting it to their particular needs and experiences. This phenomenon is most visibly articulated in Chicana art integrating feminist concerns and interweaving personal, familial, or community motifs with existing cultural representations.

Throughout this book, I refer to various forms of cultural expression of La Malinche, La Llorona, La Virgen de Guadalupe, and Mexica mother earth goddesses that contribute to recreations and reinventions of Chicana and U.S. Mexicana culture, identity, and historical consciousness. For example, representations of La Virgen de Guadalupe can be traced in a continuous stream from the first image said to have been produced in 1531 to contemporary Chicana art forms.[29] Representations of Mexica mother earth goddesses (and gods) were rendered in precolonial stone sculptures and in surviving sixteenth-century codices (often residing in museum storage, educational archives, or private collections and thus invisible to many people). By contrast with the continuous representation of Guadalupe throughout the centuries, the memory of the goddesses as sacred and vital elements of indigenous cultures was repressed for three hundred years until it was revived in twentieth-century museum exhibits and Mexican and Chicana literature and art.

During the Chicana/o civil rights movement of the 1960s and 1970s, images of the Tolteca god Queztalcoatl, depicted in murals and other representational forms, illustrated the movement's reclamation of indigenous heritage. At the same time, the largely male representations were emblematic of the patriarchal focus of the civil rights movement and its "static, ahistorical Aztec identity."[30] Consequently, many Chicana writers and artists recovered images and narratives of the historical figure of La Malinche and Mexica mother earth goddesses whose multiple aspects signify powerful, creative, sexual beings. As with Chicana artistic renderings of La Virgen de Guadalupe, images of the goddesses are not mimetically reproduced as reflections of Mexica deities. Rather they are refigured to represent the concerns and desires of contemporary Chicana feminism. The writers and artists redraw the goddesses to overcome the monstrous, defeated, and degraded positions they were sculpted into by the Mexica warring leadership. For example, the Chicana artist Santa Barraza's 1986 refiguring of the mother earth goddess Coatlicue as a source of life and spirituality is shown by her association as genetrix in connection with the maguey plant, a principal source of fiber and the sacred drink pulque for indigenous peoples of the central Mexican plateau region.[31] Represented with La Virgen de Guadalupe, Coatlicue is scaled larger than the Catholic mother figure and thus accorded greater significance as the originator of the genealogy and the indigenous peoples. By emphasizing Coatlicue's life-giving associations as the earth that nourishes plants vital to indigenous existence, Barraza refigures her from the wartime depiction of the beheaded Coatlicue in Mexica stone sculptures, a portrayal that justified the Mexica war games and the accompanying human sacrifice that increased during their reign. Similarly, the goddess Coyolxauhqui is represented in Mexica stone sculptures as degraded and defeated following her mythical decapitation and dismemberment by the male god of war/sun. Like Barraza's recovery of Coatlicue, the Maestrapeace muralist group including several Chicana artists re-member Coyolxauhqui in a mural on the San Francisco Women's Building. More recently, Chicana artists have begun reimagining La Llorona, changing her countenance from a demon or death figure to a real woman who is associated with the goddesses' spiritual and creationary powers.

I connect this discussion of visual representations to memory and culture to illustrate how memories of the past are transformed through Chicana artists' labor, metonymically represented by the hand that paints or writes (and the tongue that speaks) into contemporary images that refigure patriarchal portrayals of women.[32] Each re-presentation anticipates a future one even as it relies on foundational images from the past that perpetuate a recognizable, if permutational, culture. In an essay on California murals, Eva Sperling Cockcroft and Holly Barnett-Sánchez describe how the collective memory reproduced in mural art contributed to Chicana/o cultural identity in the 1960s and 1970s by transforming the past.[33] Chicana artists and authors disrupt inherited discourses that confine and degrade women by reworking the unacceptable elements in cultural symbols such as La Virgen de Guadalupe and reappropriating dormant or forgotten ones such as the complex of mother earth goddesses. Their transformations participate in the continuation of cultural memory even as they attempt to change aspects of it that negatively affect women. This paradoxical quality of collective memory that Richard Terdiman describes as the "unforeseeable *productivity* of its representation" allows Chicana feminists to identify with recognized cultural practices and symbols yet play with their contingent meanings in order to distance themselves from the damaging elements.[34] Stuart Hall characterizes the necessary but tenuous relationship of this affiliation: "Cultural identities are the points of identification, the unstable points of suture which are made in the discourses of history and culture."[35] As such, Chicana/o collective memory shows itself to be sustaining and varying, accommodating and renewing. This paradoxical model of cultural continuity explains similar processes of remembering and cultural refiguring found in the oral histories of the U.S. Mexicanas who identify with, yet refigure, elements of La Virgen de Guadalupe model. The diverse ways in which the professional intellectuals and the working-class and semiprofessional women construct relationships with these cultural symbols indicate that collective memories create differences in historical consciousness and cultural refiguring.

MEXICAN FEMALE CULTURAL SYMBOLS: *La Malinche, La Llorona, La Virgen de Guadalupe, and Mexica Goddesses*

A historical overview and analysis of critical perspectives of La Malinche, La Llorona, and La Virgen de Guadalupe makes apparent how the three figures have overlapped and interacted in Mexican history and memory since the sixteenth century to promote the interests of various political and religious groups, to maintain male dominance, or to reflect the human misery produced by violence, subjugation, and loss. Alternate readings reveal how La Malinche and La Llorona signify transgressive and resistive figures whose actions can be reinterpreted or rewritten to reflect contemporary Chicana feminist concerns. My readings also reveal how the Mexica mother earth goddesses, including Tonantzin, Cihuacoatl, Coatlicue, and Coyolxauhqui, have been recuperated by Chicana writers to represent complex, powerful, and plural subjectivities. As with the other female cultural symbols, narratives of the goddesses reflect rewritings of history by those who have access to the official record or, as in the case of the professional intellectuals and the working-class and semiprofessional women, those who want to counter it. All the revisions signify moments of change or rupture with the past, while at the same time incorporating the past into their new vision. Some refigurings serve as counterdiscourses that compete with the dominant versions for a place within the collective memory. The result is that the symbols themselves continue over time, but their representations (visual, oral, and written) are transformed to mirror particular concerns and interests composing the dynamic conception that is Chicana/o and Mexicana/o culture.

Mother Earth Goddesses

Although La Malinche, La Llorona, and Guadalupe are sometimes mentioned and often act as subtexts in Chicana literary works by Anzaldúa, Castillo, Cisneros, Moraga, and Villaneuva, they do not figure as prominently as Mexica mother earth goddesses. In fictional and autobiographical works, the mother earth goddesses serve as spiritual, physical, and emotional inspiration for the authors or their female characters. One reason the goddesses are more readily recuperated is because they bridge dualistic divides that structure the other figures. In Mesoamerican religious thought, the concept of paired oppositions—a complementary duality recognizing "the essential interdependence of opposites"—exists as a fundamental structuring principle in the representation of the gods and goddesses.[36] Nothing exemplifies this principle better than the mother earth goddesses who are known for both their creative and destructive capabilities, and for whom gender ambiguity is an important feature. Symbols of life and death (womb and tomb), growth and decline, martiality and domesticity, carnality and repentance, they are associated with the earth, water, corn, maguey, weaving and other art forms, childbirth, snakes, sexual sin, human sacrifice, the night, the moon, and the underworld, to name a few of the most significant aspects.[37] The serpent snake is a significant feature of the mother earth deity. Representing carnality and divinity and existing above and below ground (land of the living and the dead), the serpent snake signifies rebirth and transformation. In the Mexica historical narratives, the goddesses Toci/Tonan, Cihuacoatl, Coatlicue, and Coyolxauhqui are linked genealogically and sometimes interchangeably as grandmother, mother, sister, and wife of Huitzilopochtli (Hummingbird on the Left), the Mexica sun and war god. They are also the structural equivalents of the woman of discord. The accounts of the goddesses intertwine the historical movements of the Mexica peoples and the origin stories of the Mexica gods who are instrumental figures in the Mexica journey to dominance in the central plateau region. Humans are integral figures in the narratives along with the gods. In the specific narratives of these goddesses, history and cultural memory interweave to explain the Mexica rise to power, the origin/justification for the prominence of their god of war/sun, Huitzilopochtli, and concomitant denigration of the mother earth goddesses, and the increase in human sacrifice in the period just prior to the Spanish conquest. The Mexica's cyclic conception of history and cosmology requires the repetition of traditions that invoke the past. Each repetition of the sacrifice of the goddesses (woman of discord) included in the historical genealogical accounts (codices) narrates a different stage in the Mexica cosmological or historical sequence. Most importantly, Gillespie writes, each sacrifice represents "the point of greatest uncertainty and instability [in the Mexica journey to power]. This point is thus represented by a female, the antithesis of male hegemony expressed in masculine rule," which causes disruption of the status quo and unification of the past and present.[38]

Toci (Our Grandmother) and Tonan (Our Mother), commonly known as Tonantzin, the suffix -tzin signifying veneration and respect, are virtually identical in their attributes and represent the ultimate genetrix, the earth, source of life. I consider them here together in order to pursue an understanding of the significance of Tonantzin as a mother earth deity, a woman of discord, and her association with La Virgen de Guadalupe. The latter association relates primarily to their similar names, Our Mother, and life-giving functions. The narrative of Toci/Tonan begins with a mortal woman, a Culhuacan (Tolteca) princess, who later becomes manifest as the grandmother/mother goddess. The Mexica, originally a faction of the northern nomadic Chichimecas, moved from the north into the central Mexican plateau region through a series of stays in different regions where they would intermingle with the local people before moving on.

During their stay in Tizaapan, Culhuacan territory, the Mexica settled and coexisted harmoniously even intermarrying with the Culhua. Noticing their happily settled existence, their god, Huitzilopochtli, feared they would not continue the journey he had planned for them to a promised land. To break the peaceful ties, he instigated a plot that would cause a war. He commanded his priests to search for the "woman of discord," who was identified as the daughter of the Culhuacan king. Huitzilopochtli told his people to invite the king's daughter to come live with them as their mistress and his wife. The king agreed, pleased at the prospect that his daughter would be considered the living goddess. But when she arrived at the Mexica temple, instead of honoring her as his wife, Huitzilopochtli ordered that she be killed and the skin flayed from her body. When the king, her father, came to make an offering to his daughter goddess, he saw instead a priest dressed in her skin. Horrified and infuriated, he ordered his people to drive the Mexica from Culhuacan territory. Thus, the Mexica were forced to continue their wanderings as Huitzilopochtli desired. In this narrative, the king's daughter is none other than Toci/Tonan, a reigning mortal who became a goddess upon her death. Huitzilopochtli identified her as such in instructing his people to find the woman of discord, declaring that she was to be known as "my mother, my grandmother." Her relationship in this version as his wife, mother, and grandmother, and in another version as his sister, completes the merging of the four kinship roles in one woman.[39] Furthermore, the element of sexual ambiguity of the god/desses is expressed through the depiction of a male priest wearing her flayed skin.[40]

In her aspect known as Cihuacoatl (Serpent Woman), the mother earth deity was considered Huitzilopochtli's sister. Cihuacoatl is goddess of midwifery and women who died in childbirth. Images of her often include spears and a shield representing a warlike aspect referring to the belief that women giving birth were warriors taking a prisoner (the child) captive. Midwives counseled women to exhort Cihuacoatl's name during childbirth and to consider themselves engaged in battle as they violently expelled the child from the womb. Representations of birth goddesses show them standing up or squatting and raising their warrior batons as the child issues forth. Cihuacoatl's significance as a fertility goddess also relates to the earth and is manifested in her designation as patroness of the farming and lake region Chinampaneca, south of Tenochtitlan. Cecelia F. Klein designates Cihuacoatl as the mother earth goddess that reigned during the final tenure of the Mexica, observing that they turned her into a monstrous deity with a voracious appetite for human hearts and blood, a feature that earned her a reputation as evil and relentless.[41] Closely related to Cihuacoatl, Chalchiuhtlicue (She of the Jade Skirt) is the goddess of water and birth. Her name is a metaphorical reference to a shining expanse of verdant water, such as in lakes and rivers. The watery nature of the womb also connects Chalchiuhtlicue to birth ceremonies such as baptism. The visual representation of this goddess includes infants in a birth stream flowing from her uterus.[42] Both Cihuacoatl and Chalchiuhtlicue provide elements of the La Llorona legend discussed below.

Coatlicue (Serpent Skirt), closely related to Cihuacoatl in name and the death feature, is the best known of the goddesses today because of the colossal stone sculpture of her that resides in the National Museum of Anthropology in Mexico City. In the sculpture dated to the late postclassic period (thirteenth to sixteenth centuries), she wears a skirt of woven rattlesnakes and a necklace of severed hearts and hands representing human sacrifice. A snake and skull waistband symbolizes life and death. In place of her head, two snake heads rise from her severed throat in the form of gushing blood representing her beheading and the fountain of life (see figure 1). According to Mexica originary stories, Coatlicue was the mother of Huitzilopochtli, the god of war, who was born during a battle in which he emerged victorious. The story begins with Coatlicue's miraculous impregnation. One day while sweeping at the top of Coatepec (Serpent Mountain), Coatlicue placed a stray ball of down in her bosom. Later that day she realized she was pregnant. Upon learning of Coatlicue's pregnancy, her children, Coyolxauhqui (Painted with Bells) and the Centzon Huitznahua (Four Hundred Southerners), were furious at their mother's sexual transgression and decided to kill her. Still in the womb, Huitzilopochtli learned of the plot and spoke to his mother, reassuring her that all would be well. When the battle began, Coyolxauhqui beheaded her mother Coatlicue. However, at the moment of Coatlicue's death, Huitzilopochtli emerged from the womb fully armed, decapitated his half sister, Coyolxauhqui, and routed his half brothers. He then threw Coyolxauhqui's body down the mountain, resulting in her dismemberment. In a different version similar to the Toci/Tonan story but accounting for a different leg of the Mexica historical migration, Coyolxauhqui and the Centzon Huitznahua (in this version unrelated to each other) are depicted as resisters to Huitzilopochtli's desire that the Mexica move from

1. Coatlicue (goddess of the earth), late postclassic period, thirteenth–fifteenth century. Stone sculpture. Reproduction authorized by the Instituto Nacional de Antropologia e Historia, México, D.F. CONACULTA.-INAH.-MEX.

Coatepec mountain. Considering them traitors, Huitzilopochtli punishes them by killing them and eating their hearts, the first depiction of the ritual human sacrifice the Mexica practiced. In this version, Coyolxauhqui was considered Huitzilopochtli's mother and was beheaded, thereby assuming the same position as Coatlicue in the narrative of the god's birth. Following their killings, Huitzilopochtli caused a drought that forced the Mexica to move from Coatepec and continue their peregrination to the land he promised them.

In 1978, a massive eight-ton stone sculpture depicting Coyolxauhqui's decapitated head and severed limbs was discovered in Mexico City (see figure 2). The discovery prompted excavation of a section of the Templo Mayor, the primary Mexica temple in Tenochtitlan razed by the Spaniards and overbuilt with a cathedral. The Mexica had built the Templo Mayor as a reproduction of Coatepec (Serpent Mountain), where the mythical Coatlicue-Coyolxauhqui-Huitzilopochtli battle occurred. The Coyolxauhqui stone sculpture was discovered in a location at the base of the temple, thereby representing in sculpture the defeated position she occupied in

2. Coyolxauhqui, late postclassic period, thirteenth–fifteenth century. Stone sculpture. Reproduction authorized by the Instituto Nacional de Antropologia e Historia, México, D.F. CONACULTA.-INAH.-MEX. Courtesy of the © Foundation for the Advancement of Mesoamerican Studies, Inc., www.famsi.org.

the narrative after Huitzilopochtli threw her down the mountain. Every human sacrifice conducted at the Templo Mayor repeated this scenario of Coyolxauhqui's public humiliation. Her connection to human sacrifice is exemplified in another sculpture remnant that shows a fiery serpent weapon piercing her heart. The sculpture of Coyolxauhqui decapitated and dismembered resides as the featured display in the Templo Mayor museum. The museum brochure explaining the sculpture states that the Huitzilopotchli-Coyolxauhqui battle, reenacted in ritual human sacrifice, depicts the "everyday struggle of light against darkness, between day and night, the repetition of something that happened in a mythic time." This explanation implies a solar-lunar-astral interpretation of the narrative. "Huitzilopochtli is the sun, who, at the moment of his birth—rising from the earth (Coatlicue), conquers and disperses the moon (Coyolxauhqui) and the host of stars of the southern firmament (Centzon Huitznahua)."[43] Based on this interpretation, Coyolxauhqui is often referred to as the moon goddess, although there is nothing explicit in her representation to link her to the moon.[44]

However, the solar-lunar-astral explanation in the museum brochure, offered as the official story, overlooks the historical, social, and political underpinnings of the Mexica narratives and fails to acknowledge the militarism of the Mexica toward their neighboring city-states, the increase in human sacrifice they instituted, and the patriarchal significance of Coyolxauhqui's defeat. The contradictions between the Mexica representations of Coatlicue and Coyolxauhqui and more benign representations of the two goddesses are related to the god of war, as remarked by Mary Miller and Karl Taube. "In Huitzilopochtli's company, female goddesses become hideous, subjects for dismemberment."[45] For example, Coyolxauhqui's image in the Mexica stone shows an old and conquered woman, whereas many narrative representations characterize her as a young beauty. Similarly, the Mexica's grisly stone image of Coatlicue beheaded and wearing a necklace of sacrificial hearts and hands contrasts with other sculptured images, which focus on fertility features and her revered status.

Klein, who considers Coatlicue and Coyolxauhqui as avatars of Cihuacoatl, argues that the rise of the war/sun god Huitzilopochtli was concurrent with the increasing dominance of the Mexica in the central plateau region. In a social political analysis of the significance of Cihuacoatl to the imperialistic Mexica, Klein describes the Coyolxauhqui sculpture as presenting "the goddess in a state of obvious defeat."[46] She characterizes Coyolxauhqui and other images of Cihuacoatl/Coatlicue as manifesting multiple signs of capture, defeat, and shame, including nudity, bindings on limbs, and decapitation. Klein relates these images to the Mexica defeat of nearby city-states where the cult of Cihuacoatl was prominent and concludes that the goddess and her cult were appropriated forcibly as a sign of victory. Consequently, associated with the Mexica Cihuacoatl obtained a monstrous reputation for her appetite for human hearts and blood, a feature also attributed to Coatlicue and Tonantzin. Klein argues that Cihuacoatl's carnivorous aspect was magnified and used to justify military expeditions that contributed to the fame and fortune of the Mexica military leader who had adopted Cihuacoatl's name. By contrast, the Mexica commoners experienced poverty and hardship because of the continuous wars and tributes that were exacted. Moreover, the Mexica rulers appropriated Cihuacoatl to justify human sacrifice and the commoners increasingly viewed Cihuacoatl "as a cruel, relentless creature" representing death, hard work, and poverty.[47]

Klein's observation that class differences accompanied gender stratification echoes June Nash's earlier argument that with the rise to power of the Mexicas the culture was transformed along class and gender lines. "The history of the Aztecs provides an example of the transformation from a kinship-based society with a minimum of status differentiation to a class-structured empire" accompanied by the simultaneous conversion from a matrilineal to patrilineal-based royalty "supported by an ideology of male dominance, and the differential access to its benefits between men and women."[48] Over a period of three centuries societal changes included division and rigid classification of male and female labor, isolation of women and commoners from power-making positions and state functions, consolidation of power and property in the hands of the ruling elite, and a shift from the production economy of the commoners to a "parasitic economy of war." Structural changes were paralleled by theological shifts that moved from the worship of multiple and complementary deities characterized by the principle of balanced opposites to first the "emergence of a single god at the apex of a hierarchy of male gods, and second, the eclipse of female deities related to fertility, nourishment, and the agricultural complex."[49] Although the female deities were officially subjugated, Nash observes that they persisted among the commoners as major figures of worship. Ultimately, she concludes that all these changes contributed to the defeat of the Mexica by the Spanish because the Mexica could not rally the alienated commoners or the neighboring city-states that composed their empire to fight on their behalf.[50]

Klein's, Nash's, and Gillespie's interpretations reveal the patriarchal and imperialistic motives underlying Mexica denigrations of the powerful mother earth goddess complex, whereby the goddess/woman of discord challenges the male god of war but ultimately, and necessarily in order to support male rule and Mexica militarism, is defeated and degraded. Drawing on Klein's liberatory metaphor, however, I argue that Chicana writers and artists "invade the prison and cut the bonds" of the mother earth goddesses,[51] recovering them from more than five hundred years of imprisonment and misrepresentation, first by the Mexica and then the Spaniards.

For example, Santa Barraza's 1986 depiction of Coatlicue restores the life-giving aspect to the complementary dualism of the mother earth goddess, which was devalued during the Mexica reign. In portraying Coatlicue as producing and emerging from the sacred maguey plant, Barraza preserves and emphasizes Coatlicue's significance as an earth and fertility goddess.[52] In addition, Coatlicue's meaning as a divine, rather than monstrous, figure is emphasized by her association with La Virgen de Guadalupe, who appears above as if birthed from the fountain of Coatlicue's life-giving blood.

Coyolxauhqui is visually refigured in the San Francisco Women's Building mural by a collective of seven female muralists (see figure 3). Referring to the Mexica narrative and stone sculpture in which Coyolxauhqui is decapitated and dismembered by her half-brother, the war god Huitzilopochtli, the mural re-members Coyolxauhqui as a whole human being (see figure 4). She is no longer a disembodied and disempowered object of patriarchal myths and sculptures. Instead, she is breaking out of the stone casing (literally the sculpture) that surrounds her in an active movement of liberation (compare figures 2 and 4). In her lower hand she clutches paintbrushes signifying the creative and political power of the artists to re-present women as active agents creating their own subjectivity. Coyolxauhqui emerges from a maguey plant cradled in the palm of Rigoberta Menchú, the Quiché woman from Guatemala who won the Nobel Peace Prize in 1992, whose visage tops the mural. Both female figures symbolize dynamic, outspoken actors for indigenous and Third World women's rights. The mural group, Maestrapeace, whose name is a feminist and pacifist refiguring of the word "masterpiece," includes the Chicana muralists Juana Alicia and Irene Pérez.

Malintzin Tenepal (La Malinche)

Malintzin Tenepal is an actual historical figure who lived at the time of the conquest and is the only woman named in historical accounts of that period. Commonly referred to as La Malinche, she was the interpreter for and sexual subject of Hernán Cortés, the Spanish conqueror. What is known about La Malinche comes from the Spanish chronicles of the conquest rather than from a firsthand account about her life. Not only are the details of her personal history scarce and obscure but the absence of her voice is ironic given the major role her linguistic abilities played during that liminal period. She was highly regarded by both the Spaniards and the indigenous peoples for the translating and leadership roles she assumed during the conquest period. In her role as mediator between the two cultures she became associated with and signified by the act of speaking. Known as "la lengua" (language, tongue), her subjectivity was defined by the speech act, even as she herself was desubjectivized and left no traces of speech. However, the accolades others paid her during and after the conquest were short-lived. She quickly became the scapegoat for the Mexica defeat, an unwarranted attribution that continues to resonate

(above) 3. Maestrapeace mural, San Francisco Women's Building, Lapidge Street façade, 1994. Maestrapeace: Juana Alicia, Miranda Bergman, Edythe Boone, Susan Kelk Cervantes, Meera Desai, Yvonne Littleton, and Irene Pérez. Courtesy of the artists. All rights reserved.

4. Maestrapeace mural, detail: Coyolxauhqui. Courtesy of the artists.

today. In her study *La Malinche in Mexican Literature: From History to Myth*, Sandra Messinger Cypess finds that "La Malinche has been transformed from a historical figure to a major Mexican and Latin American feminine archetype, a polysemous sign whose signifieds, for all their ambiguity, are generally negative."[53]

The few facts about her life can be summarized in one paragraph. For example, two different locations and times are listed as Malintzin's place and date of birth by the Spanish chroniclers yet neither has been definitely ascertained. Most likely she was raised in a wealthy or royal family, which would explain her linguistic knowledge and cultured manner, although this too is unsubstantiated.[54] Exactly how she came to be a slave also is not known. Cypess and others speculate that after the death of her father she may have been stolen or sold into slavery as a young woman.[55] Eventually, she was presented along with twenty other women to Cortés as a gift from a Tabascan chief. Cortés first gave her to one of his men, then took her for his companion upon learning of her linguistic abilities. Because she spoke both Nahuatl and Maya and learned Spanish readily, she quickly became an essential figure in Cortés's understanding of and communication with the indigenous peoples. In 1522, La Malinche bore a child by Cortés, named Martín. Soon thereafter, Cortés married her off to one of his lieutenants, Juan Jaramillo, and endowed her with land, the encomienda of Xilotepec. In 1524, Cortés took her and Jaramillo on an onerous overland trip to Honduras during which she became pregnant and birthed a daughter by Jaramillo.[56] After her work translating on this expedition, however, she disappears from the historical record.

That she was instrumental as Cortés's guide, interpreter, and confidante is apparent from the responsibility she was given to meet alone with indigenous leaders to convey the Spanish position, and from the adulatory recognition accorded her by the indigenous chroniclers who named her *"la lengua de los dioses,"* "the tongue of the Gods."[57] Images of her drawn by indigenous artists also depict the significance they attributed to La Malinche and her strategic importance as mediator. Cypess writes that in codex Lienzo de Tlaxcala, La Malinche stands "with her arm outstretched, pointing as if she were helping direct the events" (see figure 5).[58] Tzvetan Todorov describes her central position in the Florentine Codex, in which she stands between Cortés and Moctezuma, as characteristic of her role in negotiating between the Europeans and the indigenous peoples: "the two military leaders occupy the margins of the image,

5. Malintzin Tenepal (La Malinche), Lienzo de Tlaxcala, sixteenth-century reproduction of lost cloth original. Paint wash and ink on handmade (amate or maguey) paper. Courtesy of Benson Latin American Collection, University of Texas, Austin.

6. Malintzin Tenepal (La Malinche) between Cortés and indigenous leaders, Florentine Codex XII, sixteenth-century reproduction of lost cloth original. China-ink on European paper. Courtesy of Biblioteca Laurentiana, Florence.

dominated by the central figure of La Malinche" (see figure 6).[59] In these illustrations, the indigenous historians give her a principal position in relationship to both groups. Ironically, though she was Cortés's slave, La Malinche's elite status was restored by those who first enslaved her, the indigenous peoples. She is referred to frequently in indigenous accounts that tell of her direct participation in meetings with indigenous dignitaries. Consequently, Cortés is referred to as "El Malinche,"[60] thus linguistically subjugated to Malintzin. Yet the esteem with which she is regarded in indigenous representations lasted for only a brief period of history; respect would quickly turn to a notoriety that evolved with ever-increasing negativity into the twentieth century.

Few Mexican Americans or Mexicans consider Malintzin Tenepal to be a positive female figure today. Two of the women whose oral histories I gathered heard negative ideas associated with her name. In her oral history, Ventura Loya notes the contradictory ways La Malinche is conceived in Mexican history textbooks and in popular culture. The differing conceptions Loya discusses represent the ambivalent and still changing position that this historical female figure occupies in Mexican culture.

> What I know about Malinche is that she was an Indian who was the interpreter for Hernán Cortés when he was in Mexico. She was his lover. Somehow learning the language, she was able to communicate with the two sides. But for some reason, people talk about, "hijo de la Malinche," like "son of the bitch." Or sometimes there are little jokes about that. But I never heard explanations about why they would say that Malinche was considered bad. In [books taught in Mexican history classes], she was the woman who learned the language and helped Hernán Cortés communicate [with the indigenous peoples]. And then also how she enabled the Indians to communicate [with the Spanish]. . . . The way that the history books described her is that she was a smart woman who'd been able to learn and help.

Irma Vásquez remembers that "Malinche was a free Indian," but that her name has also come to signify a traitor. She relates that people say, " 'Don't be a malinchista' because the Malinche was on the other side, not with her people. For instance if I am more attracted to American than Mexican ways, they can call me a malinchista." Loya and Vásquez are the only oral historians of the working-class and semiprofessional women who could identify the historical significance of La Malinche. Several of the other women conflated her with las soldaderas, women who fought in the Mexican Revolution, 1910–20. This misrecognition with las soldaderas, however, suggests the similar sexual terms under which women were circumscribed even as they served important, independent roles in Mexican history. Like las soldaderas, La Malinche went from heroine to betrayer/whore in the public sentiment. Because these historical figures acted independently and supposedly voluntarily slept with more than one man, they were branded unreliable and impure.

The transitive position La Malinche has occupied in indigenous, Spanish, and Mexican history and her transformations in the collective memory are signified by the various names by which she is known that refer to her changing status from one period to another. Following traditional Nahuatl naming practices, Malinal and Malintzin are formed from the Nahuatl name for the day, malinalli (twisted grass), on which she probably was born.[61] Upon being given to Cortés, she was immediately baptized and christened Marina (a reference to the sea). In writing his sixteenth-century account of the conquest, Bernal Díaz del Castillo refers to her as Doña Marina, the title "doña" conferring the respect due a Spanish lady, a portrayal Díaz took pains to cultivate in his vivid and glowing accounts of La Malinche's character and services.[62] By contrast, Cortés and Francisco López de Gómara, a loyal follower of Cortés, referred to her only as Marina, which speaks more about her status and Cortés's view of her in "strategic and military" terms as a "faithful slave girl."[63] The uncertainty of her original name as a sign of identity and subjectivity suggests the tenuous position women occupied in precolonial and conquest Mexico, where even wealthy or royal indigenous women could become slaves, object commodities for exchange between warring tribes, a practice also acceptable to the Spaniards.[64]

Cypess elaborates how La Malinche was transformed from historical figure to a negative feminine archetype. In the early colonial period immediately following the conquest, the name Doña Marina represented positive attributes in accord with chivalric Spanish literary heroes and biblical figures. Symbol of the syncretism of cultures and races, she was portrayed as the mother of the first mestizo. After the 1810 War of Independence, the criollos who came to power felt compelled to distance themselves from all things Spanish and to create a version of history that accorded with their view of Mexican nationalism. "The Spanish conquistadors had read La Malinche as Doña Marina, an object of desire—of male dominance of the female, of desire for the land newly conquered. . . . The new reading of the mother figure projected the resentment of the children for their progenitors and the system they had created." In the representation of the new nation, Doña Marina became La Malinche, a Spanish corruption of Malintzin, the name signified by "the snake and the Mexican Eve, the traitor and temptress."[65]

When La Virgen de Guadalupe came into prominence as the nationalistic sign of the liberated Mexico, La Malinche was rewritten as the anti-Virgin, the traitor-whore. Her supposed renunciation of the indigenous male in favor of the foreigner (Cortés) is named malinchismo. As Vásquez stated above, it is a term used even today to condemn the actions of any Mexican who rejects the homeland and its people by crossing the border literally or figuratively to the other side. During the civil rights movement, Chicanas who married European American men, embraced feminism, or pursued higher education were called "malinches" for adopting Eurocentric ideas. The appellation "vendido" or "vendida" (sellout)—synonymous with "malinchista," a person who engages in malinchismo—is explored by the Chicana/o writers Cherríe Moraga and Luís Valdéz.[66]

The concept of traitor and whore associated with La Malinche is further magnified in Octavio Paz's identification of her as La Chingada, the violated Mother. Paz's phallocentric explication of the Mexican psyche in *The Labyrinth of Solitude* constructs an active/passive dualism along strict gender lines that valorizes aggression and domination. The chingada (female)—loosely translated as the fucked one or one fucked over—is described in opposition to the aggressive male, the chingón, who rips her open. In Paz's view, the female is defenseless and entirely passive.[67] Paz relates the violation of Mexico by the Spanish to Malintzin's sexual relationship with Cortés, which he believes was voluntary on her part. Further describing the passivity of la chingada as "nothingness," a loss of name and identity, Paz extends this metaphor to all women: "she is the cruel incarnation of the feminine condition."[68] By his reasoning, not only is La Malinche condemned for sleeping with (being forced to sleep with) the enemy but she and all women are responsible—by their alleged passivity and openness—for violations committed against her, themselves, and Mexico. Men are absolved of responsibility, and the motivations of greed and power that propelled the conquest of Mexico by Spain—enabled by the dominant Mexica conquest of other indigenous peoples—are forgotten.

Women are robbed of subjectivity, agency, and identity; if not for their abject bodies they would be obliterated from being. The repercussions of this thinking for Mexicanas and Chicanas as the "symbolic daughters of La Malinche" is that "their sexuality, whatever its form, is stigmatized."[69]

Malinal, Doña Marina, La Lengua, La Malinche, La Chingada. Representing object of exchange, object of desire, object of language, object of contempt, object of violation, these overlapping significations of Malintzin's name have sustained generations of patriarchal rule. Yet the reverence accorded her by the indigenous peoples as "la lengua," and the esteemed position the Spaniards awarded her as the mother of the mestizo race, serve as counterpoints to the disapproving significations. Consequently, in the second half of the twentieth century, Chicana and Mexican writers began restoring La Malinche's name by reviewing her place in history, revealing her as a cultural and gender scapegoat, and representing her as a historical subject-agent. In a series of articles, the Chicana feminist scholar Norma Alarcón explores the significance of rewritings of Mexican female cultural figures and the construction of a Chicana identity through "the appropriation of history, sexuality and language for themselves." Maintaining that masculine conceptions of La Malinche have affected experiences of many U.S. Mexicanas and Chicanas, Alarcón describes how Chicana writers redefine and reinvent their own experience beyond negative stereotypes and rigid gender roles.[70]

In contrast to the saintly Guadalupe, the figure of La Malinche represents the transgressor who speaks as a sexual being and steps outside her role as mother. As a transcendent figure, Guadalupe is disembodied and desexualized, limiting her potential within language as a symbol for resistance. Embodied and racialized as an indigenous woman, La Malinche is readily appropriated by Chicana writers and artists because she can be refigured as a linguistic agent who passes on her agency as a speaking subject. This move legitimates Chicana discourse by grounding it in Mexican/Chicana/o culture and by positioning them as her offspring, "her [Chicana] daughters."[71] Chicana writers' revisions of La Malinche gave them a means by which to recover language and their experiences as women of color. Furthermore, by recuperating her, they could avoid the ambivalence of Guadalupe's religious femininity.[72]

Not only is La Malinche positioned in oppositional terms to La Virgen de Guadalupe; she is also seen as the negative counterpart to Cuauhtemoc, the last Mexica male leader, who is considered a symbol of indigenous resistance to the Spaniards.[73] In this comparison, she is blamed as the sole person responsible for the downfall of the indigenous civilization. Mary Louise Pratt argues, however, that if not for male dominance, whereby women were used as objects of exchange among men, La Malinche would not have been delivered into the hands of the Spaniards in the form of war chattel.[74] If not for the betrayal of Malinche by her own people, Cortés would not have had access to a multilingual indigenous translator and may not have conquered Tenochtitlan. Pratt argues the Malinche myth positions the conquest as a battle between invading Spanish colonizers and heroic indigenous males, rather than considering the internal conflicts that caused many indigenous peoples to side with the Spaniards. La Malinche disrupts the notion of conquest and resistance as male-gendered activities by inserting a female presence into the male homopolitical relations between the Spaniards and the Mexica and among the indigenous factions.[75] These historical facts provided Chicana writers, especially poets during the 1970s and 1980s, an opening to refigure La Malinche as an active agent with a purpose and vision beyond patriarchal domination. In particular, Carmen Tafolla's poem "La Malinche" provides a radical refiguring of Malintzin Tenepal as a woman with a futuristic vision beyond the narrow power plays of the male antagonists. The poem's persona speaks as Malintzin Tenepal: "I began to *dream*/ I *saw,*/ and I *acted!*" In this poem, La Malinche, historically silenced, is given voice and speaks as a self-determining subject who imagines the grander project of a new mestiza/o world.[76]

In the 1990s, visual artists began recuperating Malintzin, the woman and La Malinche, the symbol. Santa Barraza's painting *La Malinche* portrays a strong, self-reliant indigenous woman pregnant with child blossoming from a maguey plant that grows seemingly from her uterus or from which she grows.[77] In this representation, La Malinche takes on the life-giving powers of a mother earth goddess. A much smaller Hernán Cortés stares voyeuristically from the distance, but La Malinche's back is to him and she gives complete attention to the fully formed male fetus as if to focus on the future rather than the past. In the background, Spanish conquerors ravage the landscape of earthly and human riches.[78] La Malinche's face bears a pensive look signaling knowledge of the difficult life her mestizo child will lead. Santa Barraza says her artwork is inspired by "the indomitable women who lived in the harsh environment of the Borderlands. My Karankawa great-great-grandmother, Cuca Giza, who married her Spanish conqueror, has become my Malinche."[79]

Most recently, two new books feature La Malinche in their titles. In 2006, Mexican writer Laura Esquivel published *Malinche: A Novel*, which portrays an ambivalent Malintzin who, though she has sex with Cortés willingly at first, also recognizes his narcissism, greed, and hunger for power. To write the novel, Esquivel had to imagine Malintzin's everyday life, including what food she liked, what it meant to light a fire, and what gods she sought comfort in. She realized that Malintzin's images of the gods would have come from a codex or sculpture. Inside the book jacket of the hard-cover edition, Esquivel includes a codex "that Malinche might have painted," which tells the same story in pictographs that Esquivel writes in the novel. She notes that "the codex symbolizes a process of mediation" unifying the mental work of writing rational events with the creative, emotional, and spiritual process of painting concrete forms. "In this manner, I try to conciliate two visions, two ways of storytelling—the written and the symbolic—two breaths, two yearnings, two times, two hearts, in one." Esquivel creates a facsimile codex of Malintzin's daily life to replace the absence of knowledge about her in historical codices. In addition, she re-members herself—as an indigenous woman—in the memory of Malintzin the actual woman: "two hearts, in one."[80]

Chicana writer Michelle Otero refigures Malinche in a collection of essays about the sexual abuse of young women. *Malinche's Daughter*, also published in 2006, focuses on the trauma of sexual violation and the silencing of victims. Otero considers Malinche a survivor of sexual abuse, in contrast to historical writings that indicate she was Cortés's lover, a voluntary and mutual partner. She rewrites Malinche's history and story exposing how Malinche and Chicana/Mexicana victims of sexual abuse were betrayed by fathers, brothers, uncles, family friends, or authority figures. "I wanted to call things what they are. The Spaniards didn't *arrive* in the Americas. They *invaded*. Malinche was not Cortés's *lover*. She was his property. He owned her. Their relationship wasn't based on equality, but on domination. Where there is domination, there is no love. I wanted Malinche to know across time that someone has her back." In an interview with Carolina Monsivais, Otero, who was sexually abused at age five, discusses how she had to "unlearn the mistrust" of speaking the truth. "There's a saying in Spanish, Te vez más bonita cuando te quedas callada

(You look prettier when you keep quiet). Even though no one ever said this to me directly, I received and internalized the message that something bad happened when women spoke their truth. . . . But no one ever talked to me about the ways these silences eat at our hearts and destroy us." In addressing Malinche's misrepresentation, Otero says she began to "un-twist" her own feelings of inadequacy and confront those who called her a betrayer. "This is what I've wanted when I've felt the backlash of speaking the truth about racism or sexism or patriarchal violence, someone who will say, 'I hear you,' and will stand by you as people call you disloyal or ungrateful."[81]

Otero's writing shows that of all the Mexican female cultural figures, La Malinche stands as the real woman and symbol through whom Chicanas and U.S. Mexicanas begin to make sense of their mestiza existence. As the title of Otero's book suggests, Malintzin Tenepal is the originator of a "second generation" of transgressive women, who disrupt the colonialist patriarchal legacies of the Mexicas, the Spaniards, and Mexican Catholic culture. In the genealogical line of the woman of discord, the authors, artists, and oral historians in this study are part of her legacy.

La Llorona, the Weeping Woman

The legend of La Llorona derives from precolonial mother earth goddess stories and indigenous Mexica conquest stories involving La Malinche. With colonialism, European folktale themes intermixed with indigenous elements to produce the popular contemporary legend. La Llorona also resonates as a Mexican maternity symbol and, like La Malinche, she obtained negative significance in contrast to La Virgen de Guadalupe. The contemporary story line depicts La Llorona drowning or stabbing her children because her husband or lover, often a man of higher class status, leaves her for another woman. This version resembles the Medea myth and emphasizes the European elements of the syncretic tale. The drowning variation, especially prevalent in the U.S. Southwest, in which La Llorona weeps for her children by the water, is told as a ghost story. Often parents use it to warn children away from waterways or to keep them from going outside at night. Cordelia Candelaria relates a common parental admonition: "Settle down and behave or La Llorona will come and get you!"[82]

Hundreds of variations of Wailing Woman narratives exist, but the stories generally fall into three thematic groupings: (1) an indigenous mother earth goddess (or La Malinche) is heard crying, often in mourning for her lost people; (2) a beautiful woman or siren-like figure lures men to illicit sex or men and children to death, often in water; (3) a woman is betrayed by her lover/husband who leaves her for another woman. She kills her children, herself, or both, and then weeps and wails while she wanders looking for them. The first two have roots in indigenous creation narratives, while the third draws from European folktales.

La Llorona's roots in indigenous symbology are significant.[83] Her name and weeping feature stem from a precolonial myth describing the creation of the earth. An indigenous originary goddess called the "Hungry Woman" generated the earth from her body and cried constantly for food to sustain her as she worked.[84] La Llorona's wailing also may be derived from the mother earth goddess Cihuacoatl, who represents midwives and women who died in childbirth. Birthing mothers were encouraged to cry out Cihuacoatl's name in a war call. Another aspect of Cihuacoatl, Chalchiuhtlicue, the fertility goddess of lakes and streams, represents La Llorona's common association with water. As the goddess of childbirth, Chalchiuhtlicue is summoned to ceremonial purification rituals, including the baptizing of children in lakes,[85] which bears consideration in the interpretation of variations in which La Llorona "drowns" her children. Cihuacoatl's death aspect, the Cihuateteo reproductive demons, also account for La Llorona's wandering, fearsome behavior. The Cihuateteo haunted crossroads, waiting to prey on children and seduce men to commit adultery or other sexual transgressions.[86] Cihuacoatl is said to have looked for "naughty children, sometimes carrying a cradle with nothing in it but a bloody dagger."[87] This death aspect explains why children are taught to fear La Llorona and why she sometimes appears to men at night as a beautiful young woman and ultimately reveals herself as an old witch or La Muerte, death personified.[88]

In indigenous narratives the Cihuateteo fulfilled the role of what Sarah Iles Johnston describes as "reproductive demons," the "souls of women who died as virgins, died in childbirth, or died shortly after the deaths of their own children."[89] Because they have not fulfilled the reproductive cycle they inflict the same fate on other women by killing infants and young children and sometimes pregnant women or new mothers. In the colonial period, the Cihuateteo appear to have metamorphosed into La Llorona, child killer and, in some variants of the legend, male seducer and killer. Johnston notes that female figures such as Medea and La Llorona evolved from reproductive demons that killed other women's children, like the Cihuateteo, into demons that killed their own children.[90] In the case of the Llorona legend, the Cihuateteo evolved to a figure more European and Catholic in form.

One of the earliest recorded stories of the weeping woman figure is associated with the indigenous goddess Cihuacoatl, who warned her people of impending doom prior to the Spanish conquest. Spanish chroniclers recorded these indigenous versions in the sixteenth century. Fray Bernadino de Sahagún relates her story in several of his sixteenth-century chronicles. "She was in white . . . in pure white. . . . By night she walked weeping and wailing, a dread phantom foreboding war."[91] "Oh, my children, your destruction is at hand. . . . My children, whither shall I take you so that you will not utterly perish?"[92] Other Spanish chroniclers recorded similar versions that foretold the fall of the indigenous peoples. Bernal Díaz del Castillo wrote of a woman's voice in the night wind saying, "Oh my children, we are now lost!" or "Oh my children, where shall I take you?" In a similar way, La Llorona's wailing holds particular significance for Chicana/o culture, symbolizing children lost through "assimilation into the dominant culture or because of violence or prejudice."[93] From these perspectives, La Llorona may be considered as a benevolent goddess warning her people about the Spanish and American invasions.

During and after the conquest, connections were drawn between La Llorona and La Malinche, who mourns the loss of her people or "eternally laments the betrayal of her people."[94] In La Malinche versions containing the infanticide theme, La Llorona's actions function as resistance to European conquest and white and male dominance. One early version, re-enacted annually in Mexico as a play, represents La Llorona/La Malinche using violence to defy a greater violence. This variation of the story depicts her as an indigenous woman who drowns her child in the symbolic act of saving her family, her culture, and her people from subjugation by the Spanish conquerors. The conquerors capture her and put her to death, but her spirit roams the streets of Mexico crying for her lost children, symbolically, the indigenous peoples.[95] As mentioned earlier, submergence into a lake or river represents ceremonial purification and association with the goddess Chalchiuhtlicue. For this reason, the "drowning" of the children could be considered as a sacred ritual rather than a crime.

A similar story depicts La Llorona as La Malinche in love with Hernán

Cortés. In this version, Cortés refuses to marry Malinche or take her with him to Spain because "she was an Indian," but he wants to take their son to Spain because of his "Spanish blood." When Cortés comes to take the boy by force, La Malinche/La Llorona stabs the child and herself to death with an obsidian knife, evoking ritual sacrifice to the gods.[96] In yet another variation, La Llorona is depicted as a mestiza, a mixed-race woman, who is raped by a Spaniard, then spurned.[97] Similar to Toni Morrison's *Beloved*, which responds to the power realized by white male slave owners over black women and their children, these La Llorona/La Malinche variations reflect anticolonial and antipatriarchal themes in which indigenous women demonstrate defiance to presumed white male supremacy.

The Europeanized features of the legend include Western folklore themes of a woman with children who is betrayed by an adulterous husband. She takes revenge by killing her children and then wanders in anguished repentance searching for them. This revenge theme is familiar from depictions of the Greek Medea and the Judaic Lilith. Regarding the Medea legend, the infanticidal revenge theme became accepted as the "true" version with the advent of Euripides's play *Medea*, written in 431 BCE. Before the existence of Euripides's play, many Corinthian Medea stories did *not* contain acts of infanticidal revenge, and Medea was viewed as a complex being.[98] Significantly, as with the stories of Medea and Lilith, the earliest recorded versions of La Llorona do not represent her killing children. Rather, in early versions of all three figures' stories, social-political or religious forces kill their symbolic or actual children. La Llorona, Medea, and Lilith, who have come to represent the ultimate "bad" mothers/women, originally took form as revered fertility goddesses in pre-Christian cultures.[99]

La Llorona narratives serve as a model of how women should act as mothers, wives, and lovers and relate the repercussions for women who do not accept their roles as reproducers and servers. Mirandé and Enríquez explain that La Llorona serves as a negative cultural symbol, an example of a woman who "strayed from her proper role of mother, wife, mistress, lover or patriot."[100] Like La Malinche, La Llorona represents the negative pole of dualistic thinking that compares them to the idealized mother, La Virgen de Guadalupe. As Gloria Anzaldúa notes, "in the case of La Llorona, the culture projects all of its negative fears and how it feels threatened by women onto her and she is made the bad mother that kills her children."[101] Because La Llorona repents and mourns her actions, Shirlene Soto observes that she is a somewhat more sympathetic figure than La Malinche, yet both figures engage in independent and resistive behavior considered unacceptable for women. By emphasizing that the consequence of "disloyalty" is eternal condemnation or isolation, the legends are used to socialize women into traditional roles, control their conduct, and define what constitutes Mexican femininity. The message conveyed is that independent women are dangerous and treacherous. Ironically, the legend also demonstrates that women have tremendous power.

In relating her own childhood experiences, Anzaldúa reveals the regulatory effects of the Llorona legend and later how La Llorona liberated her to refigure patriarchal and heterosexist narratives by "speaking out" a different reality for women and girls. "Llorona was the first cultural figure that I was introduced to at the age of two or three years old. My grandmothers told me stories about her. She was a bogeyman. She was the horrific, the terror, the woman who killed her children, who misplaced her children. She was used to scare us into not going out of the house at night, and especially to scare the little girls into being good little girls. If you were a bad little girl la Llorona was going to come and get you. To me she was the central figure in Mexican mythology, which empowered me to yell out, to scream out, to speak out, to break out of silence."[102] La Llorona's transgressive scream, reflecting those of the Mexica goddesses and La Malinche and contrasting with La Virgen de Guadalupe's silent demeanor, provides Anzaldúa a metaphor for her creative and theoretical writings.[103] In her children's book *Prietita and the Ghost Woman/Prietita y La Llorona*, Anzaldúa refigures La Llorona from a scary figure capable of evil to a kind and helpful spirit. When Prietita gets lost in the woods looking for a medicinal herb to heal her mother, La Llorona helps her find the herb and her way out of the woods. Anzaldúa overwrites the reproductive demon story of infanticide and the nightmarish witch that children must fear, portraying instead a female figure who acts as a role model. Other Chicana authors have rewritten La Llorona as a resistive figure. Sandra Cisneros's well-known short story "Woman Hollering Creek" represents La Llorona as a calming, liberating, and joyful influence for an abused woman. Two other works, Alma Villanueva's short story collection *Weeping Woman: La Llorona and Other Stories* and Moraga's play *The Hungry Woman: A Mexican Medea*, examine the struggles women encounter in meeting their personal and sociopolitical needs and desires. I examine the latter texts in chapter 4 along with La Llorona stories told by the oral historians, several of whom experience Llorona moments or emulate her transgressive behavior.

In the 1990s and into the new century, La Llorona began to be recuperated and revised in visual art and mass media. In 1994, Carmen León's painting of La Llorona appeared on the cover of Villanueva's *Weeping Woman* (see figure 7). This depiction represents La Llorona as a reflective and compassionate woman who extends her hands toward the viewer, offering a gift of a seashell. Her upper torso emerges from the swirling water of a lake or stream and is clothed only in a loosely woven shawl revealing her as a sexual being. León says this depiction represents Villanueva's view of La Llorona, one that contrasts with narratives of her as an infanticidal, hysterical figure.

Santa Barraza also began recuperating La Llorona in the mid-1990s. Like the painting *La Malinche*, Barraza's series of La Llorona drawings and paintings features a bare-breasted indigenous woman who merges with the life-giving elements of maguey and water. The earliest painting, completed in 1993, situates La Llorona next to the corn goddess, another sign of fertility.[104] Barraza's 1994 retablo, *Apparition of La Llorona*, features a two-headed woman. One face appears asleep with a tattooed hand of death covering her mouth, symbolizing her silence. The other open-eyed face wears a tattoo of a Chicana/o farmworkers' eagle, a symbol of resistance and voice. The two heads may symbolize the indigenous duality of life and death, creation and destruction, victimization and agency. The Mayan goddess of healing, childbirth, and the moon appears in the background.[105] A charcoal drawing of the same woman completed in 1995 is titled *Teotl*, which means "sacred vital force." This drawing also contains a dismembered Coyolxauhqui whose arm extends down to La Llorona "as if passing on her memory—her final act to empower womankind."[106] Barraza's 1995 oil painting *La Llorona II/The Weeping Woman* portrays a symbolic mountain with a spear embedded in it signifying conquered territory and relating La Llorona to La Malinche and all mestizas who lived through the conquest.[107] A 1996 silk-screen represents La Llorona and the Cihuateteo as the same figure. This painting, *Cihuateteo con Coyolxauhqui y la Guadalapana*, is identical to *La Llorona II* in its representation of the woman, maquey, water, and the symbol of conquered territory. However, the stone of the dismembered Coyolxauhqui and La Virgen de Guadalupe are added in the background, rising from the earth and overlooking La Llorona.[108] In these paintings, Barraza depicts the interrelationship

7. Carmen León, *Weeping Woman*, 1994. Acrylic on canvas. Courtesy of the artist.

of La Llorona with the three other Mexican female cultural figures, in which all four figures represent real women's experiences. In depicting them as brown-skinned indigenous women, she asserts their strength and beauty conveying the colonial, racial, and gender ideologies that have affected real and symbolic female experiences and representations. For Barraza, La Llorona represents the lives and experiences of actual women such as Malintzin Tenepal as well as Barraza's own sister, mother, grandmother, and great-grandmothers.[109]

The painter and graphic artist Maya Christina Gonzalez produced the illustrations for the 1995 publication of Anzaldúa's children's book *Prietita and the Ghost Woman/Prietita y La Llorona*, depicting La Llorona as a source of wisdom providing "light" or knowledge. In Gonzalez's representations, La Llorona appears at night dressed in white tinged with yellow, evoking the moon goddess, Coyolxauhqui. A yellow halo surrounds her body, suggesting the cloak of La Virgen de Guadalupe. The book's biographical description of Gonzalez says she "feels a deep connection with the figure of La Llorona, viewing her as a metaphor for Prietita's, as well as her own, creativity and spiritual growth."[110]

In the early twenty-first century, La Llorona themes also began appearing on television. The PBS television series *American Family*, about several generations of a Mexican American family living in East Los Angeles, featured a Llorona theme in two episodes of its 2002 season. In the first episode, the Llorona legend is introduced to the young boy Pablito by his uncle Cisco as an explanation of why the wind howls during a storm. A cyber-expert, the sixteen-year-old Cisco shows Pablito Internet illustrations depicting the legend. The dialogue between Pablito and Cisco slightly revises the Llorona legend when Pablito calls the legendary husband a "jerk," condemning him for leaving his wife and children for another woman. At the same time, Cisco's cyber-story maintains La Llorona as an infanticidal crazy woman, and her story performs a disciplinary function when Cisco warns Pablito to stay away from rivers and lakes.

The main story line of the two episodes follows two women portrayed as modern-day Lloronas who lose their children. One plot features Pablito's mother, Laura, who has lost custody of her son to his paternal grandparents because her drug addiction has endangered Pablito's life. Pablito's grandfather Jess encounters Laura staring at Pablito from outside the school yard and warns her to stay away from him. "You're so hooked you're lost and you know it."[111] The theme of lost women is continued in an interwoven plot about an undocumented immigrant who loses her husband and newborn child to U.S. immigration authorities. The characters, Elena Bonilla and her husband Emilio, originally from Guatemala, are deported separately to Mexico. Their American-born child is put up for adoption in California. The second episode follows Elena's arduous journey crossing the U.S.–Mexico border and walking through the desert to Los Angeles to find her husband and child. Both stories of loss are unresolved; neither Laura nor Elena is able to recover her child. However, Elena's brave actions crossing the border refigure the evil mother version of the legend as Elena acts to reunite the family rather than kill the child or herself. In addition, the male figure in the Llorona legend is also revised by depicting Emilio's separation from his wife and child as a result of social and political forces rather than adulterous behavior. The story line implies that the boss who hired Emilio to do "garden" work conspired with "la migra" so that he would not have to pay for Emilio's stoop labor in a cilantro field. The two episodes critique U.S. government policies toward Mexicans, Central Americans, and other undocumented peoples who labor at jobs European Americans are unwilling to perform. The final image fosters sympathy and compassion for undocumented women or any woman who has lost a child through no fault of her own. An image of Elena Bonilla reaching out for her lost child is transformed into the La Llorona cyber-image Cisco accessed on his computer to tell Pablito the legend. In a sympathetic voice, Cisco concludes: "La Llorona. She never found her children even though she still wanders the night looking, always looking."[112]

Also in 2002, a team of U.S. Latina graphic art students from the Art Center College of Design in Pasadena produced a "Got Milk" commercial featuring La Llorona. Sponsored by the California Milk Processors Board, the thirty-second advertisement begins with a wispy, ethereal woman in white walking through a family's house at night. The soundtrack features her weeping and builds suspense in the manner of a horror film. She passes through the sleeping parents' bedroom as if she is looking for the children. However, the kitchen is La Llorona's destination and she cries because she is hungry and thirsty. She opens the refrigerator and her facial expression changes from forlorn to ecstatic at the sight of a carton of milk. La Llorona takes a big bite of pan dulce and prepares to gulp down the milk. Then she realizes the milk carton is empty and begins to weep again.[113] In this parodic and humorous depiction, La Llorona's loss is neither significant nor tragic. Nor is it caused by male betrayal or her violent actions. Although La Llorona is appropriated for the purposes of capitalist consumption in this context, the advertisement avoids depicting her as an evil, infanticidal mother who kills her children and suffers eternal damnation. In contrast to the main theme that encourages Latino/as to buy milk, a subtheme reflects the reality of hunger and malnutrition among the greater Mexican and Central American population. While it may not have been the conscious intent of the art team, La Llorona is refigured as the "hungry woman" in the indigenous narrative of the creation of the earth.

In 2003, Alma López's artwork *La Llorona Desperately Seeking Coyolxauhqui in Juárez* appeared on the cover of Alicia Gaspar de Alba's collection *La Llorona on the Longfellow Bridge: Poetry y otras movidas*. The title of Lopez's work alludes to a contemporary serial crime, the decade-long rape, mutilation, and murder of more than five hundred young women in Juárez, Mexico. The art presents a young woman in a rose floral dress with a tattered cloak and veil covering her head in the image of La Virgen de Guadalupe. Her eyes are downcast like Guadalupe's but not in submission; she is searching the water of the Rio Grande for the bodies of murdered young women. The woman is barefoot and her arms and neck are badly bruised as if she has been held captive, a victim who survived, or alternately that she was murdered and her ghost haunts the river like La Llorona's. The bridge across the Rio Grande between the United States and Mexico is featured in the background and the woman walks in the middle of the river on the submerged stone sculpture of the dismembered body of Coyolxauhqui. Looking down at Coyolxauhqui and reaching toward her, the brown-skinned young woman appears to will Coyolxauhqui to power. She re-members Coyolxauhqui as she remembers other Juárez women like herself. As discussed earlier, the Coyolxauhqui sculpture represents the misogynist patriarchal rule of the Mexicas that denigrated female goddesses. In Lopez's artwork, Coyolxauhqui also signifies the young brown women who are victims of the NAFTA-produced border economy, which exploits their labor in the maquilas and their sexuality through often lethal activities such as pornography and prostitution. In titling the main figure La Llorona, López suggests not only the pain and suffering the woman experienced within this racist and sexist late-capitalist social order but also the fortitude of a survivor or ghost who seeks to uncover the bodies and expose the unsolved crimes.

A serigraph using the same female model and similarly titled, *La Llorona Desperately Seeking Coyolxauhqui*, shows a close-up of the woman's face crying and looking straight out rather than down (see figure 8). In this image, the figure does not wear Guadalupe's cloak. Instead, a shadow form of La Virgen with her arms raised stands with her back to the woman as if to suggest that Guadalupe has deserted her. Or maybe Guadalupe has turned her back on the male representation of god and is pleading for another higher power, a goddess, to intervene. The young woman is wearing a strapless gown of roses echoing the swimsuit of roses in López's earlier depiction of Guadalupe *Our Lady* (see figure 14 on page 67) and indicating the woman's embodied sexuality in contrast to Guadalupe's virginity and noncorporeality. Or, in another possible interpretation, the shadow form may represent the mother of a violated young girl who is mourning or searching for her child like La Llorona and La Virgen. The decapitated head of Coyolxauhqui is tattooed on the woman's shoulder and Coatlicue's (serpent/snake) fangs are stenciled over her nose and mouth. Also stenciled on both sides of her face are the open-palm hands and organs Coatlicue wears on her breast. At first glance the stencil

8. Alma M. López, *La Llorona Desperately Seeking Coyolxauhqui*, 2003. Digital print, printed at Sam Coronado Studios, Austin, Texas. Courtesy of the artist. Special thanks to Coral López.

appears to represent a death mask, but the woman's open eyes suggest life, although heavily lidded with pain and sorrow. Has Coatlicue also abandoned her? Is Coatlicue depicted here as the traitor affiliated with the war god who has slain Coyolxauhqui? Or is Coatlicue also a victim of patriarchal violence like the women of Juárez? These Llorona figures echo the history of La Malinche, whose body also represented a site of exploitation and violent interactions among men. The fact that both La Llorona and Guadalupe are seeking Coyolxauhqui in these two works by López suggests the recovery of the ancient female image and spirit and the remembering of women past, present, and future.

La Virgen de Guadalupe

Although a number of versions of Guadalupe's story exist, the basic details I relate here are contained in all the versions. On December 9, 1531 (ten years after the fall of the Mexica center, Tenochtitlan, to the Spaniards), an indigenous man named Juan Diego who had recently converted to Catholicism was walking on Tepeyac, a hillside near Mexico City. La Virgen appeared and instructed him to inform the bishop of Mexico of her desire to have a church built on the site. In the days that followed, Guadalupe appeared to Juan Diego twice more, making the same appeal. During the third visitation, Juan Diego told her that the Catholic officials did not believe his story and wanted proof of her appearance. She told him to pick flowers from a nearby rose bush miraculously blooming in winter and take them to the bishop to show her intent. When Juan Diego gained entrance to the bishop's office and unfolded his tilmatli (cloak) to show the flowers to the bishop, the image of Guadalupe appeared imprinted on the cloak. This image (or what subsequently became the recognized image) of La Virgen de Guadalupe and her apparition story annually draw thousands of Mexicans on pilgrimages to Tepeyac to celebrate Guadalupe's December 12 feast day (see figure 9). Others who cannot make the journey celebrate the feast day by holding an all-night prayer vigil beginning on December 11.[114] Through the year, individuals, families, groups of workers, and tour groups from all over the world visit the basilica where the image resides. Of all the Mexican Catholic saints, La Virgen de Guadalupe is probably the major source of mandas, promises of a sacrifice to be made in return for a request fulfilled, such as the restoring of health, love, or emotional well-being to oneself or others. Such mandas to Guadalupe are the basis of Sandra Cisneros's short story "Little Miracles, Kept Promises" discussed in chapter 2.[115] Additionally, because the figure in the sacred image has black hair and olive skin, Guadalupe is referred to as "la virgen morena," the brown virgin, and is considered a representative of indigenous and mestiza/o peoples.

Two related narratives connect Guadalupe to the indigenous peoples of ancient Mexico. The first suggests that Guadalupe is an avatar of the indigenous mother earth goddess Tonantizin, because the hill where she appeared and requested that her church be built was the site of a former temple to the goddess. In worshipping La Virgen de Guadalupe at this site, the narrative suggests, the indigenous peoples were able to continue their spiritual practices and appease the Spaniards' demands that they convert to Catholicism. The second narrative relates that in the sixteenth century Guadalupe was a tremendous force in converting to Catholicism the thousands of indigenous peoples who flocked to worship her because of her association with their own goddess, Tonantzin.[116] In

9. La Virgen de Guadalupe, sixteenth century. Oil and tempera
paints on maguey cactus cloth and cotton. Basilica of Guadalupe,
Tepeyac, Mexico.

his comprehensive review of the origins and sources of La Virgen de Guadalupe, Stafford Poole questions many of the assertions represented as truths by the Catholic Church and religious historians. His research has shown that no evidence exists to connect the Tepeyac site with Tonantzin; the story of Juan Diego's appearance did not emerge until a hundred years after 1531; and the indigenous peoples did not flock to the Tepeyac site. Rather, he concludes, a planned effort to convert them occurred only in the eighteenth century. The factual history of the religious and political uses of the Guadalupe story and image is largely unknown, ignored, or considered irrelevant by Guadalupe's steadfast believers. Attempts to adjust the popular narrative have been resoundingly refused, as attested by the furious public outcry that greeted Mexican Abbot Guillermo Schulemberg's statement in May 1996 that "Juan Diego is a symbol not a reality."[117] The story's significance for many Mexicans rests in the replication of Juan Diego's experience in their own lived reality and the hope Guadalupe inspires for deliverance from harsh economic and social conditions. Beyond the religious significations, Guadalupe has been used to propagate numerous ideological visions. Poole summarizes the various and often interwoven discourses that have shaped understandings of La Virgen. "Guadalupe has had various meanings: indigenism, religious syncretism, respect for cultural autonomy, the struggle for human dignity, or conversely, submission and subjugation, whether of Indians or women. Most frequently Guadalupe is associated with mexicanidad [Mexicanness]."[118]

Visual representations of La Virgen de Guadalupe are a prime example of how dominant discourses initially shaped her image and how Chicanas have responded with the production of counterdiscourses. Since the colonial period, La Virgen has resonated with political and social significance for Mexican peoples. In an article that examines artistic images of Guadalupe through four centuries, Jeanette Favrot Peterson discusses how Guadalupe's various representations signify the interests of the artist or individual/group that commissioned the work. She observes that the original sixteenth-century image, modified from the classic Spanish Marian image to include olive skin and black hair, in its "humble attitude and pious gesture . . . conveniently reflected the colonial church's image of the native population that it sought to bring under its control" (see figure 9). Likewise, an early-seventeenth-century representation commissioned by the bishop to help raise funds for a new basilica named after Guadalupe records "miracles worked on behalf of the ruling white class" but fails to include any "on behalf of her native constituency."[119] Peterson's analysis shows how in the sixteenth, seventeenth, and eighteenth centuries Guadalupe functioned as a symbol of the powerful, the Catholic Church, and the Spanish elite. Later appropriations of her image were carried out in the name of the poor and indigenous populations. In 1810, the criollo priest Father Miguel Hidalgo carried a representation of La Virgen de Guadalupe to proclaim the Mexican War of Independence from Spain. In this instance, he managed to unite upper-class criollos with indigenous peasants in the fight for Independence. In 1910, Emiliano Zapata's forces used her image in asserting land reform as the aim of the Mexican Revolution.[120] In 1965 in Delano, California, when Chicana/o farm workers led by César Chávez carried an image of La Virgen de Guadalupe at the head of a protest march, they followed the earlier liberation traditions of uprisings against exploitative landowners. Peterson's analysis concludes that Guadalupe is "a symbol of liberation as well as one of accommodation and control."[121]

However, the presence of a female symbol of liberation did not ensure equality or liberation from traditional roles for Chicanas who participated in the Chicana/o civil rights movement. As the idealized opposite to La Malinche and La Llorona, Guadalupe implicitly represents the domesticated and quiescent roles women were assigned within the movement: cooking food, taking care of children, and standing behind their man.[122] From this perspective, Guadalupe's symbolism assumes meaning contrary to the liberatory significance. Women raised within Mexican Catholic culture grapple with characteristics attributed to La Virgen that encourage acceptance and endurance, rather than self-determination, and reinforce restrictive gender and sexuality roles. As the long-suffering mother of Christ she is considered a passive, submissive role model for Mexican Catholic women, one which encourages piety, purity, virginity, and unquestioning obedience in their primary roles as wife and mother. For this reason, Guadalupe is an ambivalent figure who could not "emerge as a cultural heroine for [Chicana feminist] authors without some transformations."[123] In contrast to the absence of Guadalupe in early works by the Chicana writers discussed in this study, the working-class and semiprofessional women express enduring faith in Guadalupe. Yet as their oral histories attest in chapter 3, they also challenge and resist some of the confining attributes associated with her.

Following the civil rights movement, Chicana artists (although not writers) were inspired to refigure Guadalupe to reflect what Chabram-Dernersesian calls the "*mujer valiente*" (valiant woman).[124] In the mid- to late 1970s, transformations of La Virgen de Guadalupe emerged with Ester Hernández's and Yolanda López's visual portrayals of Guadalupe as productive, active, and independent. Hernández and López took Guadalupe off her pedestal, depicting her as real working women actively producing their own subjectivities. Hernández was the first Chicana to visually refigure Guadalupe, depicting a woman as a karate-kicking warrior surrounded by Guadalupe's cloak of stars and rays of sun and held up on a pedestal by an angel. In this 1976 etching, titled *La Virgen de Guadalupe Defendiendo Los Derechos De Los Xicanos/La Virgen de Guadalupe Defending the Rights of the Xicanos*, the Chicana martial arts expert actively fights for her people. Unlike the religious depiction of Guadalupe with hands folded in prayer and eyes downcast, this Chicana does not wait passively for help from God or anyone else. She provides for her own well-being and that of her people through active self-defense. In addition, her kicking leg extends outside the cloak and sun rays as if breaking through religious and cultural stereotypes of women's roles.

In 1978, Yolanda López created a series of paintings that replaced the Catholic visage of La Virgen with depictions of her grandmother, her mother, and herself (see figures 10–13). In each of the portrayals, the cloak of sun rays that radiates around Guadalupe in the traditional image is an element of López's refigured image. The cloak signifies the spiritual import the artist attributes to each real woman in the painting and reaffirms a cultural connection to Mexican working-class identity through Guadalupe. In the painting of her grandmother, Victoria F. Franco, the elderly woman holds a knife and the flayed skin of a snake (see figure 10). The determined, yet worn, look on her face suggests the struggles she has overcome throughout her life. Here is a woman who has endured considerable hardship and has survived. The flayed snake and knife she holds represent the battles she has fought and won. These symbols also signify her recognition of indigenous heritage and an affiliation with indigenous culture through the goddesses who are associated with the snake as dweller of earth and underworld. The painting is a tribute to her fortitude and strength in overcoming the racism, sexism, and colonialism she has experienced throughout her lifetime. The second painting shows López's mother sewing La Virgen's traditional cloak for herself. López explains that "she's not waiting around for anyone to bestow honors. She's making her own cloak" (see figure 11).[125] This image celebrates the work Chicanas and Mexicanas do in the home. It also depicts a woman who celebrates herself and revels in the conception of her subjectivity as a creative and spiritual being. In the third painting, López's image of herself shows the artist assertively gripping a live snake and leaping off Guadalupe's pedestal. In the process she steps on the male angel that holds up La Virgen in the traditional image (see figure 12). López says this portrayal makes a statement that "she doesn't need anyone to hold her up or hold her down."[126] Her self-portrait also evokes images of a woman warrior like the goddess Coyolxauhqui or birthing mothers considered warriors. López grasps the snake as a weapon or as a captured enemy, indicating female power. The snake might also represent female sexuality, appearing as a vital element of the woman's self-concept. A second self-portrait depicts how López battles negative representations of women with her artistry. The paintbrushes held in her hands with her muscular arms upraised show the strength and vitality she brings to her work and to the fight against misogyny and racism. This figure also expresses the joy of creative endeavors (see figure 13).

The four images together characterize three generations of Chicanas and U.S. Mexicanas proudly asserting their strength and endurance and convey how women of different generations have faced the challenge of being a woman of color. In contrast to the traditional depiction of Guadalupe with hands clasped in prayer and eyes humbly lowered, the women are gazing forward, asserting their presence and significance in the world. In the first image of the grandmother, a quiet but deep resilience is portrayed; this is a woman who has survived the assault of imperialistic powers on her culture, race, and gender. The second image of the mother shows how Chicanas reinforce their self-worth within the domestic sphere using the tools they have access to in the home. The sewing machine represents the means by which this U.S. Mexicana fashions an identity from a significant religious and cultural symbol, Guadalupe, yet redefines the patriarchal and colonialist meanings associated with it to portray herself as a valued member of society. The third and fourth images of the artist show an active, independent young woman who proudly asserts her Chicana identity, confronting anyone who dares to challenge it. In addition, this Chicana leaves the private, domestic sphere to enter fully into public life. The absence of male figures in each of these portraits defies the idea

10. Yolanda López,
*Victoria F. Franco: Our
Lady of Guadalupe*, 1978.
Oil pastel on paper.
Courtesy of the artist.

11. Yolanda López,
*Margaret F. Stewart: Our
Lady of Guadalupe*, 1978.
Oil pastel on paper.
Courtesy of the artist.

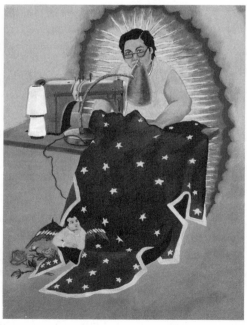

12. Yolanda López, *Portrait of the Artist as the Virgin of Guadalupe*, 1978. Oil pastel on paper. Courtesy of the artist.

13. Yolanda López, *Tableaux Vivant: Guadalupe Series*, 1978. Photo: Mogul. Courtesy of the artist.

that women only gain significance through association with a man as Guadalupe (Mary) does through Jesus.

These re-presentations of strong and combative women exist in stark contrast to the traditional image of the long-suffering Mexican Virgin who does not have the power to act and who bears all suffering and injustice without complaint. Inspired by the Chicana/o civil rights movement and Chicana feminist activism, the artistic renderings of the mujer valiente indicate passionate female resistance to sexism, racism, patriarchy, and economic exploitation. They also reveal diverse manifestations of Chicana feminism and the culturally significant groundings from which the artists draw and through which they re-member their divine and indigenous selves.

Ten years later Hernández created another work in the traditional image of Guadalupe, although the context of this representation contributed to its radical interpretation. In *La Ofrenda* (*The Offering*, 1988), Guadalupe is painted on the back of a naked woman with a punk haircut. The arm of another woman holds a rose up to Guadalupe at approximately the location of the virgin's uterus. *La Ofrenda* has been interpreted as a symbol of lesbian desire and appeared on the cover of the anthology *Chicana Lesbians: The Girls Our Mothers Warned Us About*, edited by Carla Trujillo and published in 1991. In an interview with Theresa Harlan, Hernández says that she did not create the painting as a sexual image. Rather, she drew the image on her compañera's back as a reaction to the transgression of women wearing tattoos. "In reflection much of our cultural legacy, we literally carry on our backs. That's a part of our makeup; both good and bad, and makes us who we are. People read more into the symbology than I intended. I did not see *Ofrenda* as overtly sexual although it has been discussed as sexually symbolic. It was an offering. Certainly there is a little blood I am offering, but that is another story."[127]

Unlike Chicana artists, Chicana writers were unable to refigure Guadalupe at all during the 1970s and early 1980s, standing as she did for "blind devotion."[128] Tey Diana Rebolledo discusses identification with Guadalupe as a dilemma for many Chicana writers. "Notwithstanding the Virgin's strong image in popular culture, she is represented in a problematic manner by many Chicana writers, and at times even—ironically—as a symbol of failure. On the negative side, La Virgen is often seen as not active enough, a somewhat passive figure created by the patriarchy, an image giving them mixed messages: How can one be a mother and a virgin too?"[129] Although Paz describes La Malinche as a passive object, it is most often La Virgen who sets the example for women to be meek and accepting of their circumstances, just as the Virgin Mary suffered and accepted the torture and death of her son, Jesus. La Virgen's desexed and bodiless state is regarded as a model of miraculous birth and sexual denial by means of her immaculate conception. Thus, passive and disembodied, Guadalupe could not provide spiritual or symbolic inspiration until, beginning in the late 1980s, several writers and artists recuperated her image as a site for lesbian desire and Chicana feminism by locating her within the genealogy of indigenous goddesses.

Of the major Chicana writers, Denise Chávez was among the first to create short stories intertwining Guadalupe with real women's lives. Guadalupe was the thematic inspiration for *Novena Narrativas* in 1987 and the one-woman performance piece *Women in the State of Grace* in 1989, which Chávez took on tour in the 1990s. The latter performance included an altar containing a frontispiece banner of the Mexican Virgin's image. Chávez's characterizations of marginalized Latinas, who exist in "a state of grace," capture a sense of female spirituality, a feminist metaphysics, similar to the popular religiosity inspired by La Virgen de Guadalupe. Chávez describes the characters as "survivors," struggling to keep their lives together. She emphasizes Guadalupe as the significant aspect in the character's lives; however, she also refigures Guadalupe as God. "She comes out of the tradition of Catholicism but she is bigger than that tradition. She has to do with the concept of God being a woman, having more feminine aspects than the traditional Catholic or Protestant angry God with the lightning coming out of his head. I identify her more as a spiritual being in which the mother is the core."[130] In *Borderlands/La Frontera*, published in 1987, Gloria Anzaldúa also began a feminist revisioning of Guadalupe, equating her with indigenous mother earth goddesses. In the 1990s, other Chicana writers incorporated Guadalupe in their writings and worldviews. I discuss specific works by Cisneros, Moraga, and Anzaldúa in chapter 2. Interestingly, when other Chicana authors eventually refigured Guadalupe in their writings, they also adopted her image for their personal and professional lives. Sandra Cisneros's house in San Antonio features a representation of Guadalupe painted on the outside wall near the front door. Ana Castillo's stationery contains a

Guadalupe image on the envelope in the return address position above Castillo's name. Castillo also edited a collection of essays published in 1996 on the significance of Guadalupe as "the goddess of the Americas."

In 1999, the revisioning of Guadalupe took another radical step artistically and bodily. The artist Alma López produced a digital photo collage of a real woman as Guadalupe clad in a swimsuit of roses, surrounded by indigenous goddess iconography, and held up by a bare breasted female "angel" (see figure 14). The work *Our Lady*, featured in the 2001 exhibit "Cyber Arte: Where Tradition Meets Technology" at Santa Fe's Museum of International Folk Art, produced a storm of controversy. Prayer vigils were held by hundreds of Catholic protestors and Archbishop Michael Sheehan of New Mexico demanded that the work be removed from the exhibit, asserting that the artist portrayed the religious icon as a "tart." López says "the image in Santa Fe is very much about a strong woman standing there with an attitude and wearing flowers. It has nothing to do with sex or sexuality. . . . It's about showing alternative identities that illustrate more the lived realities of Chicanas."[131] In fact, Raquel Salinas, the actual woman photographed as Guadalupe wearing a swimsuit, says her motivation for modeling Guadalupe was to advance her own healing process after being raped at age eighteen. Burdened with guilt and shame, she underwent a long process to reclaim her psyche and body. "I feel good about my body [now]. I carry no shame anymore." Nonetheless, Salinas was unsettled by the controversy. She practices an indigenous spirituality that considers Guadalupe as Tonantzin: "I respect her. I would never do anything to disrespect her."[132]

In 2004, Alma López painted another Guadalupe representation, titled *Coyolxauhqui Returns Disguised as Our Lady of Guadalupe Defending the Rights of Las Chicanas*, which contains an obvious reference to the title of Hernández's groundbreaking 1976 etching of the karate-kicking Guadalupe. In López's painting, a middle-aged, pregnant indigenous woman wears a halo around her head signifying both the holiness of Guadalupe and the moon symbolism of Coyolxauhqui. The star-strewn blue sky background invokes Guadalupe's cloak. In this artwork, López includes a postmodern self-referential nod to her earlier controversial work *Our Lady*. The indigenous woman's bright orange dress slips slightly at the shoulder to reveal the strap of a floral bikini or bra. The glimpse of the floral bikini indicates López's embodied and sexualized refiguring of the religious icon in *Our Lady*, making her point without renewing the controversy.

14. Alma M. López, *Our Lady*, 1999. Digital print. Courtesy of the artist. Special thanks to Raquel Salinas and Raquel Gutiérrez.

The woman holds up one hand as if to stop an injustice from occurring, while she brandishes a sword in the other hand. With the position of the hand in the center of the painting and the placement of the sword in the lower half, the woman seems to be indicating that peaceful engagement and dialogue are preferred over violence. However, like the mother earth goddess Coyolxauhqui and La Llorona, she will resort to violence in defending women of color from harm. López's title differs from Hernández's in focusing solely on the defense of "Las Chicanas," women, rather than "Los Xicanos," which includes men. López also distances this Guadalupe from the iconography that traditionally identifies the Mexican Virgin; one must look closely at details or the title to recognize the association. At the same time, López "disguises" Coyolxauhqui as La Virgen, revealing Guadalupe in the genealogy of the mother earth goddess and signifying the "return of the repressed" in the form of the indigenous goddess and woman.

The most recent Guadalupe art controversy occurred in December 2006, when Anna-Marie López's painting, *Virgen*, was pulled from a Guadalupana exhibit at the Centro Cultural Aztlan in San Antonio, Texas. López's painting was removed from the art exhibit celebrating La Virgen's feast day just days before it opened because of its "pagan interpretation." Her painting portrays a nude woman with Guadalupe's blue mantle draped over her shoulders and arms and a strategically placed serpent wrapped around her loins and breasts. The Guadalupe figure stands behind a barbed wire fence and wears a necklace with a tiny human heart hanging from the chain to indicate her relationship with the indigenous goddess Tonantzin. López says even before she submitted the piece for the show, she self-censored the portrayal by covering up the full-frontal nudity of her original figure and removing some of the symbols that would be considered "more ferociously pagan." She wanted the painting to reflect Mexico's rich cultural and religious heritage, including its indigenous legacy, "not just the traditional folk-art Catholicism. It's richer than that."[133] From an austere albeit hybrid symbol of religious morality intended to convert indigenous peoples in the 1800s, Guadalupe has been transformed, like other Mexican female cultural symbols, into a twenty-first-century feminist icon whose corporeal and sexual connotations remain taboo.

This brief analysis of the representational discourses surrounding the four Mexican female cultural symbols reveals the social and political forces that have determined their reception and influence. In the most recent re-presentations, Chicana artists and writers and U.S. Mexicana oral historians engage in cultural refiguring expressing their late-twentieth- and early-twenty-first-century existences as indigenous mestizas. The agency of cultural refiguring arises from the interrelated processes of revising history and recovering memory (re-membering). Following the example of the woman of discord, Chicana writers and artists disrupt the dominant discourses binding La Malinche, La Llorona, La Virgen de Guadalupe, and Mexica goddesses. Their writings and artwork unearth a collective memory of female confinement, mistreatment, and resistance and intervene in official histories that deny or demote women's existence and contributions. A different but no less significant re-membering takes place among the working-class and semiprofessional women for whom La Virgen de Guadalupe functions as the primary female cultural symbol. For them she represents a source of resistance and identity connecting them to the culture, history, and religion that signifies Mexican identity. In this respect she serves to mitigate the unrelenting assimilationism of American culture and the sometimes blatant but more often insidious racism that accompanies their existence in the United States. Yet, as with the Chicana authors and artists, the working-class and semiprofessional women do not simply reproduce the Mexican cultural or official Catholic representations of La Virgen. As their oral histories testify, they refigure her as a "real" woman who fights back subversively or defiantly as the occasion demands. They re-member Guadalupe in the image of themselves. Re-membering is the element of cultural refiguring that sutures the past onto the present, providing the means by which subjects identify themselves and subvert constructions that attempt to define them.

The authors' and oral historians' cultural refigurings function, like the woman of discord, to connect the past with present and future visions of transformation. Following La Malinche's lead, they become women of discord through their pivotal and transgressive actions to reform images and choices available to women. This diversity of cultural change strategies presents Chicana feminist thinking along a spectrum of positions. Consequently, in rewriting their histories, recovering their memories, and renewing their spiritualities, they renew indigenous and mestiza subjectivities. More so, cultural refiguring recreates historical, cultural, and spiritual genealogies that inform collective memories and, ultimately, alters political and material conditions.

chapter two

 CHICANA FEMINISM

Spirituality, Sexuality, and Mexica

Goddesses Re-membered

In *The Last Generation,* Cherríe Moraga describes a spiritual epiphany she experienced while watching an eclipse of the sun from the ruins of a pyramid high above Tepoztlán, Mexico. Likening the eclipse to a "deep silent feminine darkness" associated with Coyolxauhqui, the moon, "She Who Has the Power to Put Out the Sun's Light," Moraga realized a profound reverence for the sacred—"a power utterly beyond my control."[1] Moraga's spiritual vision of a female god, rooted in a consciousness of Mexican American women's experience, "drives me to write: the search for Coyolxauhqui amid all the disfigured female characters and the broken men that surround them in my plays and poems. I search for a whole woman I can shape with my own Chicana tongue and hand. A free citizen of Aztlán and the world."[2]

For Gloria Anzaldúa, Coyolxauhqui is a metaphor informing her struggle to rewrite the myths and fictions that have been used against women and people of color "to control, regulate and manipulate us." The Mexica's symbolic dismemberment of Coyolxauhqui suggests patriarchal and colonial violence against women's bodies and souls that requires refiguring. "I think the reason this image is so important to me is that when you take a person and divide her up, you disempower her. She's no longer a threat. My whole struggle in writing, in this anticolonial struggle, has been to put us back together again. To connect up the body with the soul, and the mind with the spirit. That's why for me there's such a link between the text and the body, between textuality and sexuality, between the body and the spirit."[3]

While both make use of goddess images in their writings, Moraga's and Anzaldúa's conceptions differ in their theoretical underpinnings. Moraga's emphasis on the feminine and on male/female difference, also found in Ana Castillo's and Alma Villanueva's works, promotes a woman's counterculture that reclaims and reaffirms "female" or "feminine" principles generally associated with peaceful and nurturing qualities. Anzaldúa's writing resists claims of inherent behavior, emphasizing instead the diversity of subject positions available to Chicanas through the complex of Mexica goddesses.[4] By some standards these differences would set the writers in distinct feminist camps; yet their shared commitment to exposing and opposing intersecting oppressions such as racism, classism, sexism, and heterosexism, which characterize the experiences of women of color, unites them in the theory and practice of U.S. Third World feminism. Chicana feminists, along with other feminists of color, have engineered a challenge to the white, middle-class-dominated second wave movement and its unified gender strategy through an insistence on combating multiple injustices and on affirming the varied experiences, self-definitions, and resistance practices women of color engage. The first publication of *This Bridge Called My Back* in 1981 marks the date of collective, public articulation of this differently theorized feminism, which, Chela Sandoval observes, "remained just outside the purview of the dominant feminist theory emerging in the 1970s, functioning within it— but only as the unimaginable."[5] U.S. Third World feminism recognizes power dynamics as interwoven and rules out a facile understanding of gender—often coded as white, middle class—as the only or primary injustice women face. As Moraga writes in her 1983 multigenre collection *Loving in the War Years,* "In this country lesbianism is a poverty—as is being brown, as is being a woman, as is being just plain poor. The danger lies in ranking the oppressions. *The danger lies in failing to acknowledge the specificity of the oppression.* The danger lies in attempting to deal with oppression purely from a theoretical base."[6] Chicana feminist writers contribute to a refiguring of the feminist movement by advocating a variety of resisting and proactive strategies and by locating domination and resistance historically, racially, and culturally through the genealogy of the Mexica woman of discord.

In this chapter I situate writings on Mexica goddesses by Anzaldúa, Castillo, Moraga, Villanueva, and Sandra Cisneros within several inter-related feminist discourses of the second wave movement including anthropology, spirituality, and radical/cultural feminist debates about sexuality, woman's culture, and universalized gender oppression. I show how these five writers emphasize the significance of indigenous heritage to Chicana subjectivity and cultural refiguring. They convey the diversity of creative and theoretical refigurings of sexuality, spirituality, and subjectivity in their re-presentations of Mexica goddesses.

Although it is a subject deserving attention, one conversation that isn't elaborated to its fullest extent here is a comparative analysis of the use of indigenous goddesses in Chicana and Mexican women's writings. I digress somewhat from the main argument of this chapter to consider the differences between Chicana and Mexican women's writings. The primary reason Mexican women writers have not served as role models for Chicana writers is that Mexican authors have not overtly featured indigenous goddesses in their works, although they sometimes serve as subtexts. While some writers, including Rosario Castellanos, Elena Ponia-towska, and Elena Garro, project an identity based on the cultural history of Mexico much like the Chicana writers do,[7] my sense in a preliminary review of the literature is that goddesses are not significant concepts or images for most Mexican women writers for several paradoxical reasons. First, living in Mexico they are steeped in their heritage—what anthropologists have chronicled as Olmeca/Tolteca/Maya/Azteca history and memory—and therefore do not need to foreground it as Chicana writers do in tracing a connection to an indigenous and Mexican identity. However, even as Mexican writers are steeped in it, the racist and classist denial of all things related to indigenous identity (language, skin color, cultural practices, land rights) by the Mexican government and upper-class elite, and the continuing strong influence and presence of the Catholic Church, have relegated indigenous practices and thoughts and contemporary indigenous peoples to the margins. A poem by Rosario Castellanos, "Silence Near an Ancient Stone,"[8] refers to this sense of a buried or repressed history and memory the poet is unable to retrieve. Castellanos, who was raised in the southern Mexican state of Chiapas, cared for by an indigenous nanny, and later worked for the National Indigenist Institute in San Cristóbal de las Casas, more than any other Mexican woman writer strove to represent indigenous experiences and beliefs in her writings.

Her novels *Balún-Canán,* translated into English as *The Nine Guardians; Ciudad Real,* translated as *City of Kings;* and *Oficio de tinieblas,* translated as *Book of Lamentations,* are the primary examples. While a number of prominent male and female writers such as Castellanos, Carlos Fuentes, and Octavio Paz feature indigenous god themes or symbols in their works, the writers themselves do not identify as indigenous or come from working-class backgrounds as do many Chicana and Chicano writers.

Finally, in comparison to Chicana writers' uses of indigenous goddesses as symbols of feminist resistance, sexuality, and spirituality, many Mexican women writers are, in the words of Poniatowska, "mosquitas muertas" regarding feminist activism.[9] Their writings, with the exception of works by Castellanos, Poniatowska, Garro, and Sor Juana Inés de la Cruz, often fail to deliver what U.S. writers and critics consider oppositional feminist critiques that challenge systems of gender domination, much less of race, class, or sexuality.[10] The title of Debra Castillo's book *Talking Back: Toward a Latin American Feminist Literary Criticism* alludes to what she describes as the reticence of writers and academics to align themselves with a women's rights agenda or call themselves feminists.[11] That is not to say, however, that stinging criticism of repressive class- and government-based practices or of Mexican patriarchy has never been presented by a Mexican writer. Poniatowska exhibits social and political awareness in her journalistic works. *Hasta no verte, Jesús mío,* published in English as *Here's to You, Jesusa!* moves toward an understanding of class differences through the portrayal of the life experiences of a poor woman. *La noche de Tlatelolco: Testimonios de historia oral,* published as *Massacre in Mexico,* exposes the horrific government-ordered massacre of student demonstrators protesting wage decreases and human rights violations, a tragedy kept from international media on the eve of the 1968 Olympics. The Taller de Literatura Feminina Mexicana (Workshop of Mexican Women Writers) held each summer at the Colegio de México espouses a feminist approach and encourages the participation of North American feminist scholars. In addition, from the 1950s until her untimely death in 1974, Castellanos's poetry, essays, and plays reveal an acute awareness and pointed disclosure of the systems of domination that enclose women, the poor, and the indigenous in Mexico. Moreover, in a book of essays published in 1973 exploring the condition of women, Castellanos describes the very issues that Chicana writers engage. "The boldness of exploring one's self; the need to become conscious of one's bodily existence or the unheard-of pretension to confer a meaning on one's spiritual existence are severely repressed and punished by the social apparatus. The latter has proclaimed, once and for all, that the only legitimate attitude of femininity is that of waiting."[12]

Another reason that this conversation is not as immediate as the others is that Mexican (or any Latin American) women's writings, with the exception of Castellanos and Sor Juana,[13] did not inspire or inform Chicanas. This is primarily due to a lack of encouragement and support for Mexican women to write beyond domestic fiction and the difficulty in getting their works published by Mexican publishers, much less having them translated into English for North American readers.[14] For Chicanas, access is much greater to Spanish-language copies and English translations of the works of such Mexican male writers as Paz or Fuentes.[15] The problem is compounded by the fact that many Chicanas were/are not schooled in written (or spoken) Spanish. Full-length English translations of the works of the three best-known Mexican women writers, Sor Juana, Castellanos, and Poniatowska, appeared in the United States only in the late twentieth century, and translations of younger or lesser-known writers are few and far between, with the exception of Laura Esquivel's recent works. The editors of the anthology *Cuentos: Stories by Latinas,* including Moraga, identify the lack of literary antecedents as a gender issue. While many male writers' works from "El Boom" have been translated into English and are well known in North America, few, if any, female Latin American writers' works were translated until the late twentieth century. At the same time, the editors of *Cuentos* note that race and class differences between Chicana writers and their Latin American female counterparts reflect different perspectives. "The question remains, however, to what extent can most Latin American women writers be considered our literary legacy when so many, like their male counterparts, are at least functionally middle-class, ostensibly white, and write from a male-identified perspective."[16]

Another factor is a historical lack of reciprocated interest in Chicana/o literature or knowledge of Chicana/os on the part of Mexican writers since 1848, when the northwest territory of Mexico was appropriated by the United States, a point made by the editors of the 1972 anthology *Literatura chicana: Texto y contexto.* "While Chicanos may have viewed Mexico as a model, there seems to have been little corresponding interest from Mexico, as her writers dealt with Mexican themes and remained aloof from the Chicano problems in the United States."[17] Indeed, my conversations with literary scholars in Mexico suggest that Chicana/o literature still is little known, rarely available in translation, and considered second rate if written in Spanish because of "poor" or "improper" usage. These considerations may be changing as I write, given recent translations into Spanish by major publishing houses of acclaimed works by several Chicanas/os.

In the mid-1980s, a series of exchanges between Mexican and Chicana feminists took place that opened avenues for communication and understanding. In her 1994 book *Massacre of the Dreamers*, Ana Castillo relates that Mexican feminists are beginning to realize that "despite American citizenship and certain gringo acculturation, the mestiza in the United States has been prevented from benefiting from many of the privileges available to gringos due to racism, sexism and their poor to working class backgrounds."[18] Although she notes that many Chicanas, because of their working-class backgrounds, feel they have more in common with the domestics that work for the middle- and upper-class Mexican writers, nonetheless "there is now a deliberate effort among feminists on both sides to reach across the border to each other for an unprecedented understanding of the very particular ways sexism has affected all of us."[19] Yet class and race issues have impeded open, honest dialogues between Chicana and Mexicana writers and scholars. In a 1995 article Norma Alarcón relates the circumstances of a conference in Tijuana, Mexico, aimed at encouraging dialogue between the two groups, which instead resulted in the marginalization and silencing of the Chicanas. In a scathing critique, Alarcón summarizes the attitude of Mexican women writers' and scholars toward Chicanas. "Few upperclass Latin American women would admit to being a colleague to someone who could have been the household maid but for the grace of a minoritizing education in the United States."[20] In addition, she insinuates that U.S. colleges and universities function similar to maquiladoras in exploiting Chicana/o labor. Given these circumstances, analyses of the intersections and variances among Mexicana and Chicana literary works regarding use of goddesses and other indigenous symbols would provide needed insight into their respective positions.

If Mexican women writers maintain silence concerning the "ancient stones" that represent their female ancestors and the women's issues connected to them, Chicana writers, artists, and activists, in contrast, embrace the mighty, sensual, and fecund spirituality of Mexica goddesses and are vocal participants in debates among U.S. feminists that concern the purpose and direction of the movement and issues of feminist epistemology and ontology. The memory of goddesses and the concept of a "woman's culture" it entails has been a topic of considerable debate among U.S. feminists. Adherents of "radical feminism" denounce goddess worship as essentialistic, as backsliding into a conservatism that figures woman through biological rather than constructionist terms. "Cultural feminists" identify an often universal Mother Goddess as a nonpatriarchal source of spiritual sustenance, valuing qualities identified with women and proving the existence of previous female-governed societies. Some feminists maintain an interest in goddess worship while subscribing to the radical feminist position of opposition to forms of domination. Others argue that there is little difference between radical and cultural feminist politics as both affirm the superiority of women over men.[21] Chicana feminists, along with other women of color, reorient the issues by making use of various strategies and theories to accomplish their aims. They diverge from singular and ahistorical approaches, which, for example, categorically dismiss provisional essentialism as a strategic position, figure a universal deity, or focus only on gender oppression. They apply diverse strategies and theories simultaneously and provisionally to outmaneuver various adversaries. Nor is there a unified field of Chicana feminism or U.S. Third World feminism. Each activist, each writer, charts her own course based on her particular experience and vision.

WOMAN'S CULTURE AND SECOND WAVE FEMINIST DEBATES

Alice Echols's extensive comparisons of radical and cultural feminisms carefully elaborate important critiques of the divisive issues and diverging streams of thought marking the second-wave feminist movement. Yet her works firmly situate this history as white and middle class. The participation and positions of women of color, such as Cherríe Moraga, Audre Lorde, Angela Davis, and Chrystos, among others, are not included among the forty women she interviewed for her book *Daring to Be Bad*, although each was active within the movement. That they are not regarded as significant figures points to their marginalization as lesbians and women of color and speaks to the multiple positions they articulate and their own ambivalence about the strategies mainstream feminism adopted.[22] Moraga's engagement in the movement and critique of second wave feminism is well documented, yet her viewpoints are not part of Echols's accounts. Moraga was a participant in the 1982 Scholar and the Feminist Conference: "Towards a Politics of Sexuality" at Barnard College, where the "sex wars" escalated into a "sex-panic."[23] Her writings appeared in the two significant anthologies resulting from the sex war debates, *Pleasure and Danger: Exploring Female Sexuality,* published in 1984, and *Powers of Desire: The Politics of Sexuality,* published in 1983, both of which included essays by Echols.[24] The anthology *This Bridge Called My Back,* edited by Moraga and Anzaldúa (1981/1983), predates any of Echols's publications and reveals the multiple and contradictory positions of women of color in relation to the feminist movement. In *Loving in the War Years,* published in 1983, Moraga elaborates on the shortcomings of radical feminism:[25]

> In failing to approach feminism from any kind of materialist base, failing to take race, ethnicity, class into account in determining where women are at sexually, many feminists have created an analysis of sexual oppression (often confused with sexuality itself) which is a political dead-end. "Radical Feminism," the ideology which sees men's oppression of women as the root of and paradigm for all other oppressions allows women to view ourselves as a class and to claim our sexual identity as the *source* of our oppression and men's sexual identity as the *source* of the world's evil. But this ideology can never then fully integrate the concept of the "simultaneity of oppression" as Third World feminism is attempting to do.[26]

In emphasizing a materialist focus, Moraga identifies universalization as the heart of the problem with both radical and cultural feminisms, the failure to consider multiple and simultaneous oppressions and to place them in historical perspective. While Echols pointed out radical feminisms' failure to confront issues of race and sexuality, she nonetheless reinforced this single-minded perspective of the feminist movement in writing her history of it. Katie King describes and criticizes the tendency of feminist histories, such as Echols's *Daring to Be Bad,* to "give over 'origins' to white women." King encourages reading the "lacquered layerings" of diverse texts to reveal what connects and/or distinguishes them and to place their struggles within specific locations and moments of power.[27]

Feminist historical research shows a relationship between woman's

culture and late-eighteenth- and nineteenth-century women's movements in the United States and Great Britain. In a 1980 symposium on
politics and culture, Ellen DuBois describes the existence of a dialectical
relationship between nineteenth-century woman's culture and feminism.
She draws on the political ideas of Elizabeth Cady Stanton that reveal
"how woman's rights feminism grew out of a critique of what we are
calling women's culture." DuBois also considers Nancy Cott's work that
shows "the development of women's consciousness of themselves as a
group, which was a necessary prerequisite for the emergence of a feminist
movement." However, in studying the first wave of feminism DuBois
cautions that it is "important not to confuse woman's culture and feminism, or to assume a simple and direct development out of one into the
other."[28] Responding to DuBois and other members of the symposium,
Temma Kaplan stresses the need to situate studies of woman's culture
within broader political, cultural, and historical perspectives. "Women's
culture, like popular or working-class culture, must appear in the context
of dominant cultures. Sometimes, it is a variation upon the ruling culture.
Sometimes it is created from the shards of broken tribal or peasant cultures. Sometimes the alternative culture grows in opposition to the dominant culture."[29]

Reconsidering cultural feminism and the concept of woman's culture
in the 1990s, Verta Taylor and Leila Rupp illustrate how lesbian feminism,[30] which came to be identified with cultural feminism, rather than
depoliticizing the second wave feminist movement, preserved and nourished feminist "impulses" during lulls in activism caused by an unfavor-
able political climate. They argue, against Echols, that lesbian feminist
communities "have forged a rich and complex resistance culture and style
of politics that nourishes rather than betrays the radical feminist vision."[31]
In particular, they discuss "private ritual and the politicization of everyday
life," considered by critics to be the most egregious aspects of cultural
feminism, as having "political consequences" through the display of commitment to the lesbian feminist community and resistance to dominant
society. In an observation also countering bell hooks's narrow profile of
cultural feminists, they note that self-presentations reflect the "preferences of working-class women, women of color, and young women," in
other words, those who are underrepresented within an already marginalized population.[32]

Drawing upon these insights and my own study of working-class and semiprofessional U.S. Mexicanas' oral histories and Chicana professional intellectuals' writings, I propose viewing woman's culture not as a unified field but rather as composed of numerous, diverse, and simultaneous units, incubation sites that are specific to their historical, spatial, and temporal context. While each site maintains the shared assumption of female-oriented concerns and interests, such as resisting male domination, supporting survivors of breast cancer, or sharing women-only activities, locations may also amalgamate other common characteristics that connect the site participants but distinguish, and sometimes alienate, them from the larger identity frame of "feminism." The raced and classed positions of U.S. Mexicana and Chicana culture sites function in this way. Woman's culture sites possess the potential to incorporate a range of individual and group positions from embryonic consciousness of women's oppressions to insurgent feminism. Woman's culture nurtured in churches and kitchens, YWCA activities, lesbian softball teams, women's studies programs, writing groups, or social reform activities may contribute to a feminist agenda and consciousness even though specific groups (or individuals within a group) may not mark themselves as feminist or may advance positions that critique dominant feminist discourse or practice. Rita Felski's theorizing of social change and the "counter-public sphere" in feminist literature provides a means by which to further elaborate the diverse and incubatory functions of woman's culture. She describes the women's movement as generating an "oppositional public arena" that articulates women's needs through critical opposition to a male-defined society.[33] The feminist public sphere supports a dual function, internally generating a "gender specific identity grounded in a consciousness of community and solidarity among women" and externally seeking to "convince society as a whole of the validity of feminist claims."[34] The women's movement itself, while constituted on the common factor of gender oppression, nonetheless is fragmented and dynamic. Felski notes that it oscillates between the ideal of a unified collectivity and women's reality of gender experience which conflicts with a range of alliances such as race or class.[35] Within the feminist movement, then, incubatory sites of woman's culture, often formed upon multiple alliances of gender and/or race and/or class and/or sexuality, may also function as counterdiscourses within the women's movement. They have a dual purpose as well, produc-

ing both the affirmation of "woman" vital to maintaining the empowerment of the shared umbrella politics and the critique (race, class, sexuality)
that challenges its constricting effects.

Finally, a view of woman's culture as actually or potentially oppositional
rests on the recognition that women often are able to participate in resistance activities only through networks of empowerment that offer
seemingly paradoxical support. Ann Ferguson relates this predicament in
her study of the alliances and activities of Nicaraguan lesbians. She found
that the financial support of family and friends, who do not recognize or
approve of their sexual identity, is nonetheless as critical to their ability to
work in resistance movements as is the support of radical leftist and
lesbian groups. Going public as lesbian is not desirable and may even
be counterproductive. In the United States the same may be true for
working-class and semiprofessional Mexicanas for whom financial support or family ties are too important to forgo. Therefore, woman's culture
sites may provide important avenues of support and resistance for some
women who may not claim feminist, lesbian, or oppositional identities
in public.

The following descriptions of two different groups conceptualize the
diversity of woman's culture sites among Chicanas and U.S. Mexicanas.
Mensajeras de Salud (Messengers of Health), sponsored by the Tucson
YWCA and partially funded by grants from the Avon Corporation, is a
cancer and education support group that raises awareness among lower-
income women (and men) about the need for breast and cervical exams to
reduce the incidence of cancer. While the counseling done by the six paid
"messengers" sometimes challenges specific imbalances of power between women and their partners, it does not challenge systems of domination such as those within the institution of marriage or the Catholic
Church, which contribute to women's lack of awareness of their bodies
and of medical care. In addition, neither the Mensajeras nor the women
they counsel identify themselves or their work as "feminist." Yet the Mensajeras refigure attitudes toward women's bodies, sexuality, and domestic
abuse in addition to conveying valuable health information and services.
Moreover, discussions that occur in the cancer support group attended
by breast cancer survivors challenge stereotypes of passive, desexualized
women.[36] The Mensajeras' discourse may not publicly challenge domination systems or enter the feminist counterpublic sphere (although the
ideas they dispense surely have been influenced by the latter), yet it circu-

lates within the Chicana, U.S. Mexicana, and Mexican immigrant communities of Tucson and South Tucson. The materialist concerns they address contribute to empowering women who are otherwise silenced or dispossessed.

Mujeres Activas en Letras y Cambio Social (Women Active in Writing and Social Change), known as MALCS, was founded in 1983 as a support system for Latinas in academia. MALCS, whose membership primarily consists of U.S. Latinas associated with higher education including faculty, professional staff, and students, holds an annual summer institute that includes research-sharing and empowerment workshops. A 1988–89 survey of MALCS members found that the majority identify as Chicana feminist—although the type of feminism varied from liberal to cultural nationalist to insurgent—and have participated in activist work and women's organizations.[37] The organization maintains an indigenous women– and Latina-only policy for its workshops, in order to provide for its members a nurturing and supportive space rarely available within the academy.[38] MALCS also fosters literary and scholarly efforts that contribute to the oppositional and multipositional discourse of U.S. Third World feminism. Ideas incubated in the relatively safe space and nurturing atmosphere of MALCS seminars eventually become part of the feminist public sphere serving to critique the limitations of mainstream feminism and male dominance within Chicano and European American dominant cultures.

Comparatively, Mensajeras de Salud and MALCS differ significantly in their identity positions. The Mensajeras identify as Mexican or Mexican American, implying a primary affiliation with their racial and cultural group rather than with gendered oppression. MALCS members identify as Chicana or Latina feminist, signifying an alliance around women's issues and a political consciousness of the intersections of race and class with gender, issues formalized in the "MALCS Declaration" of 1983.[39] Mensajeras de Salud is institutionally located, supported by capitalist ventures, and subject to the whims of such support, whereas MALCS is an independent organization supported and directed solely by its membership. MALCS members publicly recognize and oppose racism, classism, and heterosexism within Chicana/o and Mexicana/o cultures while the Mensajeras do not. However, the designation "feminist" (or "not-feminist") clearly has little correspondence with the significance of the feminist-oriented work each group contributes to the needs of its constituents. As different as these two groups are in class, identity, location, feminist historical consciousness, and activist strategies, nonetheless they both render important services that address the material, emotional, and psychic needs of their constituents. Each responds to the particular concerns and issues of its own community—lower-income U.S. Mexicanas and Mexican immigrants with little knowledge of or access to medical help, and upwardly mobile Chicanas and Latinas in education who are alienated and marginalized within the system—and, at the same time, generates a broader consciousness of gender issues.

Chicana feminist writers' contemplations of spirituality, sexuality, and identity through Mexica goddesses constitute another example of a woman's culture site, although one that differs in some important aspects from earlier feminist conceptions surrounding goddess identification. Grounded in the genealogy of resistance and refiguring that marks the woman of discord and relating a historical consciousness of racial, cultural, and religious commonalities, Chicana recoveries of Mexica goddesses challenge a monolithic woman's culture based on a universalized and essentially peaceful Mother Goddess. In particular, the reworking of the pacific goddess/woman expands conceptions of female empowerment. Rather than discount or deny the violent aspects attributed to Mexica goddesses, Chicana writers integrate violence into complex portrayals of female subjectivity, spirituality, sexuality, and activism. In so doing, their writings refigure subjectivities through the full spectrum of physical, emotional, and spiritual possibility. Conceiving pain as an element of sexual passion, envisioning destruction as an element of social change, imagining self-mutilation as an element of transcendent spirituality, Chicana writers include violence within the range of transformative potential.[40] In contrast to the limited range of female potential forwarded by patriarchy and by cultural feminism, the appeal of Mexica goddesses for the writers is based on the possibilities they provide for characterizing complex, active Chicana subjects.

By these examples I suggest several important considerations about woman's culture sites: their diversity in identity, form, location, and practice; their significance to the women's movement regardless of direct or nondirect affiliation and identification; and the importance of essentialistic identities (woman, Chicana) as provisional strategies available to combat multiple oppressions. Woman's culture sites are specific to time, place, and context; they are dynamic and diverse, positional and provisional in the service of a U.S. Third World feminist politics. This examination of woman's culture sites finds that specificity, difference, and multi-positionality are what critiques of cultural feminism, such as Echols's, overlook.

Woman's culture is only one strategy among many drawn upon by Chicana feminists and other women of color who have redefined the terms of feminist struggle. Not only does multipositionality refer to diverse understandings of oppression but it also characterizes various resistance strategies and possible subject positions. Chela Sandoval's concept of differential consciousness responds to charges that women of color have not developed influential feminist theory, or that feminists of color do not commit to "the cause."[41] Her answer is that, on the contrary, feminists of color commit when and as necessary depending on their readings of the "current situation of power," "a survival skill well known to oppressed peoples." Here Sandoval alludes to the connection between subjectivity, identity, and political activism. She characterizes the urban guerrilla approach of differential consciousness as "tactical subjectivity" wherein "subjugated citizens can either occupy or throw off subjectivities in a process that at once both enacts and yet decolonizes their various relations to their real conditions of existence."[42] In a critique of European American feminisms' obstinate adherence to a unitary subjectivity and to a gender-only focus, Norma Alarcón writes that the recognition of "multiple registers of existence" by women of color "is an effect of the belief that knowledge of one's subjectivity cannot be arrived at through a single discursive 'theme.' Indeed the multiple voiced subjectivity is lived in resistance to competing notions for one's allegiance or self identification."[43] Subjectivity is intimately related to the mode of political strategy women of color engage. Chicana feminists adopt variable strategies and subjectivities to negotiate the conundrums of their specific existence, recognizing the multiple systems of power that affect them, recognizing themselves and their experiences as transcultural and diverse. It is no coincidence then that they identify Mexica goddesses as their primary representational symbols. The numerous aspects of the mother earth goddesses, including Cihuacoatl, Coatlicue, and Coyolxauhqui, portray various behaviors and many narratives depict their strategic resistances. Similarly, the woman of discord—who is integrally interwoven with these goddesses—represents an interweaving of plurality and opposition: "one woman and many women at once, a means of achieving union but representative of opposition, a source of power yet also of chaos."[44]

Chicana feminist writings do not theorize solely an oppositional sub-jectivity but a dynamic process that braids diverse ways of being and resistance activities into a transformative subjectivity. Just as the woman of discord opposes patriarchal domination in her various incarnations transforming indigenous, Mexican national, and Chicana/o history and genealogy, Sandoval's "differential consciousness" and Anzaldúa's "mes-tiza consciousness" refigure feminist and racial-cultural concepts of iden-tity and political struggle. Like Sandoval, Anzaldúa defines mestiza con-sciousness as necessarily chameleon, a redefinition of both subjectivity and political activism. "Deconstruct, construct. She becomes a *nahual*, able to transform herself into a tree, a coyote, into another person. She learns to transform the small 'I' into the total Self."[45]

These conceptions of a transformative feminism allow for diverse activ-ities including the risky work of coalition building; the sustaining and resistive space of woman's culture; the analytical work of deconstruct-ing patriarchal and Western histories, religions, dichotomies, cultural na-tionalisms, and limiting constructions of women; the foundational work of reconstructing collective female histories; the radical activism of ex-posing and protesting material oppressions and systems of domination; and the visionary work of reimagining the past, present, and future through a spirituality that makes room for female and lesbian sexuality and eroticism.

CHICANA FEMINIST SPIRITUALITY AS EROTIC POWER

Alarcón argues that in invoking the memory of indigenous goddesses, "which implies continuance rather than nostalgia" in the words of Paula Gunn Allen, Chicana writers emphasize the necessity of remembrance and of spirituality in theorizing subjectivities that provide "vitality, auton-omy and self-empowerment."[46] She cites Allen in arguing that "a pro-found spiritual kinship with the 'lost'" has "resistant political impli-cations" if focused on feminist change.[47] In the essay "The Neglect of Female Genealogies," Luce Irigaray reflects on the loss of spiritual geneal-ogies transmitted from mother to daughter that connected women to a female divine and served to establish their identity.[48] Irigaray considers a female genealogy—in other words the history and memory of woman as divine—necessary to restore woman as speaking subject. In a 1984 speech titled "Divine Women," she reflects on divinity as the basis of being. "Divinity is what we need to become free, autonomous, sovereign. No human subjectivity, no human society has ever been established without the help of the divine. . . . If she is to become woman, if she is to accomplish her female subjectivity, woman needs a god who is a figure for the perfection of *her* subjectivity."[49]

Although Irigaray predicts that "a *female* god is still to come,"[50] Chicana writers insist that their subjectivities are located in the already existing memory of female gods, who endure as historical, cultural, and racial markers of their subjectivity. Recalling multiple deities from their cultural past, rather than a singular, all-encompassing deity, and taking an empowering rather than passive and lacking ("still to come") position in determining their future, Chicana writers create a feminism that hopes to transform gender role and sexuality stereotypes and systems of power that maintain racism, classism, and colonialism.

As Alarcón notes, the referent "Chicana," "the name of resistance," has profound implications for change through the recovery of the "lost." It is precisely this term rooted in the history of a people and allowing "cultural and political points of departure and thinking through the multiple migrations and dislocations of women of 'Mexican' descent" that distinguishes Chicana feminisms' differential consciousness.[51] Chicana feminist appropriations of Mexica mother earth goddesses as transformative subjectivities respond to manifold oppressions countering the enslavement, violation, and impoverishment of indigenous women from preconquest to the present. Critiquing the devaluation of Mexican female cultural figures and, by association, all Chicanas in historical, cultural, and literary representations is one focus of Chicana writers' works. Others include identifying U.S. neocolonialism, the sexism of the Chicana/o civil rights movement, the ethnocentricity of second wave feminisms, and institutionalized sexism, heterosexism, racism, and classism in the Catholic Church.[52] As a resistant feminism focused on change, transformative subjectivity also looks to the future with utopian intent, not to disengage from the material conditions of the present but to renew power and overcome the injustices of the past. It is a response to the fear of loss of culture and identity through assimilation and dispersion, what Michael Fischer describes as "the fear not merely of being levelled into identical industrial hominids, but of losing an ethical (celestial) vision that might serve to renew the self and ethnic group as well as contribute to a richer, powerfully dynamic pluralist society."[53]

Consequently, Chicana feminists recognize the indigenous goddesses as possessing spiritual power that can renew feminist and racial-cultural consciousness. Moraga finds a direct connection between spirituality and political activism, observing how historical movements such as the civil rights movement were propelled by a spiritual imperative. "Spirituality which inspires activism and, similarly, politics which move the spirit— which draw from the deep-seated place of our greatest longings for freedom—give meaning to our lives."[54] The writers I discuss reject institutional religions such as Catholicism as the means through which to refigure spirituality and instead begin the work of fashioning an alternative religious discourse.

In the past, much feminist religious thinking has been diverted from profound speculation. Catherine Madsen observes that feminist thought is inadequately developed because women's religious "discourse and creative energies are generally focused on the public and liturgical rather than private and speculative." Rather than focusing on the development of religious concepts, feminists concerned themselves with "healing the wounds of women in religion" as a reaction to misogynist doctrines, sexist practices, and masculine liturgical language. Rather than reacting solely to exclusion and mistreatment, Madsen encourages feminists to form their own relationships within the universe through direct study and thought.[55]

While there is evidence of the kind of reactionary discourse Madsen describes, particularly in Alma Villanueva's work, for the most part the writers featured in this study produce considerations of a deeper nature. Anzaldúa's, Castillo's, and Moraga's writings reveal indications of what Madsen defines as "direct observation of bodily and spiritual states and the active development of personal and political ethics, not simply the more traditional study of philosophies and sacred texts."[56] In particular, Anzaldúa's essays "Entering into the Serpent" and "*La herencia de Coatlicue:* The Coatlicue State" convey an introspection that weaves bodily sensation, psychic suffering, and metaphysical awareness into a political mysticism that figures her as a woman of discord, one in a long line of divine, mortal, and resistant women.[57] Her work is recognized as contributing to feminist religious discourse through its inclusion in the anthology *Weaving the Visions: New Patterns in Feminist Spirituality*, edited by two highly regarded feminist religious scholars, Judith Plaskow and Carol P. Christ.

Among all the Chicana writers, a primary aspect of their religious vision includes the refiguring of spirituality as erotic—a passion experienced in body and soul—that has been lost in Western religions' split of the mind and body. The Catholic theologian Elisabeth Schüssler Fiorenza describes the "dualistic anthropology" that structures Catholic thought into hierarchized oppositions of male: mind superior to female: body.[58]

Anzaldúa, whose writing develops a philosophical consideration of the connection between mind and body, rejects institutionalized religion because it "impoverish[es] all life, beauty, pleasure." She writes that Western religion "fails to give meaning to my daily acts, to my continuing encounters with the 'other world.'" In particular, she critiques Christianity for maintaining false dualisms. "The Catholic and Protestant religions encourage fear and distrust of life and of the body; they encourage a split between the body and the spirit and totally ignore the soul; they encourage us to kill off parts of ourselves. We are taught that the body is an ignorant animal; intelligence dwells only in the head. But the body is smart. It does not discern between external stimuli and stimuli from the imagination. It reacts equally viscerally to events from the imagination as it does to 'real' events."[59]

For Moraga, bridging the material and the metaphysical is a political effort that Third World feminism alone has confronted and embraced. "Women of color have always know[n], although we have not always wanted to look at it, that our sexuality is not merely a physical response or drive, but holds a crucial relationship to our entire spiritual capacity. Patriarchal religions—whether brought to us by the colonizer's cross and gun or emerging from our own people—have always known this. Why else would the female body be so associated with sin and disobedience? Simply put, if the spirit and sex have been linked in our oppression, then they must also be linked in the strategy toward our liberation."[60] Moraga's reference to patriarchal conceptions of the female body as being associated with sin and disobedience recalls the constructions of Eve and La Malinche, whose sexual relations marked them as "sinful" according to Catholic doctrine. However, considering Chicanas and U.S. Mexicanas as women of discord, like the Mexica goddesses who defied sexual prohibitions, their actions also are strategies of resistance to domination and subordination.

Although the Chicana writers have rejected institutional Catholicism, its religious doctrines are embedded in Mexican and Chicana/o cultures and shape cultural practices, collective memory, and identity. The Church's official positions on sexuality continue to limit choices and uphold unequal relations. Rosemary Radford Ruether argues that the Church's "underlying presupposition is that sexual relations are relations of dominance and submission, not mutual relations between peers to express love through pleasure."[61] She notes that the Church condemns homosexuality for the same reason it condemns contraception, because it is sexual pleasure without procreation. When female homosexuality is considered, "it raises another anxiety for patriarchal males: namely, the possibility of female sexual (and social) autonomy of males altogether."[62] Although practice and acceptance of contraception, sexual relations outside marriage, and homosexual relations in the United States diverge sharply from official Vatican policy, within the Chicana/o culture parental control and cultural stigma continue to affect the choices made by women, lesbians, and gay males.

In opposing patriarchal domination, sexuality is a point of dissension for the writers in this study, all of whom espouse a Chicana lesbian politics or identity.[63] Carla Trujillo explains that lesbians are forced to reconcile their sexuality. "If we did not bring our sexuality into consciousness, we would not be able to confront ourselves and come out." She adds that "[a] Chicana lesbian must learn to love herself, both as a woman and a sexual being, before she can love another. Loving another woman not only validates one's own sexuality, but also that of the other woman, by the very act of loving. Understanding this, a student in a workshop Cherríe Moraga and I conducted on lesbian sexuality stated, 'Now I get it. Not only do you have to learn to love your own vagina, but someone else's too.' "[64]

Lesbian sexual awareness and fulfillment is rarely supported within Chicana/o culture and many Chicana lesbians must leave their families and seek support within mainstream lesbian communities. As a light-skinned Chicana who was able to "pass" as white, Moraga writes that she "gradually became anglocized" because it was easier to resist sex roles "in an anglo context than in a Chicano one."[65] However, the initial price she paid was estrangement from family and culture and the denunciation that she was a *"vendida"* (sell-out). Ultimately, however, Moraga's confrontation with lesbian oppression brought her to an understanding of racial and class oppression through the memory of her Mexican mother's experiences.[66]

In positioning herself as a Chicana lesbian, an identity that implies choice, pleasure, and resistance to multiple injustices, Moraga acknowledges that her sexuality is inexplicably tied up with her cultural heritage. While her autobiographical writings speak of the struggle to reconcile lesbian desire within the Chicana/o culture, her message is aimed at a collective Chicana audience. In challenging and refiguring limiting notions of sexuality, she and other Chicana feminist writers address issues that affect all U.S. Mexicanas based on the commonalities that lesbian and heterosexual women share: the "status of *woman*" and the "universal of the body."[67] Moraga fights for Chicanas to take pride and pleasure in their sexed and raced bodies and their attendant desires rather than repress, deny, or be ashamed of them.

In exposing Western misogynist social constructions, Chicana feminist writers also relate how these conceptions have been brought to bear on the specific historical, religious, and economic contexts of Mexican and Chicana/o cultural constructions. The refigurings of La Malinche, La Llorona, La Virgen de Guadalupe, and Mexica goddesses acknowledge the legacy of both European and indigenous thought. By historicizing the goddesses who metaphorically represent the splitting of the divine and the mortal in the construction of the female figure, Anzaldúa illustrates the patriarchal superiority that governed both Mexica and Spanish colonial thought.

> The male-dominated Azteca-Mexica culture drove the powerful female deities underground by giving them monstrous attributes and by substituting male deities in their place, thus splitting the female Self and the female deities. They divided her who had been complete, who possessed both upper (light) and underworld (dark) aspects. *Coatlicue*, the Serpent goddess, and her more sinister aspects, *Tlazolteotl* and *Cihuacoatl*, were "darkened" and disempowered much in the same manner as the Indian *Kali*.
>
> *Tonantsi* [Tonantzin]—split from her dark guises, *Coatlicue*, *Tlazolteotl*, and *Cihuacoatl*—became the good mother. . . . After the Conquest, the Spaniards and their Church continued to split *Tonantsi/Guadalupe*. They

desexed *Guadalupe,* taking *Coatlalopeuh,* the serpent/sexuality, out of her. They completed the split begun by the Nahuas by making *La Virgen de Guadalupe/Virgen María* into chaste virgins and *Tlazolteotl/Coatlicue/la Chingada* into *putas* [whores]; into the Beauties and the Beasts. They went even further; they made all Indian deities and religious practices the work of the devil.[68]

The feminist theologian Nelle Morton observes that Goddess as "metaphoric image" exposes the hierarchical relation of God to man to woman. If, as Morton suggests, "we act out of images rather than concepts,"[69] Anzaldúa's writings substantiate the significance of artistic images for individuals and cultures. The plurality of indigenous goddess images releases her from the Western monotheistic and militaristic Mexica male divine and allows her to move toward an immanental (earth and body based) spirituality that brings together bodies, minds, and spirits, the light and the dark, in the conception of subjectivity. In Anzaldúa's immanental spirituality, the body partakes in the activity of transcendence. The materiality of the body, its fears and desires, pervades the spirit even as it overcomes them. In rereading Sartre and Beauvoir, Judith Butler poses a similar rethinking of the mind/body dualism. She considers the body not as a "static or self-identical phenomenon, but a mode of intentionality, a directional force and mode of desire."[70] For Anzaldúa, this intentionality is the desire to empower her Self through the re-membering of mind and body, understanding disembodiment and embodiment as coexisting states of realization. "I see *oposición e insurrección.* I see the crack growing on the rock. I see the fine frenzy building. I see the heat of anger or rebellion or hope split open that rock, releasing *la Coatlicue.* And someone in me takes matters into our own hands, and eventually, takes dominion over serpents—over my own body, my sexual activity, my soul, my mind, my weaknesses and strengths. Mine. Ours. Not the heterosexual white man's or the colored man's or the state's or the culture's or the religion's or the parents'—just ours, mine."[71]

In refiguring transcendence through the body, Anzaldúa refutes the overdetermined female body as inferior, as incapable of divinity, as subject to male control. She conceives in her Self what Irigaray only imagines, "the possibility that God is made flesh as a woman."[72] Anzaldúa reveals that woman is god. In seeing the image of goddess as her Self, she further constructs a plural subjectivity that revels in the erotics of its own matter, in the power of its own erotics. Anzaldúa's writings, and those of other Chicana feminists, reiterate Audre Lorde's uses of the erotic as empowering creative energy, profound knowledge, and political action. The erotic also prefigures subjectivity, as Castillo states, because "sexuality and our spiritual energies" constitute "who we are."[73] By taking "matters into our own hands," these Chicana feminist writers fashion transformative subjectivities based on the knowledge of their own bodies and personal and ancestral histories, the realization of their desires, and the potential to remodel Self and culture through their words and images.

The Ultraviolet Sky: Alma Villanueva

In *The Ultraviolet Sky*, Alma Villanueva's character Rosa describes "racial memories" that link her to the past through the little-known goddess Quetzalpetlatl (The Precious One).[74] "And even closer to their racial memories was Quetzalcoatl, the Feathered Serpent, God and Goddess . . . and didn't Quetzalcoatl have an older sister, with the same qualities, who never stepped forth in the myth at all."[75] Rosa's racial memory functions to recall cultural and religious belief systems that have been denied significance by the Spaniards and Western culture. In addition, by naming the "older sister," Quetzalpetlatl, Rosa calls the goddess and indigenous women into being. "To create, she thought, what has never been before. No not quite from scratch, but a kind of remembering. A remembering into being."[76] Not only does Rosa remember herself and the goddess into being; she assumes a subjectivity that engages the multidimensional attributes common to indigenous mother earth goddesses including sexuality, martiality (birthing mothers were considered warriors), maternal and earthly fertility, and artistry—weaving, painting, and sculpting.[77] Rosa indulges herself sexually through self-exploration and multiple relationships, arms herself with a knife against muggers, and fends off her husband's abusive attempts to confine her to culturally prescribed roles of wife, mother, and passive object of desire. She becomes pregnant and in the nine-month gestation period, during which she is separated from her husband, she gives birth to herself and the child. In the act of birthing, she defies the doctor's orders to lie still, leaps to her feet, letting out a warriorlike yell, and births her daughter in the standing squatting position depicted in numerous indigenous figurines.[78] In so doing, she creates "Chicana" and "mother" as speaking subjects who challenge and refigure the social constructions of Mexican mother by defining their own sexuality, autonomy, and identity.[79] Moreover, she reproduces cultural memories and a female genealogy, painting a self-portrait including her daughter and the Yaqui grandmother by whom she was raised. Cultural memories also appear in the painting Rosa works on throughout the novel, depicting an intricate black shawl surrounding the earth, which she imagines weaving as she paints. She calls it Quetzalpetlatl's shawl, representing night and darkness in complementary opposition to Quetzalcoatl, the morning star. The painting symbolizes for Rosa both the recovery of the denigrated feminine, because "everything that was feminine, she felt, was in danger of being destroyed by the masculine," and the breakdown of dualisms. She attempts to reproduce the merging of opposites signified by her husband and herself and by Quetzalpetlatl and Quetzalcoatl in painting a perfect lilac sky above the shawl-covered earth. "Lilac was the color of beginnings and endings, of opposites merged momentarily before the night."[80] This theme of merging of opposites is forwarded throughout the narrative. With Quetzalpetlatl and Quetzalcoatl, a sexually ambiguous couple in indigenous originary narratives as exemplars,[81] Rosa envisions that she and her husband might each attain and value both masculine and feminine qualities. However, she constantly changes the color of the sky in her painting because she is unable to "see" the right color and ultimately realizes that, like ultraviolet, the perfect union of opposites is invisible; it can never be seen, only experienced through transformation.

The Ultraviolet Sky doesn't seek to overcome gender differences as much as it envisions the day when males will value the "feminine" within themselves and others. In this way, it reinforces essentialistic conceptions of masculinity and femininity and valorizes the feminine as superior. In addition, the female protagonist wages an individualistic struggle for empowerment and self-definition in the traditional bildungsroman fashion of a liberal humanism/feminism. Essentialism and individualism are major criticisms of cultural feminism, and neither The Ultraviolet Sky nor Villanueva's subsequent writings work to complicate this perspective. Villanueva's conception of sexuality, however, does differ from cultural feminism's in that she liberally advocates the pleasures of heterosexuality and autoeroticism (and lesbianism and bisexuality in other writings). The downside of this "liberated" view of sexuality, which in The Ultraviolet Sky involves the protagonist, Rosa, in a progression of sex scenes, threatens to reduce male/female relationships to sex only. Nonetheless, the novel functions as a significant challenge to and refiguring of limiting constructions of gender roles and sexuality for Mexican American women. The novel's vision of a female god that inspires the protagonist's creative energies and ethical musings about violence and war, even if it too simply dichotomizes these issues, also takes a step toward alternative feminist religious thinking.

Sapogonia: Ana Castillo

In a twist on Villanueva's novel of female empowerment, Ana Castillo's *Sapogonia* represents the female character Pastora as the revered and feared goddess Coatlicue through the eyes of the male protagonist/narrator Máximo, who wants to possess and control her. Unable to do so and haunted by her image, Máximo attempts to contain Pastora's power and sexuality by sculpting her as a bronze statue, Xalaquia, a personification of Coatlicue. The sculpture, which "had no heart, but a void in the area of the chest and abdomen," represents Máximo's depiction of Pastora as heartless, incapable of feeling.[82] In addition, it represents the Mexica sacrificial practice of cutting the hearts from live victims, an act which Máximo performs or dreams he performed on Pastora's surrogate after a night of lovemaking.[83] Both of these acts, the statue creation and the sexualized death (recalling similar scenes in Shakespeare's *A Winter's Tale* and *Othello*), signify what Valerie Traub characterizes as "masculine anxiety towards female power." Traub describes these acts as strategies of psychic containment of "the threat of female erotic power" by "means of metaphoric and dramatic transformation of women into jewels, statues and corpses."[84] In *Sapogonia,* Castillo suggests that possession and control of women are primary features of the negative version of "machismo," which Máximo enacts and which is echoed in his name. Unlike Shakespeare's aforementioned plays, which Traub argues psychically contain the threat of female power, Castillo's novel depicts Máximo's efforts to minimize masculine anxiety by containing women in sculptures as contributing to his self-destruction. Pastora retains her own agency apart from Máximo and constructs a subjectivity located in the divine within herself: "What I have been doing over the years is separating parts of myself, the so-called energies that my soul has carried into this life, and given them names, manifested them into clay figurines, not unlike the

Mayas or the Greeks. Yes, this is my pantheon and when I need courage, I call upon the figure that symbolizes courage, and when I need strength or patience, I do likewise."[85]

In addition, the novel explores issues of identity in characterizing Pastora as valuing and embodying a Yaqui (indigenous) identity and heritage that Máximo is determined to escape through assimilation or destroy through sacrificial murder. Recognizing his self-negating tendencies and predicting his desire to kill Pastora (representing his indigenous heritage), his Mayan grandmother warns him that wanting someone else to die and wanting to die oneself are the same thing: "¿No sabes, hijo? Es la misma cosa" (Don't you know, son? It's the same thing).[86] He denies his Mayan ancestry and flees his strife-torn homeland, Sapogonia—*a distinct place in the Americas where all mestizos reside*"[87]—relentlessly pursuing pleasure, power, and wealth through assimilation. His conflicted self is unable to forget or accept his indigenous and Spanish (conqueror) subject history. As if an epitaph to Máximo the novel's final chapter concludes with the words "All that is past, is past and all that is lost, is lost."[88] However, an epilogue recovers Sapogonian indigenous and mestiza/o history and memory through Pastora, who remains true to her working-class and Yaqui roots in political action and cultural affiliation, and who ensures their continuance in the future through the resistive agency of mothering.[89]

Like Villanueva's *The Ultraviolet Sky, Sapogonia* is primarily the story of the isolated individual and her personal struggle. One brief scene places Pastora as the member of a politicized women's group; nonetheless, she alone faces a cynical city government with the group's concerns. Still, Castillo moves toward the representation of a collective and politicized struggle through Pastora's work with the sanctuary movement aiding dissident refugees and through her music, in which she sings of human rights struggles similar to those occurring in Central America in the 1980s. What distinguishes *Sapogonia* significantly from *The Ultraviolet Sky* is the way it plays with temporality, spatiality, and subjectivity through the nonchronological ordering of the chapters, the indeterminate boundaries of the country/region Sapogonia, and the mystery of who Máximo murdered and whether he actually committed the act or dreamed it. These strategies present a sophisticated understanding of writing and reading strategies and an awareness of the disruptive and resistive potential of narrative. In addition, Castillo's conceptions of spirituality are sophisticated, combining philosophical elements of East Indian and indigenous Mexican religions.

The Last Generation: Cherríe Moraga

If Villanueva's and Castillo's narratives portray individual female agents who are raced, gendered, and sexualized subjects, Cherríe Moraga's vision expands the subjectivity positions to provide for alternative sexual identities for both Chicanas and Chicanos and to foster collective agency. In *The Last Generation,* Moraga reinterprets the myth of Coyolxauhqui and recuperates the goddess from misogynistic renderings by re-membering her dismembered body as a symbol of creative power in the form of political activism. In the Mexica creation story, Coyolxauhqui is mutilated and dismembered by her brother after she tries to prevent his birth by killing their mother, Coatlicue. However, Moraga refigures the "evil" Coyolxauhqui, as she is often referred to in Mexica narrative accounts, describing her instead as the "savior" who tries to kill her brother, Huitzilopochtli, the Mexica god of war, to "save the culture from [the] misogyny, war, and greed" of the Mexica rulers.[90] In this characterization, the moral judgment of Coyolxauhqui's act is transformed from murder (in the patriarchal narratives) to salvation and, ultimately, her martyrdom inspires others to collective action. Moraga dedicates her writing to Chicana artists and calls upon them "to pick up the fragments of our dismembered womanhood and reconstitute ourselves."[91] In Moraga's hands—as with the artists who painted the mural on the San Francisco Women's Building in which the goddess appears—Coyolxauhqui is re-membered and embodied as artistic power, her own and that of other Chicana artists, which draws on the memory of the past to recover the sacred and the transformative (see figures 3 and 4 on page 36). "She is the Chicana writer's words, the Chicana painter's canvas, the Chicana dancer's steps. She is motherhood reclaimed and sisterhood honored. She is the female god we seek in our work, la Mechicana before the 'fall.' "[92]

Moraga exposes the patriarchal social constructions that hold La Malinche, Coyolxauhqui, Eve, and by association all "Mechicanas" responsible for moral "fall[s]" from grace and refigures Coyolxauhqui as "savior." She resurrects the goddess as the Christlike figure who sacrificed her body to inspire future generations to rebellion. The refiguring of a female god as savior and mother also points to the inadequacy of La Virgen de

Guadalupe as a resisting agent, active and embodied. Moraga's emphasis on Coyolxauhqui's embodiment and her use of the communal "we" acknowledges "a collective female experience" of physical violation and "a cultural and psychic dismemberment that is linked to imperialist racist and sexist practices" traced from precolonial times to the present.[93] While Moraga's "we" contains the memory of past and on-going oppressions, it also locates the transformative power of collective activism through a "dialectic of oppression and activism."[94] Framing this dialectic as a "spiritual quest" for Chicana artists to create "a portrait of sexuality for men and women independent of motherhood and machismo,"[95] Moraga advocates a refiguring of sexuality located in the bodily reality of Chicanas, including lesbians, and Chicano gay males.

Like *Loving in the War Years*, Moraga's later work, *The Last Generation*, is a multigenre work that defies simple categorization. The disjunctive quality created by the uneasy movement from autobiographical nonfiction to lesbian poetry to anti-imperialistic essays disturbs the complacency and equilibrium of linearity just as it ruptures classificatory interpretation. The occasional tendency in the poems or essays to depict goddesses/ women as essentially peaceful and nurturing is offset by other characterizations, such as Coyolxauhqui's violent act, that refigure women as destructive, albeit for good reason. Ultimately, Moraga is less interested in the metaphysical possibilities of the divine—hence her sometimes simplistic evocations—than in refiguring narratives of Mexica goddesses to represent her ethical and utopian visions of an egalitarian society.

One year after Moraga's *The Last Generation* was published, the mural on the San Francisco Women's Building depicting the physical rememberment of Coyolxauhqui was completed (see figures 3 and 4 on page 36). Recalling Traub's analysis of women contained in statues, jewels, or corpses in Shakespeare's plays, the mural artists reveal the significance of Coyolxauhqui's sculptured confinement to a five-ton stone by the Mexica male rulers. The mural shows her breaking out of the stone circle and lifting her arms in empowered liberation. The goddess/ woman, who almost succeeded in killing the god of war/her warlord brother, was too much of a threat to the Mexica patriarchal war culture represented by Huitzilopotchli to be permitted to live freely. Not only did she need to be killed but her disempowered representation had to be forever molded to serve as a warning to other women. In freeing Coyolxauhqui, in writing as Moraga does and visually as the mural artists do, the goddess's powers and those of all Chicanas and U.S. Mexicanas symbolically are restored.

Borderlands/La Frontera: Gloria Anzaldúa

In *Borderlands/La Frontera*, Gloria Anzaldúa draws on personal and collective memory to rewrite Chicana/o history and construct a Chicana genealogy through the memory of her grandmother and Mexican female cultural symbols. Recognizing the artifice of Western thought that hierarchizes history over memory, reason over imagination, and mind over body, she deconstructs dualities, metaphorically releasing creative, sexual, and spiritual energies held captive. Her construction of a multifaceted subjectivity located in the memory of the divine, bridges the split between corporeal and spiritual, human and divine, and attends significance to psychic experiences long denigrated as "primitive."[96] "I've always been aware that there is a greater power than the conscious I. That power is my inner self, the entity that is the sum total of all my reincarnations, the godwoman in me I call *Antigua, mi Diosa,* the divine within, *Coatlicue-Cihuacoatl-Tlazolteotl-Tonantzin-Coatlalopeuh-Guadalupe*—they are one."[97] In reclaiming her multiple identities Anzaldúa regains sexuality, "the heart in my cunt starts to beat," which was denied when the Spaniards "desexed *Guadalupe,* taking *Coatlalopeuh,* the serpent/sexuality, out of her."[98] The transgressive act of "naming the unspeakable"[99]—her sexuality, spirituality, and multipositionality—speaks against the boundaries that organize Mexican and American cultural knowledge and simultaneously voices a discursive strategy that elaborates her differences. "I will no longer be made to feel ashamed of existing. I will have my voice: Indian, Spanish, white. I will have my serpent's tongue—my woman's voice, my sexual voice, my poet's voice. I will overcome the tradition of silence."[100]

Anzaldúa theorizes this positioning as the "new *mestiza*" whose "first step is to unlearn the *puta/virgen* dichotomy and to see *Coatlalopeuh-Coatlicue* in the Mother, *Guadalupe.*"[101] By linking Guadalupe to the embodied and sexualized goddesses, Anzaldúa refigures La Virgen as spiritual *and* material, disembodied *and* embodied. This move to heal the paradoxical split of body and soul breaks down the Western subject/object duality and provides for alternative subjectivities that recuperate and refigure the female body and spirituality.

Anzaldúa successfully weaves revisionary history, autobiographical testimony, deconstructive philosophy, and mystic vision into a complex conception of the physical and metaphysical conditions of a borderlands subject. Through all of this she manages to convey both the sense of her individual struggle from working-class roots through the turmoil of self-discovery as lesbian, writer, theorist, and the collective struggle of Chicana/o peoples, especially women, to account for all facets of their cultural, racial, linguistic, and historical heritage. Her writing displaces borderlands subjects as singular national citizens, anticipating the Mexican government's decision ten years later to allow dual citizenship, and challenges readers' ethnocentric proclivities through the interlacing of proper, regional, and pocho Spanish with English.[102] Anzaldúa's reflective conception of spirituality expands on the model of medieval monotheistic mysticism to envision her divine self as multiple gods. She has created the most thought-provoking conception of Chicana feminist spirituality and subjectivity to date.

Woman Hollering Creek: Sandra Cisneros

In Anzaldúa's writing, and in Sandra Cisneros's short story "Little Miracles, Kept Promises," Guadalupe can be recuperated in a female genealogy and transformed through association with the goddesses. In Cisneros's story, the character Chayo associates La Virgen, "Mary, the mild," with the passivity she sees in her mother, who accepts her father's drunken abuse. She wishes La Virgen were more like the goddesses, powerful, active, and sexual: "I wanted you bare-breasted, snakes in your hands. I wanted you leaping and somersaulting the backs of bulls. I wanted you swallowing raw hearts and rattling volcanic ash. I wasn't going to be my mother or my grandma. All that self-sacrifice, all that silent suffering. Hell no. Not here. Not me."[103]

However, in resisting gender roles, specifically the cultural role of passive mother, Chayo is forced to endure the taunts "Malinchista" (sell-out) and "Malinche" (traitor) that act as "enforcement" to hold her within culturally regulated boundaries. Eventually, she rejects the Guadalupe/ Malintzin oppositional ideology through a recognition of her indigenous heritage. She realizes that Guadalupe is also Tonantzin, the indigenous goddess whose name means "Our Mother" and whose temple is thought to have been located at the site in Tepeyac where the church honoring

Guadalupe was built. In recovering her indigenous heritage through Guadalupe, Chayo excavates the palimpsestic layers of Native Mexican, Mexican colonial, and U.S. American memory to reveal the discursive signification of her mestiza—indigenous and Spanish—faith and identity.[104]

> When I learned your real name is Coatlaxopeuh, She Who Has Dominion over Serpents, when I recognized you as Tonantzín, and learned your names are Teteoinnan, Toci, Xochiquetzal, Tlazolteotl, Coatlicue, Chalchiuhtlicue, Coyolxauhqui, Huixtocihuatl, Chicomecoatl, Cihuacoatl, when I could see you as Nuestra Señora de la Soledad, Nuestra Señora de los Remedios, Nuestra Señora del Perpetuo Socorro, Nuestra Señora de San Juan de los Lagos, Our Lady of Lourdes, Our Lady of Mount Carmel, Our Lady of the Rosary, Our Lady of Sorrows, I wasn't ashamed, then, to be my mother's daughter, my grandmother's granddaughter, my ancestor's child. . . . When I could see you in all your facets . . . I could love you, and, finally, learn to love me.[105]

Again, as with Anzaldúa, it is the unearthing of the "lost" spirituality of the indigenous goddesses and its reunion with that of the Spanish Catholic Virgins, however uneasy ("those who suffer have a special power, don't they?"), that allows Chayo's subjectivity to emerge and find fulfillment.[106] Chayo's evocation of "loving herself" is coded as self-acceptance of cultural identification and of lesbian desire. The unspeakable is represented literally as something that can't be voiced: "This thing between my legs, this unmentionable" or the even more abstract "down there" Cisneros discusses in "Guadalupe the Sex Goddess."[107]

Moraga's, Anzaldúa's, and Cisneros's writings also articulate a radical recuperation of La Virgen as a site of female and lesbian desire associated with the vulva. Cherríe Moraga's poem "Our Lady of the Cannery Workers" vividly depicts what Chayo could not name.

> Sequoia Virgen
> I see you in every crevice
> of your burnt red flesh
> vagina openings split
> into two thick thighs
> of female eruption.[108]

Moraga's discursive naming calls to mind the serigraph by Ester Hernández, titled *La Ofrenda* (The Offering) and depicting the image of La

Virgen de Guadalupe tattooed on a punk lesbian's back, which appeared on the cover of the first edition of *Chicana Lesbians* (1991).[109] In its entirety, Hernández's image of Guadalupe can be viewed as the female vulva, while the detail shows the hand of another woman placing an open rose at the site of La Virgen's vulva. The offering of the rose, itself a revision of popular representations of heterosexual desire, suggests the radical embodiment and sexualization of Guadalupe as lesbian and locates the agency of pleasure as issuing from woman.[110] In Chicana writings and artworks, Guadalupe becomes the site of female and lesbian desire. In Cisneros's personal essay "Guadalupe the Sex Goddess," La Virgen becomes "a goddess who makes me feel good about my sexual power, my sexual energy, who reminds me I must, as Clarissa Pinkola Estés so aptly put it, '[speak] from the vulva . . . speak the most basic, honest truth,' and write from my *panocha*."[111]

I include this brief discussion of Chicana writers' refigurings of La Virgen de Guadalupe to illustrate a shift by several writers toward recuperating Guadalupe as a Chicana feminist symbol through the genealogy of the indigenous goddesses and as an embodied sexual being. As noted in chapter 1 and as suggested by the writers themselves, the Catholic Church's continued use of Guadalupe to encourage female passivity and submissiveness, as well as the absence of physicality and sexuality implied by her divinity and the immaculate conception, contributed to the writers' initial difficulties in seeing Guadalupe as a symbol of empowerment. The move toward refiguring Guadalupe occurred in the late 1980s and early 1990s, perhaps in recognition of her enduring significance as a cultural symbol. However, this shift was made possible at that particular time because the writers already had recovered the goddesses, which enabled them to see Guadalupe in a different light. Their thinking about her changed by imagining her first as an indigenous goddess and second as a sexual being. The first move, seeing her as an indigenous symbol, Tonantzin, releases the Catholic, more specifically Western Christianity's, hold on her. This move disrupts the mind/body separation and restores her "body," allowing her to be a sexual being. Thus reincarnating her, the writers embrace her as a significant Mexican Catholic symbol in the popular religious tradition and in the genealogy of indigenous female spiritual symbols.

The professional intellectuals' initial adoption of mother earth goddesses as their primary female cultural symbol suggests a social status differentiation separating them from their working-class and semiprofessional counterparts due to educational attainment.[112] With the integration of the working-class symbol, La Virgen de Guadalupe, into the pantheon of female divinities in the late 1980s and early 1990s, their rewritings bridge the past and the present, the religions of the indigenous peoples and the Spanish, and social class differences among scholars and less-educated women. At the same time, their leftist, feminist, and antiracist rewritings, also products of postsecondary education, formulate rebellious discourses imagining widespread cultural and societal changes. The refigurings of indigenous goddesses and La Virgen de Guadalupe reject Western patriarchal discourses aimed at controlling brown and female bodies and diverge from second wave U.S. feminist discourse intent on positing undifferentiated gender oppression. The oppositional and transformative ideology represented in Chicana writers' and artists' refigurings differs significantly from that of the working-class and semiprofessional women's refigurings, which maintain allegiance to church and state and work within institutions rather than attempting to dismantle them. The professional intellectuals' identification with indigenous culture and thought based on a genealogy of Mexica goddesses signifies a rupture with the dominant discourses of the past five hundred years, as well as with precolonial patriarchal thought. Ultimately their critiques separate them from the working-class and semiprofessional women, who identify more with the Mexican national and Catholic religious discourses that compose their worldview. A common theme remains, however, in the writers' and oral historians' shared, although substantively different, resistance to limiting gender roles and control of the female body.

chapter three

 LAS HISTORIAS

Sexuality, Gender Roles, and La Virgen

de Guadalupe Reconsidered

While Chicana writers have embraced La Virgen de Guadalupe as one in a pantheon of indigenous goddesses that inspire them, the working-class and semiprofessional women center their belief system on Mary/Guadalupe as the female divine. A hybrid symbol, Guadalupe resonates with Spanish and Mexican Catholicism as an aspect of the Virgin Mary. Her visual representation also carries relatively unknown indigenous religious symbology resembling that of the mother earth goddess, Tonantzin.[1] In addition, her image casts her as La Virgen morena, the brown virgin, likening her to indigenous and mestizo/a peoples.

All the women whose oral histories I gathered—Minerva Godoy, Evelyn Gonzales, Aurora Harada, Ventura Loya, Mary Ozuna, Vicki Rivera Reyes, Cindy Siqueiros, Virginia Urias, Irma Vásquez—have heard the general account of how Guadalupe appeared to the indigenous man, Juan Diego, in central Mexico.[2] They tell stories of how she has helped them or family members in times of hardship or crisis. The four women who were born and raised in Mexico—Godoy, Loya, Urias, and Vásquez—hold an unwavering faith in Guadalupe and Catholicism formed in childhood, although the manifestation of their faith in practices governing their own lives differs from person to person. Siqueiros, who was born in the United States and has lived in Mexico for periods of time, also bases her faith in Guadalupe. Gonzales, Rivera Reyes, Harada, and Ozuna, second-

(or more) generation Mexican Americans whose grandparents or great-grandparents immigrated to the United States, were raised with the Virgin Mary rather than Guadalupe. However, they cited parents or other relatives for whom Guadalupe was significant, and two of them had significant experiences with the Mexican Virgen later in life. La Virgen's name, whether Mary or Guadalupe, inspires statements of reverence and profound belief from each woman.

Their stories about the Catholic Virgen reinforce the findings of other similar studies.[3] The feminist theologian Jeanette Rodríguez's study of twenty second-generation Mexican American women in the San Francisco Bay area revealed "a deep faith statement that the women make surrounding the story, image, and experience of Our Lady of Guadalupe."[4] Rodríguez explains that for many women, Guadalupe represents both Mexican culture and a valued woman: "Our Lady of Guadalupe provides them with a spiritual form of resistance to the sociopolitical negation of Mexican-American women."[5] Like Rodríguez's, my study reveals that religion is not only deeply interconnected with culture but often is an integral element of U.S. Mexicana identity. More than a symbol of Catholicism, the image of Guadalupe represents Mexicanness.[6]

Irma Vásquez of Tucson, Arizona, considers Guadalupe the primary religious figure of Greater Mexico and beyond. Guadalupe holds ethnic and cultural significance for Vásquez, who was born in 1929 in Mexico and immigrated to Los Angeles in 1962. Although she has lived in the United States for more than forty years and is a naturalized citizen, Vásquez identifies as Mexican and regards Guadalupe as an element of Mexican identity. "[She] is something very important for us, Mexicans, and I think for all Latin American people. [Her appearance] was in Mexico, and it's considered part of our tradition. I learned about Our Lady of Guadalupe when I learned my first little words. She is part of our lives, our faith."

Many different images of La Virgen are venerated in Mexico, but Cindy Siqueiros of Muscatine, Iowa, considers Guadalupe the most powerful. For Siqueiros, born in 1972 in Houston, Texas, Guadalupe signifies pride in Mexican culture and identity, and her name epitomizes dignity and respect. She relates how the Muscatine Mexican community retained autonomy of religious practice and proved its business acumen in a city where Mexicans and Mexican Americans are regarded primarily as manual laborers. "My father is particular to la Virgen de San Juan de los Lagos. There are a lot of different Virgins. Some people are very devout to one

Virgin or another, but *everyone* is devout to La Virgen de Guadalupe. Even here our church is called La Misión de Guadalupe. And our church is the only Hispanic church in this area that has a priest from Mexico and is run solely from our revenues. We run our church all by ourselves. We bought our own church, and we have a Mexican priest."[7] Siqueiros observes that her affiliation with the Mexican Catholic church, located near her house in Muscatine, is an important source of cultural affirmation that gives her the strength to resist the racist affronts she witnesses and experiences in her neighborhood and elsewhere. Although Siqueiros indicates that she doesn't believe in many of the rules the Catholic Church prescribes for its members, such as prohibiting abortions and birth control, nonetheless, she considers the church an important community and individual re-source.[8] Vásquez's and Siqueiros's concepts of La Virgen de Guadalupe can be understood as "popular religiosity," a culturally embedded system of folk customs and expressions of faith, which contrasts with the aliena-tion of institutional Catholicism.[9] In its everyday expression, Rodríguez notes, popular religiosity relates resistance to assimilation as it preserves Mexican culture, history, and identity.[10]

Furthermore, La Virgen functions as a female "metaphor for God in popular religious form."[11] Vicki Rivera Reyes relates that La Virgen's sym-bolic meaning as a woman is more important than her name or visual representation.

> I would have to say I identify more with the Virgin because she is a woman. I mean no one ever knows who or what God is, but most perceive him as a man. And I don't think there's anything wrong with that, I mean I believe in the Lord, I believe in Jesus, but I believe it all started with the Virgin Mary. It's interesting because to be able to know her story, just the fact that she could conceive a child without having sex, I mean, that's just incred-ible. It's beautiful. It really is. It's the purest form of love. That's what I think of when I think about her and identify with her, that she is the purest form of love and what a good person she must have been for God to have chosen her to conceive a child out of pure love. I just think she's beautiful. Because she has many faces, you know, many images, many pictures that portray her. But I never identify her with a particular face. Whenever I think of her I always think of her outline or when you look at shrines or pictures of her, but I never identify her face because, in my mind, I just think she's the most beautiful woman ever. The purest.

La Virgen is not a statue or a representation for Rivera Reyes; she is a "woman," a living human being. Rivera Reyes's conception of La Virgen suggests a model of the ideal self, "the most beautiful woman ever," which she strives to achieve. Having given birth to her first child two months before our meeting, Rivera Reyes remained in awe of women's creationary powers. In considering La Virgen as a living being, like herself, Rivera Reyes identifies what Irigaray and Anzaldúa consider the divine within oneself. Her recognition of female divinity produced a strong sense of herself as a spiritual being and an empowered adult. In considering the "many faces" of La Virgen, Rivera Reyes conceptualizes women, and men, as divine.

Although Rivera Reyes refuses to particularize her image of the female divine, for many U.S. Mexicans Guadalupe's specific image and iconography hold singular relevance. Since the mid-1960s, when striking farmworkers and activists and artists in the Chicana/o civil rights movement appropriated Guadalupe's image as a potent political and cultural symbol of resistance to assimilation and injustice, it is common to see representations of Guadalupe publicly establishing the presence and culture of Mexican Catholic peoples in the United States.[12] Clifford Geertz writes that art is a cultural system that conveys meaning and gives life to a social group.[13] For many Mexicans and Mexican Americans, being Mexican is synonymous with being a Guadalupano. Guadalupe art is the public expression of that identity, an expression that produces community and reproduces collective memory based on the sign: Guadalupe equals Mexico. Her image adorns locations that aren't commonly thought of as art or religious sites, which nonetheless make statements of personal and public participation with culture and community. Guadalupe's image appears painted on ranflas (low-rider cars), street murals, and outdoor walls of houses. It is etched on windows of houses and stores and on arms or backs as body tattoos. It is handmade as folk art objects; mass-produced as statues, candle holders, prayer cards, dress pins, t-shirts and other memorabilia; and displayed in altarcitos and nichos.[14] A number of Mexican communities celebrate Guadalupe's feast day, December 12, with music, dance, and performance.[15] As Evelyn Gonzales, who was born in 1933 in Tucson, says, "Everywhere I go now there's a Virgen de Guadalupe, which when I was growing up, there wasn't. It was just the Virgin Mary." Virginia Urias's home in Tucson is one example. Entering the front door of the ranch-style home she and her husband, Ricardo, built, visitors are greeted by a two-foot-high painting of La Virgen de Guadalupe in the foyer. A string of Christmas lights surrounds Guadalupe's painting and photographs of Urias's grandchildren are stuck in the frame. On the table beneath stands a painting of Jesus Christ, flowers, and other religious and personal memorabilia.

Although the public display of Guadalupe's image wasn't as prevalent prior to the 1960s, nonetheless La Virgen has been an integral element of some families' religious and social experiences since the nineteenth century. In the expanded catalogue for an exhibition of Tucson folk art, James S. Griffith refers to Ramona Franco of Tucson, whose home altar contained an image of Guadalupe that dates to 1895. He writes that "her family has had a devotion to Our Lady of Guadalupe since at least the days of her paternal grandfather, who gave his son an image of the *Virgen morena* around the time of his marriage in 1880." Born in 1902 on a ranch east of Tucson, Franco remembered that her family honored La Virgen de Guadalupe every year with a feast to which all the neighbors were invited.[16] This memory of Mexico actively constructed as a social and cultural process articulates, enhances, and produces a sense of community.[17] In so doing it reproduces and recreates collective memory and group identity throughout Greater Mexico from Tacoma, Washington, to St. Paul, Minnesota, to Charlotte, North Carolina. The images have the effect of creating, as Stuart Hall writes, "an imaginary coherence on the experience of dispersal and fragmentation, which is the history of all enforced diasporas."[18] As such, they function as material evidence of resistance to assimilation and preservation of cultural identity.

In "The Undocumented Virgin," Rubén Martínez writes that recent waves of immigrants have brought renewed Catholicism to the United States in the form of La Virgen, who "is at the center of the Mexican soul." Martínez adds that he has noticed an increase in miraculous apparitions of Guadalupe on both sides of the border that he attributes to the economic and political conditions Mexicans and Chicanos face. "It's no coincidence that She's been appearing more often lately. In times of crisis, She's always there. Today, the crisis is on both sides of the border." Rather than despair, however, he views the pervasiveness of her symbol as an expression of hope by immigrants who cross the border for a better life and by college students who stage hunger strikes and marches supporting immigrants and their own culture.[19]

Guadalupe's image and the pilgrimage sites dedicated to her function as *"lieux de mémoire,"*[20] memory sites, challenging histories that continue to devalue Mexican ethnic and racial identity and threaten its erasure. The shrine to Guadalupe in the basilica at Tepeyac, Mexico, is the heart of Guadalupe devotion for Mexicanas and Mexicanos, including those who live in the United States. Evelyn Gonzales became aware of La Virgen de Guadalupe when she married her husband, Carlos, a fervent believer. She says Carlos always kept a statue of La Virgen in their home. Although Gonzales did not pay homage to Guadalupe, she used money inherited from her brother to schedule a group tour for her and her husband to visit the basilica in Tepeyac on Guadalupe's feast day, December 12. When Carlos became seriously ill, he urged her to make the pilgrimage without him. He told her, " 'I want you to go see La Virgen de Guadalupe because I can't go. I want you to go for me.' " In representing her husband's belief, Gonzales found that the memory site at the basilica brought her to a greater understanding of Guadalupe's significance and power.

> And so I went and that night [Carlos] went into the hospital, and he almost died. [My children] told me not to come home; if he got worse they would tell me. I was gone for twelve days and I saw the Virgen de Guadalupe and I was very enthusiastic and everything. And when they told me you know that he was sick, I was there with the Virgin. That night [the tour group] went to the basilica. It was the 12th of December. . . . When I was up there on the balcony, I kept praying for Carlos to get well, and then I kept looking at the Virgin, and all of a sudden the rays of the Virgin would get brighter for me. They would go and come and go and come. . . . And to me, it was like telling me not to worry, that Carlos was going to be all right, because I was praying for him. "He'll be all right." . . . Then I promised the Virgin, "If he gets well, I'll promise to come and see you again, because right now I'm all worried about him." . . . So I came home, and then he had gotten well.

Gonzales's experience of direct communication with La Virgen reveals the semiotic capability of religious icons to evoke feeling, emotion, memory, spirituality, and artistic or imaginative production. In her study "The Cultural Semiotics of Religious Icons," Kay F. Turner elaborates the process by which "Icons are brought to life by people who speak to them because they believe in them." Turner finds that icons contain significant "evocative power" as second-order signs, signs of signs, because they refer back to first-order symbols, the historical religious personages (Mary, Christ, humans canonized as saints) who established the basis for Christian belief.[21]

Icons of Guadalupe and other saints, found in many Catholic churches, evoke spiritual communication with believers to the extent that the icons receive messages and reply to them. As Gonzales relates, Guadalupe established direct contact with her through images of oscillating light rays "going and coming." Even more significantly from a semiotic perspective, Gonzales "hears" this as a speech act from Guadalupe: " 'He'll be all right.' " Gonzales then replies to the image as if to a real person: "If he gets well, I'll promise to come and see you again." This communication process results from the icon's *langue*-based function, establishing a visual language based on the particularities of the static image, and its transformation to an active *parole* function, establishing psychological and linguistic interactions, or speech acts, with the believer.

What Gonzales saw and heard while praying to Guadalupe was not a lifeless object, an image on a woven cloth. In contrast, the historical personage of the Virgin Mary/Guadalupe communicated with Gonzales that night just as she did with Juan Diego in the Guadalupe origin narrative. In order for an icon to cultivate such significant interactions, codified events such as apparitions and the performance of miracles must be part of the icon's narrative. Turner explains that such events "mak[e] historical personages seem less remote (in the earthly sense they come alive again in apparitions) and imbu[e] the Icons with the living presence of their signifieds."[22] Guadalupe took on human characteristics when she first appeared to Juan Diego as described in the apparition narrative, which serves as a model for the sight and sound interaction that Gonzales experienced. Such apparition narratives function to establish personal intimacy with the signified, in this case both Guadalupe, who appeared in Mexico, and the historical figure of Mary, who birthed Jesus Christ.

The interaction Gonzales experienced with Guadalupe was developed in advance through the establishment of universal and local appeals related to Guadalupe's specific image. Her universal appeal results from the story and visual representation of the incarnation of the Virgin of the Immaculate Conception.[23] The sign for this manifestation of La Virgen, representing her impregnation without sexual intercourse, is represented by the sash draped around her midsection that tells believers she is pregnant (see figure 9 on page 57). Gonzales's upbringing in the Catholic

Church taught her the universal manifestation of Mary the Immaculate. Later, through her husband's belief system, she became familiar with the "local" appeal of Guadalupe, the Mexican Virgin.

Guadalupe's local and regional appeal comes from the apparition and miracle narrative placing her in the distinct geographical location of central Mexico. Icons lay claim to a local territory and its inhabitants by appearing in a specific place or adopting significant features that believers can identify with and speak to. Turner emphasizes that "by becoming locally identified, the Icon further achieves the communicative potential of iconicity, which is in this case the achievement of intimacy and personality."[24] With Guadalupe, intimacy and personality have been established with indigenous and mestizo peoples, visually, by the olive tone of her face and hands and, narratively, by her appearance to Juan Diego, a recently converted indigenous man. That she appeared at a site near Mexico City, the former seat of the Mexica culture (Tenochtitlan) and contemporary seat of Mexican culture, is also significant in securing her identification as the Mexican (national) and even Latin American (transnational) Virgen. Gonzales's husband, Carlos, identified strongly with Guadalupe perhaps because of his half-blood Yaqui ancestry.[25] Even though Gonzales was familiar with the Guadalupe story and image, it was only when she went to La Virgen's memory site in Tepeyac and interacted with Guadalupe's image that she was able to establish a personal relationship for herself with La Virgen. In the larger semiotic context, Gonzales's experience invokes both *langue* and *parole* moments. As described above, the Guadalupe icon's visual language, *langue*, told Gonzales that the icon belonged to an established Roman Catholic instruction and information system. Gonzales's prayers, belief that La Virgen would restore Carlos's health, and, further, her experience of La Virgen communicating back constitute a *parole* interaction.

The interaction between Gonzales and Guadalupe forms a mutual exchange, which repeats the bartering act that occurred between Guadalupe and Juan Diego in the Mexican Virgen's origin narrative. When Guadalupe asked Juan Diego to convey to the bishop that she wanted a church, a "home," built for her, she established a human need and began the bartering process. This request also connected her with the Virgin Mary, who searched for a home to birth Christ. Rather than birthing a Christ child, Guadalupe's request for a church was intended to birth and nurture the Catholic faith among indigenous peoples, who were seen by the Spaniards as "childlike." In return for Juan Diego's service, Guadalupe promised to heal his uncle and, more generally, to protect him and his people from harm. The origin narrative serves as a model for the mutual exchanges that Guadalupe and believers have made since the basilica was built as a memory site. The cultural practice of la petición and la manda, a petition for help and a promise of service, constitutes the most common interaction between Mexican Catholic believers and Guadalupe even today. Guadalupe established her humanness with Gonzales by signaling with light rays that she was listening compassionately to Gonzales's prayers. Gonzales recognized Guadalupe's signal, petitioned Guadalupe for Carlos's health, and promised to return to the memory site, Guadalupe's home, if her petition was granted. The communication cycle between Guadalupe and Juan Diego establishing humanness, intimacy, petition, and promise of service is repeated between Guadalupe and Gonzales.

While Guadalupe is the best known, other Virgen icons have established presence and personal relationships with U.S. Mexicans. Rivera Reyes's oral history relates a family tradition of honoring and appealing to La Virgen de San Juan de Los Lagos at her shrine in San Juan, Texas. The family's visits to this public shrine of La Virgen also exemplify the petition and promise tradition and describe a sense of a lived expression of faith, something more than weekly attendance at Sunday mass.

You know, my parents prayed very strongly to the Virgin. We would take a lot of trips down to the valley, to the shrine in San Juan. And I never really knew why we would take so many trips, you know, but as I got older and started asking—to give you an example, when my nephew was born, my brother's son, he was two months premature. So he was born very, very small and very sick. And my father prayed to the Virgin Mary and basically asked for his life, that he would be spared. And when everything turned out okay with him, we made a trip to the valley. Mother said that it was because he had made a promise to the Virgin that if Andrew, my nephew, lived he would go down to the Virgin and go to her altar on his knees. And he did. And we made—gosh, I'm trying to remember—it was always because someone was sick or there was some big need or big problem, something that needed to be resolved. And my parents would always pray to the Virgin, and if their petitions were answered, they would always honor their petition and we would go to San Juan.

. . . It's beautiful, it's beautiful out there. Very peaceful, and it was always a nice trip. And it always made my parents so happy. And I think that's where I got most of my belief from. Because they wouldn't just go down to the neighborhood church and thank her there, they would make the long trip to see her.

Rivera Reyes reveals that visits to the Texas memory site of La Virgen de San Juan de los Lagos resulted in a profound faith conviction and a deep-seated sense of peace and well-being for her family that could not be found in the local church in San Antonio. The personal relationship Rivera Reyes's family fostered with La Virgen de San Juan supplied them with enough sustenance to face the day-to-day struggles of being Mexican American in Texas. A replica of the statue of La Virgen de San Juan de los Lagos was brought to San Juan, Texas, in 1949, sculpted in the image of the original icon located in San Juan, Jalisco, Mexico.[26] The Texas memory site, like its counterpart in Jalisco, draws thousands of pilgrims each year. For Rivera Reyes and her family, visits to the shrine in Texas allowed them to practice the popular religiosity of Mexican Catholicism apart from the mainstream Church. These visits reinforced a Mexican identity, established by La Virgen de San Juan's apparition narrative in Mexico, which counteracted the assimilating forces of American and European influence. The relatively close location of the Texas shrine to Rivera Reyes's family home provided an economically viable way to communicate with the Virgin. The three-hour drive from San Antonio to San Juan was an affordable day trip, whereas the long drive to and housing near the original memory site in the state of Jalisco would have been financially taxing.

As with the Guadalupe icon, the San Juan icon resonates for Catholics through the universal narrative of the Immaculate Conception shown by the elaborate gown and crown indicating that she is the Queen of Heaven and by the half moon indicating female fecundity (see figure 15). La Virgen de San Juan also achieved local and regional signification in the miracle narrative that took place in San Juan, Jalisco, Mexico, in 1623.[27] Again, this narrative established La Virgen's humanity when she requested clothing and shelter. Essentially, she asked for spiritual devotion framed in terms of practical human needs. Found in a deteriorated state in an unused shrine, this icon petitioned residents for a home and promised them protection in return. The people of San Juan de los Lagos fulfilled their part of the agreement; the icon was repaired, provided with clothing, and permanently placed in a new home, the San Juan church. In

15. La Virgen de San Juan de los Lagos, sixteenth century. Line art drawing, ink on paper. Courtesy of the Library of Congress.

LA SANTISIMA VIRGEN
DE Sn. JUAN DE LOS LAGOS

addition, she was named after the town and claimed as its patron saint, giving her local and regional significance. In the circulation of the petition and promise narrative, San Juan residents and multitudes of people from northern Mexico maintain an intimate relationship with her, requesting aid and promising a sacrifice in return. The mutual exchange of the apparition narrative is repeated. La Virgen de San Juan, like Guadalupe, fulfills her part of the agreement daily by providing solace and serenity for believers. Although no apparition narrative exists for La Virgen de San Juan's second local and regional memory site in Texas, an elaborate official ceremony by the Church, including a pilgrimage of San Juan, Mexico, residents who conveyed the icon replica, established her "home" in San Juan, Texas, in 1949. In this way, a second devout audience of Mexican Americans was created in southern Texas, including Rivera Reyes's family.[28]

Both Gonzales's and Rivera Reyes's stories exemplify the evocative potential of the Virgen icon and the mutual interaction sequence of petition and promise that is repeated daily at the memory sites. Gonzales asked La Virgen de Guadalupe for her husband's recovery and promised to return to visit Guadalupe. Rivera Reyes's father petitioned La Virgen de San Juan to save his grandson and promised to walk to her on his knees. In fulfilling their promises to return to these memory sites, Gonzales's and Rivera Reyes's families continue the performance of the other half of the exchange, La Virgen's petition to them. Whether visiting her at Tepeyac, Mexico, or San Juan, Texas, they and others who return to the memory sites continually assure La Virgen that they will provide her with a home and dedicated worship.

The evocative potential of the Mary/Guadalupe icon results from the instability of the sign, at one moment an image or statue and at another the personification of the historical Virgin. More generally, as Turner explains, "this instability results from the oscillation between the Icon's potential as either active or passive personification of the signified." When Gonzales visited the basilica of La Virgen de Guadalupe, she understood that she would be viewing a passive image. What she didn't expect was the active communication that took place between her and the historical figure. This oscillation between passive and active icon generated a strong belief response from Gonzales. However, instability and oscillation can produce responses other than strong belief. As Turner notes, there is a "range of attitudes and meanings particular Icons are capable of eliciting."[29]

For example, Ventura Loya believes in Guadalupe as a cultural and religious symbol, but she does not accept the icon's human or evocative potential. Basing her philosophy of life on stories of "real" experience, Loya refuses the idea of Mary/Guadalupe as a role model for women. "Like La Virgen de Guadalupe, who is the Virgin of Mexico, there isn't anything in her history other than that she appeared in Mexico. I don't remember hearing the story of her life in the world. A Virgin is a Virgin of God and they just appear in the world whenever they are a Virgin already. So how can a woman get a comparison of her behavior in the world? Saints have lived in the world and later they become saints. But a Virgin, no. A Virgin is God. They just appear in this world and there is no background story about how they lived as little girls or as a woman or anything." Loya knows Guadalupe solely as a sacred being with no human history in contrast to saints, humans who were canonized as divine after death, whose humanness she can identify with. Her personal experiences allow for belief in the Catholic symbol but not in the evocative potential of human-to-human interaction that Gonzales and Rivera Reyes obtain with Guadalupe.

The icon of La Virgen de Guadalupe is unstable not only in its evocative potential but in its symbolic meaning for women of Mexican origin or ancestry. On the one hand, Guadalupe is a liberatory figure identified with independence and reform movements. On the other hand, she represents the piety and compliance expected of women in a culture bound up with Catholicism. This contradiction results in a condition of uncertainty that the working-class and semiprofessional women exploit to produce alternative meanings. I argue in this chapter that La Virgen de Guadalupe exists as a source of identity, inspiration, *and* subversive refiguring for the working-class and semiprofessional women, even as the promotion of her image by the culture and the Church reinforces traditional roles of dutiful and subservient wife, mother, daughter, sister.[30] Because of Guadalupe's ambivalent and multiple significations, she provides a window of opportunity for the women to reformulate their conditions of existence.

GUADALUPE: *Symbol of Virtue and Virginity*

Representing a gendered position, La Virgen de Guadalupe is indeed complex and contradictory. Her symbolic meaning oscillates among characteristics of strength, liberation, collective identity, and passivity, idealized purity, and confinement. Conflicting elements of empowerment, mediation, and repression coexist in Guadalupe's image, encompassing a range of representational positions for Chicanas and U.S. Mexicanas, including liberatory sexual politics, labor activism, cultural identification, nationalism, religious devotion, confinement, repression, and, at worst, victimization. Each of these positions carries significant positive and negative material ramifications for Chicanas and U.S. Mexicanas.

The Mexican upper-class promotion of Guadalupe's pacifying characteristics is a means of preventing lower-income Mexicans from revolting into class warfare in Mexico and in the United States. During its forty year reign, the Mexican political party PRI (which represented the rich upper class) sponsored annual pilgrimages to her shrine, supplying food and drink for lower-income Mexicans.[31] In addition, the Catholic Church's promotion of Guadalupe's symbolism as mother and server also restrains demands for legalization of birth control, abortion, and divorce in Mexico and keeps many women confined in the home caring for too many children and under the rule of often abusive spouses.[32] The effects of this unrewarded (re)productive labor on lower-income women include lack of education and alternative work possibilities, resulting in the inability to earn an income that could support them independently. It also contributes to exploitation in U.S. factories and farm fields on this side of the border or in maquiladoras just across the border.[33]

Because of the Catholic narrative of the Immaculate Conception, which emphasizes purity, women's lives are often regulated by Church teachings that advocate sex solely for reproduction and otherwise cast sex and displays of sexuality as sinful. The control of sexuality and reproduction is manifested in the regulatory agencies of virginity and monogamy, which have their basis in both indigenous and Indo-European cultural norms.[34] In a historical review and class analysis of attitudes on sexuality that affect "Hispanic/Latin" women, Oliva Espín found that "the honor of Latin families is strongly tied to the sexual purity of women. And the concept of honor and dignity is one of the essential distinctive marks of Hispanic culture." This concept is related to social class in that the upper classes, concerned about social status, "tend to be more rigid about sexuality" because of the implications of patrimony—"a man needs to know that his children are in fact his before they inherit his property." However, with families where property is not a concern, "the only thing left to a family may be the honor of its women and as such it may be guarded jealously by both males and females."[35] Although such values may not be adhered to as strictly in the twenty-first century, Espín writes that virginity before marriage is still a "cultural imperative" reinforced by the model of the Virgin Mary/Guadalupe, "who was a virgin and a mother, but never a sexual being."[36] Espín has found that when families immigrate to the United States attitudes toward sexuality sometimes become even stricter because of the myth that "all American women are very free with sex" and parental fear that daughters will become "Americanized" and adopt liberal sexual habits. "Sexuality and sex-roles within a culture tend to remain the last bastion of tradition."[37]

The women's religious or spiritual convictions in La Virgen and their utterances, performances of themselves as material beings, result in a paradox that must be negotiated between disembodiment and embodiment. For a conviction in La Virgen—who gave birth to the son of God—as a *virgin* relies on acceptance of the doctrine of the Immaculate Conception. More profanely, that means conception without copulation, implying that sex is a debased mortal activity with its attendant bodily expulsions—heat, sweat, blood, vaginal fluid, semen—that entail from physical contact between man and woman. Removed from the corporeal, the unruly, the irrational, La Virgen exists as a phantasm, without substance or materiality. Disembodied. She is denied sexuality, physicality, and therefore is disassociated from the material consequences of being virgin or not-virgin, a reality that several of the women remarked upon as having significant effects on their lives.[38] Writing about women's autobiographies, Sidonie Smith argues that rational Western thought in shaping the universal (autobiographic) "I" operates on a similar principle of evacuating the "I" of its "colorful" elements, thereby claiming that the masculine "I" serves as the universalized "noncorporeal soul." Individuals associated with "colorful" elements, overdetermined by their bodies, become "identified culturally as other, exotic, unruly, irrational, uncivilized, regional, or paradoxically unnatural."[39] For U.S. Mexicanas, cultural unruliness is constructed as la puta (whore), la chingada (traitor), La Malinche (traitor and whore), or La Llorona (bad mother), in opposition to La Virgen (good mother and patron saint).

These restrictive positions regarding sex before marriage translate to a denial of female sexuality and a shame concerning female reproductive processes such as menstruation. The culture of silence about sex and sexuality results in women's lack of knowledge about their bodies and the sex act but does not ensure abstinence. Vicki Rivera Reyes reveals in her historia that her parents never discussed sex with her and she didn't feel she could talk with her friends about it. This lack of knowledge and support led her to engage in sex with her boyfriend even though it wasn't fulfilling.

DEBRA BLAKE: You talked about having sex when you were sixteen years old. Did your friends know about this? What would your family have thought? Is there a real stigma when girls have sex?

VICKI RIVERA REYES: I don't know if my parents ever really knew, but they definitely were not going to ever find out for sure. I knew that. That's why they never asked me.

DB: They didn't want to know?

VRR: Right, I'm sure of it.

DB: What about your peers?

VRR: Among my peers, I would say that most of my peers were having sex. But I was not anxious to share that I was also. . . . I didn't really know anything about relationships so I just thought that's the way all relationships progressed. And I never shared it with my friends, even with my closest friends. I really didn't know that that's not the way other people did it. So when I finally did share it with friends, I realized that I really didn't have to have sex just to have this relationship and stuff. . . . But if I had been more honest, I guess, with my friends, you know my girlfriends, and talked about it more, I think I might have avoided having sex. . . . But see I never wanted to share it and I think in a way, I was not proud of the fact that I had sex. . . . I thought of myself as, like I said, a bad person, you know, for having sex because you're not supposed to have sex until after you get married. And I had done it, you know, and stuff. So I wasn't proud of the fact. I surely didn't enjoy my early sexual experience, because I always felt like I had done something bad.

DB: A lot of guilt, huh?

VRR: Yeah, a whole lot of guilt. A whole lot of guilt.

Rivera Reyes's "shame" derives from religious and cultural prohibitions regarding sex outside marriage, a standard enforced only for women. Her inability to enjoy sex stemmed from the idea that the primary purpose of sex is reproduction rather than pleasure. She adds that she was particularly concerned about not disappointing her father. In referring to her teenage years, she constructs herself as a "bad," not-virginal young woman who has disobeyed the Law of the Father/father (God/her parent) and can only be seen through the lens of virgin/whore duality. Within the sociocultural norms that provide for male authority and respect, the Law of the Father/father, his "honor," and by association the entire family's, may come into question if the daughter's betrayal becomes public. Ironically, the family's silence and the cultural taboos against talking about sex contributed to Rivera Reyes's decision to engage in it. When she breaks the silence and talks to friends, she determines what is best for herself, alleviating the guilt by ending the sexual element of the relationship. However, in this instance, guilt effectively nullifies the possibility for female sexual pleasure and for self-determination outside the parameters of the Guadalupe/Malintzin duality.

In addition, Rivera Reyes admits she and her boyfriend did not use any birth control methods. She never considered that sex could lead to pregnancy. While the absence of birth control would follow the Church's teachings, the expected result, pregnancy outside of marriage, would be contrary. Although she attended a sex education class in junior high school, she says the diagrams and explanations of male and female reproductive parts did not make explicit the connection between intercourse and pregnancy.

Nor do sex education classes acknowledge the clitoris as a sexual organ, the site of female pleasure. Many women reveal a lack of awareness about the female body and the achievement of sexual pleasure. Carla Trujillo cites a sexuality study conducted by Lourdes Arquelles in which half of the 373 Latina immigrants surveyed "possessed little knowledge of their reproductive systems or their own physiology."[40] Even when married, women are not always able to express themselves as sexual beings. Espín notes that the cultural qualities prized for women including sexual purity, subservience to males, and self-renunciation, imply that "to enjoy sexual pleasure, even in marriage, may indicate lack of virtue." This negative view of sex leads some women to view it as an "unwelcome obligation toward [their] husband[s] and a necessary evil in order to have children." Moreover, some women maintain this attitude as a virtue and express pride in their lack of pleasure or desire. The judgment that women who enjoy sex lack virtue does not apply to men, for whom sexual prowess is a sign of manhood.[41] From another perspective, however, J. Jorge Klor de Alva acknowledges that some changes have occurred in sexual norms and that "variations in Chicana sexuality have had an impact on changes in the relationships between males and females. These, in turn, have caused changes in the divorce rate, age of marriage of both partners, and have led to sexual anxieties among Chicanos [males]."[42]

Ventura Loya came to Muscatine, Iowa, in 1975 with her husband. In 1995, she divorced him for the second time, after which he again attempted to sweet-talk, bully, and belittle her into coming back to him. Her historia is filled with her own and other women's experiences of domestic abuse. In contrast to her idea of the Virgin Mary as without human history or body, Loya's life story is grounded in her female body, which her husband, and to a certain extent she herself, regulates according to the Guadalupe/Malintzin ideology. The cycle of verbal abuse, physical violence, and resistance that she experienced throughout her marriage began when her husband accused her of not being a virgin. At that time they had been married in a civil ceremony but were living separately until they could get married in a church wedding.

> VENTURA LOYA: A woman has to be a virgin. A man does not have to respond to or marry the woman if she's not a virgin.
>
> DB: Do you associate this concept with the Virgin Mary, then, or is it a separate issue?
>
> VL: Oh, no. I don't think it's something that would be related. It's just that a woman has to be a virgin. She has to prove that she hasn't had a relationship with anyone else. And one of the things that I didn't know when I was going to get married, that I heard, was that women are supposed to bleed whenever they have a relationship for the first time. And then some people told me, "No, some women bleed, some women don't." And I said, "Oh, so there's a difference here." And I had to find out because my husband said to me when we were getting married, "If you're a virgin I'll treat you like a queen. But if you're not, you're going to have a miserable life."

Like the cultural construction of Malintzin as a traitor for consorting with the conqueror, Loya was suspected of betraying her husband by sleeping with other men before their marriage. The patriarchal defloration narrative her husband invoked frames the reputation of a woman, and thus her desirability and worth, by the presence or absence of virginity. Embedded within the male narrative is an essentialized female script written in dualized terms as blood or no blood judged in equally dichotomized terms: good or bad, keep or reject, treat like a queen or a whore. But as Loya discovered, there is ambiguity in this narrative that calls the patriarchal judgment into question—"some women bleed, some women don't"—which allows her to maintain a counterdiscourse based on personal experience despite her husband's arguments: "So we started fighting and I knew that I was a virgin."[43]

As a divorced woman, Loya acknowledges the injustice of double standards for men and women. Yet she still feels obligated to meet the cultural scrutiny that defines a "good" woman by censuring her activities.

> VL: But I still have in my head that I'm not supposed to do many things by myself. For example, if I feel like going to a party I don't do it because I don't want to give a bad impression. I did it a few times

before and then I felt guilty. And even my daughter says to me, "Mom there's nothing wrong with that." So I went three times in a row to dances. And then I felt that it wasn't right. I mean it's all right to go once in a while but so many times. I just don't like to give people who know me something to talk about.[44]

DB: It's as if you're not supposed to be happy and have fun, right?

VL: Yeah. Because what men and women in this culture say is, "Oh, if she's going to dances she is looking for a man. That's what she's doing." And some people think they don't have to respect you because you don't deserve any respect. Because you're going to look for a man. That's what you're doing. That's what the eyes in this culture say, "You're looking for a man. That's what you're doing." But if you go with your husband, it's all right. "She's just going to have fun." But that's the impression that everybody gets.

DB: If you're looking for a man, what does that mean?

VL: You're supposed to be in your house and taking care of your stuff. And the real word for that is a prostitute, because if you are looking for a man you are not a good woman.

Loya's historia emphasizes the circulation of multiple, interacting power dynamics. While she has escaped the control of an individual, her husband, the culturally provided subjectivities enforced by the community gaze are more difficult to resist. Such subjectivities construct women as dangerous (or endangered) if lacking male supervision and maintain public space as male regulated, confining women to the domestic space. The regulatory gaze, both actual and imagined, serves to circumscribe Loya's actions outside the home, similar to the way her husband circumscribed them when she was married. Loya's story shows how the virgin/whore dichotomy and the mythology that women can't be trusted operate to control the activities of an available woman. An unmarried woman is dangerous because she has the potential to "lure" the men of the community into illicit acts, whether the men are "available" or not. The onus for upholding female virtue and the judgment for deviation (or suspected deviation) are placed solely on the woman. As Loya indicates, censure takes the form of ostracization or condemnation, which in her case are sufficient to provoke self-enforcement and repression of pleasure and desire.

However, Loya's story also emphasizes the importance of community and cultural identity for U.S. Mexicanas. As is the case in Muscatine, the Mexican community is often perceived as the only defense against the onslaught of racial hostilities and assimilationist pressures directed at lower-income, Spanish-speaking immigrants by the larger community and dominant culture. Loya was willing to forgo a male relationship and even the custody of her youngest son for a while to achieve peace and cultivate a sense of self. She was unwilling to risk the loss of her cultural base and support system, other members of the Mexican community.

U.S. Mexicanas also are compelled by what Castillo terms the "mandate of motherhood" that considers reproduction and mothering as women's primary roles and implies that they are not fulfilled as human beings until they have given birth.[45] Anzaldúa has written that "women are made to feel total failures if they don't marry and have children."[46] The stakes are high for women who refuse the role of mother in order to pursue self-interests because they "may be stigmatized with the 'Llorona Complex,' that is, they may be shunned as a result."[47] The gendered construction of "mother" additionally is informed by an emphasis on the ideal of the "good mother," signified by the Virgin Mary/Guadalupe, as one who puts her children's (and husband's) needs ahead of her own. In a study that examined constructions of mothering and female employment, Denise Segura writes that "among Chicanos and Mexicanos the image of *la madre* as self-sacrificing and holy is a powerful standard against which women often compare themselves."[48] In her historia, Cindy Siqueiros says she discovered the hard way the high standards set for mothers in Mexican culture.

> There is this role that you have to play as a mother that is so perfect. I guess I heard a lot of talk about [La Virgen] and the way that she mothered Jesus and how important it is to be completely devoted to your children. I thought I was a perfectly good mother until I went to Mexico and I realized what a crappy mother I really was. Because everybody told me. I remember when I was living here [in the United States], I did everything that everyone else did normally with their kids. And when I went to Mexico, my god-mother—she had a baby about the same age as mine, one month apart—she came over to the house and she brought her child and she had all of these little Gerber bottles. . . . And I said to my grandmother and aunt, "You know, how come she feeds her child Gerber and you're always giving me flack about feeding my child out of a bottle?" Then they said, "She

prepares her child's food." And they always asked her, "What is your child eating today?" And she'd say, "Oh, I made chicken-something with peas and carrots," or "liver and onions." All of these, like, meals and then she'd blend them up and stick it in a jar. She'd cook his three meals and carry them around with her. She'd bake apples with cinnamon and sugar and puree them for him. She would make him juices. . . . She did not use Pampers. She did not waste her money on Pampers. She carried cloth diapers. . . . There are so many women in Mexico that all they use is cloth diapers. They put themselves through the torture of having to use cloth diapers all the time. . . . The sacrifices that mothers make are incredible.

Siqueiros's description of her godmother as the "perfect mother" encompasses both her incredulity at the standards set for mothering and her resistance to this standard being imposed upon her. Having escaped the judgment of her immediate family in Iowa regarding her divorce by moving to Mexico, she found herself subjected to another judgment regarding motherhood by her extended family in Mexico. The basis of the good mother ideology assumes that mothering is a woman's primary role and that she devotes all her time, in effect her life, to caring for and raising children. Furthermore, a woman's self-worth is tied up in the performance of good mothering. If a woman doesn't perform to expectations, she is a "bad" mother, unlike the Virgin Mary/Guadalupe. Siqueiros's characterization of herself as a "crappy" mother finds her lacking the self-sacrificing characteristics that her godmother exhibits as a "good" mother. However, for Siqueiros complete devotion to and self-sacrifice for one's children is not only a limiting standard but one that is impossible for her to attain as a divorced woman who must work outside the home to support herself and her daughter. Her move toward independence and self-determination, freeing herself from an abusive marriage—something a "good" (passive) wife would not do—subjects her to yet another constrictive gender-role conception, good mothering. This standard not only judges her capacity as a mother by how much, or how little, she does for her child but attempts to limit her ability to provide for her daughter. In effect, a good mother must be married, completely dependent on her husband for financial support, and must forgo any desire for self-fulfillment outside children, husband, and home. After living in Mexico for a year, Siqueiros decided her relatives' critiques of her mothering capabilities and the blatant and persistent sexism she encountered in the workforce were too much to handle, and she crossed the border again, returning to Iowa, where her immediate family had softened their views of her divorce.

Because of the strict regulations governing the expression of female sexuality and the emphasis on woman's procreative role, lesbians may be stigmatized more harshly than heterosexual women who defy rules and roles, or they may be judged more critically than homosexual males.[49] Castillo states that "most lesbians of our culture have not politicized their desires nor openly declared them as a way of life. The traditions of our heritage, the rules of the Church, and importantly, economic dependency, still make most women who feel themselves to be lesbian or bisexual opt for a heterosexual lifestyle." Connections to family and community often are important to a sense of identity, intensified by "Anglo alienation," and Latina lesbians may choose to negate or hide their desires rather than break these ties.[50] Mariana Romo-Carmona, writing in *Compañeras: Latina Lesbians*, observes that Latina lesbians who choose to pursue their desires must find support outside the culture. "Being a lesbian is by definition an act of treason against our cultural values. Though our culture may vary somewhat from country to country, on the whole, to be a lesbian we have to leave the fold of our family, and to seek support within the mainstream lesbian community." Moreover, she adds that lesbian mothers are seen as a contradiction in terms. "To this day there is no support for lesbian motherhood, or motherhood without the presence of a man to legitimize the relationship."[51] None of the working-class or semi-professional women identified as lesbians in their historias; however, several expressed their views about homosexuality, which range from guarded acceptance and pity to disgust and condemnation. Virginia Urias, for example, follows Catholic doctrine in denouncing homosexuality as perverse and unnatural because it violates strict conceptions of gender and sexuality roles.

> VIRGINIA URIAS: To tell you the truth, they make me sick to my stomach. But I feel sorry for them. I feel sorry for them. Because I don't know if it's true that they are all like that. I don't know if it's true that they do it because they're nasty, or because they want to. Like the Pope said, he's against it. He said God doesn't bless the homosexuals. And I'm wondering, in my childhood years we never heard of anything like that. There wasn't anyone. I never heard anything. Why are there so many now?

DB: How do you view homosexuals as people?

VU: I don't think they're not good people. Like I said, they make me sick to my stomach but I feel sorry for them. They are good. Most of them are very nice, they are very loving, you know, I see them in the family. And that's when I feel sorry for them, when I see that they are so good to their mothers, to the family. When I see them acting like a woman I feel sorry for them. And I'm wondering if they were born like that, or if they made it up themselves.

DB: What about women, lesbians?

VU: I don't get it? I don't like that. I don't understand and it's worse to me than homosexual men. They make me sick to my stomach worse. I don't want to say anything because I don't want to hurt anyone. But that point I don't understand at all.

DB: I guess I'm not sure what you mean.

VU: Well, because a woman is different, you know, from a man. And I said, "What can they get from one woman to another? What joy? What pleasure can they get?" I don't understand. Maybe I need to see it to understand. Probably. Because otherwise I don't ask. I don't want to know. But sometimes it goes in my mind, because these women I know got married; they fell in love. I'm wondering, "What can they do?" And one day the Mensajeras had a lady come to the YWCA to a meeting and she talked about that.

Urias's statements, derived from a heterosexual culture that constructs female desire in relationship to male physiology, are predicated on the penis as the sole source of female pleasure. Lesbianism defies the Law of the Father and the double "subject" position of the historical woman named the Virgin Mary. Both the subject defined as "virgin" and a female subjected to male dominion are rejected. In addition, lesbianism refuses the phallic basis for sexual pleasure, locating it instead in female hands and sexual organs. As Urias expresses, following the Law of the Father (God and Pope), lesbianism is both perverse (sickening) and unimaginable (beyond understanding). Yet she allows that there must be something to it, although, like the biblical doubting Thomas who refused belief in Christ's resurrection, she would have to "see it" to believe it. However, the possibility of revelation is so frightening because it disturbs accepted notions of female sexuality and subjectivity that ultimately she does not want to know. Knowledge is denied in order to maintain the status quo.

The cultural constructions mapped out above must be viewed as generalizations and ones that are often defied. It would be a grievous error to assume that all U.S. Mexicanas are constricted and desubjectivized.[52] Many factors may contribute to how rigidly women are defined within, submit to, or mediate the parameters outlined above. For example, studies indicate that nineteenth-century women in northern New Mexico and southern Colorado had a greater degree of autonomy and power than women in other parts of the Southwest, due to their relative isolation from Mexico.[53] U.S. Mexicanas also have a history of participation as labor activists that challenges notions of them as passive women confined to the home. From pecan workers in Texas, to textile workers in Texas and California, to cannery workers in California, to mine workers in Arizona and New Mexico, to migrant farm workers in many states, to mothers in East Los Angeles, U.S. Mexicanas have fought for better working and living conditions and wages.[54] Although usually conducted under the auspices of bettering the family's economic or social condition, at the same time, activism may agitate conceptions of gender roles and contribute to refiguring the dynamics of personal relationships within the context of what Maxine Baca Zinn calls "political familism."[55]

GUADALUPE: *Symbol of Identity and Resistance*

For many Mexicanas, subjectivity is necessarily tied up with virginity, marriage, and motherhood. Luce Irigaray asserts that constrictive conceptions of sexuality, marital status, and maternity occlude the construction of female subjectivity. In "Divine Women," Irigaray argues that woman is "constituted from outside in relation to a social *function*, instead of to a female identity and autonomy. Fenced in by these functions, how can a woman maintain a margin of singleness for herself, a nondeterminism that would allow her to become and remain herself?"[56] The writings of the Chicana intellectuals I discuss in chapter 2 suggest subjectivities generated through indigenous goddesses, of which La Virgen de Guadalupe is an aspect. For the U.S. Mexicanas who maintain affiliation with the Catholic Church, La Virgen de Guadalupe provides a feminine aspect to an otherwise patriarchal God, an aspect that gives them a margin of error—created by her ambivalent significations—within which they can negotiate, and even resist, the empirical parameters of the socio-symbolic contract. The Catholic Church may have one meaning for Mary/Guadalupe as a role model for women, but believers find a wide range of meanings. While maintaining immense respect for religious understandings of La Virgen, the working-class and semiprofessional women simultaneously interpret her as validating their independent behavior.

Their reliance on personal experience and insight indicates a resistance to provided subjectivities and a renegotiation of social and cultural standards to include choices such as rejection of marriage and motherhood, divorce, motherhood outside of marriage, premarital sex, and acknowledgment of a sexual body. These choices speak, literally, as Smith observes about women's autobiography, of an " 'experientially based' history of the body that breaks the old frames, the old discourses of identity."[57] When women tell the stories of their bodies, tell their own stories, embody themselves, unruliness becomes a tool that serves the resisting subjects they create. For example, in her historia, Evelyn Gonzales, who facilitates the Grupo de Apoyo para Mujeres con Cancer (Support Group for Women with Cancer) sponsored by the YWCA in Tucson, notes that the meetings sometimes lapse into conversations about sex.

> EVELYN GONZALES: I bring them to the support group and there they can talk about anything they want to. And I'll tell you one thing, a lot of them are very sexually knowledgeable. Like I said, they're not that dumb anymore.
>
> DB: You mean that the women feel free to experience themselves as sexual beings?
>
> EG: Yes. They enjoy it. And they'll tell you they enjoy it. Sometimes those meetings go haywire. I say, "Now, now, we're talking about cancer, not sex!"
>
> DB: That seems to be somewhat of a change from years' past—that women, first of all, didn't talk about sex, and secondly they would never admit to enjoying it, right?
>
> EG: Yeah. So, like I said, they're more modern, if they've lived here long enough.

Gonzales's observations confirm that the support group members construct themselves as desiring subjects and as agents of self-fulfillment. Not only do these women refigure the passive, submissive female ideal; they challenge common conceptions of desexualized subjectivities and unfeminine bodies resulting from cancer treatment, during which a breast or uterus—symbols of female sexuality and male desire—is often re-moved. Gonzales notes that recent Mexican immigrant women are more likely to be subjected to patriarchal restrictions. However, for the women involved in the cancer support group, generally middle-aged or older, who were born or have lived in the United States many years and have survived a life-threatening illness, sexual enjoyment is not regulated by concep-tions of a good or bad woman.

Likewise, Virginia Urias does not accept a passive construction of fe-male heterosexuality or subjectivity, rather affirming that "yes, of course" women should enjoy sex. She notes throughout her historia that, although La Virgen endured the suffering and death of her son, women do not have to suffer at the hands of men and should take action to "defend them-selves." Urias, born in 1929 in a small town in Sonora, Mexico, recalls how she took a stance against her mother when she wanted to marry. When she was a girl her mother wouldn't allow her to play with boys, not even talk to them, until she was thirteen or fourteen years old. Even when Urias was in her twenties, her mother did not allow men to visit her at their home. When she met her future husband, he had to make surprise visits with her nephew, because her mother would not give permission for him to visit. The first time he paid a surprise visit, her mother was "furious" and told Urias that he could not come back. But she says, "At that time I was determined to defend myself," and she told her mother, "Well, you tell him. I'm not going to tell him." When her husband asked her to marry him, again her mother refused to give her permission. Urias says she thinks her mother did not want her to get married because then she would be alone. Her mother also told her that she did not want any man to "touch her in a special manner" because she did not want her to be unhappy or to suffer. But Urias was determined not to experience an unhappy or suffer-ing marriage. Just as she defended herself by speaking out against her mother's restrictions, she also prevented the possibility of an abusive marriage by speaking out to her fiancée. Urias, who always wears a neck-lace medallion with La Virgen de Guadalupe on one side and Jesus on the other, says La Virgen represents mothers, yet she doesn't agree that women should submit to suffering at the hands of their husbands.

DB: Do you think La Virgen is a role model for women?
VU: Yes.
DB: In what way?

VU: In the way that she's a mother, the way she suffered all that they did to her son. I think that's where the idea of a mother came from, you know, from her. Because of all that she's been through. Of course, she is a model mother. But we are all model mothers. . . .

DB: Does she represent a model for women to endure suffering in their lives?

VU: No, no. Especially not in the way that they should stay with men who don't treat them right. But some women won't go for help, for example, some women whose husbands beat them. You know, they just accept it. They don't go get help. They don't leave. That's what I was telling my husband. . . . And I said, "Why don't they go get help? Because I would have. If you were beating me, I would go and ask for help." But it seems that they like it.

DB: Or they don't know what to do.

VU: Or they don't—but what do you mean they don't know what to do? There is public assistance. If you need help, you know, there is help. Because if my husband hit me or anything, I would just separate from him. He might hit me once, but not twice. Not a second time. I might forgive him the first time and talk to him, tell him, "Once more, that's it." But this is one thing I told him when he asked me to marry him. I said, "I'm going to take everything except two things." And he said, "What is that?" "I'm not going to accept it if you hit me and I'm not going to accept another woman. I'm going to accept it if we move, if we're poor, whatever we suffer through, both of us. But those two things I'm not going to take. The first time you hit me, that's it. It doesn't matter how much I care for you or love you, that's it. We're going to be separated." And I told that to him in front of the priest.

DB: Oh, so you laid down the rules right from the beginning.

VU: Right. And thanks to that, never. Not that it never happened, like I said, I'm not saying that he might not have been with another woman, but not that I know of. Okay? Not that I know of. A lot of wives know that their husbands have a second woman, but I've never known about anything. I'm not saying he's a saint or that he might not have been with someone else. That might be the case, but not that I'm aware of.

DB: Not that you would accept.

VU: I've never noticed anything different with him, never, never. Either he's been a good husband or he's been very careful to do things. I tell him that and he laughs.

Urias's resolute rejection of the passive, submissive roles that encourage women to stay in abusive or unhappy marriages mediates her consideration of La Virgen de Guadalupe as an ideal role model. Although she displaces the responsibility for abuse onto women who stay in violent relationships, she favors alternatives to the role of long-suffering wife and mother. The terms of marriage she declared to her husband upon their engagement in the 1950s and her explanation that their marital relationship has been "fifty-fifty" in sharing the decision making indicate her long-standing refusal to accept a subservient or quiescent position. Furthermore, Urias refuses to grant La Virgen exclusive rights to model motherhood. Instead, she shares this favored position with all women, an acknowledgment of the effort and dedication that good parenting requires.

The experiences discussed above document the women's struggles with and everyday resistances to confining gender roles and sexualities and reveal the cultural refigurings that they implement in their own lives. While individual resistances change the circumstances of a single person's life, three women participate in the activities of a Tucson organization, Mensajeras de Salud (Health Messengers), which aims to better the lives of many U.S. Mexicanas and Mexican immigrants. Their actions have far-reaching consequences for the health and well-being of lower-income women in Tucson. Their work as health messengers educating women about the need for cervical and breast examinations raises awareness about women's bodies and about the importance of attending to them. The experiences they relate going door-to-door and talking with women identified as at-risk for cancer reveals how various cultural prescriptions prevent women from taking care of their bodies and how the Mensajeras combat these passive beliefs. Irma Vásquez tells the story of one woman who had not seen a doctor for ten or twelve years and was afraid to touch her own body.

> We have a plastic or silicon breast that we use to teach them. They can touch it and feel where the tumors are. And she didn't want to touch it. She didn't want to do it. "No, no, no, no, I don't, put this away. I don't want to feel it." But we insisted and so I grabbed her hand and put it on it, "Just touch this." "Ah!" she said. "What's that?" And I said, "Maybe you could have something like this, but you never touch your breasts." So we start joking with her and finally she did it. That night she found five lumps. Three on one and two on the other.

So she called Alicia [another Mensajera]. Alicia said she was scared, that poor lady. So Alicia made an appointment for her, and she got in right away, because sometimes the clinics will make the appointments for a month later. And they got her in right away and thank God everything was okay. And then she said, "I'm so thankful that you came to teach me how to do this." And we see a lot of things like that. They don't want to touch it or they don't know how to do it. They don't have the money. They don't have much insurance.

The woman's reluctance to perform a breast self-examination, or even touch a simulated model of a breast, suggests a deeply embedded fear of the female body derived from cultural and religious interdictions against homosexuality and female pleasure. The Catholic Church teaches that to touch one's body is a sin, an unnatural act. The prohibition is intended to prevent masturbation, which is thought to be a sign of homosexuality, and reflects the Church's long-standing condemnation of homosexuality. Masturbation also is considered a selfish act, an attitude reinforcing that sexual pleasure is intended only for heterosexual, married couples who experience it as a by-product of or an incentive for reproduction. In the face of these negative social constructions, Vásquez convinces this woman, and others like her, that touching her body will be beneficial rather than harmful. In demonstrating preventive health care procedures, she provides women with a mode of acting and thinking that overcomes social restrictions and empowers them to take care of themselves.

While Vásquez's experience relates how fear of religious and cultural condemnation contributes to women's fear of their bodies, other Mensajeras found that male control of female bodies contributes to a high incidence of cancer and venereal disease among U.S. Mexicanas in Tucson. Gonzales suggests that lower-income and recently immigrated Mexican women are especially at risk.

Like I said, I haven't dealt too much with women that are real poor. I do visit several that are poor, but they don't have husbands. But when my other co-workers, when they go out talking, like down to the downtown section, they do find lots of people from Mexico, and they do say that the men are machistas. The men give their wives venereal diseases, and the women don't want to go see the doctor because they're sick. Then when they go see the doctor, he gives them medicine, but that doesn't help it because the husband doesn't get the medicine, and he doesn't want to go see the doctor, so that's it. But I'm not in that situation. Like I said, my co-workers were in that. Every Friday all of the Mensajeras meet, and we have discussions of what we come across and ways that we can help or advise one or the other of what can be done. And that's when I heard about those things. That the man is very machista, and that they don't want their wives to go see the doctor, and they don't want them to have pap smears and things like that.

Gonzales's comments expose the patriarchal authority that some men use to keep women ignorant of their bodies and helpless in taking care of them. Not only do they hinder awareness and prevent treatment; the men also deny responsibility for their own behavior and its repercussions and decline to accept responsibility for their own health. The men's refusal to see a physician about an illness associated with the male sex organ suggests possible homophobia through the fear of another man touching their penis. Gonzales's story further exemplifies the double standard that allows men to have multiple relationships, while monogamy is expected of women. The Mensajeras combat patriarchal control by openly addressing bodies and health care issues with women and men.

As Gonzales's story details, some men prohibit their partners from seeing a doctor. The Mensajeras also find that some women fear how their partners might react if they talk to them about health care. Urias relates that the Mensajeras address the men's concerns about losing their authority to another man, and the women's concern's about abuse that might result.

VU: There are a lot of men who don't want their wives to have mammograms, because they don't want them to be seen by a male doctor. So we [Mensajeras] have to explain, we have to talk to the husband, and say, "Sir, there are not only men doctors but we have some women doctors who can take care of your wife." [And the men ask] "But why do they have to have an exam?" I said, "This is for your own good." So we have to explain everything about [breast and uterine] cancer and what we're trying to do. Some men accept that and others say, "No, no, no, no." So when we get the ladies by themselves, we say, "You have to defend yourself. We're not trying to tell you not to do whatever your husband tells you. No. But for your health and for your kids you have to take care of yourself. I'm not telling you to go do it behind his back, but talk to him and make him understand." And sometimes they tell us, "You talk to him."

DB: Because they're too afraid to?

VU: They're afraid. So I say, "Okay, next time. You tell me when I can come and talk to him." And we find that some of the men understand. They do understand. And some are kind of, "No, no, no, no." But by the second time we make them understand. We tell them, "Think it over, and let us know. Think twice what you're doing to yourself and to your children, too."

DB: And then you go back?

VU: Then we go back, and they change their minds. They even say, "I'm sorry, forgive me but I was so stubborn. I didn't know anything about it. I've never heard these things." I say, "Yeah, but you've heard about cancer? Cancer is curable if we catch it in time." And that's what we're trying to do. Make him understand why we tell his wife that, "You have to take care of yourself with a self-exam, and if you feel something go right over to the doctor." I tell him, "If you don't want her to be seen by a male doctor, you can always ask for a lady." And they agree. They say, "Oh yes, go ahead and give her the [reduced fee] card and she can go and have a test."

Urias's account reveals multiple social constructions that must be counteracted to provide for the women's basic health needs. The women she describes are subject to the control of their partners, who decide what they can and cannot do. The men's refusal to allow their partners to see a male doctor implies that the women's bodies are their property and they alone have access to them. In addition, it suggests that the men suspect male doctors of desiring female patients' bodies and that their partners may be potentially unfaithful by having a relationship with the doctor. In other words, like La Malinche, all women are suspected of betrayal, and, like Cortés, all (white) men are suspected of using indigenous women and mestizas for their pleasure, the latter not an insignificant fear given the history of white men's behavior toward women of color. In this respect, the men's suspicions may be warranted. However, Urias's testimony also reveals that the women fear negative, perhaps even physical, responses from their husbands if they attempt to assert their needs. Urias's approach appeals to the emotional pain that might result or the possible loss the men might incur if their partners were to become seriously ill with or die from cancer. This subversive strategy focuses on the effects on the men even as it aims, successfully, at gaining mobility and power for the women.

Urias's, Vásquez's, and Gonzales's work as Mensajeras acknowledges the intersections of race, class, gender, language, and, less forthrightly, sexuality by addressing multiple arenas of power circulating to restrict and regulate the lives of lower-income Mexicanas living in the United States. As Urias notes, Mensajeras de Salud enables women of limited economic means, who have little or no health insurance coverage, to seek medical care. The organization has contracted with several Tucson health clinics to provide cancer screening services for reduced fees, including mammograms for twenty dollars. Mensajeras are available to accompany Spanish-speaking women to appointments or to make hospital visits to aid them in communicating with health professionals. In addition, the cancer support group, conducted in Spanish, is the only one of its kind in Tucson. While the goal of Mensajeras de Salud is prevention and early detection of cancer—as well as educating women about sexually transmitted diseases, menopause, diabetes, and nutrition—through their work Vásquez, Urias, and Gonzales also participate in refiguring the cultural terms of who has control over women's bodies.[58] Their efforts suggest multiple, overlapping beneficial effects on the lives of Tucson Mexican American and Mexican immigrant women. They expose regulatory forces that confine women. They refigure women's conceptions of their bodies and men's conceptions of power over women's bodies. They encourage the use of disease-prevention methods that can result in greater physical freedom and sexual pleasure. Most importantly, their efforts empower women to think and act for themselves.

For the Mensajeras, the Catholic Church is an ally. Urias and Gonzales describe meetings, sponsored by Mensajeras de Salud and held in the church hall after services, where they show videos about cancer and venereal disease detection that promote women's awareness of their bodies and the use of condoms for disease prevention. They note that sometimes these meetings turn into counseling sessions where women discuss the problems they have in convincing their male partners to use condoms and to seek medical care. Urias says that sometimes the priest opens the meetings with a prayer and parish announcements, thereby endorsing the proceedings. Not only do they gain power and authority by working through the Church but the messages they transmit often counter Church doctrine. In this instance, advocating the use of condoms within a church setting gives permission for women to use them despite official Catholic doctrine forbidding artificial birth control methods. The use of condoms for disease prevention serves secondarily to prevent pregnancy and provide for sexual pleasure without the fear of pregnancy. Similarly, Minerva Godoy, a licensed practical nurse who volunteers at a free medical clinic in Muscatine, Iowa, both subverts and exploits Church policy to reinforce the advice she gives patients. She encourages abstinence and, if that fails, condoms, for men and women to prevent the transmission of AIDS and venereal diseases. She explains that she advocates abstinence as a positive solution primarily because the Catholic Church also promotes it, adding, "I'll use anything I can" to prevent disease.

These accounts suggest that the working-class and semiprofessional women derive individual and collective power from association with the Catholic Church and their respective Mexican communities. They work within and through the church and their communities to negotiate cultural refiguring. As the primary symbol of Mexican Catholicism and as the female face of god, La Virgen de Guadalupe is an essential element of this power base. Affiliation with the Catholic Church provides the women a measure of power to change conceptions about women's roles and bodies within the culture. Their insider status as members of the Church and as mothers assures them of the support of the institution and the respect of other members of the Mexican community, enabling them to promote rethinking of some cultural norms.

For some women, activism in social and economic struggles leads them to activist work regarding gender issues. In her published life history, *Forged under the Sun*, the labor activist Maria Elena Lucas tells how her work organizing farmworkers in Michigan, Illinois, and Texas led her to a recognition of injustices against women. Despite battling the debilitating physical effects of pesticide poisoning, she began to challenge sexism, sexual abuse, and harassment within the union and in her personal relationships. As a result, she devised a new vision of La Virgen de Guadalupe.

> I'd have her pregnant and in jeans and with a farm worker shirt with the sleeves rolled up. She'd have a scarf like we use when we work in the fields and a hat also, but underneath the hat, she'd have her veil with the stars. And instead of her hands together like in prayer, I'd have one hand on her chest by her heart holding a document, and her other hand would be holding a rifle that was resting against her. Her eyes would be strong and looking forward, saying something like, "You'd better behave." Or I could

have her arm thrust forward with the document, like, "Here, this is the law." The rifle wouldn't be a symbol of violence but a symbol of enforcement of that law. Like, "Either you abide or you're in trouble."

The document she would be holding would say, "Justice. Power to women. No barriers between countries. Freedom in the world for all people." Then, instead of having Juan Diego holding her up, I'd have a farm worker with a basket of tomatoes and signs of the harvest. That's how she looks to me.[59]

As Lucas's consciousness of injustices to farmworkers and their rights grew through her work as a labor organizer, so did her awareness of gender oppressions and women's rights. Rather than rejecting La Virgen de Guadalupe as a symbol of this oppression, Lucas refigured her "feminine God" to affirm her own recreated subjecthood, one that is powerful and empowering. The feminine face of God is herself. She imagines Guadalupe not as a disembodied, ephemeral being but in her own image as a laborer, an activist, and a visionary who conceives an oppression-free, borderless world. Recognizing that many lower-income women have contributed to the economic support of their families while pregnant, Lucas represents Guadalupe as a working woman who bears children but is not limited to motherhood as her sole avenue of fulfillment. The document and the gun serve dual purposes, first, exposing the lack of power women of color experience in a white, male-dominated world, and second, appropriating available law and legal authority venues for the empowerment of women of color.

Most of the working-class and semiprofessional women's historias do not refigure La Virgen as directly or boldly as Lucas or the Chicana professional intellectuals do. In their historias, they don't subscribe to an overtly activist or feminist position, yet in their own distinctive ways they refigure the desexualized and idealized Virgin mother model. Moreover, the historias formulate the women as agents who speak out and talk back in attempting to fulfill their desires. Rodríguez states that the women she interviewed for her study on the significance of La Virgen de Guadalupe were "unaware" of the resistive quality that belief in La Virgen entails.[60] However, the historias I collected document variation and creativity in the meaning the women assign to Guadalupe's traditional associations. As Turner elaborates, a sign remains viable only if it is capable of changing with cultural and historical fluctuations that influence the meaning of the signified for different eras.[61] Chicana artists' paintings of contemporary women standing within Guadalupe's cloak of stars are examples of late-twentieth-century revisions of the Catholic Virgin. They indicate changes made in order for Guadalupe to represent the changing status of women. Similarly, the working-class and semiprofessional women refigure Guadalupe to accommodate what Gonzales calls "modern" women. Contrary to the religious and cultural image of Guadalupe as a speechless female with downcast head and eyes, they reimagine her in their own images with forthright gaze, speech, and dynamic manner.

Aurora Harada of San Antonio says La Virgen de Guadalupe helped build her confidence and show her a new life, even though she was more familiar with the Virgin Mary. By the age of fifteen, Harada had two children whose father abandoned them and her. Throughout her narrative, mental depressions are associated with times when she was living with or relying on a man. Her most severe depression occurred during and after her marriage to a Japanese American military officer, who expected her to conform to the traditional role of wife and mother. He opposed her desire to take classes, to work, or even to visit the neighbors at the air force base where they lived in Washington, D.C. Harada describes their relationship: "I was the maid and he was the provider." Eventually, he divorced her, "kidnapped" the children—her first two, whom he had adopted, and the two the couple had together—and took them to Turkey. She didn't see them again for eleven years. During this time when she turned to alcohol and "couldn't find herself," two experiences with La Virgen de Guadalupe helped her. The first one was a cathartic homecoming to her childhood church, where she wept out her struggles in front of statues of the Virgin Mary, La Virgen de Guadalupe, and other saints. In this representation, Harada is La Llorona, the crying woman who was "lost." Unlike La Llorona, Harada did not remain forever lost and crying. Instead, she recovered her Mexican and female self with the help of La Virgen de Guadalupe. The second experience freed her from a relationship with a man who asked her to wait for him while he served time in prison.

AURORA HARADA: It seemed like when he was gone it wasn't there. It was like an illusion. I really didn't love him. I could do so many things on my own, because I was holding back when I was with him. Like going back to school. Like going to work and stuff like that. And dressing up, he didn't want me to dress up. . . . So I went to la Virgen de Guadalupe and I prayed. I remember writing a note and pinning it to her dress and saying that if it was her will for us to get back together, then I would wait for him. And if it was not her will, then I would go ahead with my life. But that I was putting all that in her hands and I was going to, you know, not worry about it. I was going to go ahead with my life. And I got involved. I went back to get my GED. The kids, we were living with my mother, we got a house, a rented house. I got transportation. A lot of things were happening. I was making plans to go into college after I got my GED. Taking art classes. And I mean, it was like my vision was open. There were horizons that I hadn't seen before in the world, and I wanted to get over there. He wrote me a couple of times, maybe I wrote him a couple of times. I went ahead with my life. . . . I was with him for two whole years and since I was not used to having friends with my ex-husband, I didn't have any friends with him. You know, he was my companion the whole time. Like he influenced my whole life the whole time.

DB: And this was after he was gone, you could develop other friend-ships?

AH: I could. My own identity. And this happened with La Virgen de Guadalupe.

Harada's awakening in the "hands" of La Virgen de Guadalupe further reveals Guadalupe's semiotic potential. It also suggests the strength that women derive from La Virgen as a female religious symbol. Two impor-tant communicative qualities structure this interaction. First, Harada felt La Virgen listened to her prayers and considered her circumstances in the letter she wrote. Second, Guadalupe answered the pivotal question of whether it was "her will" or "not her will" that Harada wait for the man to get out of prison. In contrast to Gonzales's interaction where the Virgin responded in verbal language to Gonzales's prayers, the acceptance that Harada needed took the form of a lack of response from Guadalupe. La Virgen gave Harada tacit approval for her to "go ahead with my life." Harada's abdication of responsibility to Guadalupe, however, was sym-bolic, because, as she relates, she had already made the decision to take matters into her own hands and pursue her own interests. In describing her recreated self, Harada defines a subject-agent, rather than an object, signified by her use of first-person pronouns and active verbs. "I was going to go ahead with my life." In contrast, passive negative verb constructions and sentences placing the male pronoun as the subject characterize descriptions of her life with men. These redefining experiences also gave her increased awareness of a collective female experience.

> Women shouldn't have to do that. They shouldn't have to marry just because men will provide for them and their children. I don't know how long this help has been going on, like the Pell Grant and the food stamps and all this. I understand it hasn't always been available, but now it is. And I took advantage of it. At first I didn't want to. I was not used to asking for help. I had this kind of pride in myself, you know, that I didn't want to ask for help. But it was either that or sink. So I'm glad I did. . . . I see a lot of women that don't. They believe whatever men tell 'em. You know, "You're not going to go anywhere" and "You're never going to amount to anything." And, you know, the husbands tell them, "Without me you won't do anything." I see that. I see how they speak to each other and there's no respect. And that's why I'm by myself, because I will not let a man talk to me that way. I will not. I will not let him degrade me. No. Because I am a human being.

Harada's interweaving of her own personal experiences with her observations of other women's subjection to male authority recognizes the relationship between an individual and a collective female struggle. While she suggests that many women are unable to free themselves from the confinement of the cultural norm that defines women through men, her self-determining statements announce a subjectivity that rebels against regulation of women's bodies and treatment of them as subhuman. Harada's defiant claim to humanness restores the self-respect and selfhood that she felt was undermined in her relationships with men. Her recognition that she could determine her own self-worth apart from men released her from the colonizing patriarchal prison. In addition, she freed Guadalupe from similar confinement, conceiving La Virgen as supporting women's self-interests and self-fulfillment.

In Harada's refiguring, Mary/Guadalupe is addressed as the sole source of resolution for her requests. The official Church narrative represents Jesus/God as the source of miracles, the ultimate authority figure. Mary/Guadalupe is said to intervene with him on behalf of her petitioners.[62] However, Harada bestows upon Mary/Guadalupe the power to determine what is best. Harada's use of "her will" or "not her will" speaks directly to La Virgen's authority. The assumed male "God" of Catholic doctrine is not a significant element in Harada's belief system. In fact, the Church has been alarmed by increasingly strong Virgin worship in Central and South America and has made attempts to reinforce that Jesus is the primary deity. For example, Urias stated that her parish priest in Tucson gave a sermon emphasizing that worship and prayers should be directed to the Father/Son and that Mary the Mother is secondary to their rule. For the women in this study, however, Mary/Guadalupe remains the divine figure they admire and respect most.

Similar to Harada's refiguring of Guadalupe, Irma Vásquez changes the concept of the long-suffering Virgen. Her own life decision to remain single also refigures the terms by which a woman can create a female subjectivity outside marriage and motherhood. Vásquez believes La Virgen is a role model for women, but she has her own definition of what that means.

> IRMA VÁSQUEZ: Yes. She was sent. Está humilde [She is humble]. But she was strong at the same time.
>
> DB: So humilde doesn't mean that you have to be weak?
>
> IV: No. Humilde means to say the truth, whatever it is. For me, this is what it means to be humilde. To know what you want, what you believe, what you—Santa Teresa, do you know about her? Santa Teresa de Ávila. She was a very strong woman and she says humilde is to talk the truth.
>
> DB: I'm wondering if you think other women can have a different definition of humilde?
>
> IV: They say humilde is agacharse [to submit]. And they'll accept "whatever they want to do to me, cause I'm humilde." No!
>
> DB: But that's not your definition?
>
> IV: No, it's not my definition. It's not my definition.

Here, Vásquez refashions La Virgen as a model of strength and truth, rejecting the definition of humility as submissiveness, "agarcharse," and the conception that women must endure whatever suffering life brings. Vásquez focuses on the historical figure of St. Teresa of Ávila, whose historicity and materiality fleshes out what Ventura Loya noted was lacking in La Virgen de Guadalupe, the history and story of La Virgen's experience as a human being before becoming divine.[63] Not only was Teresa of Ávila an embodied woman, in contrast to the disembodied Virgen, but she is also a speaking subject whose writings are widely acclaimed as veritable treatises on mystical experience, thus giving her words the weight of truth. And it is this telling of the truth, telling what one thinks, believes, and desires, that Vásquez argues defines "humilde." By this definition, she provides women the agency to act on their desires and to define themselves, rejecting the construction of women as subservient to others' needs. Vásquez is equally firm in her belief that the unequal standards of sexual behavior for men and women are unfair, and that women should be allowed to make their own decisions about working outside the home. Vásquez characterizes herself as "a happy single," saying she came close to marrying but is glad she didn't. Her self-description refutes the idea that women need men, need to marry, need to have children to be fulfilled. Instead of following the cultural prescriptions for female subjectivity (marriage and motherhood), she defines herself apart from the patriarchy as single and without children. For her, this position is not a lack or a loss but a fulfilling existence.

The working-class and semiprofessional women do not explicitly refer to La Malinche in word and deed, yet the majority of the women's historias refigure the Guadalupe/Malinche dichotomy. Their historias reveal a complexity of thought and behavior that the stifling dichotomy does not contain. What becomes clear in reading the women's self-representations is not only that they refigure Guadalupe but that they emulate Malintzin by translating cultural and religious tenets into less rigid thinking that reflects the lifestyles and beliefs of borderlands women in the late-twentieth- and early-twenty-first-century United States. Performing as interpreters, their words and actions are acts of translation between and within ideological systems, a strategy Malintzin employed to gain power, however limited, in her changing sixteenth-century world. Even if they have never heard of Malintzin or think of her in negative terms, their speech and actions nonetheless bear out her history as a living, speaking female agent. Their historias negotiate the collisions and collusions of sixteenth- and twentieth-century beliefs about race, class, gender, and sexuality. The working-class and semiprofessional women maintain their affiliation with religious and cultural belief systems that continue to idealize limiting gender roles and sexuality positions, depriving women of agency. Yet their words and deeds revise these ways of being without severing the affiliations that define their identity as U.S. Mexicanas, Malinche's symbolic descendants. Their refigurings recall the codex representations of Malintzin Tenepal in her role as "la lengua" before the "fall" (see figures 5 and 6 on page 38) and Yolanda López's paintings of her mother and grandmother as Guadalupe (see figures 10 and 11 on page 62). While Guadalupe represents Mexicanness for them and spiritually inspires them as the feminine face of God, they themselves embody and reproduce the history of Malintzin Tenepal and her daughter. This union of the metaphysical and physical, Guadalupe, as the female divine, and Malintzin, as the embodied female agent, is an appropriate representation of the women's portrayal of their own Mexican Catholic spirituality and identity.

Mary Ozuna's representation of her life exemplifies this complex refiguring process. Ozuna identifies as Mexican American but when she fills out forms, she checks the "Other" box to acknowledge her mixed heritage—German, Spanish, and Mexican. This defiance of being boxed into categories also figures prominently in her life view. She was the first woman in her family and among friends who bought a car, moved out of the house, went to college, and worked out of state at a migrant workers' summer camp in Minnesota. With an elementary education degree and a master's degree in special education, she wants to use multicultural literature to show other women that they have choices: "It's hard as a woman to make a choice as it is because of being put in a box."[64] Her given name, Mary Magdalena, after the biblical "fallen" woman whom Christ redeemed, is ironic given her beliefs and actions.[65] As she tells of her ambivalent feelings about La Virgen as an ideal for women and of her defiance of traditional roles—she is a single mother—other subversions of her virginal name occur.

As a woman working in an auto business with a lot of Mexicanos, and even the Anglos that worked there, they would try to put you in a slot. What a woman was and what you were supposed to take. . . . And then I got pregnant. . . . By that time I had established my specific, you know, Mary, as what I was, which wasn't a street lady. Literally, that's what they would call you. So everyone knew, the salesmen that came in, the mechanics, because we sold to a lot of people in town, they already knew who I was. So they were friendly, but they weren't over-friendly and they weren't ugly. It had to be established ahead of time. It was real hard to do that too. But I didn't tell anybody until I was six months pregnant. . . . I finally told my mother and she couldn't believe it. She was like, "What?" It was almost like a paradox. I was the one that finished college, you know, "Mary always got A's in school," except once in sixth grade. Math was my worst subject. That was a trauma for me. But "Mary always did this. Mary always did that." At the same time, she didn't like the independence in me, so when that happened it was like, I fell off the pedestal. . . .

When I went to the hospital to give birth, it really wasn't negative. It was a small hospital, but it was quite different. There were friends around, people around, all my girlfriends, we all went to high school together. And they kept saying, "Well, what do you want?" One of them is a nurse, she's in charge of nursing at the nursing school here in town. She's one of the top people. And she goes, "What do you want us to bring?" So I said, "A Bloody Mary." So here they bring this Bloody Mary and my aunt and everybody is there and my friends were trying to hide it. It was so wild.

Ozuna's account of her "fall" from heavenly disembodiment to earth(l)y body is signified in the graphic metaphor of the "Bloody Mary," not only in its relation to the flesh and blood passion and pain that is signified by intercourse and birthing but also by the defiance of convention which her request for the alcoholic drink implies. In addition, her re-vision of La Virgen (Mary/Guadalupe) model challenges the construction of a "good" woman. She is no "street woman," yet she defines herself as a sexual being. Her "bloody" body represents the site over which patriarchal ideology and female experience struggle and suggests her own (re)birth as she overcomes the Guadalupe/Malintzin duality to construct her own meaning of the name "Mary."

When Virginia Urias says that women "must defend themselves," she describes a position that opposes patriarchal authority and control of female bodies; when Mary Ozuna, the straight-A student, decided to have a child outside marriage, she toppled long-standing notions of a "good" woman; when Irma Vásquez defines humilde (humble) as strength and honesty rather than submissiveness, she recreates the definition of women's roles; when Aurora Harada and Ventura Loya decide that to live alone is better than living with men who degrade them, they stand up to systems of power that define women through relationships with men. Minerva Godoy's rhetorical question, "What gives [men] the right [to judge women]?" expresses a similar oppositional consciousness. It also acknowledges how ideological power functions in gender and sexual relations to maintain cultural representations of good and bad female conduct, restricting physical mobility and bodily pleasure. These women negotiate and refigure the uneasy cultural terrains of disembodiment and embodiment, marriage and autonomy, and virginity and sexuality in relation to La Virgen de Guadalupe.

As seen through the historias related in this chapter, La Virgen remains a positive symbol of cultural identity and spiritual inspiration for working-class and semiprofessional women, even as they refigure the representations associated with her that contribute to the disempowerment of women. In individual, everyday resistances and local group subversions, they create new meanings that represent their philosophies of what it means to be a U.S. Mexicana in the late-twentieth- and early-twenty-first-century United States.

chapter four

 CULTURAL ANXIETIES AND TRUTHS

Gender, Nationalism, and La Llorona Retellings

Circulating across ages, geographic spaces, and class and educational locations, La Llorona's name sparks memories of childhood and adult encounters by the working-class, semiprofessional, and professional intellectual women in this study. All of them are familiar with one or more versions of the Wailing Woman's legend often heard in childhood as a ghost story or cautionary tale warning children to behave. In their oral histories, the U.S. Mexicanas relate their own or a relative's experience with the eerie woman dressed in white. For the Chicana writers, La Llorona is featured as a character or theme in stories, poems, and plays representing the anguish and anger of a betrayed and battered Chicana or as an indigenous goddess offering solace and support. In each instance of La Llorona retellings, cultural anxieties and "truths" are revealed about Chicana and U.S. Mexicana experiences and imaginings.

La Llorona differs from the Mexican female cultural figures discussed in previous chapters in that she is neither a historical figure nor a direct source of spiritual inspiration. With a historical figure such as Malintzin Tenepal, facts can be assembled to prove the legitimacy of her existence as a real person. With spiritual figures such as La Virgen de Guadalupe and indigenous goddesses, semihistorical narratives and ancient images or sculptures promote belief in their real existence and faith in their symbolic authority. As the subject of a legend, La Llorona carries ambivalent significance; some listeners may believe La Llorona's story is true, others may not. However, the legend's purpose is not necessarily to evoke belief but to make people contemplate truth value. Elliott Oring writes that a legend "is concerned with creating a narrative whose truth is at least worthy of deliberation; the art of legendry engages the listener's sense of the possible."[1] La Llorona's appeal persists within Greater Mexico because Mexicans and Mexican Americans find in her stories a number of "truths" worth deliberating, including economic, political, racial, and gender realities. At the same time, her story, as with any legend, "requires the audience to examine their world view—their sense of the normal, the boundaries of the natural,"[2] and perhaps see things from a different perspective.

In the first two sections of this chapter I examine the working-class and semiprofessional women's oral narratives to show the various ways La Llorona provokes deliberation of Greater Mexican reality, especially in terms of what it means to be a Chicana or U.S. Mexicana, that is, a woman or girl. I analyze the legend's disciplinary function for children and its regulatory message regarding female sexuality. I examine "Llorona moments," instances of profound sorrow or loss that the women relate about their lives. And I discuss how several variations reflect oppressive neocolonial conditions and imply that La Llorona works as a resistance figure for women. In the final section of the chapter, I read fictional writings by Alma Villanueva and Cherríe Moraga that depict La Llorona's origin as an indigenous goddess and refigure the misogynist view of La Llorona as a gendered infanticidal fiend or a Mexican "national" terror.

LA LLORONA'S SELF-REGULATING FUNCTION

For most of the U.S. Mexicanas, the mention of La Llorona's name conjures memories of frightful stories told by parents or relatives. As a young girl, Evelyn Gonzales remembers hearing a generic version of the legend intended to scare her and other children from playing near waterways. "My relatives would tell us stories especially so we would get scared and mind. The story is that she killed her children, and she was crying for them. She would come by and if she saw some kid she would try and take him away with her. At that time there was an acequia downtown near Congress Street [in Tucson]. The Santa Cruz River is there and about a block down was an acequia, a cement thing with water for the fields. So they would say, 'Llorona will come either to the river or to the acequia.' "

Gonzales's narrative consists of few details about the figure or story of La Llorona. Her ungarnished account is provided as an explanatory afterthought for someone who might not know why the legend would frighten children. Yet she repeatedly mentions the two geographical locations, the river and the acequia, which exist as appealing but dangerous play sites for children. Rather than focusing on the story of La Llorona, Gonzales's account explicates the legend's purpose and function as a behavior-regulating mechanism for children. The basic information of the legend —a woman kills her children—is presented as truth. What listeners' must deliberate is whether or not La Llorona will abduct and harm all children. Gonzales tells this story from the perspective of a child who deliberates and determines there is enough truth value to "get scared and mind." As Gonzales implies, she accepted the veracity of the legend as a child. She then provides a cross-generational perspective on the Llorona message, that of an adult parent who no longer believes in the legend's truth value but presumes her children will believe in it. "I used to tell my kids, 'The bogeyman will get you.' Or, you know, el viejo. 'El viejo is going to come by and pick you up if you're out there.' I would tell it in both English and Spanish, both La Llorona and the bogeyman." To ensure that her borderlands children understand the message, Gonzales fashions the message from the two cultural perspectives that influence them. She uses the Mexican Llorona and the American bogeyman to reinforce her disciplinary point. And she tells her bicultural and bilingual children the lesson in both languages to reinforce its reception. Most importantly from Gonzales's perspective, the legend is not a gendered story that she relates to as an adult female but a message intended to control her offspring and protect them from particular geographical hazards.

Virginia Urias also remembers being told La Llorona stories that scared her during harsh winters in the Sonoran mountains of northern Mexico where she grew up.

My mom used to tell us [the story] and we were very, very afraid to go outside. Those times, those years, the kids were never out at night. They all went in the house early because they were afraid of the Llorona. Especially in the wintertime, because you know the wind blows and it's so dark and so cold. It makes you feel frightened. And when the winds blow like that you can hear "Woooooohhh." And my mom used to tell us that the Llorona does "Woooohhh." And we used to hear that in the mountains because of the wind. Now, I've figured out it was the wind. We thought it was the Llorona, you know. And I said, "Why is she crying?" And then they used to tell us that she had two, three kids, I don't remember, but she drowned the kids in the well. And that's why she was crying. Looking for them and crying because of what she did. She drowned them in the water of a well.

Like Gonzales, Urias describes a specific geographical location, the Sonoran mountains, to supply the reason the story was told: "the wind blows and it's so dark and so cold." And she focuses primarily on the legend's emotional and disciplinary effect: "It makes you feel frightened." Again in this telling, the truth value of the legend went unquestioned and the children stayed indoors at night. Yet both Gonzales and Urias describe the move from childhood naiveté to adult skepticism and suggest that the story's effectiveness as "truth" is a factor of age and experience. Urias says, "Now I've figured out it was the wind." She acknowledges childhood belief and fear and foregrounds adult disbelief and reality. "Of course I don't believe it's true now. But those years we did believe. And like I said, when we went out our skin used to get like chickens [goosebumps] when we heard that noise through the mountains. Wooooohhh."

However, Urias's second Llorona story challenges absolute distinctions of belief by age, nationality, or ethnicity. "But once I was in California, and my [older] cousin went to the beach and when she came back, she said they were all scared because they heard the Llorona. I said, 'Do you believe in that?' And she said, 'Yes, we heard [her wailing] and all the people left the beach.' And I said, 'Even Americans?' 'Everybody,' she said, 'everybody.' And I said, 'I thought it was just a story in our little town over there.' And she said, 'No, everybody left, they were scared.' It was at night, too." Urias's cousin's insistence that "everybody"—youth and adult, Mexican and American, Spanish- and English-speaking, believers and nonbelievers—left the beach implies that the possible truth of the Weeping Woman's story causes deliberation (and action) across differences of age, culture, race, ethnicity, and other signifiers.

Even more so, what the oral histories reveal is how the Llorona legend achieves the power to regulate and control people's behavior. Both Gonzales and Urias recognize the effectiveness of La Llorona stories in deterring children from potentially life-threatening situations, precisely because they remember the self-policing effect La Llorona stories had on them in their youth. Michel Foucault's discussion of how surveillance by a

"Great Observer" resulted in self-regulating behavior for prisoners and quarantined plague victims suggests how the legend works.³ In Gonzales's and Urias's stories, La Llorona's surveillance takes the form of a "faceless gaze," invisible and omnipresent, observing children especially when they are outside the home or beyond their parents' sight.⁴ If children venture to potentially dangerous locations, the story implies, La Llorona will see them and kidnap or possibly kill them. Not only does La Llorona possess the power to discipline; her legend implies that she also has the power to punish. The two components combine to incur fear and induce self-regulation. La Llorona becomes a surrogate parent regulating children even when the parental watch guards are not present or the story has not recently been told. La Llorona also performs as a horrific mother figure, the binary opposite of the loving, nurturing Mexican mother, aunt, or comadre. Children project their fears onto La Llorona rather than associating them with their real mothers. In turn, children's anger and resentment at being disciplined is deflected away from the mother or guardian, although the discipline still is meted out by a mother figure and therefore gendered as feminine.

Further, La Llorona's legend becomes inculcated in children's minds and the disciplinary message can be provoked by phenomena other than the story itself. Most significant for Urias was the wailing sound, "woooohhh," the sensory sign for La Llorona that became associated with fear and danger. As Urias later realized, the wailing sound alone is enough to provoke self-regulation, even for cultural outsiders at the beach who may not know the story of La Llorona but are familiar with the potential truth value of legends. Functioning similar to the perceived presence of prison guards in the Panopticon, La Llorona stories insinuate to individuals and even groups of people in a common circumstance that they are vulnerable to a higher power, a secular god-demon that must be obeyed or they will be sacrificed.

The Llorona legend also signifies different messages for individuals at different stages of life. Vicki Rivera Reyes's narrative suggests that the overt warning to stay away from dangerous sites also provides a lesson to curb adolescent desires.

One story we heard about La Llorona, "the crier," was that she was a Hispanic woman who was on her own; she didn't have a husband or a male figure in the household. She had several children and then the husband or the father left. She couldn't afford the children and basically she had gone down to the river and had drowned the children. She was crying by the creek, because she had killed her children. And so the story at school was that there was an alley at one part of the field where we would have recess. It was a big, long alley in the middle of a city block where the houses were back to back. So long that you really couldn't see the end of it; all you could see was the brush so it would end up looking black. It was a pretty deserted alley. Whenever we would go on recess, everyone would say that La Llorona lived in the alley and that at night you could hear her crying. I never heard anything, but it was good enough for me to believe it and not go down the alley. Kids would always—I guess if maybe someone saw a bum in the alley or something like that—they'd come into class, "I saw her, I saw her!" For a while there, the belief in these stories was pretty intense.

Significantly, this schoolyard Llorona variation was prevalent when Rivera Reyes and her schoolmates were entering puberty. Unlike previous variations that featured waterways or weather conditions as overt dangers, in Reyes's variation there is no specific danger identified, only vague suggestions about darkness and "bums." In addition, a parental figure does not directly convey the story; the young teenagers tell it among themselves. In this variation, the "big long alley" and the blackness at the end of it represent the unknown path to adulthood down which the children must eventually walk. The alley represents the burgeoning sexuality of young teens who may consider venturing down its shadowy lane to experiment with sex, drugs, alcohol, and other rebellious activity. In this respect, the alley is both tantalizing and terrifying. For young women, in particular, the specters of pregnancy and rape haunt the alley. The latter is signified by the figure of a "bum," the stereotypical alcoholic, unmarried, and unemployed man who lurks and looks for young girls to satisfy his lust. La Llorona's invisible presence serves as a disciplining mechanism by which the teens regulate themselves and others. Like the bum, La Llorona is intriguing and dangerous; both figures are frightening because they do not fit into prescribed categories of gente decente. As Reyes relates, La Llorona is "a Hispanic woman who was on her own; she didn't have a husband or a male figure in the household." Because her sexuality was not controlled by a man, she would be interpreted as a dubious character. The children transfer their qualms onto the questionable figure, which Reyes identifies as "intense" belief, because they have learned not to acknowledge their growing sexual desires or their uncertainties as prospective adults in a changing world.

In Mary Ozuna's retelling of her mother's experience, the ambiguity of the danger also is couched in vague terms about nighttime darkness, which again suggests the use of La Llorona as a sexual disciplining mechanism for girls.

> My mother used to live out in Poteet, which is a little town south of San Antonio, in a small farmhouse where the dairy workers lived. The outhouse was far away from the house. If she had to go to the bathroom at night, she wouldn't go out there, because they would tell her about this lady that would be coming looking for her children. (And she never really told us that that was La Llorona. She would just tell us the story about the woman that was looking for her children, because this horrible thing happened and she had killed her children, and now she was looking for them.) So my mother always had this story in her head [when she was young], and she'd say, "And I didn't want to go out there to the bathroom—it was horrible! I'd be up all night. I would wait until the sun was just coming up and then I'd *run* and go to the bathroom and *run* back, cause nobody else was awake." And nobody would go with her out there.

Although no visual or aural sign of the Wailing Woman manifests itself in this story, the idea of surveillance and punishment motivated Ozuna's mother to self-regulate even when bodily functions were pressing. However, the plaintive last line of Ozuna's account, "And nobody would go with her out there," conveys additional meaning, which moves the La Llorona legend from a story about a frightening supernatural being to one about a real girl's experience. From Ozuna's perspective and presumably her mother's when telling the story, her mother was neglected and conditionally abandoned when her parents or older siblings would not accompany her to the outhouse at night. From this perspective, Ozuna's mother became a Llorona, abandoned and fending for herself.

As she continues her oral history, Ozuna's extended family's experiences during the colonial aftermath of the U.S. conquest of Mexico provide additional layers of Llorona meaning. José E. Limón argues that La Llorona stories often reflect the social and psychological needs of the Mexican folk masses who have been subjected to hegemonic, hierarchical, patriarchal, and capitalist social orders throughout Greater Mexico.[5] Ozuna explains that when her mother experienced fears of La Llorona, her family was living on a dairy farm outside San Antonio, where they worked for a European American farmer. From a class context, rather than neglecting their daughter's needs at night, Ozuna's mother's parents might more accurately be understood as exhausted manual laborers. All their strength and energy would have been spent for the economic benefit of the white, landed capitalists who took the land, often through illegal or dubious means, from the Mexican and indigenous peoples.[6] Their reality as landless wage-workers also can be understood within the racial and social hierarchy that existed in southern Texas after 1848. Ozuna's grandparents had fled the border town of Laredo early in the twentieth century to escape racial tensions. One of her grandmother's brothers had been shot in the street by an American sheriff and the family feared that the sheriff would come after the other brothers. They left their livelihood behind and were forced to seek wage labor on the dairy farm. It is important to note that Ozuna's relatives thought very highly of those specific dairy owners. She says, "My mother always raves about the Mavericks, a lot of the Hispanic people do" because "he championed the Mexicans" and encouraged the children to go to school. Yet her grandparents' view of European Americans most likely would have been altered by the murder of a family member. In this story, La Llorona themes reflect the loss of a brother and the family's independent existence due to the racist and classist late-nineteenth- and early-twentieth-century border economy. La Llorona would be used to warn children from not only natural dangers such as waterways or the unknown dangers of the night but also hostile Americans right outside their doorstep.

CULTURAL ANXIETIES AND LLORONA MOMENTS

Not all women interpret La Llorona as a frightening ghost. Limón found that working-class women in South Texas identify with La Llorona as a real woman, like many they know, who has been betrayed by her lover or husband. The responses of the women Limón interviewed indicate that they do not judge La Llorona for killing her children but instead blame the husband or lover for his deceitful behavior.[7] In her oral history, Minerva Godoy recalls a Llorona variation featuring a man who betrays his mate and abandons the family. "Actually, La Llorona is a story of love and death. I can't remember very well. I think she killed herself and her children because of jealousy for her husband. I think she found out he was seeing another woman at a ballroom dance and she went home and whah! killed everybody. And now the legend is that she goes down the rivers screaming for her kids." Although Godoy is not particularly sympathetic to La Llorona in her dramatic retelling of the story, this version includes a specific explanation for infanticide. A simple reading might suggest revenge as the motive, but race, class, and gender domination due to the Spanish colonization of Mexico are implied themes. The man's betrayal and La Llorona's discovery of his infidelity take place in an upper-class setting, an elegant ballroom dance, which La Llorona's husband attends with another woman presumably of the same upper-class status. The story contains no racial descriptors, but race, class, and gender intertwined to determine the status of indigenous and mestiza/o peoples in colonial Mexico. This narrative echoes the historical record of Malintzin Tenepal, the indigenous woman who conceived a child with Hernán Cortés and later was abandoned by him when his upper-class Spanish wife arrived. Godoy's story implies the sexual use of indigenous or mestiza women first by the Spanish conquerors and later by criollos, Spaniards born in "New Spain." The story's focus on the female figure as the perpetrator of violence overlooks the underlying violence of hierarchical interpersonal relationships that resulted from colonialism. More European in context, set in a ballroom, this version might also be read as containing implicit European religious and moral judgments against working-class, non-Christian mestiza or indigenous women. La Llorona is doomed to a purgatory-like existence, forever searching for the children and never able to achieve internal peace or Christian redemption. The story also implies cultural anxieties about racial and class mixing.

Other Llorona variations respond to cultural anxieties about female and male sexuality and economic and social status. Aurora Harada's first two versions of the legend position the Wailing Woman as a sexual predator of men, the ubiquitous femme fatale.

> I heard stories from my male cousins. They would be out drinking and instead of going home they would stay on grandma's porch and fall asleep there. They said that they were sitting there rocking in one of the chairs, you know, they were drunk, and all of a sudden this lady passed by. She wore a tight, white dress, and had long, black hair with a scarf around it. And her high heels click, click, clicked against the sidewalk, which meant

she was a prostitute. My cousin Armando said that he had been out drinking one time, and he saw this beautiful woman from the back, he heard the click, click, click, click of the high heels. He was falling asleep on the porch, and he opened his eyes. He said, "I saw this glowing white beautiful woman, long hair." He says that he followed and called her, but she would not answer. And then he was hurrying and she would hurry too, you know. You could hear the high heels click, click, click. And he was going by her and then he said that she just disappeared. Disappeared into thin air. She wasn't crying, but he said, later on, he heard her crying, and he figured that it must have been the Llorona. And then he passed out.

Then my other cousin Enrique said that he also saw her. He just saw the white going by. But he recognized the click, click from the high heels, so he went up behind her and he tapped her. And she turned around and her face was really ugly, it was like her skin was falling off. It was La Muerte, death.

Harada's narratives depict adults, this time males, who assign ambivalent truth value to the legend, seeing first a real woman who is both idealized and denigrated, and then an apparition expressing cultural anxieties about gender and sexuality. These variations perform humor in a self-deprecating manner that acknowledges and mocks male sexual desire and impotency expressed by the men's drunken states: "then he passed out." However, the description of La Llorona also represents a sign of desire beyond sexuality, especially in Harada's first story about cousin Armando. For working-class Mexican American men, a beautiful, well-dressed woman may represent a desire to attain the American Dream of a stable middle-class income, which is absent from Harada's description of their neighborhood: "I don't know if you heard but that's supposed to be the worst part of town." Although in many variations La Llorona characteristically is dressed in white, here she may represent the unattainable white woman who signifies the higher living standard, social status, and power associated with the American Dream. Armando's words, "I saw this glowing white beautiful woman," stress the ethereal, almost saintly quality of a figure in a dream or vision, which contrasts sharply with the earthly reality of his manual labor job and his own brown skin. South Texas's deep divisions in economic class, education, and social status, racially hierarchized in terms of positioning European Americans above Mexican Americans, provide a ripe environment for internalized racism,[8] whereby the values of the white male become manifest as the desires of the mestizo. Only after Armando's pursuit of the woman, who just "disappeared into thin air"—like the American Dream that Harada aspired to as a young girl—does he hear La Llorona crying for her children lost to assimilation or internalized racism. While no discipline or punishment is outwardly manifested in Armando's story, in cousin Enrique's narrative, sexual and economic desires are severely and immediately disciplined when the white woman reveals herself as death. La Llorona may function here as a warning to males to avoid adultery or sex outside marriage as well as the false hope of the American Dream.

Ironically, while the romanticized, noncorporeal "glowing white beautiful woman" is desired by the men, she also is bodily sexualized and demeaned as a "prostitute" in their stories. If male-oriented narratives idealize sexual and economic desire for white or light-skinned upper-class women and status, they also demonize female sexual and economic desire as "immoral." Labeling a woman a prostitute alleviates male social, economic, and sexual responsibility for his own actions and for the well-being of his family. At the same time, male virility, control, and domination are reinforced when the woman is made inferior by assigning negative value to her behavior. The responsibility for any transgression is placed upon the woman, effectively disciplining her for attempting to achieve economic independence and sexual fulfillment.

In their oral histories, the working-class and semiprofessional women generally dismiss La Llorona's significance in their adult lives. Yet a number of their encounters with La Llorona reveal cultural anxieties about gender role limitations and female sexuality. In addition, several of the women's self-representations contain Llorona moments, such as profound sorrow when they have been abandoned and abused or rage arising from incidents of danger or injustice. Harada's third story not only gives agency to La Llorona but also alludes to Harada's own Llorona moment.

> I remember when we were little, we used to hear a lot about, "Oh, la llorona esta llorando" [the Weeping Woman is crying] at night. We used to sleep out in the porch, believe it or not, right there on Guadalupe Street. "Don't sleep out in the porch, because va pasa la Llorona." You know, "the Llorona's going to pass by there." So they would try to scare us to come inside. When company came over, we could stay up late and we sat on the front porch exchanging stories. And I remember my grandmother or my mother or the mother of my cousins, saying, "You better come inside, you

know, because La Llorona is going to pass by Guadalupe Street after midnight, going to the arroyo," which is the river. It seems like she had left her husband, and she had children, and her boyfriend or her lover didn't want the children. So she drowned them. And then she wanted them back, so she would cry and go looking for them in the night at the river. She would be crying and crying and crying.

Harada interprets the legend from the perspective of a woman, like herself, who has experienced significant loss. Her telling of the legend reinforces the disciplinary function of the Llorona figure for children and suggests compassion for the woman who searches endlessly for her children. Although La Llorona's sexual desires and violence toward children generally would be interpreted negatively as moral and religious transgressions, this variation suggests female agency in the woman's desire for and pursuit of another man and her choice of the boyfriend over the husband and, although misguided, the children.

Despite the evidence that La Llorona is the betrayer in this variation, Harada's sympathies lie with the Weeping Woman because of the repetition of the word "crying." In chapter 3 I mentioned Harada's experience as a Llorona when she cried out the story of the loss of her children and husband before the icons of La Virgen. At that time, she was the one who was "crying and crying and crying." Yet her personal story digresses significantly from La Llorona's. Harada does not kill her children or herself. She does not become the reproductive demon who tries to snatch other children. In Harada's oral history, the betrayers are clearly the two men who fathered her children: the former lover, who abandoned her and their two children when she was still a teenager, and later her former husband, who divorced her and "kidnapped" the adopted and birth children. As Tey Diana Rebolledo writes, La Llorona's legend portrays the "tragedy" of lost women and children.[9] Certainly circumstances in Harada's life could be considered tragic, but Harada's response to abandonment, loss, and poverty did not determine her entire existence or subjectivity as in the Llorona legend. Although it took her several years, she eventually recovered from psychological depression by enrolling in U.S. government education and medical care programs. Rather than replicate the legend's portrayal of women as murderous adulterers and tragic figures, Harada refigured herself as a woman who regained her own sense of self apart from husband and children. Her oral history reveals that La Llorona served as a role model, along with the Catholic Virgins, Mary and Guadalupe, to whom Harada cried out her pain and fear. Her crying saved her from desperate acts such as suicide or infanticide. For Harada, the Llorona moment was a cathartic experience that led to positive changes in her life.

Unlike the interpretations of the oral historians above, Ventura Loya does not find any truth value in the legend of La Llorona. The stories she tells, however, indicate that she and other members of her family have experienced Llorona moments reflecting significant events in their lives. Her first Llorona moment occurred when she was four years old.

> My parents were religious fanatics and especially my mother. No matter what the economic situation was or the distance my mother would go to what was called the holy house in the hills. And she would stay there for up to a month. Sometimes, my father would also go with my mother, both of them. All that time, my siblings would stay alone. I was the youngest of my whole family and I remember that we would lock ourselves in and we would listen to La Llorona cry. But I think that more than anything, I would hear my siblings cry with fear. They would say, "It's La Llorona," and they were telling stories, that so and so saw her and that she was seen over there. I was very young.

In Loya's historia, her siblings not only hear La Llorona weeping, which provokes their self-regulation—"we would lock ourselves in"—but they also take on the role of parental watch guards, repeating the scary stories to each other to reinforce the self-policing message. They become Llorona figures in two respects: first in disciplining each other by telling the stories, and second in crying out with loneliness, hunger, and fear because they are left without a primary caretaker. Loya's story insinuates the psychological and physical affects of abandonment on children who are uncertain whether or not their parents will return and who may feel guilty that they are responsible for their parents' absence. Bess Lomax Hawes found that stories about the Weeping Woman were told by female teenagers at a residential correction facility in Los Angeles. She concluded that La Llorona stories represented the girls' plight of indefinite incarceration, their own type of purgatory. Hawes notes that the unresolved nature of La Llorona's situation—constantly searching for but never finding her children or achieving a settled state of existence—mirrored the girls' own disequilibria.[10] Similarly, Loya's recollection of her siblings crying like La Llorona and repeating the legend mirrors their uncertainty about whether their parents will return. Hawes's conclusion about the girls at juvenile hall also applies to Loya and her siblings. "Maybe they are not so much children of fear as they are children of loss, children of need, children of lack."[11]

From Loya's perspective, her mother was a "religious fanatic" and her actions were irresponsible and untrustworthy. While leaving children alone for any period of time cannot be condoned, her mother's religious retreats also could be understood as resistance to the female gendered role of continuous reproduction idealized by the Catholic Church and Mexican culture. Given that she had birthed thirteen children, Loya's mother's leaving could be considered respite from child care and domestic duties so that she could engage in religious or intellectual contemplation, activities that women are discouraged from pursuing. When Loya was older, her mother told her about a personal experience she had with La Llorona. Her mother's narrative suggests the effects of strictly enforced gender conventions for women.

> But later my mother told me, because I said to her, "Mom was it really La Llorona?" Because everyone talks about La Llorona down at the river. And the river was so close. And I said to her, "Is there a Llorona? Why does everyone speak of La Llorona? Does she haunt people? What does La Llorona do?" I wanted to know if I should fear her because everyone feared her. And then she said to me, "Yes, I saw her." And then well, my mother, I trusted her; she couldn't be lying to me. I was four years old when my mother left us alone, but when my mother told me about La Llorona I was about thirteen, fourteen, around there.
>
> We lived in a part of San Luís Potosí close to the Rio Verde, a famous river, and my mother would do the laundry in the river all the time. She told me that sometimes she wouldn't have enough time in the day to do all of her work, so late at night she would go to the river to wash clothes. And she says that she almost always heard La Llorona crying and it was something so common that everyone heard her. But they didn't see her. Then one night there was a very bright moon when she was washing and she clearly saw a woman approaching dressed in a long dress. She thought, "Oh good, someone is coming to keep me company so that I won't be alone, so we can be here chatting and washing." When she turned to greet her and to see who it was—because generally they knew each other, the people who lived on the ranches close by—and when she turned to look the woman, the figure,

didn't have a face. And she got so frightened that she wanted to run but she was paralyzed. She couldn't scream; she couldn't speak; she couldn't do anything. Then she started to walk and had only walked a short way when suddenly there was nothing. And that was the story she told me.

Departing from the accounts that consider only children's belief in and fear of La Llorona, this narrative clearly represents an adult believer who has determined truth value in the legend. Although Loya's mother "almost always heard La Llorona crying"—a sound "so common that everyone heard her"—the sound alone was not enough to frighten her or to induce self-regulating behavior. Initially the image of another woman coming to keep her company is comforting, but instead what appears is "a woman without a face," a phantom. La Llorona's visual appearance and especially her "faceless gaze," similar to Foucault's description of the Great Observer, suggest that Loya's mother experiences surveillance guilt and fear. Loya's mother registered the rural community's disapproval of a woman's independent actions, being out alone at night, as Loya later felt the judgmental community gaze when she went to a dance alone after her divorce. The blank face her mother saw could be read as mirroring various gender anxieties that might flit through her mind including guilt and fear because she lacked a male protector or because she left her children home alone. As proposed earlier, if the religious retreats she took functioned as an escape from limiting gender roles, the blank face could indicate an existential crisis related to nothingness or death. Terror would result from seeing the specter of nothingness, mirroring her own absence of subjectivity outside wife and motherhood. Death, an unconscious wish to "kill" her children in order to create her own subjectivity or kill herself to escape, might also be mirrored in the blank face. "A woman without a face" also could signify any woman or every woman in similar circumstances and provide an opportunity for independent self-construction and identification. This interpretation suggests resistance to and rejection of patriarchal norms that subordinate women to caretaker status. However, any ideas of resistance would likely vanish—"suddenly there was nothing"—when La Llorona's punishment of being exiled from family and community came to mind. The latter element is crucial to the interpretation of the legend's disciplinary function for women. Relationships with family members or a community of friends often are deemed vital to the development and maintenance of a healthy female subjectivity. The threat of exile from family and community and the fear of loss of a support system serve to keep women close to home, husband, and children. Exile would be akin to nothingness, a loss of self—"a woman without a face."

Loya refuses to assign any truth value to her mother's story and cannot imagine her mother's desires. She rejects the plausibility of the legend and of her mother's sighting, considering the incident as a delusion, something unreal. "Now, I've read a lot on how the mind functions, and I think maybe when a person is very scared, they see things." At the same time, however, she uses the science of psychology, which allows for the possibility of apparitional visions as part of the unconscious, to explain the phenomenon. The use of a psychological or scientific explanation provides oppositional interpretations. On the one hand, Loya's mother's vision of La Llorona is dismissed as the result of an "unhealthy" mind. On the other hand, the vision contradicts Loya's rejection of the truth value of the legend by supporting the occurrence of visions "when a person is very scared." Unlike her mother, Loya refuses to do what Elliott Oring says legends demand of listeners: "to examine their world view—their sense of the normal, the boundaries of the natural."[12] If her mother escaped the patriarchal real world for one moment and saw La Llorona outside at night by the river, Loya will not allow herself to contemplate the transgressive possibility of such a vision.

However, Loya does allow herself to perform transgressive behavior. She relates a Llorona moment when she cried out against her husband's attempts to beat her. The first time her husband hit her she had been talking to evangelists from a non-Catholic religion, an act he considered similar to "going to another man." Ironically, the evangelists had encouraged her to be more subservient to her husband so he would not abuse her. Yet when she practiced subservience, her husband became suspicious and began hitting her. She describes her Llorona moment as an unconscious act of self-defense.

> Somehow in my personality, I am usually very easy or—I do not know what the word is—but anybody can do anything to me except touch me. And when he hit me, every good thing went out of me. And I started screaming and yelling, and I started saying awful things back to him. Oh, when he hit me, I was like somebody else, I was not thinking in the normal way. I just got really aggressive and started throwing things at him, cause he hit me and made my face bleed. . . . And then he changed in that moment.

Loya refigures La Llorona's sorrowful wailing to one of justifiable rage. "I started screaming and yelling . . . saying awful things back to him." Her powerful self-defense reaction to his violence succeeded in changing the power dynamic of male domination: "And then he changed in that moment," sparing her from further injury. Loya's fighting spirit recalls La Llorona's genealogy through the mother earth goddesses Cihuacoatl, who represents the warrior aspect of birthing mothers, and Coyolxauhqui, who fought the war god Huitzilopochtli. Similar to Rosa in Alma Villanueva's *The Ultraviolet Sky*, Loya stands up to her abuser, using words as her sword. This act and others that followed position Loya in the genealogy of the woman of discord.

> And I said, "This is the first time he has hit me and this is the last time he will hit me, because I'm leaving right now." And I started taking my stuff and taking Cindy, and anyway he started apologizing and being completely different. And well I ended up staying because I didn't have ways to get out of there. You know in Mexico you don't have a car, you need to walk far away to get a bus, and it depends on the hour if you can get a bus or not, and if you don't have enough money. . . . I mean, it's just crazy to do nothing like I did. But I ended up staying.

Many Llorona variations portray a woman left to support her children without any means of income when her husband betrays her by going to another woman. Similarly, Loya is betrayed by the failure of a social or economic network to support her and her child after her husband betrayed their marriage vows to love and honor. Loya's experience exemplifies the inadequacy of social welfare systems to assist women in leaving abusive partners.[13] Resourcefully, Loya continued to act to effect change. She resorted to transnational migration as a strategy to overcome her isolation and her husband's control, moving back to the United States to be close to her family. Loya transmigrated, like La Llorona, back and forth between Mexico and the United States, using covert and overt strategies to gain control of her life and preserve the integrity of her mind and body. Furthermore, she challenged the legend's infanticidal representation of mothers by acting in the best interests of her children as well as herself.

As discussed in the introduction, I include La Llorona in the genealogy of the woman of discord, which served as a disruptive force in Mexica history to break connections with the past and engender a new era. Similarly, Llorona moments in the lives of the working-class and semiprofessional women serve as a disruptive force to indicate an epiphany or new life strategy. Vicki Rivera Reyes's introduction to La Llorona in the dark alley inaugurates her entrance into adolescence and secret sexual activity. Aurora Harada's wailing moment releases her from the past and allows her to pursue new experiences based on her own personal interests and needs. Ventura Loya's screams disrupt her husband's act of violence and encourage her to pursue transnational migration to change the terms of their relationship. Llorona moments such as these represent U.S. Mexicanas' agency to effect individual or social change.

LA LLORONA: *Disrupting Gender Relations and National Narratives*

While the working-class and semiprofessional women's oral histories depict La Llorona's disciplinary function, cultural anxieties, and individual Llorona moments, the professional intellectuals' fictional works continue to refigure indigenous mother earth goddesses with whom the wailing woman story originated. Domino Renee Pérez argues that Gloria Anzaldúa's poem "My Black Angelos" revises La Llorona from a tragic mother to a powerful goddess and in the process reclaims La Llorona's "Aztecan antecedents."[14] In the two works I examine below, Alma Villanueva's short story collection *Weeping Woman: La Llorona and Other Stories* and Cherríe Moraga's drama *The Hungry Woman: A Mexican Medea*, La Llorona also is refigured as an indigenous mother earth goddess. As do the oral narratives, these writings reveal La Llorona's significance as a woman of discord. They portray real women's experiences interwoven with those of symbolic Mexica queens or goddesses. More importantly, they represent Chicana characters disrupting the status quo, particularly in gendered relations and in historical narratives of American and Chicano nationalism. In these writings, the authors forgo the characterization of La Llorona as a frightening infanticidal fiend. Instead, she becomes involved in struggles more representative of the experience of Chicanas and U.S. Mexicanas in the late twentieth and early twenty-first centuries.

In the title story of *Weeping Woman*, Villanueva draws on the originary story of La Llorona as Cihuacoatl, the mother earth goddess who mourns for her lost children, the indigenous peoples killed in the conquest. Villanueva dedicates the book to her daughter, "who dreamt La Llorona years ago, in the rain, scooping the world's tears with her black lace shawl." La Llorona's act of collecting the world's tears symbolizes her mourning for the injustices humans perpetrate against one another. In the painting by Carmen León featured on the book's cover, those tears appear as a gleaming seashell, a repository of memory and history, which La Llorona holds in her extended hands (see figure 7 on page 51). León notes that her visual depiction reflects Villanueva's view of La Llorona. Instead of taking life (hers or children's), La Llorona gives the seashell to individuals to strengthen their resolve and sense of self. Villanueva's refiguring challenges the sexism of the Llorona infanticide version, which poses the weeping woman as a bad mother figure, and shows how she represents Chicana and U.S. Mexicana contemporary experiences.

In the first story in Villanueva's collection, the conquest of Mexico is symbolized as a "great flood" of destruction that occurred when the Spanish conquerors came from the ocean. Rather than a destroyer of life, La Llorona acts as the savior of her children. The grandmother character, Isidra, explains to her granddaughter, Luna, that La Llorona "turned her children into fish . . . 'It was the only way to save them.' "[15] In addition to Cihuacoatl, Villanueva's Llorona is based on an indigenous creation story featuring the water goddess Chalchiuhtlicue, who presided over the fourth sun era. The fourth sun era ended in a flood whereby the human inhabitants were transformed into fish by the gods. When the fifth sun appeared, the bones of those who perished in the flood were retrieved from the underworld and brought to life, forming the present race of people.[16] In Villanueva's story, La Llorona possesses the divine power of the goddess Chalchiuhtlicue to save her people from the conquerors. The grandmother Isidra tells Luna that when La Llorona cried and extended her black shawl into the water like a net "her children could appear one by one."[17] Villanueva also may be refiguring the goddess Matlaciuatl, whose name means "the woman with the net," to positively alter her previous depiction as "a vampire-like creature who stalks desolate places preying and feeding on men."[18]

Villanueva also revises the perspective that indigenous Mexicans largely are extinct, the discourse of American and Mexican historical and political mythology.[19] Like the transformed fish people, symbolically representing mixed-race peoples, Chicanas and Chicanos respond to La Llorona's call as cultural memory. They do not forget where they came from or the source of their spiritual sustenance. In Villanueva's revision, La

Llorona is a benevolent, protective figure offering a gift, the seashell, to those who seek her. Yet she is not afraid to fight back. She not only takes action to protect her people; she also is prepared to avenge their loss. Isidra explains to her granddaughter that "if her children will not be scooped into her shawl, La Llorona kills as many people as she can. Mostly men, but one never knows." Here, Villanueva refers to the conquerors, largely men, yet suggests the role white women played in the conquest and colonization. She also refers to Chicanos or men of any race who mistreat and subordinate women or to women who mistreat children. Although Isidra fears La Llorona's power, she nonetheless understands the pain and rage that causes La Llorona to fight to recover her people. "I don't blame her. She has reasons to be so angry, and she has every reason to weep."[20] Finally, the memory and history of mestiza/o and indigenous Mexican peoples is preserved in the precious seashells she collects in her shawl and gives to the female characters as a symbol of their strength and endurance.

The story reflects further on the harmful effects of colonization and oppression by portraying a character who has internalized racism. Isidra's daughter, Carmen, has been corrupted by European American thinking to devalue herself and her people. Carmen denies her racial and cultural heritage, dyeing her hair red, wearing makeup to lighten her skin color, and prostituting herself with white men. She perpetuates the history of violence against indigenous and mixed-race peoples by treating her mother as a servant and beating her when Isidra resists this role. She is a "fish the river took away" and Isidra, a curandera, has "no magic" to recover her. She is one of the "lost" children that La Llorona mourns. While Carmen has lost the ability to love herself and others, her daughter, Luna, appreciates the love and cultural wisdom her grandmother imparts. Modeling La Llorona's warrior aspect—Luna's name references the moon and warrior goddess Coyolxauhqui—Luna fiercely defends her grand-mother from Carmen's abuse. "Don't touch her or I'll kill you! I'll kill you if you touch her again! I'll kill you!"[21] Threatening violence to protect her grandmother from harm, Luna fights back against the forces that endanger the one person she knows to be true and kind. In this scene, Villa-nueva creates Luna as a resister who will use force, even against her own mother, if necessary to defend a vulnerable loved one.

However, the seven-year-old Luna is unable to protect herself from harm when she is molested by a teenager in the park. The trauma is reenacted at the doctor's office when she must undergo questioning and an examination, and especially when her mother, Carmen, refuses to recognize her pain. "Keep this to yourself. Nothing happened to you anyway, cry baby."[22] Carmen's words reflect the attitude that girls and women bear the blame for sexual assault ("she asked for it"), and that they must keep their "shame" to themselves or risk being labeled a whore. In this scene and the one in which Carmen assaults her mother, Villanueva does not hesitate to portray the harsh truth that women also must be held accountable as abusers and as abetting abuse through denial even as they themselves are abused.[23] Although Villanueva suggests that the reason for Carmen's abusive behavior toward her mother and daughter is self-hatred due to racial hierarchies, she doesn't attempt to excuse away the abuse or recover Carmen. However, La Llorona mourns Carmen's loss of Mexican heritage and identity through assimilation.

In this story, as in *The Ultraviolet Sky*, the grandmother, rather than the mother, provides a vision for the future. The grandmother represents a direct connection to a lived cultural belief system and indigenous Mexican identity, derived from belief in the goddesses Cihuacoatl/La Llorona and Coyolxauhqui/Luna. Understanding the need for healing, Isidra takes Luna to the ocean, where they wait for La Llorona. Appearing as a figure of strength and hope who weeps in recognition of Luna's pain, La Llorona transforms the pain into healing through song. La Llorona acts as a change agent in this story, altering the harmful effects of gendered violence by providing empathy and hope for the future. Although Carmen could be considered the violent Llorona of legend because she physically abuses her mother and psychologically neglects her daughter, in Villanueva's story the character of La Llorona is liberated from the damaging portrayal as a monstrous child killer. Instead, Villanueva creates La Llorona as a complex figure who absorbs emotional loss, heals psychological wounds, and acts creatively as a woman warrior to protect her people from harm and women from gender violence. Only those who have "lost" the belief in the goddess, such as Carmen, cannot be saved.

Throughout this short story collection, Villanueva returns again and again to La Llorona as a figure of solace and strength, history and memory for the female characters. In some stories, the characters interact directly with La Llorona, who presents them with the gift of a star-shaped seashell. In other stories, the characters find a seashell or locate a star in the sky, which metonymically connotes La Llorona and her reinforcement of individual self-worth. The seashell or star represents many things in these stories: the precious self each female character needs to cherish; a mature woman who enjoys sex with a younger man; memories of specific children who have died; the history of the colonization and the peoples' acts of resistance; and the individual humanity of the characters despite what they have done or has been done to them.

In the last four stories of the collection, Villanueva continues the story of Luna and her grandmother, "La Llorona/Weeping Woman," which opened the book. The title of the four stories is the same, "El Alma/The Soul," except for the sequential numbering of each as One, Two, Three, or Four. In each version, Luna is an adult turning fifty, a "half century,"[24] reflecting back on her life experiences and what she has become. In using this title, Villanueva invokes her own name, Alma, as if to suggest a biographical quality to the stories. However, she subverts such a reading by situating Luna in different adult experiences in each story. In these depictions, Luna represents the experiences of many Chicanas in the late twentieth century and reveals how their life choices are different from those of their mothers or grandmothers. "El Alma/The Soul" also suggests the spiritual and philosophical depth of Luna's character and reveals Chicanas as brown women of working-class origin who have survived childhood abuse, deprivation, and violence. In this series of stories, La Llorona functions as a source of life and love, guiding Chicanas through existential questionings of midlife and beyond.

In "El Alma/The Soul, One," fifty-year-old Luna is portrayed as a high school music teacher and accomplished pianist, who also took up surfing on a boogie board in her forties. Similar to Rosa in *The Ultraviolet Sky*, she is an educated woman who practices her art and who challenges herself physically in the outdoors, an adventurer. At the same time, she expresses doubts about her life, especially her two failed marriages. " 'Why do I feel like a failure!' Luna ate her tears as they slid into her mouth. 'Did I fail to become my possibility? The possible? I sure haven't found everlasting love' " (140). She also laments the suicide of Bobby, one of her talented music students, and wonders if she could have done something more to prevent it. The narrator notes that long ago Luna's grandmother, Isidra, also "had felt like a failure, that her magic had failed her, until that night she'd taken Luna to the stormy ocean" (143). As if the grandmother is speaking, the narrator says, "How could Luna know the moment of failure is the magic moment . . . when failure opens her mouth and weeps, singing." When Luna walks along the ocean in a storm, she hears "a thin, high singing, then weeping, then singing" and realizes that her childhood encounter with La Llorona had influenced all the actions of her life. "It was all for you, wait." In this second encounter, La Llorona asks, "Do you have it?" and unconsciously Luna holds out the star-shaped seashell La Llorona had given her when she was a child. Luna's question "Have I failed you?" is answered in the glow of inner light produced by the sea-shell and La Llorona's soft laughter (143). These semiotic signs tell Luna that she has lived according to her own philosophical compass and that she cannot disappoint La Llorona no matter how she has lived.

In this version, La Llorona appears as a "tall, strongly built" woman whose wet cloak clings to her body. The description indicates she is fully embodied, rather than an apparition, and that she is not a weak or dependent woman. Her ageless and "unbearably beautiful face" reflects sorrow and peace, simultaneously representing her knowledge of the suffering of her people and acceptance of her role as a woman of discord. This depiction suggests that La Llorona is a model for Luna, who must shrug off external judgment and self-doubt and stay true to her inner self, symbolized by the glowing seashell. It also suggests that her grandmother came to the same understanding when she took the child Luna to meet La Llorona. The grandmother's magic did not fail then, nor was she disappointed in Luna's life choices to leave unfulfilling marriages and thereby challenge religious and cultural traditions of submissive and long-suffering women. Both Luna and her grandmother act as Lloronas by practicing indigenous beliefs and refiguring women's roles of mother and wife.

In "El Alma/The Soul, Two," Luna, a photographer, documents the lives of disenfranchised people, among them dark-skinned teenagers smoking a joint on the beach and a homeless family cooking hotdogs over a beach fire. She identifies with both groups, remembering her own difficult past. Version Two expands on the initial "La Llorona/Weeping Woman" story that opened the collection. It details the sexual violence Luna experienced as an adolescent and the subsequent harsh realities that led her to become a "lost" soul. In a flashback she remembers: "*I was only thirteen when he raped me*, my mother's boyfriend, he was living with us, my grandmother dead. I was the cook, housekeeper, everything my grandmother had done" (original emphasis; 145). Luna was forced into the roles of servant and sex slave at an early age, but she did not accept them even then. When her mother would not believe that she had been raped, she ran away and hung out with other cholas and cholos who used drugs to forget their pain and traded sex for comfort and pleasure. As the youths grew older, they became political allies "against It, what kept pressing down on our sad-assed brown necks—It, the White People's System, the Men's System, the Welfare, the Food Stamps Line, the Housing Project, the Clinic where the Doctors—were they Doctors?—never *looked at you*, the County Home where Mamacita died, where the poor, the unwanted, the homeless die because no one wants them" (original emphasis; 146).

When the father of her two children, who had been her ally against oppressive systems, began to beat her, she threw him out and became a sex worker to support her children, because "the Welfare and Food Stamps [were] not enough to feed a dog." Through the years her sense of self-worth kept eroding, and an attempt to escape by taking heroin, "just a little bit to forget It owned all of me," washed away the little faith in herself that remained. Waking up screaming in a jail cell years later, she could not remember her name or the children she had lost. However, as the narra-tor/grandmother in "El Alma/The Soul, One" noted, the act of screaming restores her identity as "L U N A," the moon goddess, Coyolxauhqui. Using Coyolxauhqui/La Llorona's association with the moon and the moon's physical effects on earth's tides, Villanueva gives Luna her life back literally through a flood of light.

> When I heard my name in the moon's sad music and saw her tidal wave pouring back to earth, I knew that there was something stronger than It, stronger than all the Systems, stronger than what I always thought I was. Nada. Just a brown woman, an uneducated, junkie-woman, a raped girl-woman, a whore of a woman. Nada. But the moon said L U N A, loosing her tears, her flood, her music just for me, just for me, and then and there, I got an inkling, just an inkling, that me, a nada woman, might be *todo*. Me, a todo, and I laughed. (original emphasis; 146)

In this stream-of-consciousness style, Villanueva restores Luna to whole-ness, "todo," emphasizing her return to subjectivity in the all-capitals spelling of her name. In addition, Villanueva refigures Luna/La Llorona as a hollering, crying, and ultimately laughing woman as Cisneros does in "Woman Hollering Creek." Through an enlightened gringa named Linda who exposes Luna to 1970s-style feminist books, she learns of sec-ond wave woman's culture thinking, including a universalized goddess and presumed matriarchal world system. She comes to understand that "AWOMAN, I say—get it, not amen—AWOMAN" can achieve "the whole body thing," that is, appreciation for her body as a sexual being. Furthermore, the goddess readings lead her to see herself as a "VIRGIN," even at the age of fifty, overwriting the violent loss of virginity she experienced when raped by her mother's boyfriend. In this way, Luna recovers her former self and renews her inner spirit. She remarks, "Sometimes my TODO is so good I laugh *and* cry" (original emphasis; 147), which suggests that La Llorona's legendary crying may not reflect only despair. Laughing and crying overlap in producing catharsis, joy, and wholeness. Returning to the present moment, Luna sees playfulness in the eyes and actions of the cholos and cholas as she photographs them, a playfulness she must have had before the rape. She mourns the loss of her son, who died or was killed in a state youth prison, and daughter, who she hopes is alive, and the realities of her life actions haunt her. "My poor, innocent children, my babies, I failed you, how can I pretend it's not true" (149). Similar to her appearance in version One, the sounds of weeping and singing conjure La Llorona. This time Luna recognizes her unbearable beauty as awesome potential, "so complete, so perfect, so filled with TODO, with every human possibility" that it "teetered on the edge of terror." This mirror reflection of herself, her own potential, is frightening, but she also sees playfulness in La Llorona's "night-sea eyes" as she sings the question, "Do you have it?" (150). This encounter with La Llorona emphasizes that laughter and playfulness are important remedies and necessary emotions, even at the age of fifty, to achieve psychic wholeness. The glowing star-shaped seashell, which emerges from Luna's solar plexus, site of a powerful chakra or life force, and La Llorona's laughter at the sight of it, reinforce that Luna has not only survived great physical and emotional harm but has managed to thrive in midlife.

In "El Alma/The Soul, Three," Luna's character at age fifty has stepped far outside the boundaries of traditional Mexican Catholic womanhood. She is a medical doctor specializing in children's illnesses and has decided not to have children of her own. She lives with her lesbian partner, Mara, and they regularly attend Wiccan Circle of Goddess worship. In terms of class, Luna overcame poverty and lives an upper-middle-class lifestyle. She defied the gender roles of mother and heterosexual wife by choosing not to have children and by partnering with another woman. And she chose a spiritual practice that fit her feminist vision, rather than patriarchal and hierarchical Catholicism. Her invisible burden is that she has killed someone. Similar to Luna's childhood circumstances in version Two, in this flashback Luna's stepfather attempts to rape her. She heard him beating her mother during drunken lovemaking and locked herself in her bedroom. When her stepfather manages to open the door and come after her, Luna stabs him with the knife her grandmother had given her before she died—"Hide it, sleep with it, niña, no te dejes nunca, niña, cabrones" ("don't ever let them, niña, those bastards"; 152). After the trial in which her mother testified in her defense, Luna is adopted by a white couple. They send her to Denmark to live with their relatives, and there she eventually feels accepted and loved and receives a good education. Villanueva implies that women and children, especially lower-income women and children of color living in the United States, do not receive the resources they need to recover from abusive or violent experiences. In a utopian impulse, Villanueva plots Luna's migration to Denmark, where progressive national policies of universal health care, family-oriented work schedules, and more open-minded racial politics are put into practice. As with any migration, Luna's move was not easy, but it was beneficial. "Dark-skinned, dark-haired, dark-eyed, she'd arrived to live in a household of light-skinned, light-haired, light-eyed people, but they succeeded, finally in making Luna feel special and beautiful because of her difference" (153). The family members even learn to speak Spanish as she learns Danish and buy piñatas to celebrate her birthday. In this accepting environment, Luna received the attention she needed to thrive. Ironically, Luna can only achieve the American Dream of a good education, financial security and independence, a loving relationship, and her own image of the divine by migrating to a new nation. Villanueva subverts the long history of immigrants coming to the United States to gain the idealized benefits of democratic citizenship and social and economic mobility by plotting an American citizen's migration to another country for the same reasons. This plot device is not as far-fetched as it may initially seem because Luna had already been living in "another country" within the United States, to use James Baldwin's metaphor for the dystopia of internal colonization.

On her fiftieth birthday, still in Denmark, Luna mourns her mother, whom she left in the United States. "And when you began to cry, your horrible sobbing, I wanted to hold you and comfort you, but I couldn't. I couldn't reach you. My arms never did reach you. It was too late, mother.

And it was too soon. I was only thirteen and then I came here to be a brand-new person and I gladly left you behind" (154–55). Her mother symbolizes disenfranchised women of color who continue to live in the internal colony, receiving little social or financial support from the U.S. government. Although Dolores had not been a good mother to Luna previously, her court testimony that Luna killed in self-defense was the first step toward righting the previous neglect. Nonetheless, Dolores was declared an unfit mother and lost custody of Luna. Rather than provide support and rehabilitation to keep mother and daughter together in a healthy relationship, the U.S. social services system punished them both with separation. Villanueva suggests that Luna is one of the lucky ones who "got out"—out of the barrio, out of poverty, out of an abusive family, out of the United States. Dolores, whose name signifies pain and sorrow, was sacrificed by a nation and nationalism that claim equality and happiness for all but care little for indigent U.S. Mexicanas. In this version, Dolores is a tragic Llorona who has been failed by her adopted nation.

In this story Americo Paredes's concept of Greater Mexico crosses not only national borders but half the world as La Llorona transmigrates to Denmark to reinforce Luna's cultural and racial identity. As in the other versions, La Llorona appears singing "Do you have it?" She wraps Luna in her black lace shawl and assists her in birthing the star-shaped shell. Here, La Llorona serves as a cultural midwife rather than a murderer, helping Luna to rebirth herself, symbolized by the pulsing seashell that emerges from her uterus. Cradling Luna in her "infinitely powerful, protective arms," La Llorona sings "a mother you've become to death and life" (155). This refrain refers to the complementary dualisms of life and death powers possessed by indigenous mother earth goddesses, including Luna/La Llorona. Now Luna has performed in the ongoing cycle of life and death. She killed her stepfather, in order to save her own life, and she gave birth to herself, confirming her status as divine goddess.

In the final story, "El Alma/The Soul, Four," Luna is a poet living in California, like Villanueva. She has been invited to participate in a symposium of women poets of color at Stanford University and wonders whether their voices will be heard. "How about bleeding women poets of color turning blue, purple, from shouting into the wind." She feels rewarded when audience members "get it" and appreciate her poetry "that varied, tortured, exquisite, brutally beautiful language of the soul" (156–57).

Walking along the beach reviewing her life at fifty, Luna remembers her elderly grandmother, who continued to perform poetry on the bare stage of a Spanish-speaking Baptist church. The act transformed her aging body and renewed her soul. "When the poetry rolled from my grandmother's mouth her back was straight, her beautiful gray hair was long and loose, down to her waist . . . and her eyes were shining, shining, burning, because she looked out at us and *saw*" (original emphasis). Her grandmother's wise vision beheld the beauty of the indigenous culture and people that the Spanish and Anglo oppressors had devalued. Rather than despair, Luna's grandmother found perfection in every living thing and conveyed that in her poetry. "And her voice created silence; her voice made people weep, remembering what they, too, once saw" (158). Villanueva suggests that the grandmother took on the role of a curandera. Her poetry served a healing purpose, keeping the people psychically alive by recalling their magnificence and that of the natural world.

Luna wonders what impact her poetry will leave on the world. She bemoans her failure to gain greater recognition and reward and doubts that career poets make a significant contribution. "Who would actually miss my little exclamations! Really, Luna, she told herself, a Professional Poet?" (159). Villanueva critiques the devaluation of poetry in U.S. society and the capitalist economy that forces poets to professionalize their art rather than view it as artistic creation and philosophical reflection. When Luna bitterly denounces her lack of "grants and genius awards" and calls herself "a failed Professional Poet,"[25] La Llorona appears, laughing and asking for the seashell. In coming face to face with La Llorona, Luna sees the exquisite beauty her grandmother saw. Luna sees a mirror image of herself. "She'd come to the conclusion that her body wasn't bad for fifty. It had a secret: sensuality. But she wasn't prepared for what she saw—the most perfect woman she'd ever seen" (159). Villanueva describes La Llorona/Luna as strong, dark, and graceful, wearing "a delicate, well-made black, lace shawl float[ing] in the wind as though it were a part of her hair" (see figure 7 on page 51) and implies that Luna and La Llorona are one and the same, human and divine. "It was as though she saw through you with the power of the sun. Her cheek bones were high and her mouth was lush and full, smiling with eternal self-satisfaction" (160). La Llorona tells her, "I know you are," and Luna responds, "I know I am." Expanding on Descartes's philosophical truth from *Discourse on Method*, "I think therefore I am," Villanueva brings Luna to a similar conclusion.

Seeing herself through the divine Llorona, Luna recognizes her self-worth. Not only does Villanueva create Luna in the image of the divine, she also fulfills Irigaray's imperative that women must have a female image of the divine to achieve subjectivity. The star-shaped seashell appears on Luna's forehead in the position of a sage's third eye, revealing her wisdom as a vision seeker and a repository of history and memory. In this final version, Luna reaches up to give the seashell to La Llorona, but she is stopped. In that instant Luna understands her role is similar to her grandmother's. "She was to make people remember." She emphasizes that the role is so important she would fight, even kill, to ensure its fulfillment. Unlike Descartes, who posits human beings isolated from history, Villanueva insists that humans are connected in the past, present, and future. She places Luna in a female genealogy echoing Villaneuva's own family history, from which Luna draws strength and courage. "I am the granddaughter of a woman who . . . saved her husband's life. . . . I am the daughter of a woman who refused the old ways to live in the new ways. . . . Her medicine was laughter. I am the great-granddaughter of a woman who was known for her healing powers. . . . She was an undefeated Yaqui Indian. She was a bruja, as was her daughter, my grandmother" (160–61). Accepting and valuing her foremothers' histories, Luna/Villanueva claims her subjectivity and her purpose in life. "I know who I am" (161). Similar to the other Chicana writers I discuss, Villanueva places Luna/La Llorona in a genealogy of strong and independent indigenous and mestiza women. In previous works such as *The Ultraviolet Sky*, Villanueva's characters and goddess figures fell into the essentialist trap that Fregoso and Chabram call "static, ahistorical Aztec identity." Many Chicana and Chicano activists, writers, and scholars have done the same, including Moraga, Anzaldúa, and Cisneros, in part because a record of their indigenous ancestry has been lost through conquest, intermixing, and racism.[26] However, in this final story Villanueva names the particular indigenous peoples, Yaqui, from which Luna originates and their distinct history of rebellion against the Mexican and Spanish forces. "She was an undefeated Yaqui Indian."[27] In doing so, she makes an important early move in this 1994 text to overcome a universalizing tendency that presents all indigenous Mexicans with the same history and culture.

Villanueva's reclamation project in the Luna/Llorona five-story sequence is manifold.[28] She preserves and diversifies Chicana history and experience by creating more than one Luna story and experience and by integrating elements of her own female family history. She distinguishes indigenous ancestry by identifying Luna as Yaqui and noting the particular Yaqui history of rebellion as different from that of the Mexica and other indigenous peoples. She rescues La Llorona from the one-sided depiction of despair and destruction that usually accompanies her legend. She restores La Llorona's significance as related to beloved fertility goddesses Cihuacoatl and Chalchiutlicue through the birthing metaphor of the star-shaped seashell. She also reinstates the deities' complementary dualism (life giving and life taking) by associating La Llorona with childbirth and water. Finally, Villanueva revises women's roles and sexualities to account for late-twentieth-century Chicana and U.S. Mexicana autonomy and self-determination. In these stories, La Llorona and the Chicana characters to whom she appears are firmly rooted in the genealogy of the woman of discord, causing chaos, disruption, and change and linking the past to present and future. Villanueva also portrays transnational migration as a means of survival and restoration of culture. In "El Alma/The Soul, Three," Luna transmigrates to Denmark, which provides distance from the violence of her home life and allows her to value her heritage and culture. References in "El Alma/The Soul, Four," to Luna's and Villanueva's Yaqui grandmothers also signal a women's history of migration for escape and survival.

The most complex retelling of the Llorona legend appears in Cherríe Moraga's play *The Hungry Woman: A Mexican Medea*. Moraga intertwines La Llorona with the Greek Medea, creating "a Mexican Medea." In keeping with her recovery of goddesses in earlier writings, Moraga also figures La Llorona within a pantheon of indigenous female deities. Like La Llorona/Cihuacoatl, the Greek Medea originated as a fertility goddess and is depicted in mythology and drama as a woman who commits infanticide. From Euripides' *Medea*, Moraga borrows the names of the primary characters and several major themes including (1) how the Greek and Mexican Medea's actions are affected by the social and political drives of her husband, Jason/Jasón; (2) the outsider status Medea holds within the nation-state (Crete/Aztlán); and (3) the betrayal and infanticide elements. In addition, similar to the Greek chorus in Euripides' *Medea*, four characters assume the role of the chorus sympathetic to the Mexican Medea. Moraga casts them as the Cihuateteo, women warriors who died in childbirth and obtained divinity as aspects of Cihuacoatl. Moraga's play also adapts elements of the Llorona/Malinche story in which La Llorona has a child with Hernán Cortés, the Spanish conqueror, who attempts to take their son away from her to Spain. Nationalism, racism, and colonialism are subtexts of this Llorona variation. Cortés imposes "Spanish"-only ancestry upon their son, colonizes the child as his subject, and simultaneously robs the indigenous people and state of one of their own. Moraga's play considers similar issues, portraying Jasón, like Cortés, as Medea's land-greedy husband in the semblance of a hetero/sexist Chicano nationalist. Moraga's Mexican Medea is a rebellious woman modeled after Llorona and other mother earth goddesses. She is exiled from Aztlán, the Chicana/o homeland she helped create. Similar to Euripides' Medea and the La Llorona narrative of Malinche/Cortés, the Mexican Medea faces the loss of her child/children.

The play's subtitle also draws on Western patriarchal discourses that portray Malintzin as the Mexican Eve, a traitor who sold out her people to align with the conqueror. All four figures, La Llorona/Medea and Malinche/Eve, represent models of powerful women who stepped outside the norms of appropriate female behavior. Although popular and religious lore severely castigates them as "bad" women, traitors to the patriarchal nation-state or culture, Moraga's depiction highlights the complex social and political arena in which Medea's mestiza character exists and the agency in her deeds struggling against oppressive forces. In addition, Moraga foregrounds the interconnections in the narratives of La Llorona, Cihuacoatl/Coatlicue,[29] Coyolxauhqui, and the Cihuateteo, all of whom represent life and death forces and act as warrior women. These figures symbolize the revolution Moraga hopes will fulfill the needs and desires of women of color and Chicana lesbians. In the foreword, Moraga writes that she portrays the female figures "in all their locura," "the living expression of their hungers."[30] In this statement, she isolates the double bind that lies buried within the narratives: the needs and desires that drive women to pursue their self-interests, fight for their needs, or commit desperate acts, and the knowledge that they will be labeled "crazy" or "bad" for their actions. When women express and act upon their hungers, they step outside the primary female role of caretaker by putting their own interests before those of others. The play's title, *The Hungry Woman*, comes from another indigenous Mexican originary narrative depicting a female goddess who created the earth from her own body and "cried constantly for food." She represents the first Wailing Woman, one who gave of herself, but whose needs and desires were never fulfilled.[31]

The narrative interrelationships of La Llorona, Coatlicue, Cihuacoatl, Coyolxauhqui, and Cihuateteo stories also can be considered in the context of Gillespie's woman of discord merging as one and the same to disrupt a Mexica patriarchal and imperialistic "national" narrative and create the possibility for change. Moraga's play bears similarities to the codices reinscribed by indigenous survivors after the conquest, which included the woman of discord to symbolize hope for the overthrow of the Spaniards.[32] Moraga creates a revolutionary woman warrior, who takes the form of a Mexican Medea and a rebellious Llorona, to represent the hope of a new nation-state where the expression of Chicana lesbian desire and Chicana/o and indigenous sovereignty is possible. In the postconquest codices that rewrite Mexica histories, the recurring representation of the woman of discord signaled the Mexica journey to a new homeland. In *The Hungry Woman*, Moraga addresses the importance of homeland to her imagined Mechicana/o community of Aztlán, and its relationship to female power and desire. Her reconsideration of the Medea, Llorona, and goddess stories subverts dominant narratives in which the "trope of the nation-as-woman . . . depends on a particular image of woman as chaste, dutiful, daughterly or maternal."[33] In U.S. national narratives, universalized "woman" as white and heterosexual has been used in the "defense of the mother country and of (white) womanhood . . . to bolster colonial conquest and racist violence."[34] In Moraga's play, Medea, an indigenous woman, rather than serving as passive trope and colonized subject, defies the U.S. national narrative and formulates an imagined community of Chicana/o nation, Aztlán. Medea serves as a woman warrior and revolutionary leader in the "ethnic civil war" that resulted in the formation of the "Mechicano Nation of Aztlán" as well as other ethnic nations.[35] However, the utopia falters and eventually Aztlán adopts a national narrative of male and heterosexual dominance reinstating the Chicano nationalism Moraga has critiqued in other writings. In this play, Moraga continues the project she envisioned in *The Last Generation* imagining "Queer Aztlán," a "Chicano homeland that could embrace *all* its people, including its jotería."[36] She writes, "Chicanos are an occupied nation within a nation, and women and women's sexuality are occupied within Chicano nation. If women's bodies and those of men and women who transgress their gender roles have been historically regarded as territories to be conquered, they are also territories to be liberated. Feminism has taught us this."[37]

In Moraga's imagined Aztlán, the trope of woman-as-nation that relies on male, white, and heterosexual dominance is replaced with a vision of equal power and agency. *The Hungry Woman* revolves around the tension caused by the disintegration of the narrative of an ideal Chicana/o state and a reversion to old hierarchies of gender and sexuality. The "Playwright's Note and Setting" makes clear what Homi Bhabha calls the "impossible unity of the nation as a symbolic force."[38] Moraga describes the drama as situated in the borderlands between nations, Aztlán and "Gringolandia (U.S.A.)," following a "counter-revolution" in Aztlán that reestablished hierarchies between male and female and sent queer folk like Medea, her son, and her lover into exile.[39] One of the strengths of the play lies in Moraga's astute recognition of how national narratives of womanhood and home/land are interwoven, gendered, and sexualized to assert male and heterosexual prerogatives. In particular, Moraga asserts a conception of home/land where women are acting forces in conceptualizing the nation rather than being acted upon. Although this vision is achieved only to be lost, the hope remains. Within the trope of woman-as-nation, Moraga examines various ways motherhood, especially lesbian motherhood, is narrativized and experienced, including the rendering of mother and child as colonized male possessions, which is continually contested by Medea/La Llorona. In addition, the mother-child relationship is depicted as a sexualizing experience and as related to home/land with both liberating and betrayal aspects. In this respect, the play vacillates between utopia and dystopia.

In creating a new variation of the Llorona legend, Moraga also turns the traditionally heterosexual narrative into the love of two women and two goddesses, Medea (Cihuacoatl/La Llorona) and Luna (Coyolxauhqui). Similar to Villanueva's revisioning of La Llorona through the character Luna, literally translated as "moon," Moraga names Medea's lover Luna to invoke the moon and warrior goddess Coyolxauhqui. She takes the connection to La Llorona one step further, placing the two lovers in exile from their homeland, similar to the exiled wandering state in which La Llorona exists in the legends about infanticide.

Irony permeates the play, especially with regard to Medea, who led the fight to establish the new nation based on anticolonial and anti-imperialist

principles and then was relegated to colonized pariah status, like La Llorona, because of her sex and sexuality. Throughout the play Medea struggles to regain and maintain control of the right to name and fulfill her
desires, including the right to land and love. In the first act, Medea's
grandmother, Mama Sal, explains to Medea's son, Chac-Mool, that the
queer folk have renamed their exiled land "Tamoanchán," which Moraga
defines as "we seek our home."[40] Referring to an indigenous originary
narrative, Tamoanchán is a mythical paradise, a place where the gods
fashioned the contemporary human race from drops of their blood and
the ground bones of the previous world's inhabitants.[41] In the indigenous
narrative cycle, Tamoanchán is a temporary place in which early humans
existed until the gods created earth and contemporary humans. Similarly,
Mama Sal explains that "the seeking itself became home," suggesting that
the exiles reside in a perpetual state of unfulfilled desire, a state so familiar it seems like home. "We seek our home" also alludes to ongoing
struggles by queer peoples against oppressive ideologies at the same time
as they are subjected to them. In this concept of homeland, Moraga suggests the importance of acknowledging the oppressions women and other
oppressed peoples live with even as they perform agency to free themselves.[42] As Moraga puts it, to "*Imagine freedom. . . . Write freedom*," she
must paint "pictures of prisoners on the page," which constitute the "surviving codices of our loss."[43] In other words, in order to consider the
possibility of agency and liberation, to "Imagine freedom," it is necessary
to portray women in oppressive conditions, "prisoners" who have fought
and suffered "loss."

Furthermore, Moraga addresses the significance of rethinking and rewriting "official" narratives whether they are U.S. historical accounts,
Mexica histories and cosmologies, Chicano nationalist rhetoric, or misogynist narratives about women such as the Llorona legend. When Mama
Sal begins to tell Chac-Mool about the history of radicalism and racism in
the United States, he doubts her version.

CHAC-MOOL: Is this the official version? . . . .
MAMA SAL: Yes. I was there.
CHAC-MOOL: You're editorializing, 'buela. I just need the facts.
MAMA SAL: There are no facts. It's all just story.[44]

Here, Mama Sal challenges constructed differences between fact and fiction, history and story. Her cryptic words imply that the type of story told

depends on the teller. Chac-Mool has been told the "official" story, which erases the oppressive nature of the dominant power and any resistance by the oppressed. In this play, Moraga excavates the stories of the oppressed.

The connection between home/land and homosexual, especially lesbian, desire is a major theme of the play. Moraga foregrounds how Chicano "nationalism favors a distinctly homosocial form of male bonding" in which "proper" homosociality, the nation as a "union between men," must be secured through the distancing of homosexuality and the enshrinement of the Mother figure.[45] Medea remembers that when she still lived in Aztlán, before exile, her husband, Jasón, would say, "I want a wife, Medea. It's not natural!" Moraga makes clear that what Jasón (Cortés) wants is control of Medea's (La Malinche's and La Llorona's) body and sexuality, in other words, control of what he considers his territory. "Each night I could hear Jasón circling outside our bedroom window, over and over again, pissing out the boundaries of what he knew he could never enter. Only protect. Defend. Mark as his domain."[46] Ironically, his competitor in this scene is not another woman but their infant son, with whom Medea admits she had "an insatiable love affair," a bond that grew through breast-feeding. Nonetheless, Jasón claims her body as his "property" just as he later claims her land, taking it into his custody while she is in lesbian exile. When she attempts to reclaim it, he demands that she "give up the dyke," her lover Luna, to regain her "status."[47] Here "status" relates multiple connotations including her position as his wife, the right to keep her son, her citizenship within Aztlán, and possession of her land, all of which can only be realized through the expression of normative heterosexuality and submissive femininity. Jasón dictates the terms of Medea's relationship with her son and with others even though they are separated. He assumes that she and their son are property that he can control like the land and invokes the narratives that maintain his (male, heterosexual) domination over all.

Another irony emerges with the fact that Medea possesses land in Aztlán by right of her indigenous identity even though she lives in exile. Jasón, who cannot claim indigenous identity, has access to land only through marriage to Medea or custody of their son. Moraga ironically inverts the Llorona legend in which La Llorona's/Malintzin's indigenous ancestry is rejected by Cortés, who decides their son is "Spanish." In this play, Moraga characterizes Jasón (Cortés) desiring the son's indigenous ancestry rather than rejecting it to attain land. In an anticolonial, antiracist statement, Moraga returns the land to indigenous hands and honors indigenous ancestry. At the same time, she complicates an indigenous vision of nationalist belonging by foregrounding the necessity of heterosexuality to Chicano nationalism. As in Euripides' play when Medea exposes Jason's interest in the children to guarantee succession to the crown, Moraga's Medea exposes Jasón's interest in Chac-Mool, her indigenous son, to guarantee his right to land. "He is your native claim. You can't hold onto a handful of dirt in Aztlán without him. You don't have the blood quantum."[48] But in both plays what the men have that ensures the fulfillment of their self-interest and greed is their status as male and heterosexual. Both "identities" take priority over indigenous, female, and lesbian, literally and figuratively.

The merging of Medea with La Llorona is most evident when Chac-Mool decides to leave and go live with his father in Aztlán. Medea fears that Chac-Mool, like the "Mechicano" people, will abandon her for the sexist, heterosexist Chicano nationalism that sent her into exile. As in the Mexica narrative of La Llorona/Cihuacoatl and in Villanueva's story "Weeping Woman," Moraga's Medea considers the Mechicano people her endangered children. "All the babies, they're slipping through my fingers now. I can't stop them. They've turned into the liquid of the river and they are drowning in my hands."[49] However, contrary to Villanueva's Llorona, who symbolically drowns her people to save them by converting them to fish, Moraga conceives the Mechicano people as drowning themselves in intolerance to maintain a rigid view of nation that dichotomizes them from the female and homosexual Other. Medea/La Llorona fights back to keep her son from "drowning" in Chicano nationalist thinking. In the scene that follows it appears that Medea/La Llorona has decided to poison her son rather than let him go with his father. She gives him a potion that puts him to sleep, and with help from the Cihuateteo, divine warrior women who died in childbirth, she places him upon Coatlicue's altar like a sacrificial victim. However, several elements of the scene foster ambiguity as to whether Medea actually kills her son, simultaneously calling into question the Llorona and Medea legends of infanticide.

First, the action of laying Chac-Mool on a sacrificial altar invokes an early Greek myth in which Medea does not kill her children. In this Greek version, the goddess Hera grants Medea's children immortality when Medea lays them on Hera's sacrificial altar.[50] In Moraga's play, Medea functions in this scene as a priestess and, as such, the ritual she performs sanctifies the act, whether it is an actual or symbolic killing.[51] Second, after laying Chac-Mool on the altar, Moraga's Medea enacts a symbolic ritual, not of child killing but of purification. She cleanses herself and Chac-Mool of internalized hatred by rejecting the narrative role that Coatlicue plays in Mexica mythology of aiding the male god of war in giving birth to him and demanding conquests. Moraga's Medea changes the role of the woman of discord into aiding women and queer folk rather than a patriarchal, imperialist regime, such as the Mexicas'. The cleansing ritual also implies a rejection of the hetero/sexist rhetoric of Chicano nationalism, which Medea feared Chac-Mool would embrace. Referring to an earlier scene in the play, which reenacted Coatlicue giving birth to Huitzilopochtli, who then defeated Coyolxauhqui, Medea says: "What crime do I commit now, Mamá? To choose the daughter over the son? You betrayed us, Madre Coatlicue. You, anciana, you who birthed the God of War." Medea fights back with words and refigures the stories of women warriors and betrayed wives or lovers. She tells the story from her perspective and speaks a female history and experience that is not part of American, Mexica, or Chicano nationalist discourses. She publicly tells her story of sexual abuse by her brother, Huitzilopochtli, and neglect by her co-opted mother, Coatlicue. "My mother did not stop my brother's hand/from reaching into my virgin bed./Nor did you hold back the sword/that severed your daughter's head."[52]

Medea also exhibits agency in choosing her own divine. In this speech act, Medea chooses her lover, Luna/Coyolxauhqui, the goddess of the moon, over the heterosexist husband, Jasón, the potentially patriarchal son, Chac-Mool, and the god of war and sun, Huitzilopochtli. "Ahora, she is my god. La Luna, la hija rebelde. Te rechazo, Madre."[53] Literally and figuratively, Medea chooses to live with and as the rebellious daughter, "la hija rebelde," a lesbian and woman warrior who fights back rather than submitting to the violence and colonization of the patriarchy. Symbolically, Medea rejects her son because he has chosen his father's Chicano nationalism and Huitzilopochtli's Mexica discourses and way of life. In addition, she must reject the mother, Cihuacoatl/Coatlicue, who was rewritten in the Mexica histories from a complex goddess of life and death to a monstrous symbol of war and human sacrifice.[54] Medea denounces the denigration and demonization of female "hungers" through the misrepresentation of Coatlicue and La Llorona as figures of violence. Here also Moraga rejects the depiction of Medea and La Llorona as reproductive demons who commit infanticide.

This scene performs the interpretation Moraga presented in *The Last Generation* of the Coyolxauhqui-Coatlicue myth. The "daughter [Coyolxauhqui] must kill male-defined motherhood [Coatlicue] in order to save the culture from misogyny, war, and greed."[55] The "killing" of the mother, Coatlicue, and the son, Huitzilopochtli, in Moraga's play then symbolically represents not murders but the necessity of dissociating from harmful narratives. Rather than participating in the imperialist narratives the Mexica created for Coatlicue and Huitzilopochtli, Medea takes on the role of "Coyolxauhqui's unnamed star sister," whom Luna sculpts and who embodies the characteristics of "renegade rebozo, el tambor's insistence, a warrior's lament." Moraga rewrites Medea and La Llorona in the image of Coyolxauhqui, a defiant, indigenous woman warrior who denounces controlling nationalist discourses and fights back against domination. At the same time, Moraga represents Medea lamenting those lost to rigid, oppressive histories and mythologies. Act 2 ends with Medea wailing La Llorona's lament "¡AY-Y-Y-Y! ¡MI HI-I-I-I-JO!" echoed by the Cihuateteo's pluralized cry, "¡MIS HI-I-I-I-JOS!"[56] which in turn echoes one of the earliest recorded Llorona stories of Cihuacoatl's lament for the loss of her people during the Spanish conquest.

Moraga's play implies that the conquest especially of indigenous women continues and that those who rebel suffer severe repercussions. Medea is declared "insane" and incarcerated for her renunciations and implicitly for the "killing" of her son. As in the cases of real women who kill their children, her "madness" must be contained in an institution and she must be regulated under constant surveillance because of the danger her ideas or actions pose to the state. Much of the play takes place by way of flashbacks, Medea's memories of what occurred as she sits incarcerated in a mental hospital under constant guard. The discipline Medea receives is more direct than Foucault's "faceless gaze." She is punished through confinement in a mental hospital, diagnosed as "mad" by doctors and psychologists who observe her, and finally assigned an armed guard who watches her every move. These policing mechanisms reveal that Medea is considered highly dangerous and cannot be trusted to self-regulate. But ambiguity marks the incarceration scenes too. No specific reason is given for why Medea has been institutionalized or why she is under constant surveillance by a prison guard stationed in her room. Medea admits to wanting to commit suicide to "try to join [Chac-Mool]," suggesting that her son is dead and that she may have killed him. However, the character's title, "prison" guard, and the fact that the same actor plays both the prison guard and the border guard who stops and interrogates Luna for crossing into Aztlán, suggest that Medea may be a political prisoner rather than a mental patient.

Medea herself believes or has been convinced, by the misogynist Medea/Llorona narratives, that she killed her son. When Chac-Mool appears in her hospital room to take her home she doesn't accept the reality of his presence.

MEDEA: Are you a ghost?

CHAC-MOOL: No.

MEDEA: You're mistaken. You are a ghost. You're the son I mourn, the one I pray to, that his heart may soften when I join him on the other side.

CHAC-MOOL: Mom, I'm Chac-Mool.

MEDEA: If you live, then why am I here? I've committed no crime. If you live, why then am I strapped into the bed at night? Why am I plagued with nightmares of babies melting between my hands? Why do I mourn you and no longer walk the horizon at the hour of sunset as I used to? Why are there locks and I haven't the key? Why?[57]

Medea's questions refer to narratives that identify her as Cihuacoatl—"babies melting between my hands"—and La Malinche and La Llorona—"why do I mourn you and no longer walk the horizon at the hour of sunset?" They suggest her innocence of any "crime," especially that of infanticide. Chac-Mool's answers also suggest that she has been held as a political prisoner rather than as a murderer. He describes home, the Mechicano Nation of Aztlán, through the physical landscape of cacti that populate the U.S. Southwest and Mexico's northern states. "By the full moon, you'll be looking at saguaros. You're going home."[58] His statement also implies that he has not gone over to his father's side or to an afterlife ("the other side").

This scene intimates that an all-tolerant Aztlán may still be only a vision rather than reality. In the hospital, Chac-Mool gives Medea a sleeping potion and then holds her in his arms in a pietá image, as she had earlier done with him. This image, combined with the final scene of the Cihuateteo, warrior women, dancing in the light of the moon (Luna/Coyolxauhqui), lends itself to multiple interpretations. Chac-Mool's assumption of a nurturing role suggests that he has not embraced the model of masculinity forwarded by his father and Chicano nationalism. "Home" may also be symbolic of the reunion of mother and son, especially when the son respects, rather than rejects, the mother's rebellious, independent spirit. This view is significant because Moraga does not base her vision of home/land on a female-only utopia. Her image of home/land is not exclusionary but hopes for recognition and understanding of difference, which would curtail war and violence. At the same time, the sleep-induced moon vision suggests that moon/female/lesbian/goddess identification creates a sense of "home," an imaginary community that provides a sense of safety and peace, however temporary or illusory, until male, heterosexual, white dominance subsides. Regardless of whether the return home is actual or symbolic, the play challenges popular narratives that uphold false dichotomies and denigrating images of women and men.

Immediately before Medea is arrested and taken to the hospital, Chac-Mool tells her he has decided to fight for the Queer Aztlán she helped create. "I'm gonna go back to Aztlán, and make 'em change, Mom. . . . Like those Cuban kids who went back to Cuba in the 70s and became Castro sympathizers."[59] In other words, as a symbol of the new generation he takes up her role of the revolutionary warrior and fights to reclaim Aztlán for queer folk and women so that his mother and her lover can return to their home/land. At the end of this scene, the prison guard escorts Medea out while Chac-Mool and Mama Sal are still in the room. Chac-Mool is still alive when Medea is arrested and imprisoned, revealing that the Mexican Medea does not kill her son. Moraga refigures the horrific infanticidal narratives of La Llorona, the Greek Medea, and Mexica goddesses. La Llorona and Medea are redeemed as symbols of oppressed peoples and justice fighters who struggle against entrenched and recurring forms of subjugation. Moraga's fictional narrative disputes received notions of subordinate women and forces readers to confront the spirit, strength, and even desperation of their lives and actions. Moraga's play also shows how rebellion and fighting back can be reconsidered, accepted, even admired and emulated by a younger generation of men whose consciousness has been raised by mothers, grandmothers, and their lesbian lovers. Written while Moraga was pregnant with her son Ricardo, this play expresses her hope for the future, a world where men, women, heterosexuals, homosexuals, and peoples of all races respect the right to sovereignty of mind, body, and land. As with Villanueva's fiction and the oral histories, Moraga's writing leaves no doubt that fighting back is an acceptable and necessary resistance strategy. Her characterizations of the Cihuateteo as warrior women and Medea as a revolutionary in the image of las soldaderas, women who fought in the Mexican Revolution, insist that resistance is a viable option to create new national, familial, and communal systems governed by discourses of equality and respect.

The narratives discussed in this chapter reveal many configurations of the Llorona legend: its history of inducing children to self-regulate their behavior through fear; its use as a weapon in the patriarchal arsenal to repress female power and agency by suggesting eternal exile and loss of children; its representation of cultural anxieties about independent, sexual women and gender roles, and race, class and gender hierarchies; and its depiction of colonial struggle, hardship, and loss. The legend variations that end with infanticide and exiled grieving do not provide hope of recovery for La Llorona. However, as the oral histories and fictional works reveal, Chicanas and U.S. Mexicanas refuse to remain lost and disempowered. La Llorona's legend also can be understood as defying cultural and colonialist scripts that attempt to silence mixed-race and indigenous women. Whether mournful, angry, or joyful, Chicana and U.S. Mexicana voices insist on chronicling Llorona moments, their experiences of relinquishing sorrow and resisting domination. The contemporary oral and written narratives also recover La Llorona's originary power and significance through indigenous goddesses and La Malinche. They reinvent La Llorona as an active agent, a woman of discord who ruptures the status quo and creates change. Prior to the 1990s, few popular or published narratives revised the Weeping Woman story. Now, La Llorona seems poised as the woman of discord who will precipitate change and unity in the new era of the twenty-first century. Able to evoke popular sentiment, reach mass audiences, and negotiate woman-centered and indigenous feminist critiques, the many oral and written variations of this Mexican female cultural symbol speak to and for Chicanas, U.S. Mexicanas, and many women and men of the Americas.

chapter five

 READING DYNAMICS OF POWER

Oral Histories, Feminist Research,

and the Politics of Location

Theresa Meléndez notes that the "metaphor of the book," which distanced writing and reading from daily life and from the working classes, continues to be a defining element in what constitutes literature in the Western tradition. During the Renaissance, oral traditions largely became associated with "simple" and "uncivilized" cultures and were not considered artistically refined enough to be called literature.[1] Likewise, women's experiences and stories were devalued, even when women began to write and publish. In these ways, oral narratives are multiply marginalized by their status as oral; by association with women, even more so by women of color; and by the language in which they are spoken if not Standard English, for example, Spanish, black English, or Spanish and English code switching or vernacular. Oral and life histories continue to be relegated to the sidelines, even though, like folklore, they are considered to be the inspiration for much creative and nonfiction writing. As a response to the secondary status given oral histories and life stories, I read the working-class and semiprofessional women's oral narratives as literary works of equal value to that of the professional intellectuals' written texts. In claiming their literariness, it follows, as Arnold Krupat argues about collaborative oral narratives published as Native American autobiographies, that they must be included in the American literary canon to "call into question the particular value it institutionalizes."[2] In other words, the academic canon represents primarily the white, male, middle- to upper-class, and written social order. Similarly, an expansion of the Chicana/o literary canon to include oral histories and life stories would counteract the secondary status associated with oral narratives and permit working-class and semiprofessional women's voices to be heard, rather than have their stories told in the writings of their daughters or granddaughters, as Tey Diana Rebolledo notes occurs in the works of many Chicana authors.[3]

The literariness of oral histories and life stories exists in their relationship to both autobiography and storytelling. Yet their use as sources of information in fields such as history, sociology, and anthropology and their frequent divergence from the singular subject, linear narrative of Western written autobiography confound strict genre categorizations. Even as I argue for their consideration as literary works, they are best understood as borderlands texts blurring the boundaries of narrative form and self-representational practice. Carole Boyce Davies characterizes life stories as akin to autobiography yet distinct, "a *crossover genre* that challenges the oral/written separations and unites these forms as they maintain their distinct textualities."[4] The oral histories in this study cross over several genres, simultaneously intersecting storytelling, autobiography, historical account, and testimonial.

Oral histories, although mediated by various dynamics during the interview process, provide the opportunity for an individual to articulate what Agnes Hankiss describes as "his or her own theory about the history and course of his or her life." This theory about the history and course of one's life creates an ontology of the self and its relation to family, community, and culture.[5] The working-class and semiprofessional women's oral histories reflect a conscious decision to represent themselves as "modern" women,[6] while at the same time articulating their sense of self in terms of an actual or symbolic past relationship with Mexico. Moreover, they are proud of their Mexican roots and wish to retain affiliation with Mexican identity and traditions even as they acknowledge their status as citizens of the United States.

As historical accounts the oral narratives establish both personal histories and a history of Mexican-identified women in the United States, in each instance a particularly gendered, classed, and racialized experience. Contrary to dominant stereotypes and culturally idealized notions of women giving over their lives to male or white dominant authority, the historias depict women who act on their own behalf. When societal forces compromise this ability, they perform covert, everyday resistances and overt rebellions to wrest back a measure of control. Here history making and subject making intertwine so that it's impossible to separate the formulation of U.S. Mexicana histories from that of the production of subjectivities. These women's reflections on their actions often are positioned in larger societal or cultural contexts, such as Aurora Harada's recognition that many women suffer and think they have to endure abuse in marriage as she did. Her desire to alert other women to the possibilities for a fulfilling life outside male dependency and domination speaks to historical and ethnic understandings of gendered oppression as well as the potential for change. Consequently, the historias illustrate the agency in actor-centered words "allow[ing] one to see how an actor makes culturally meaningful history, how history is produced in action and in the actor's retrospective reflections on that action."[7] Although the historias are narratives of individual lives, a sense of the collective nature of the experiences is conveyed throughout them. The narrators' reflections on their personal lives often integrate remembrances of similar incidents in other women's lives, establishing a communal record of experiences common to U.S. Mexicanas as women and as Mexican ancestry or Mexican immigrant peoples.

At times when instances of gender and racial oppression are recounted in the narratives, the discourse assumes the expression of testimonio, a Latin American narrative form generally originating as an oral account testifying to hardship, repression, struggle, and resistance. As John Beverley defines it, the subject of a testimonio is not concerned as much with the life of an individual as with a "problematic collective social situation in which the narrator lives." The testimonio may address individual circumstances, but always within the context of shared concerns, and therefore the narrator "speaks for, or in the name of, a community or group."[8] Recognizing the testimonio component within the historias acknowledges the threat and pain detailed by the narrators and situates their narratives as bearing witness to identifiable forces, material and ideological, which can be held accountable for Chicana and U.S. Mexicana suffering and struggle. Within the American literary tradition, slave narratives perform a similar function of bearing witness to the injustices committed against the greater black community. In slave narratives the forces of power are oppressive to a greater and different degree and the literary conventions often veil the narrator's and the community's repression to a greater extent than in U.S. Mexicana historias. However, such comparisons further understandings of the similarities and differences in oppressions and the representational expressions that aim to raise public awareness and establish permanent records of injustices. One published historia by a U.S. Mexicana that contains many of the conventions of a slave narrative as elaborated by Toni Morrison and other scholars is *Forged under the Sun/Forjada bajo el sol: The Life History of María Elena Lucas*.[9]

Even as historical and communal truths about the lives of U.S. Mexicanas and Chicanas emerge from the historias, the beauty of storytelling is ever present. The significance of the historias resides as much in the aesthetic value as in the truth value. More so, the pleasurable qualities of the oral narratives contribute to and expand on an understanding of the lived reality. Many of the historias contain symbols and metaphors that provide revelations concerning individual and cultural subjectivity.[10] Virginia Urias's statement, "Women must defend themselves," repeated throughout her historia, becomes a metaphor of self-actualization as she describes the defiant actions she took to make a life for herself despite her mother's overprotectiveness and the violence against women and children she witnessed.

Just as the literary conventions used in the working-class and semiprofessional women's narratives reinforce the facts of their experiences, in a similar manner the professional intellectual women's literary writings employ oral truth-telling devices to augment the creative. Chicana writings perform as historias in combining the oral and the written, history and storytelling, fact and fiction. The authors create fictional or autobiographical subjects bearing witness to historically situated gender and racial power struggles. The writings consist of personal historias, transcriptions of each author's self-representing words, and familial historias, transcriptions of family members' words. Incorporating fragments of the histories and stories told by their mothers and grandmothers who shared their struggles with the authors as lessons to be learned about life, they form a collective representation of female experience. I have argued elsewhere that Cherríe Moraga's work draws on a long and well-established Mexican oral tradition of cuentos and corridos, stories and songs, to record Chicana and U.S. Mexicana experiences of poverty, discrimination, resistance to oppression, and racial-cultural affirmation.[11] In *Loving in the War Years*, Moraga relates her mother's girlhood historia of working long hours in factories and of narrowly escaping the sexual advances of the family's Anglo benefactor. Her mother's historia is intertwined with Moraga's own testimony to sexual and cultural repression so that the individual and communal become inseparable. Gloria Anzaldúa transcribes her mother's historia in *Borderlands/La Frontera*. Through her mother's words, she tells the story of her maternal grandmother's experiences of economic and racial struggle. " 'Drought hit South Texas,' my mother tells me. *'La tierra se puso bien seca y los animales comenzaron a morrirse de se.' Mi papá se murió de un* heart attack *dejando a mamá* pregnant *y con ocho huercos,* with eight kids and one on the way. . . . A smart *gabacho* lawyer took the land away *mamá* hadn't paid taxes. *No hablaba inglés,* she didn't know how to ask for time to raise the money."[12] Anzaldúa's own testimony builds upon her mother's and grandmother's historias. "I remember being caught speaking Spanish at recess—that was good for three licks on the knuckles with a sharp ruler."[13] In transcribing their own historias and those of their mothers and grandmothers, Moraga, Anzaldúa, and other Chicana writers record a female history of common experiences. In the process, they revise distorted historical and sociological accounts written from European American perspectives, and racial, cultural, and gender stereotypes and idealizations, such as that of the passive, submissive Mexican woman. Creating historias of resistance, their narratives express a female and Chicana way of being and knowing that results in powerful and empowering female re-presentations.

The three dimensions that signify in my definition of the historias— histories, stories, testimonios—emerge as counterdiscourses articulating moments of resistance and refiguring. In defying cultural inscriptions of the body, the historias suggest a relationship between storytelling, embodiment, and empowerment. Reflecting upon and speaking about their experiences, about the forces that have acted upon their bodies, the narrators define themselves as oppositional beings, women of discord, who succeed in obtaining a measure of personal power.

READING DYNAMICS OF
POWER IN ORAL HISTORY PRACTICE

Working-class and semiprofessional women's oral histories are as significant as professional intellectuals' writings to understanding Chicana and U.S. Mexicana experience and resistance. Framed by the women's own words and ideas of themselves, oral histories provide a window into every-day and life-long realities and courses of action. Yet oral history gathering remains a sensitive practice due to power differences that generally exist throughout the interviewing and editing process and affect the outcome of the narratives and sometimes the individuals involved.[14] Recognizing power differences and the problems associated with them does not alter disparities, but it does provide understandings of the extent of the differences and their possible ramifications. My reflections on the dynamics of these relationships reveal a deep ambivalence resulting from the exchanges that took place during the gathering process and how I have made use of the oral histories—even as I continue to do so—since then.

Feminist thinking about fieldwork practices often implies that implementing democratic, collaborative, and self-reflexive practices can minimize, if not overcome, power differences.[15] The methods and methodology I contemplated in gathering the oral histories proceeded from these premises, which are critiqued below, but my oversights resulted from my incomplete understanding of the advantages I possessed and the power those advantages entailed. Prior to gathering the oral histories, I knew that power differences would exist in my interactions with the women by the immutable fact that I am white. Perhaps because of my position when I began the project as an economically struggling graduate student from a rural, working-class family, I did not foresee how a number of my assumptions reinforced inequities, especially regarding the intersections of class, education, and language, all of which are related to racial and cultural differences.

In formulating my approach to the oral history–gathering process, I attempted to develop feminist research practices that made central the race, class, and gender locations of myself, the researcher, and of the working-class and semiprofessional U.S. Mexicanas.[16] I considered how my privileges as a white person (in a society where white, middle-class values are the invisible "norm" and people of color and of other cultures are evaluated by that norm) would shape the research experiences. Early in my graduate studies, I participated in several diversity workshops that challenged constructs of white superiority and class and gender hierarchies, and this awareness, along with personal experiences of oppression, aided me in gaining the women's trust. I also considered the effects that my changing class status—as someone from a lower-income, working-class family who was transitioning to a highly educated, middle-class professional intellectual—might have on our interactions. I imagined that my working-class Catholic upbringing might aid in understanding aspects of the U.S. Mexicanas' lives but that the educational status I had achieved could be a hindrance in gaining their trust. These considerations address questions of whether white scholars, such as myself, can elicit understandings of gender and race relations, such as those experienced by the U.S. Mexicanas and Chicanas, and whether white scholars can gather oral histories without reproducing the historical subordination of U.S. Mexicanas by race, class, and gender during and after the interactions.[17] By discarding the directed interview approach and the "objective" research stance (value-free and colorblind), Margaret Andersen found that she gained the trust of black women participants and thereby gathered extensive accounts of their experiences.[18] My approach and experience collecting historias with the working-class and semiprofessional U.S. Mexicanas had similar results. Yet even scholars attentive to race, class, and gender issues may not overcome the disparities that exist.[19] The factors I did not consider beforehand that had a bearing on this study were the significance of language to the power equation; the psychological, perhaps even physical, risks for several women; and the difference between my interests and investment in the project and those of the participants.

I met with each of the nine women several times for periods of two to five hours in their home cities of Muscatine, Iowa, Tucson, Arizona, and San Antonio, Texas.[20] In each city, I was introduced to the women through a professional colleague who asked them to participate prior to my contact with them. Through referral by someone the women knew and trusted, I earned a badge of initial acceptance, avoiding refusals or overt race-based distrust that white women researchers may encounter from nonwhite women.[21] In Tucson, a medical doctor whom I had met at a language school in Mexico suggested that I interview members of a group she worked with, Mensajeras de Salud (Messengers of Health), a Tucson cancer education and support group. In San Antonio, the director of the Hijas del Quinto Sol: Studies in Latina Identity Conference (now called Latina Letters), at which I was presenting a paper, furnished me with the names of three women. In Iowa, a professor who was advising me on my research project referred me to a social worker who introduced me to several women in Muscatine, a small city in southern Iowa with a significant Mexican immigrant and Mexican American population.

As did Andersen, I found that being honest and open about my positions, beliefs, and values and encouraging the women to talk about what was important to them enhanced my relationships with the participants and the candidness of the information they shared.[22] My thinking was that by engaging an oral-history, storytelling approach the women would feel greater power and control to represent themselves according to their own self-image and narrative strategies. At the same time, I also defined the research relationship by controlling the process, initially seeking English or bilingual speakers and directing their narratives by my questions. I also controlled the agenda, wanting them to talk about specific and sensitive topics, some of which might have put one or two women at risk. Initially, I also controlled the narrative method by asking starter questions such as Where were you born? What are your childhood memories? How did you or your ancestors come to live in the United States? These types of questions reflect linear, chronological thinking characteristic of Western, male autobiographical writing and positivist "objective" scientific practices. Only in the post-fieldwork stage, after reading Catherine Kohler Riessman's analysis of how an Anglo interviewer misunderstood a Puerto Rican woman's nontemporal narrative strategy, did I recognize how my questions might have influenced the structure of the women's historias. Some of the women immediately resisted my move toward temporality and linearity, instead presenting their life stories in episodic, circular, or repetitious patterns that I read as thematic organizations of their experiences. In other cases, I discontinued the questioning as the women became involved in their own stories. Although I had a list of prepared questions, I rarely referred to it, and the conversations flowed and ebbed according to each woman's desire to talk. When their own stories moved in these directions, I asked questions related to racial and cultural identity, discrimination, gender roles, work, education, male-female relationships, domestic abuse, sexuality, Mexican female cultural symbols, and Chicana writings. Several of the women seemed to welcome the opportunity to tell their lives and were reluctant to end the interviews. Overall, the women expressed appreciation that I was interested in their particular experiences and concerns and that I considered U.S. Mexicana issues important.

As an outsider to the culture and race, I was not sure how I would be received by the women, especially given that I was interested in personally and culturally sensitive issues. The anthropologist and literary studies scholar José Limón encouraged me by saying that the women might be more comfortable talking to me than to "insiders," members of their own culture, because of cultural taboos against such talk.[23] Indeed Patricia Zavella found "there may be great reluctance to discuss [personal problems] with a researcher" who is both an insider, a Chicana, and an outsider, someone who has received an elite education and thus is perceived to have a higher class status.[24] Although there are significant differences between myself and the U.S. Mexicanas, including race, culture, education, class status, and, variously, first language and age, there are also several intersecting perspectives that may have contributed to my acceptance as enough of an insider for personal stories to be shared.[25] Primary among these are my knowledge of the Catholic religion, having been raised in a strict Catholic family, and Mexican culture. After living in Mexico during several summers and studying Chicana/o literature, art, folklore, history, and political and social movements, I had come to "see the world through the experiences of others."[26] Because I indicated in advance my interest in stories related to Mexican female cultural figures such as La Virgen de Guadalupe and La Llorona, the women came prepared to share their stories about these figures with me. In addition, they often volunteered information or responded at length when I asked questions about sensitive issues such as sexuality and domestic disputes, including physical and verbal abuse. Perhaps, in part, they were willing to do so because I had informed them beforehand that these were topics of interest, and therefore I did not "project my taboos" as occurred when Elizabeth Jameson interviewed women in Colorado mining towns.[27]

Yet the U.S. Mexicanas' openness about sexuality, and perhaps about domestic abuse, has a cultural component. In a comparative study, Yvonne Tixier y Vigil and Nan Elsasser found significant differences in responses to questions about sex depending on the ethnic identity of the listener. "The respondents perceived that the entire subject of sex was a less personal and less taboo subject in American culture than in Chicano culture and conversed accordingly. Women of all ages spoke more, and more freely, to the Anglo than to the Chicana interviewer."[28] Other Chicana researchers have suggested to me that domestic violence carries similar taboos within Chicana/o culture and that very little research has been done on the topic.[29] These findings indicate that cross-cultural research can be valuable in contributing to the body of knowledge about specific cultures and that conscientious white researchers can play a role. Regarding questioning about racial discrimination, Tixier y Vigil and Elsasser found that rather than avoiding or minimizing the issue with an Anglo interviewer, as they had hypothesized, the participants gave indirect answers to avoid offending the researcher. They steered the topic away from the personal realm or the geographic area and also referred to Anglo friends or positive aspects of Chicana/o and Anglo relations. The results of my study differ somewhat in that I received a range of responses. Several of the women offered detailed stories of how they or family members were the targets of discrimination, while others were circumspect or laconic with their answers. Those who spoke freely tended to be more open and explicit about all the issues discussed in their historias. The reticence of the majority of the participants to discuss this issue reminded me that, however little I want to be identified with the dominant power group, my skin color both marks me as a member and affords me the option to claim membership.

The women's willingness to discuss sensitive topics regarding sexuality and domestic violence also raised my awareness about the power dynamics occurring within families and the risks involved for those who shared family secrets. I met with a Muscatine mother and daughter, Ventura Loya and Cindy Siqueiros, together in Siqueiros's home and separately in each woman's home. Cindy Siqueiros spoke at length about her abusive father and first husband, the latter whom she had already divorced. She also revealed that her brother had come out as gay. She said his sexual orientation was no surprise to her, but that her mother had some problems with it, and she and her brother had to "educate" her about homosexuality. Loya, who was sitting in the room listening, later told me that she never would have brought up the subject of her son's homosexuality with me if her daughter had not mentioned it. She said it was not because she was ashamed of her son or judged him, but because she feared for his well-being and did not want him to have a difficult life. Loya, who was born and raised in Mexico, reflects the attitude that some family secrets are best kept within the family for the protection of its members. Her son's psychological and physical safety also was a factor. She feared that the information about his sexual orientation might be relayed to his abusive and intolerant father.

In addition, Loya's own safety was a consideration during the oral history–gathering process. Initially, she wanted to use a pseudonym, having discussed at length her relationship and recent divorce (for the second time) from her psychologically and physically abusive husband. She did not want her children to know what she had told me about the relationship for fear that it would get back to him and be used against her. When we met two years later, she readily signed forms granting permission to publish her historia under her real name, having been freed from her husband's harassment due to his remarriage. But she also said she knew that if he hadn't remarried, he would still be harassing her.

Another situation I encountered reinforces the risks women take in speaking out against their abusers and emphasizes how "fieldwork represents an intrusion and intervention into a system of relationships, a system of relationships that the researcher is far freer than the researched to leave."[30] When I first met with Alicia Córdova (a pseudonym) in the tiny apartment where she lived with her husband and five children, she became uncomfortable talking with me when her husband came home from work. She did not attend two other meetings we scheduled. The social worker who introduced me to her advised me that although she was interested in meeting with me again, her husband tended to exert strict control at times, which may have been the reason for her inability to meet with me. My brief interaction with Córdova speaks to the psychological as well as material inequalities that may exist between the researcher and the narrator.[31]

Language accentuated power differences when I exerted control of which language would be spoken in the historias. Following the initial meeting with Córdova, who spoke only Spanish, I decided to interview English or bilingual speakers. The major consideration for this decision was to avoid replicating power imbalances with U.S. Mexicanas, such as Córdova, who had lived in the United States for less than one year and whose lack of economic and linguistic resources made her more vulnerable to abuse from her husband, abuse which could be exacerbated by our contact. In requesting English speakers, I hoped to avoid circumstances that would put the women at greater risk for abuse. The issue of language was a dilemma that I agonized over for some time. Although I can converse in Spanish and have done so for periods of time while living in Mexico, I was not confident that I could catch all the nuances in extended conversations of a personal nature with native speakers. I didn't realize that the same may have been true for native Spanish speakers listening and talking to me in English. An additional factor was the translation that would be necessary if the historias were conducted in Spanish, as my field of study is literature written in English. This was primarily an economic consideration that reflects the state of research funding for graduate students and faculty in the humanities. Ultimately, I used my graduate student income to pay for translations of the historia segments spoken in Spanish. My decision was pragmatic given the effort and expense I was undertaking as a literary studies graduate student conducting field research outside the conventional realm of my discipline. Yet my emphasis on English contains multiple ethical and power-related repercussions. Exploitation and unequal exchange are elements of this interaction, stemming from how I hoped to use, and in fact am using, the women's words for professional and economic gain when the women themselves did not benefit in any similar manner. As a means of acknowledging and attempting to rectify this situation, I have pledged to donate the proceeds of this book to Mensajeras de Salud, the cancer education and support organization in Tucson with which Gonzales, Urias, and Vásquez work.

When I asked my contacts to refer me to English speakers, I thought the participants would be second- or third-generation Mexican Americans who learned English in U.S. schools. And five of the women fit this characterization. However, several of the women who were located for me were born in Mexico and educated in Spanish, although I didn't know this until the moment I met them. Each of the four had lived in the United States for more than ten years when I met her, yet for these women whose first language is Spanish my request to tape their historias in English may have circumscribed their ability to communicate their experiences and emotions comfortably, fluidly, and fluently.[32] My control of the research relationship in some instances affected the women's self-representations. Sometimes I spoke in Spanish with them informally during the historias, wanting to let them know that I appreciate and can speak their native language. Upon realizing that I understood Spanish, several of the women spoke it at length during the course of their storytelling. During other conversations, I occasionally translated Spanish terms the women used or contributed words for them when they seemed at a loss. I recognize this as an attempt both to help them through their discomfort and to put my words into their mouths. These interactions confirm the dialogic nature of fieldwork as well as the inherently unequal relationship created by a white academic with personal and professional agendas—including furthering feminist research and publishing—who collects personal narratives by immigrant women of color.[33] At the same time, the second-language English speakers, who have lived in the United States from ten to forty years, are effectively bilingual, using English daily to converse with their children, spouses, and co-workers or to transact business in their communities. Their "imperfect" English did not preclude them from powerfully conveying their emotions and experiences.

Power differences in the form of researcher control also take place in the post-fieldwork stage when the researcher is formulating the representation and writing and negotiating with editors.[34] In shaping the form of this manuscript, I considered various means by which the women's voices could be represented more or less unmediated. In particular, I wanted to minimize interference with their words by editing them as little as possible. I also wanted them to "speak first," prior to my critical analysis, in a prologue that opened the book, a move the editors rightfully opposed, noting that the oral histories were already mediated. The editors also thought that foregrounding excerpts from the oral histories at the beginning competed with the goals of an academic analysis that drew on them as evidence throughout the book. In addition, while the textual play with representation I proposed strove to decenter my power, it did nothing to resolve the real discrepancies of who has control of the women's words and for whose advantage. Having gathered more than fifty hours of taped oral histories, I ultimately include only brief segments of the life experiences and views the women narrated. Their representations of themselves are mediated by the fact that I chose to include the portions that fit my project's themes, rather than what the women may consider most important about their historias. For example, I read their historias through a feminist lens and represent the women as resisting and refiguring cultural norms, when their own interests may place more value on the struggles and pleasures of raising their children. I intend to publish the oral histories in a separate collection to provide a more complete perspective of their interests and narrative styles. Even that collection will be subject to editorial and publishing decisions made by myself and the editors. Ideally, I would like to engage the U.S. Mexicanas in decisions about the manuscripts' form and content.

Translating the oral into the written always represents a major revision of the spoken word, and my process in editing the historias is not different from other researchers' in this respect. I tried to preserve the nuances and idiosyncrasies of each speaker's presentations, but I agonized over how to represent the oral histories of the nonnative English speakers. Initially, I maintained sentence syntax as spoken and retained individual speech patterns, including some repetitions and incomplete sentences, because the speech patterns reflect the realities of bilingual and bicultural existences. Yet I do not want to misrepresent the women's thinking or speaking or to have their English-speaking ability influence the reading of their stories and subjectivities. My interest in presenting their words "as spoken" may also conflict with their interests. After reading the transcript of her historia, Loya suggested that the portions I include in the book should be made grammatically correct. I hesitated to do so because this would constitute a significant intervention in her narrative that borders on reproducing the colonial dynamics of white people "speaking for" people of color.[35] This dilemma points again to the repercussions of my decision to gather and publish the oral histories in English. This decision transformed several women who are articulate Spanish speakers into uncertain English speakers and may have altered their self-perceptions and self-representations. Ultimately, I edited Loya's historia by changing verb tenses and the structure of some sentences. On rare occasions, I inserted a different word to more accurately reflect the meaning that was being conveyed.

One of the ways I hoped to rectify somewhat the discrepancy in how much control I was exerting over the use of their words was to consider the women as collaborators in my project, although I neglected to ask them if this was a role they were willing to undertake. Before returning for another visit, I asked them to read and respond to what I had written. However, my concerns about accuracy and fair representation or about having them validate my work were not important to them. The responses of the Tucson women were instructive. When I contacted them for a second visit one-and-a-half years after our first meeting, Virginia Urias was concerned about whether she had talked equally about all of her children rather than about what I had written, and Evelyn Gonzales did not remember our first meeting when I contacted her by telephone to arrange a second. Although Gonzales later apologized profusely and told me she had remembered immediately after talking to me, her initial response was a rude awakening for me. I realized then that in transcribing their historias and writing about them, I had "lived" with the women, in a sense, and they had become important people to me, but that our interaction and my academic work were for them relatively insignificant.

I, having shared little about myself during our first meetings, was merely an acquaintance to them.

This changed somewhat with the second visit when I was invited to Urias's home, where I met her husband, photographed her in front of her altar to La Virgen de Guadalupe, gave her a copy of her transcribed historia, and told her about my hopes and disappointments for finding a job. Likewise, I attended a meeting of the Mensajeras de Salud at Gonzales's invitation where I listened intently as the group's members spoke in Spanish about their strategies and goals for encouraging women to receive breast and cervical examinations to increase early cancer detection. They were curious about my note taking and asked me to report on what I had written during the meeting. Realizing that they may be wondering how well I understood what they were saying, I gave my report in Spanish. I also shared with them my personal interest in research about women, my Catholic upbringing, and my history as an abuse survivor. At the close of the meeting, several of the women hugged me and Gonzales presented me with a gold and pink metal pin in the shape of a crossed ribbon representing breast cancer research. The well-known pin is sold by the Avon Corporation, which donates the proceeds to cancer research and awarded a large grant to the Tucson Mensajeras. In giving me the pin, Gonzales reminded me to "support our cause."

Rather than illustrating the extent of my involvement with the women, an involvement that might further "legitimate" my research, these incidents, I suggest, reveal the complicated interpersonal dynamics that oral history practice creates, including my desire for affirmation and their desire that I support their interests, financially as well as academically— certainly a fair request given the time, energy, and confidences they shared with me. These experiences also point out how the expectations and actions of the scholar, however well-intentioned, can magnify the already existing imbalances of the relationship. My interest in soliciting the women's reactions to my writings in hopes of creating a more "democratic" and thus "feminist" project failed to consider their time and interests. Not to recognize the implications of asking working-class and semiprofessional, second-language English speakers to read a fairly substantial number of typed pages written in academic prose by someone they barely knew or had forgotten was an oversight on my part. Only when I learned that the Tucson women had not even opened the manila envelopes heavy with portions of my manuscript did I fully realize the class, cultural, educational, and linguistic differences that separate us. Even the women who were native English speakers did not read the chapter sent to them, and I realized that I was asking them to use time that could be better spent in other ways. Although feminist scholarship has led the academy in questioning "objectivity" and in changing research practices, these experiences have reinforced for me the degree to which disparities exist and the limitations of an ideological position such as feminism to overcome them.[36]

Recent ethnographic literature suggests that the Western academic focus on research by individuals, especially outsiders, is a central problem. This literature proposes collective research models that directly involve the community being researched. One of the most ethical and equitable models researchers can follow focuses on volunteer participants who determine the research parameters and benefit from the research. The Latina Feminist Group came together to document and share the struggles and survival experiences of Latina academics through testimonio. Their seven-year collaboration resulted in an ongoing support system and the publication of *Telling to Live: Latina Feminist Testimonios*. Participants in the Puerto Rican women's literacy research project conducted by Rina Benmayor and her colleagues gained valuable skills such as learning to read and write during the research process. Projects that include reciprocity and the sharing of knowledge as their basis are more likely to be sensitive to a community's interests and well-being. For Linda Tuhiwai Smith, sharing research knowledge includes demystifying the way knowledge is constructed and represented.[37] In her groundbreaking work on indigenous research by Maori communities, Smith insists that indigenous peoples design, control, and disseminate research based in their own ways of knowing and being. Research by and for indigenous peoples addresses the misrepresentative and harmful effects of positivist, imperialist Western research methods and methodologies. As Smith elaborates, Maori research involves a core social unit that keeps indigenous values central to the project. It is based on collective rather than individual research and follows culturally sensitive and ethical practices that include reporting back to the community, giving voice to different entities within the community, and debating issues that impact the research. Nonindigenous researchers may be involved, performing specific activities based on a particular expertise as decided by the collective.[38]

Insider and outsider researchers must be ever attentive to how their status and location benefit them and contribute to the circumstances of those they are working with. At the same time, research conducted with respect, sensitivity, and an awareness of the historical conditions that created hierarchies and the individual and group interactions that reproduce them contributes to the potential for better understandings. The opportunity to meet and converse with the women in my study enriched my life and theirs. It opened new vistas for my understandings of women who prefer to call themselves Mexican, Mexican American, or Hispanic. It introduced them to an Anglo woman who is willing to "cross the border" to make their historias known, and to the existence of Chicana/o literature that portrays experiences similar to their own. Finally, I believe that these oral histories, which also will be archived, will contribute to future scholarly understandings of U.S. Mexicana thought and experience, as similar collections have done for me. The dynamics of power I have elaborated here are real and significant and cannot be ignored or minimized, but neither should they serve as reasons to retreat and disengage. This research and analysis process reinforced for me the importance of enlarging my understandings of power differences and my own implication in their maintenance. The narratives that emerged from the desire of a white woman to meet and talk with Chicanas and U.S. Mexicanas bear witness to the humanity of each individual and the respect and recognition that can result from sensitive face-to-face interactions.

CULTURAL REFIGURING AND THE POLITICS OF LOCATION

A number of questions kept recurring when I began thinking about the bold and radical Chicana feminist literary and artistic re-presentations of Mexican female cultural symbols. Are Chicana works read by U.S. Mexicanas outside the academy? What is the reception to Chicana feminist refigurings of gender roles and sexuality? Are symbols such as indigenous goddesses and La Malinche recognized and considered relevant to working-class and semiprofessional women? What significance do La Virgen de Guadalupe and La Llorona carry in working-class and semiprofessional women's everyday lives? What are their attitudes toward gender roles, motherhood, sexuality, and work outside the home? How do they identify themselves? What significance do they give to the multiple lineages of their heritage? How do they resist, mediate, or perpetuate cultural norms and stereotypes that regulate their lives? How do they describe their relationships with their fathers, brothers, husbands, lovers? Has verbal, physical, or psychological abuse ever been a part of these relationships? What are their experiences and understandings of racism and discrimination? These questions, derived from themes in the writings of various Chicana authors, motivated me to gather oral histories with working-class and semiprofessional women.

Many of the themes in the U.S. Mexicanas' historias coincide with those in the fictional and autobiographical writings of the professional intellectuals, for example, repression of female sexuality, limiting gender roles, inequality in male and female relationships, and violence against women. At the same time, the working-class and semiprofessional women's historias suggest a number of crucial differences between the characterizations they fashion of themselves and the professional intellectuals' self- and fictional representations. Three major differences are significant. First, the working-class and semiprofessional women identify themselves as Mexican, Mexican American, Hispanic, or American with Mexican heritage, in contrast to the more politicized identification, Chicana, that the writers use. Second, the types of resistance strategies the working-class and semiprofessional women engage focus on individual or local community circumstances, in contrast to the professional intellectuals' writings that address broad social and political concerns to a largely academic audience. Finally, but not surprisingly, the working-class and semiprofessional women's primary cultural and religious symbol is La Virgen de Guadalupe. In contrast, the early writings of the professional intellectuals emphasize indigenous goddesses. Their acceptance of La Virgen de Guadalupe came only after recovering her in the lineage of goddesses. In addition, the working-class and semiprofessional women's historias reveal that they are not aware of the existence of a body of writings called Chicana/o literature, nor have they read books written by Chicana authors. With the exception of one woman who lived near Sandra Cisneros and has read *The House on Mango Street*,[39] none of the women who spoke with me were familiar with Chicana/o authors or their writings. Four of the women indicated they enjoy reading literary works, but when they read they choose Latin American, European, or American canonized works.[40] Two of the older women, who were born and educated in Mexico, indicated familiarity with well-known Latin American male writers such as Gabriel García Márquez and Carlos Fuentes, but not with Chicano or Chicana writers, even those who have written in Spanish.[41] Two younger women, who attended high school in the United States and have taken several years of community college or university courses, had not read or even heard of Chicana/o literature. While this small sampling shows that some U.S. Mexicanas enjoy reading literary works, I would venture the premise that the working-class and semiprofessional population has little if any knowledge of Chicana/o literature.

A number of factors may be responsible for this lack of awareness: (1) Few Chicana/o writings have been published by major booksellers. Until the second half of the 1990s, most works were published by small presses and were relatively unknown outside academic circles.[42] (2) Chicana/o literature's emerging, yet still marginalized, status within both the Latin American and American canons means that it is taught infrequently in U.S. secondary schools and university Spanish or English departments and rarely, if ever, in Mexican or other Latin American university courses. In the early twenty-first century, there has been greater recognition and involvement of this body of literature within academia; however, it still is situated in the relatively unknown and disregarded position held by African American literature in the 1970s and 1980s. (3) Within Chicano studies programs begun in a few U.S. universities in the 1970s and 1980s, mostly male-authored literary works were taught, although this situation changed in the 1990s largely due to student demand and the publishing success and acclaim for Chicana authors. The larger issue is that few colleges and universities support Chicana/o or U.S. Latina/o studies programs and within many English and Spanish departments these literatures are not considered significant enough to be included as required courses in the curriculum. (4) Primary schools may not encourage Chicana/o and Latina/o children to read (or to succeed in school in general) or provide culturally relevant materials to motivate reading. A lack of quality bilingual education programs maintains high illiteracy rates among the Mexican immigrant population in the United States, especially recent and undocumented immigrants. These circumstances may be further compounded by schooling interrupted for work or to migrate to work. (5) Working-class and semiprofessional U.S. Mexicanas, like their European American counterparts, invest their time in television and cable culture rather than reading. Also, reading is an isolated individual activity that may be discouraged by an emphasis on familial activities.

The lack of awareness of Chicana/o literature by the working-class and semiprofessional women also may be related to issues of identity and various understandings of the term "Chicana/o." As noted, none of the women identifies using the term "Chicana." Moreover, seven of the nine women indicate that "Chicano" and "Chicana" contain negative connotations for them, signifying "lower-class" people, "illegal" border crossers, or individuals who lack pride in Mexican culture and identity. The differences in identification suggest variations in historical consciousness and reflect a politics of identity. Similar to the refigurings of the identities "black" and "Indian" in the 1960s and 1970s, the appellation "Chicana/o" reflects racial and ethnic pride and awareness of historical and contemporary oppressions. In particular, "Chicana/o" is a rejection of the U.S. government–adopted term "Hispanic," which refers to the European country, Spain, and its inhabitants, Spaniards, who colonized the ancient Mexican and Mayan peoples. Chicana feminist and lesbian identities, which also characterize the writers, further relate a sophisticated understanding of systemic oppressions, the intersectionality of gender and sexuality along with race and class, and the multipositional aspect of identity politics. The Chicano historian Rodolfo Acuña argues that in not using "Mexican" in the primary identificatory term, the Chicana/o civil rights movement missed the opportunity to incorporate the greater population in an ongoing struggle.[43] Moraga's use of the term "Mechicana/o" is an effort to bridge the separation of identities.

Castillo writes in *Massacre of the Dreamers* that "most Chicanas and Latinas lack *conscientización*. The majority of the populace, on either side of the border, in fact, is not actively devoted to real social change."[44] She maintains that a "sense of inferiority . . . permeates most Chicanas' self-perceptions," especially those who were born in or came at an early age to the United States and didn't develop enough identification with Mexican culture to combat American assimilation.[45] While I'm not disputing Castillo's assessment, the historias of the nine working-class and semiprofessional women in this study indicate a great deal of pride in their Mexican heritage. Several of them talked at length about the racism they have encountered or witnessed in the United States. Moreover, the fact that the women name themselves Mexican in some form indicates a conscious identification choice, which also appears to reinforce Acuña's point. Nonetheless, the women did not exhibit a historical awareness of the political, economic, and racial conditions that have caused Mexicans and Mexican Americans to deny or negate their indigenous ancestry and to seek assimilation into the dominant culture. For many who identify as Chicana/o, this consciousness is achieved through exposure to Chicana/o studies courses or Raza student center activities on college campuses, or through affiliation with local political resistance efforts and community artistic centers. For this reason, individuals who describe themselves as Chicana/os generally are or were affiliated in some capacity with the civil rights movement or intellectual, artistic, or activist environments. Through advanced education, the Chicana writers and artists have moved into class and social positions different from those of their working-class and semiprofessional counterparts.

The U.S. Mexicanas are located in a working-class and semiprofessional environment generally removed from the influences of a college Chicana/o studies program or activist politics. In their historias, they acknowledge an awareness of cultural shortcomings regarding the treatment of and expectations for women to a greater degree than racial issues. However, their greater willingness to talk about gender issues may be due to their discomfort in talking with a white person about race and racism. Their consciousness of women's issues is based in personal experiences of felt or witnessed gender oppression rather than an understanding of systems of oppression. Their resisting self-representations and actions are distinct from Chicana academic thinking yet can still be characterized as feminist and as working for cultural change. Despite the differences in social and economic locations, both the oral and written narratives express a spectrum of ideas and positions that can be situated within Chicana feminism.

As this study demonstrates, while many of the Chicana writers and artists were raised in lower-income circumstances and were the first generation to gain access to postsecondary education, the concerns and visions elaborated in their writings reflect a politicized academic orientation as well as their working-class backgrounds. They are socially concerned and yet removed from their communities or families even as they try to maintain contact. Unlike the working-class and semiprofessional women in this study, the professional intellectuals' educational opportunities and social economic locations allow them the choice to distance themselves for extended periods from their communities of origin, their families, and the Catholic Church. Consequently, they are far freer to take action against and make public critiques of oppressive institutional and cultural belief systems. In their writings, artwork, and lifestyles as out lesbians and feminists, they audaciously expose and challenge the heterosexism,

sexism, and racism of the Chicano/Mexicano and dominant cultures. My discussion here of the writers' middle-class, professional intellectual status is not intended to minimize the difficulties they overcame in achieving their current positions or the struggles they, and other Chicana/o writers and scholars, continue to face in achieving literary acceptance, funding for creative writing, or retention of academic positions. In fact, as the writings in *Telling to Live: Latina Feminist Testimonios* document, the intersecting oppressions experienced by women of color do not end when they achieve a higher economic or educational position in society.[46] Systemic oppressions are as embedded in higher education as in any other U.S. institution. Instead, I wish to highlight distinct cultural productions that arise from the different social conditions of working-class, semiprofessional and professional intellectual women while considering all of them as modes of Chicana feminism. The Chicana authors have written or spoken about their working-class origins and about the need to leave their families or communities to establish their own identities. For example, Anzaldúa, whose family eked out a meager existence by sharecropping, writes, "I had to leave home so I could find myself."[47] Yet the professional intellectuals' current locations and their revisionary strategies entail understandings and concerns somewhat different from those the working-class and semiprofessional women engage.

These differences are most apparent in their choice of representational symbols. The working-class and semiprofessional women affiliate with the Mexican Catholic Virgen de Guadalupe, suggesting their greater connection to the Catholic Church and to working-class interests with which Guadalupe often is associated. The professional intellectuals locate their primary female cultural symbol in indigenous spirituality by recovering the powerful and sexual mother earth goddesses, of which they consider La Virgen de Guadalupe an avatar. The rather late recuperation by the writers, compared to earlier efforts by visual artists, took place because the writers realized the continuing importance that Guadalupe's image asserts as a cultural identification and anti-assimilation figure for U.S. Mexicana/os.

Knowledge of the relatively unknown goddesses signals the professional intellectuals' access to books, libraries, and museums and contrasts with the responses of most of the working-class and semiprofessional women, who are unaware of the indigenous goddesses and don't consider them significant symbols in their lives. Instead, the working-class and semiprofessional women view indigenous cultural practices as ancient history, that is, as part of a distant past removed from their contemporary Mexican or Mexican American ethnic or racial existence. Castillo notes that the destruction and negation of indigenous cultural practices by the conquering Spaniards and the Catholic Church accounts for their relative obscurity. "Pre-Conquest history is probably deemed irrelevant to our daily lives by most of us. Save for scholars, most of our people can recite the Apostles' Creed but would be hard pressed to identify the Mexica (Aztec) sun god, Huitzilopochtli, or the earth goddess and mother of Huitzilopochtli, Coatlicue."[48] The responses of the working-class and semiprofessional women in this study coincide with Castillo's analysis. While sculptures of Mexica mother earth goddesses such as Coatlicue and Coyolxauhqui hold prominent places in Mexico City museums, they are not popularly embraced as emblems of contemporary U.S. Mexicana identity, perhaps in part due to the monstrous and disempowered images the sculptures represent. Indigenous representations, whether monstrous or maternal, have little meaning for women steeped in Mexican Catholicism who learned that the defeated indigenous peoples embraced the religion of the conquerors via the story of La Virgen de Guadalupe's appearance to the converted indigenous man, Juan Diego.

None of the working-class or semiprofessional women recalled the names of any goddesses, although several knew the names of male gods. However, when I mentioned specific goddesses, several of the women said they had heard of Coatlicue, Coyolxauhqui, or Tonantzin.[49] The women who grew up in Mexico consider the gods and goddesses as textbook history learned in school but not as part of the cultural memory that plays a role in their daily lives. Moreover, while they recognize and express pride in their indigenous heritage, they nonetheless distance themselves from it by saying that the goddesses were part of "the Indians'" religion. This move, placing "Indians" in the past rather than as part of the present, allows them to sidestep identification as "Indian" and avoid the racism still associated with this identity in both Mexico and the United States.[50] Lack of identification also contributes to the myth both governments have perpetuated in their national narratives—that "Indians" are "dead"—and allows the governments to abdicate responsibility for the living.[51] The five women who were educated in the United States knew nothing of the goddesses, further evidence of the effectiveness of Spanish colonial efforts to destroy the indigenous cultures, as well as the European American educational emphasis on ancient Greek and Roman civilizations. Similarly, only three women could identify La Malinche although none knew what is considered to be her indigenous name, Malintzin Tenepal.

The working-class and semiprofessional women's lack of knowledge about or identification with indigenous goddesses and Malintzin Tenepal signals how effectively indigenous Mexican female symbols and histories have been devalued and how identification with them has been denied as a viable option for Mexicanas on either side of the border. Rather than considering U.S. Mexicanas' devotion to Guadalupe or Mary as a contrast with Chicana writers' pantheistic emphasis, their beliefs must be understood in terms of the racist and colonialist history that attempted to erase indigenous beliefs and practices.

The goddesses and La Malinche hold appeal as symbols of indigenous culture and experience for those who are able to access understandings of their historical and political significance. Identification with them situates Chicanas as indigenous peoples and foregrounds the conquest and colonization of indigenous peoples in the past and the denial of indigenous existence in the present. However, because the Mexica goddesses are not significant elements of U.S. Mexicana popular memory, questions arise about their recuperation by scholars, writers, and artists regarding their broad cultural appeal and effectiveness in galvanizing popular sentiment and resistance. In a discussion of the Chicano nationalism movement of the 1960s and 1970s, which employed male god symbols to recover and show pride in indigenous identity, Rosa Linda Fregoso and Angie Chabram critique the "shortsightedness of Chicano studies intellectuals" in failing to recognize that representations of "an ahistorical 'Aztec' identity would fall on the deaf ears of an urban community versed in the rhythms of disco, *conjunto* music and *boleros.*"[52] In other words, they argue that indigenous imagery and symbolism did not evoke the sentiment necessary to rally U.S. Mexicana/os to engage in prolonged struggle because of the absence of the symbols' cultural currency.[53] Fregoso and Chabram's critique raises other questions. Can the images and symbols created by middle-class, college-educated writers and artists speak to or for working-class and semiprofessional women who have never heard of the goddesses or of Chicana/o literature? And should they be expected to?

Daniel Cooper Alarcón remarks that the ability to produce counter-discourses "may require some degree of privileged agency, such as the writers and artists have obtained through education and distance."[54] I expand Alarcón's definition to include the privileged access to publishers and the means to publish, which is generally invisible to people outside literary or academic circles. As I argue in chapter 3, however, the working-class and semiprofessional women also produce counterdiscourses through their personal acts of resistance and community-based group activities. Working toward a complex understanding of the multiple and diverse means of resistance and activism Chicanas and U.S. Mexicanas engage, I argue that each narrator's cultural refiguring strategy addresses concerns specific to the author's or oral historian's location. This perspective necessitates the acknowledgment of privileges by Chicana professional intellectuals even as they document their own marginalization within their culture as Chicana feminists and lesbians, within the European American dominant culture as women of color, and within the academy as nontenured or tenured faculty. Reassignments and firings of Chicana/o faculty and closings of Chicana/o studies programs reinforce that Chicana/o professional intellectuals struggle to achieve and maintain academic positions.[55] In other words, the same economic and political power structures that affect working-class and semiprofessional U.S. Mexicanas also are regulating Chicana scholars. The same applies for the Chicana writers who early in their careers often existed in a tenuous semirelationship with the academy conducting readings, giving speeches, or accepting part-time or temporary teaching positions. More recently, the reputations of the writers I discuss have been established such that they can command high speaking or reading fees and/or permanent affiliations with major universities.

I raise these issues not to discount the working-class backgrounds of the professional intellectuals or to call into question the authenticity of their experiences or writings. Rather, my concern is with how we in the academy view and interpret different sites of cultural refiguring. On the basis of the U.S. Mexicanas' historias (albeit limited in scope and number) and interviews with the Chicana writers and interpretations of their works, I find that significant convergences exist, especially on feminist issues. The working-class and semiprofessional women's historias reveal they are concerned about limited gender roles, autonomy, sexuality, violence against women, and female spirituality, in addition to economic concerns—all issues the professional intellectuals' writings elaborate. The similarities between the themes found in Chicana writings and the experiences expressed in the working-class and semiprofessional women's oral histories support my contention that Chicana writings portray significant issues in working-class women's lives. Even if they are not read by the women or if the theoretical nature of the writing makes them inaccessible, working-class and semiprofessional women's concerns and experiences are still being represented to a great extent. Most important, these and other Chicana writings have inspired countless women and men to imagine their own representational strategies and theories and have created awareness of Chicana *and* U.S. Mexicana lives and experiences among a broader academic and literary audience.

Rather than favoring the cultural refiguring strategies of one socioeconomic location over the other, for example, the working-class and semiprofessional women's praxis over the professional intellectual women's theory, or the oral over the written representations, I view them as existing within a spectrum of social change activities. All need to be considered to better understand the simultaneous oppression and resistance experienced by Chicanas and U.S. Mexicanas. Further study of the experiences and ideas of middle-class, professional Mexican American women, who are not part of this analysis, regarding identity politics, Mexican female cultural symbols, reading preferences, gender roles, and sexualities would provide an even more complex picture.

While there are many similarities in subject matter within the writings and the oral histories, there also are significant differences in the representational figures with which the academic-oriented writers and the nonacademic-oriented oral historians affiliate—in particular, the historical consciousness (memory) that indigenous goddesses and La Virgen de Guadalupe differently signify for each group. Consequently, I contend that the images and symbols created by the professional intellectual writers cannot necessarily be expected to appeal to or represent working-class and semiprofessional women's beliefs, even though they may. While some concerns overlap, issues distinctive to each social and economic location produce different representational and practical strategies. For this reason it is important to distinguish the discursive and material practices of change workers in various locations and consider the specific circumstances of each in assessing the effectiveness of the resistance. The cultural change strategies each group or individual favors are determined by the particular and shifting concerns and interests of each narrator's social and economic location. Cultural refiguring occurs in multiple locations and class and educational status determine the *type or means* of refiguring that is engaged.

The oral histories indicate that the working-class and semiprofessional women practice cultural refiguring in two modes of activity: (1) They participate in local service organizations such as the Mensajeras de Salud, which Urias, Gonzales, and Vásquez worked for, and the Muscatine free health clinic, which Godoy volunteered at on Saturdays. These structured group activities address concerns of community members outside each woman's familial or personal interests. Their cooperative volunteer efforts culturally refigure understandings of women's bodies within specific families or constituency groups and enhance women's dignity, autonomy, and pleasure. In addition, they contribute to the physical health, safety, and emotional needs of the larger Mexican American and Mexican immigrant community. (2) They produce individual actions and self-representations that respond to oppressive situations and ideologies as well as positive achievements each woman has experienced in her life. Such individual actions include Loya's long-term struggles to resist and eventually leave an abusive relationship. Her oral history self-representation portrays her as a fighter and a survivor. Another example is Vásquez's decision not to marry in order to work outside the home. She represents herself as "a happy single." The *oral* narrative form reflects the working-class and semiprofessional women's more immediate and action-oriented approaches. They would not think of their community work or individual actions from a U.S. Third World women's or Chicana feminist perspective, but their refigurings are woman oriented and culturally specific. Moreover, the sources from which the U.S. Mexicanas draw their power derive from their social, economic, and educational context. Several of the working-class women affiliate with local organizations such as the YWCA, the free health clinic, or the Catholic Church, which provide economic support and a space for meetings and activities. In addition, these women personally contribute by volunteering time, energy, and thought to help community members in need such as new immigrants and undocumented women and men. Others who act individually to remedy situations within their personal relationships find their power sources in personal communication with La Virgen de Guadalupe or by following a role model whom they witnessed resisting violence and control. For example, Harada credits La Virgen de Guadalupe with sustaining her efforts to live independently, get a GED, and begin artistic craft work that fulfilled her. Siqueiros followed her mother's (Loya's) contesting actions to extricate herself from an abusive marriage.

The professional intellectuals' written and artistic output performs cultural refiguring in three distinct but often intertwined modes of expression: (1) creative stories and images that represent real women's lives and dreams; (2) critical analyses that expose discourses of power and embedded hierarchies; and (3) contemplative and theoretical ideas that reflect contemporary reality and envision a new future. For example, Sandra Cisneros's short story "Little Miracles, Kept Promises" creatively imagines a Chicana character who learns to access the power of La Virgen de Guadalupe rather than the message of submission. Yolanda López's paintings visualize her mother, grandmother, and herself possessing the same dignity and respect as the revered Virgen de Guadalupe. López imagines human beings, particularly women, as divine. Gloria Anzaldúa's writings reveal and invite deep spiritual contemplation about Chicanas' relationship to the universe and to divinity. Anzaldúa fosters awareness of difference, oppression, and multicultural understanding through the theorizing of mestiza consciousness and the borderlands. Alma López's digital art creations of Guadalupe and Llorona figures simulate actual women's experiences with sexuality, body image, and violence at the turn of the twenty-first century. All these works present implied or stated critiques of long-standing, harmful discourses and representations of Chicanas. The writers and artists are especially interested in the empowering potential of memory and counterdiscourse representing sovereignty for self and community. This work has become their profession. They advocate far-reaching and sometimes radical social change from an overtly Chicana feminist activist position revealing their research-based awareness of how the histories of racism and colonialism in the Americas impact contemporary Chicanas' lives. They are inspired by the possibilities of art to enact political resistance and advocate change, and by an indigenous spirituality conceptualizing powerful women through Mexica goddesses and other Mexican female cultural symbols. They derive power from researched and critical academic thought and social justice and civil rights movements. Their work occasionally reaches a broad U.S. Mexicana/o audience through the staging of plays and readings and the exhibition of artwork in community centers or on public buildings. Yet the writers affiliate with and their works are received primarily by an artistic,

intellectual community that extends far beyond their community of residence or birth. With the exception of the mural collective Maestrapeace,
the writers and artists work individually, isolated from other authors,
painters, and their audiences. However, once the works are published or
exhibited they become public, open for examination and interpretation by
anyone who is able to access or afford them, both crucial issues.

Anzaldúa acknowledges that she writes for intellectual, artistic, and
academic audiences but defines the professional intellectuals' location as
"in between." "I think the artists—writers, visual artists, performing artists, video artists—fall somewhere between the academy and the community and many of us depend on the community to show our work, to give
us grants, to allow us to teach."[56] Here she refers to community centers
such as the Guadalupe Cultural Arts Center in San Antonio located in the
heart of the Mexican community, as well as Chicana/o studies programs
at various colleges and universities. While her use of the term "community" implies a membership including working-class and semiprofessional individuals, most of the women state in their oral histories that they
do not participate in artistic or activist events even when the programs are
sponsored by centers located in their neighborhoods. As Anzaldúa herself
notes, the community members who may be most influenced by her ideas
are the "young Latinas and Latinos working on their B.A.'s," exposed to
her writings in Chicana/o studies and women's studies courses.[57] The
ethnographic nature of much of Chicana writing and painting, derived
from insider knowledge of family and community experiences, serves to
create awareness of the experiences of an often underrepresented or misrepresented people.[58] Yet the use of abstract language or little-known
symbols and images such as mother earth goddesses suggests resource
and access opportunities based on educational and socioeconomic differences. Such differences identify the existence of and may even reinforce
inequalities between the writers and artists and their working-class kin.
Ruth Behar characterizes the tensions engendered when she writes about
her family: "In writing about my parents, I also seem to be trying to mark
the distance I've traveled, the distance that separates me from them and
gives me the power to describe our relationship."[59] Her analyses of how
race, class, gender, and nationality tensions play out within her Jewish
Cuban American family and between herself and the Mexican woman
whose life history she compiled express the complicated dynamics that
pertain when professional intellectuals move in milieus and possess aca-

demic understandings that family members or research participants can-not access. Ideally, insights shared interactively between research partici-pants and professional intellectual researchers and writers would expose commonalities of oppression and their hidden structures. Yet because academia does not reward community work or activism and because writ-ing and artistry require a degree of distance and seclusion, such under-standings are difficult to ensure, even if family or community members desire them, which oftentimes they do not. Behar notes that her parents are not interested in explanations of her analyses. A similar situation existed for Anzaldúa. After she died in May 2004, her family was sur-prised and overwhelmed by the outpouring of condolences they received. Because of ideological differences and respect for their social, economic, and educational location, she had not told them that she was a well-known and respected writer or that her published works enticed a broad reader-ship and loyal following.

Behar's and Anzaldúa's examples emphasize the importance of analyz-ing locations to grasp nuanced understandings of power, domination, and resistance. The politics of location demands that we tease out complexities which shape oral and written narratives and working-class, semiprofes-sional, and professional intellectual thoughts and actions.

✿ CONCLUSION

In broad terms, the working-class and semiprofessional women's cultural refiguring strategies address individual or local community concerns through action-oriented redefinitions of women's roles and female sexuality. Their refigurings take the form of individual resistance to domination or volunteer work in community organizations aimed at alleviating oppressive conditions. The professional intellectuals' refiguring strategies address cultural, national, and global concerns by rewriting and re-presenting denigrating ideologies and symbols of women. At times, the strategies between the two groups cross over and realize similar effects. For example, when Chicana literary writings inspire campus activism protesting racism, sexism, or heterosexism, they are achieving action-oriented results as well as new symbolic understandings. Or when the working-class and semiprofessional women's local community efforts encourage women to seek health care and view their bodies as deserving attention, they redefine the symbolic meaning of a "good woman" from someone who serves others' needs to one who fulfills her own needs and desires. These examples indicate that theory and praxis are intertwined elements of cultural refiguring. Collectively, the working-class, semiprofessional, and professional intellectual women's actions serve as exemplary models informing and inspiring other women toward self-determination and initiating changes in the way women's roles and bodies are perceived.

My analysis of privilege and power in relation to the locations of the working-class, semiprofessional, and professional intellectual women attempts to unravel distinctions that influence the choices women make in creating visions of their lives and in acting upon those visions. Besides illuminating differences along educational and economic axes, this examination divulges commonalities of struggle and reformation found in various geographical, ideological, and economic locations among oral, written, and visual texts. Regardless of Chicanas' and U.S. Mexicanas' social and economic locations, the female symbol they affiliate with, or how they identify, their narratives indicate that they are engaged in claiming and redefining power for themselves and others. That some symbols and images, such as La Virgen de Guadalupe and La Llorona, circulate in all locations with various and sometimes contestatory significations, while others, such as indigenous goddesses, retain currency limited to artistic or academic locations, testifies to the complexity of Chicana/o and U.S. Mexicana/o culture. This diversity within the culture "must be the linchpin of any political strategy or project" as the historian Alex Saragoza argues.[1] Fregoso and Chabram's statement that there are "many faces of the Chicano/Latino people" reaffirms there is not a single text, image, or meaning that represents all Chicanas and U.S. Mexicanas.[2] Particular circumstances inspire diverse practices contributing to the making of history and cultural meaning. This perspective highlights the importance of examining authorial (in the broad sense of the term) locations to better understand the political and economic ramifications of individual or group resistance and empowerment efforts. Unraveling power variances and analyzing the distinct modes of cultural refiguring that give power to each agent, as this study does, inhibits universalizing notions of Chicana/o and U.S. Mexicana/o peoples and practices. The identification of diverse responses to oppression situates the narrators along a continuum of feminist thinking and revisioning and shows how each refiguring influences or expands the lives of Chicanas and U.S. Mexicanas who exist in varied circumstances and locations.

The mutual refigurings of La Llorona and La Virgen de Guadalupe by Chicanas and U.S. Mexicanas underscore the symbols that are most salient within the culture as a whole. Guadalupe's significance as the symbol of Mexico links the Chicana writers and artists and the U.S. Mexicana oral historians to a national, ancestral, and spiritual homeland establishing their Mexicanness. At the same time, their narratives work to redefine Guadalupe's history as a confining gender role model. The oral and written narratives show how Guadalupe can be refashioned to express the issues facing late-twentieth-century and early-twenty-first-century women. The refigurings of Guadalupe to represent "modern" women's lives, to use Evelyn Gonzales's term,[3] or postmodern thought continue to be the most culturally significant and contentious alterations among the Chicana and U.S. Mexicana narratives and artwork. The December 2006 censoring of Anna-Marie López's refiguring of La Virgen de Guadalupe by the Centro Cultural Aztlan in San Antonio clearly exemplifies this point. More than thirty years of protest have followed artists' representations of Guadalupe as an embodied and sexualized being, beginning with Ester Hernandez's 1975 karate-kicking Guadalupe; to Yolanda López's 1978 Guadalupe series, which includes a dark-skinned indigenous Guadalupe breast-feeding a baby; to the turmoil caused in Mexico City in 1984 when the journal *fem* published on its cover an image of Guadalupe in high heels and a dress hemmed just below the knee; to Alma López's 1999 multimedia work of La Virgen wearing a modest two-piece swimsuit of flowers. Anna-Marie López's partially clad Guadalupe continues a tradition of refiguring La Virgen's corporeality and sexuality. Paradoxically, the Catholic Church and dedicated Marianistas decry the refigurings as profane, while Chicana feminist artists and authors revere the female body and sexuality as sacred. In the case of La Virgen de Guadalupe, the contestation of what constitutes sacred or profane representation will likely continue for years to come.

Chicana writers' and artists' refigurings of La Llorona include her within the pantheon of goddesses and embody her spirit in the faces, feelings, and flesh of real women. Even in the oral narratives, La Llorona signifies more than just a scary story of a "bogie(wo)man." She represents cultural and gendered anxieties that shift and change depending upon circumstances of place and period. Whether it is parental concern about children drowning attributed to a "bad mother" figure, male anxiety about the power of female sexuality, female concern about pregnancy or sexual abuse, teenage delinquents' feelings of loss and abandonment, masculine apprehension about losing control over women and children, or plays and short writings that challenge national and gendered myths, stories involving La Llorona traverse the psychological terrain of an active and expanding cultural production. Far from "assimilating" or dying out, La Llorona's refiguring signifies the persistence of lo mexicano in the United States, and even more broadly Latinidad. As an example of the latter, the graphic arts students who worked on the La Llorona Got Milk advertising campaign identify their ancestry or national origin from various Central or

Latin American countries as well as Mexico. The common experience among them was knowledge of La Llorona's legend. As with the refiguring of other Mexican female cultural symbols, Chicana authors' and artists' revisions of La Llorona maintain the emotion of circumstances and experiences that haunt people. However, the theme of these La Llorona revisions is redemptive, not in a religious or moral sense but from the perspective of bringing justice or hope to humanity. In the case of several fictional works, the outcome of La Llorona's story is reversed to represent gain rather than loss.

Guadalupe's and La Llorona's transnational migrations across the Rio Grande/Río Bravo and across class, gender, and generation signify their appeal as popular culture symbols and as discursive agents of cultural refiguring. In refiguring these symbols to reflect the potential and actuality for greater female autonomy and agency, the oral, written, and visual texts depict resistance to neocolonial nationalisms as well as colonizations of women's bodies within cultural and personal relationships.

These refigurings reveal the intersecting themes in the oral, written, and visual texts and among working-class, semiprofessional, and professional intellectual women's ideas and experiences. They represent the circulation of U.S. feminist and women of color philosophies at the beginning of the twenty-first century. A significant feature of the intersecting themes regards the trans-coding of meaning by reappropriating existing meanings and reassigning new ones.[4] The refigurings also convey the recurrence of past events and experiences in the present as en/countered by Mexican and U.S. Third World women.[5] Similar to the Mexica's recurring use of the woman of discord to rewrite their history, the writers, artists, and oral historians in this study rewrite history and story to counter contemporary colonization and white and male dominance. The en/counters that they depict reveal that oppressive conditions similar to those experienced in precolonial and colonial periods continue in contemporary women's lives. Like the genealogy of the woman of discord, such portrayals represent the experience of one and many Chicanas and U.S. Mexicanas, transgressive women, real and divine, who generate change. In this instance, the refiguring occurs for the purposes of feminist empowerment, rather than reinforcing Mexica conquest and patriarchal gain. That refigurings of Mexican female cultural symbols, including La Malinche and the indigenous goddesses, cross cultural and national boundaries and carry significance in two or more countries reveals that they are not only refigurations but transfigurations in the dual sense that they are continually in transit and being reimagined.

Another form of intersectionality occurs when the oral, written, and artistic representations include features of three or more of the female symbols in one characterization. For example, the authors' and artists' representations of a fictional character or artistic figure may feature La Malinche's betrayal by her own people *and* La Llorona's presence by a river *and* the life and death dualism of the goddesses of which La Virgen de Guadalupe is a manifestation. Or an oral historian's self-representation may portray a wailing woman moment (La Llorona) *and* a Coyolxauhqui warrior act *and* communication with La Virgen de Guadalupe. In other words, the depiction of one woman/character often intersects features— historical, experiential, and/or visual—which identify her as La Malinche *and* La Llorona *and* La Virgen de Guadalupe *and* a Mexica mother earth goddess. In this way, one depiction relates the symbolic and historical meanings of all four cultural figures to the present experience of Chicanas and U.S. Mexicanas, conveying the intersectionality of oppressions and identities.

This cross-dressing move performs several transgressive functions. It challenges teleologies of progress regarding sexism, racism, classism, and heterosexism in indigenous and mestiza women's experience by re-vealing that oppressions of the past continue in the present. It also re-inforces the survival and self-determination of indigenous women and mestizas into the future. As the Chicana/o, U.S. Mexicana/o, and U.S. Latina/o populations continue to grow in the twenty-first century and as technology becomes more prevalent, all four of the refigured and cross-dressed Mexican female cultural symbols may transmigrate throughout the Americas and beyond. Already, many of the revised images have be-come popular culture icons among younger members of the population for whom transnational and transcultural identities are a way of life. Pub-lic access to Chicana feminist writings and art on the Internet has national and international significance. Artists' and writers' websites and blogs discuss their works and their political concerns and convictions and ex-pose any censorship that occurs. Rather than representing a fleeting trend, cultural refiguring begun by Chicana artists and writers in the 1980s informs and renews Mexican and Chicana/o culture. This study pursues the relevancy of the revised Mexican female cultural symbols into the new millennium and in diverse locations, wherever and however Chicanas and U.S. Mexicanas live.

The persistence of indigenous peoples in the United States, Mexico, and Central America, and the significance for Chicana/os of recovering indigenous Mexican identity and history remain important themes for the artists and writers. The Chicana professional intellectuals' embrace of contemporary indigenous identity signals the greatest difference in consciousness between them and the working-class and semiprofessional women. In political terms, Chicana/os' identification as indigenous peoples contests the U.S. and Mexican governments' denials of the abiding and substantial indigenous presence in contemporary North America. As this study shows, written and artistic representations of indigenous identity also combat cultural genocide. Still, several issues emerge in the Chicana professional intellectuals' use of the ancient goddesses and the term "Aztec," and their portrayals of indigenous culture. Although most of the Chicana writers and artists in this study historicize their refigurings of goddesses linked to the Mexica domination of Central Mexico and the Spanish conquest, and several refer to the histories of specific groups such as the Yaqui, occasionally their writings romanticize indigeneity and generalize beliefs and practices. In addition, a focus on the Mexica peoples and practices or broad references to the "Aztecs," who resided in the central plateau region, overlook the varied histories, experiences, cultures—including deities, and geographical locations of the numerous other indigenous groups in precolonial and contemporary North America. At the same time, much Chicana/o and European American scholarship takes a similar approach owing in part to a lack of available or accurate information on family ancestries and in part to the Spanish chroniclers' and early anthropologists' and historians' focus on the great civilization of Tenochtitlan. The latter constitutes the primary material available for scholarly research. Greater attention by all scholars and writers to the differences in histories and cultural beliefs among indigenous peoples of the precolonial Tenochtitlan region, and to the particularities of contemporary indigenous peoples elsewhere in Mexico and the U.S. Southwest, would convey a richer, more complex view of indigenous experiences and Chicana/o heritage in the past and present.

In the twenty-first century, several Chicana/o writers have taken up this task in fictional works, depicting indigenous peoples who were not colonized by the Spaniards or for geographical reasons were not as harshly subjugated in the sixteenth century as were the peoples of the central Mexican plateau region. Instead, their histories are marked by the Mexican government's violence against them and their resistances in the late nineteenth and twentieth centuries. Among these are the Yaqui, Tarahumara, Tomochiteco, and Opata peoples living in the mountain ranges and deserts of northern Mexico, and the Lacandon, Tzeltal, and Tzotzil peoples living in the rainforests of southern Chiapas.[6] Recent writings also depict circumstances of specific ethnic and racial mixing, voluntary or violent, which contribute to understandings of Chicana/o indigenous and mestiza/o history and ancestry. As the themes of these writings indicate, the recognition of indigenous identity and the excavation of histories are ongoing. And as this study notes, the recovery of memory and history is partial, fluid, and in constant flux. I have tried to show how the professional intellectuals' refigurings of Mexica goddesses and other Mexican female cultural symbols draw on representations from earlier time periods and have contributed to particular forms of cultural production (writings and artworks) that have responded to intellectual thought from the 1970s to the present. In addition, I suggest how these forms are related to the broader production and reception of cultural meaning among Chicana/os and U.S. Mexicana/os during this period. In particular, I emphasize that the creative and inspirational qualities of these works and their ability to evoke diverse responses, from spiritual insights to angry protests, are key to understanding their power in reproducing and transforming cultural meaning.

Similarly, the self-representations of the working-class and semiprofessional women and their refigurings of symbols such as La Virgen de Guadalupe to reflect their philosophies of life are also products of their time and place. What is clear is the impact of second-wave feminisms on the self-representations by the U.S. Mexicanas even as they avoid the term "feminist." It is also clear that the oral historians participate in the wide range of opportunities contemporary U.S. society provides for women, and that they are actively working for social change. And despite criticisms to the contrary, this study shows that Chicana feminist writings continue to address significant concerns affecting real women's lives, including those of working-class and semiprofessional women, and to redefine what it means to be a Chicana or U.S. Mexicana into the twenty-first century.

✿ NOTES

INTRODUCTION

1. Anzaldúa, "Doing Gigs," 216.
2. Moraga, "A Long Line of Vendidas," 136.
3. Lila Abu-Lughod warns against feminist scholars' inclination to "romance resistance" when studying women's attempts to gain power ("The Romance of Resistance," 16, and *Writing Women's Worlds*, 13).
4. Common themes of those I located included recollections of Mexico and traditional lifestyles, women's work within and outside the home, and participation in labor struggles. Several early collections in which women of Mexican origin or ancestry are represented include Hubert Bancroft's California histories of the 1870s at the Bancroft Library, University of California, Berkeley, and the Federal Writers Project New Mexico collection of the 1930s and 1940s at the History Library of the Museum of New Mexico in Santa Fe. Genaro Padilla, in *My History, Not Yours*, notes that many personal narratives lie buried in archives and when unearthed will constitute "a huge inventory that must, and shall, overturn the ethnocentric assumption that Mexican American culture has a meager literary production" (5). However, he also acknowledges that many of the written narratives, as opposed to oral narratives, were produced by ricos, members of the landed upper class (x), and that "women's narratives were considered supplemental to men's" (111). In a survey of several university and state historical society collections in Texas, New Mexico, and Arizona, I found only a small number of archived narratives. A number of transcribed oral histories can be found at the Arizona State Historical Society in Tucson, although they are not well catalogued and one must locate them by skimming the catalogue for individual names. An excellent collection housed at the University of New Mexico Center for Southwest Research is Cecilia Portal's "Las Mujeres de la Tierra del Sol/Women from the Land of the Sun." Also, Fran Leeper Buss's "Work and Family: Low Income and Minority Women Talk about their

Lives" includes but does not exclusively comprise oral histories by women of Mexican origin or ancestry. This collection is housed at the University of Arizona Special Collections Library and at the Arthur and Elizabeth Schlesinger Library of the History of Women in America at Radcliffe College, Harvard University. Published oral histories compiled by Buss include *Forged under the Sun* and Jesusita Aragon's life history, *La Partera*. Other published oral histories include *Las Mujeres*, compiled by Nan Elsasser, Kyle MacKenzie and Yvonne Tixier y Vigil, and *Songs My Mother Sang to Me*, compiled by Patricia Preciado Martin. Scholarly works containing oral histories by Mexican-origin women include Patricia Zavella's *Women's Work and Chicano Families*; Barbara Kingsolver's *Holding the Line*; and Marilyn Davis's *Mexican Voices/American Dreams*. Recent publications include the Latina Feminist Group's *Telling to Live* and Alma García's *Narratives of Mexican American Women*. I intend to donate the oral histories I gathered to appropriate archives including the Iowa Women's Archives at the University of Iowa.

5. The oral history–gathering process took place from 1995 to 1997. Vicki Rivera Reyes is a pseudonym.

6. See García, *Narratives of Mexican American Women* 176, 188, and Smith, *Decolonizing Methodologies*, 126.

7. Edward Said's definition of the type of work public intellectuals do is relevant to the Chicana writers and artists I discuss. "The intellectual's role is first to present alternative narratives and other perspectives on history than those provided by combatants on behalf of official memory and national identity, who tend to work in terms of falsified unities, the manipulation of demonized or distorted representations of undesirable and/or excluded populations, and the propagation of heroic anthems sung in order to sweep all before them" ("The Public Role of Writers and Intellectuals," 37).

8. See Boyce Davies, "Collaborations and the Ordering Imperative in Life Story Production."

9. Scott, "Everyday Forms of Peasant Resistance," 5–6.

10. Tlahtoki Xochimeh argues, "Aztekism, the myth that all peoples from the central Mexican plateau region are 'Aztec,' leads to dehumanization." He suggests that Chicana and Chicano scholars perpetuate the myth in continuing to use the term "Aztec" in recent published books and articles.

CHAPTER ONE: THE POWER OF REPRESENTATION

1. "American" is placed within quotation marks here to recognize that U.S. citizens are not the only residents of the Americas.

2. Hall, "The Spectacle of the 'Other,'" 270.

3. Gillespie, *The Aztec Kings*, xxiii.

4. Ibid., xl–xli.

5. Ibid., 101.

6. Ibid., 24. The extant historical genealogical accounts (codices) that Gilles-pie studied were written after the conquest by indigenous writers under Span-ish tutelage. The Mexica and other indigenous peoples before them kept few permanent records of events, relying instead on oral and pictographic memory traditions susceptible to manipulation and overwriting. In the early stages of the conquest, a calculated effort was made by the Spaniards to kill all the Mexica priests who held control of the sacred memories; only later did the Spaniards realize that the indigenous priests held important keys to understanding the culture. Consequently, the Mexica survivors who were charged with represent-ing their history after the conquest were influenced by the Spaniards who oversaw this effort. Gillespie argues that the indigenous chroniclers lent their own postconquest interpretations to the writing process. For example, she says the chroniclers structured the Mexica defeat by the Spaniards as an "inevitable" repetition of a previous defeat by the Toltecas (their cultural forebears). Simul-taneously, she suggests, this "prophetic" structure expresses the indigenous chroniclers' resistance to the Spaniards by incorporating the "hope" that the descendants of the Mexica will rise again (xli). Thus, she reads the codices as another rewriting of Mexica history.

7. Poole disputes this idea as a fact (*Our Lady of Guadalupe*, 5). However, its significance remains in the story told by Catholic priests to the faithful and their belief in it.

8. Lincoln, *Discourse and the Construction of Society*, 3–4.

9. Ibid.

10. Poole, *Our Lady of Guadalupe*, 5–10.

11. Ibid., 1–2.

12. Cypess, *La Malinche in Mexican Literature*, 41–45.

13. Living in the late seventeenth century, Sor Juana is considered the first Latin American (proto) feminist. As a young girl she dressed in boy's clothes so that she could attend school. She entered the convent in order to continue her studies in math, astronomy, philosophy, religion, and literature. Her poetry is considered among the best of the Golden Age and she became known as the Tenth Muse. Today she is most famous for "La Repuesta," an essay written in reply to a religious cleric who claimed that women had no capacity to learn. Doña María Josefa Ortiz de Domínguez, also known as "La Corregidora," was a member of a criollo group that advocated independence for Mexico. On Sep-tember 16, 1810, when their plans were discovered, she alerted Father Miguel Hidalgo whose famous call to arms, "El grito de Dolores," began the rebellion against the Spanish. Teresa Urrea was a northern Mexican curandera (healer) and champion of the indigenous peoples oppressed during the reign of Porfirio Díaz in the late 1800s. Her attempted arrest by Díaz's troops sparked an indige-nous rebellion. La Adelita served as a soldier in the Mexican Revolution, 1910–

20. Emma Tenayuca was a prominent labor organizer and communist party member in Texas in the late 1930s and 1940s. Dolores Huerta is vice president and chief negotiator for the United Farm Workers, which represents migrant workers in California and other states.

14. Alarcón, "Chicana Feminism," 248.

15. Brief documentaries have been produced such as *Chicana* (1992), by Sylvia Morales, and *Adelante Mujeres* (1992), by the National Women's History Project.

16. October 2, 2004, to January 2, 2005.

17. Romo, "Mestiza Aesthetics and Chicana Painterly Visions," 24.

18. Although his initial vision was limited only to male works, Marin has championed Chicana/o art for many years and has inaugurated the "Chicano School of Painting," which portrays "a visual interpretation of a shared culture" bound together by "the DNA of a common shared experience" (Marin, "Introduction," 7). His untiring efforts for ten years to find corporate sponsorship for a national exhibition resulted in funding for an almost unprecedented five-year, eleven-city tour. He plans to reconfigure the exhibition and take Chicana/o art international.

19. Martínez, ed., *500 años del pueblo chicano*.

20. Rodríguez and Gonzales, "Teachers Suffer Consequences for Challenging Traditional History."

21. See Halbwachs, *The Collective Memory* and *On Collective Memory*; Nora, "Between Memory and History"; LeGoff, *History and Memory*; Teski and Climo, *The Labyrinth of Memory*; Terdiman, "Deconstructing Memory"; Hastrup, ed. *Other Histories*; Küchler and Melion, *Images of Memory*; Yates, *The Art of Memory*; Roberts and Allen Roberts, eds., *Memory*.

22. Nora, "Between Memory and History," 8–9.

23. Rousso, *The Vichy Syndrome*, 4, 10.

24. Lipsitz, *Time Passages*, 213–14.

25. Saldívar, *Chicano Narrative*, 4–5.

26. Gregorio Cortéz became a folk hero after successfully eluding the Texas Rangers when he was falsely accused of horse theft and shot the sheriff in self-defense. Jacinto Treviño became a folk hero after killing the Anglo boss who was beating his half brother. Like Cortéz, Treviño also eluded capture by the Texas Rangers who were brought in to search for him. Cesar Chávez was the president of the United Farm Workers, which protested working conditions and low wages of migrant workers in California. Known for his nonviolent approach, Chávez secured wage increases and union contracts with corporate grape farm owners during the 1960s and 1970s. All three men are the subject of corridos, border ballads that function as modes of Mexican pride and resistance to Anglo domination.

27. Lipsitz, *Time Passages*, 228.

28. See Halbwachs, *The Collective Memory*, 85–87; Le Goff, *History and Memory*, 98; Davis and Starn, "Introduction," 4.

29. In *Our Lady of Guadalupe*, Stafford Poole questions the manifestation of La Virgen in the sixteenth century. He notes that the first known account of La Virgen's appearance story was not published until the following century, in 1648. Its impact on the indigenous peoples is unknown, but it became very popular among the criollos, who saw themselves as marginalized (1).

30. Fregoso and Chabram, "Introduction," 205–6.

31. See plate 10, *Coatlicue*, in Herrera-Sobek, ed., *Santa Barraza*.

32. Küchler and Melion, *Images of Memory*, 6–7.

33. Cockroft and Barnet-Sánchez, eds., *Signs from the Heart*, 9. As was the case after the Mexican Revolution, the civil rights movement inspired a revival of muralism. However, this new mural movement differed in many important ways from the Mexican one. It was not sponsored by a successful revolutionary government but came out of the struggle by the people themselves against the status quo. Instead of well-funded projects in government buildings, these new murals were located in the barrios (neighborhoods) and inner cities, where oppressed people lived. They served as an inspiration for struggle, a way of reclaiming a cultural heritage, or even as a means of developing self-pride. Perhaps most significantly, these murals were not the expression of an individual vision. Artists encouraged local residents to join them in discussing the content and, often, in doing the actual painting (9).

34. Terdiman, "Deconstructing Memory," 29.

35. Cited in Fregoso and Chabram, "Introduction," 206.

36. Miller and Taube, *The Gods and Symbols of Ancient Mexico and the Maya*, 81.

37. For excellent sources on the manifestations and interrelationships of the Central Mexico mother earth goddesses, see Nicholson, "Religion in Pre-Hispanic Central Mexico," and Sullivan, "Tlazolteotl-Ixcuina." For depictions of individual goddesses, I have relied heavily on Nicholson, "Religion in Pre-Hispanic Central Mexico" and "The New Tenochtitlan Templo Mayor Coyolxauhqui-Chantico Monument"; Sullivan, "Tlazolteotl-Ixcuina"; Gillespie, *The Aztec Kings*; Miller and Taube, *The Gods and Symbols of Ancient Mexico and the Maya*; Klein, "Rethinking Cihuacoatl"; and to a lesser extent Robelo, *Diccionario de mitología Nahuatl*.

38. Gillespie, *The Aztec Kings*, 24.

39. Ibid., 59–60.

40. Ibid., 59. In visual depictions, Tlazolteotl, an avatar of Toci/Tonan originating with the Huastecs, is often represented with the flayed skin hanging loosely from the arms and legs of the male priest who wears her guise.

41. Klein, "Rethinking Cihuacoatl."

42. Miller and Taube, *The Gods and Symbols of Ancient Mexico and the Maya*, 184, 60.

43. Nicholson, "The New Tenochtitlan," 84, citing Eduard Seler, *Gesammelte Abhandlungen zuer amerikanischen Sprach und Alterthumskunde* (Berlin: A. Asher and Co., 1902–23), 3:327ff and 4:157–67.

44. Nicholson, "The New Tenochtitlan," 84.

45. Miller and Taube, *The Gods and Symbols of Ancient Mexico and the Maya*, 94.

46. Klein, "Rethinking Cihuacoatl," 241.

47. Ibid., 249–50.

48. Nash, "The Aztecs and the Ideology of Male Dominance," 350.

49. Ibid., 355.

50. Ibid., 359, 362.

51. Klein writes: "Perhaps, had time not run out for the Mexica, the repressive nature of the 'new' Cihuacoatl would have led the people to invade her prison, and to cut her bonds" ("Rethinking Cihuacoatl," 250).

52. See plate 10 in Herrera-Sobek, ed., *Santa Barraza*.

53. Cypess, *La Malinche in Mexican Literature*, 2.

54. Cypess draws from the writings of three Spaniards who provide source material on Malintzin's life: Cortés, who mentions her role as interpreter only briefly in his letters; Francisco López de Gómara, Cortés's official biographer, who represents her "as a faithful slave girl"; and Bernal Díaz del Castillo, who provides vivid and descriptive, if somewhat romanticized, accounts of Malintzin (32). Cypess also notes that Malintzin was mentioned frequently in the indigenous accounts "written after the conquest and by means of images recorded in the codices" (36). She makes this point to emphasize Malintzin's importance to Cortés despite his failure to acknowledge her contributions.

55. Cypess, *La Malinche in Mexican Literature*, 33. Popular accounts say that Malinche was sold into slavery by her mother, a version that condemns her mother for the act and reinforces the theme of female betrayal.

56. Karttunen, "Rethinking Malinche," 308–9.

57. Cypess, *La Malinche in Mexican Literature*, 34. Some scholars have conjectured that the Spaniards were considered gods by the indigenous peoples based on the promised return of the god Quetzalcoatl.

58. Ibid., 35.

59. Todorov, *The Conquest of America*, 101.

60. Cypess, *La Malinche in Mexican Literature*, 27.

61. Cypess says that it is "generally accepted" that Malinche was born in either 1502 or 1505 "on the day called Malinal (or Malinalli) hence her indigenous name *Malinalli*." However, she cautions that "it is important to remember

that the records can only suggest the naming process; we should not think we know with certainty her original name" (33).

62. Diaz's writings were intended as an overall corrective to Cortés's accounts and those of his official chronicler, Francisco López de Gómara, thus exemplifying the dynamic history approach I have outlined. See Cooper Alarcón's "The Aztec Palimpsest" for further analysis of how Diaz's rewriting functions to disturb a unitary perspective of Spanish conquest history.

63. Cypess, *La Malinche in Mexican Literature*, 27–37.

64. Ibid., 33.

65. Ibid., 9.

66. Moraga, "A Long Line of Vendidas," 90–144; Valdez, "Los Vendidos," 35–49.

67. Paz, *The Labyrinth of Solitude*, 77.

68. Ibid., 86.

69. Mirandé and Enríquez, *La Chicana*, 28.

70. Alarcón, "Traddutora, Traditora," 83, 72.

71. Ibid., 83.

72. Ibid., 71.

73. Pratt, "Yo Soy La Malinche," 860.

74. Ibid.

75. Ibid.

76. See Pratt's analysis of Tafolla's and several other Chicana feminists' poems in "Yo Soy La Malinche."

77. See essays and plate 30, *La Malinche*, in Herrera-Sobek, ed., *Santa Barraza*.

78. Barraza, "Santa C. Barraza," 10.

79. Ibid., 49.

80. Esquivel, *Malinche*, vii–viii. Interestingly, Esquivel's son Jordi Castells designed the Malinche codex included with the book.

81. "An Interview with Michelle Otero," e-interview with Carolina Monsiváis. Summer/Fall 2006. Institute of Latino Studies, Momotombo Press, University of Notre Dame. http://www.momotombopress.com/. Accessed July 9, 2007.

82. Candelaria, "Letting La Llorona Go, or Re/reading History's Tender Mercies," 112.

83. For an examination of indigenous roots in Gloria Anzaldúa's poem about La Llorona, see Pérez, "Words, Worlds in Our Heads."

84. Bierhorst, ed., *The Hungry Woman*, 25.

85. Miller and Taube, *The Gods and Symbols of Ancient Mexico and the Maya*, 60–61, 184–85.

86. Ibid., 61. Rebolledo refers to them as "Cihuapipiltin" (*Women Singing in the Snow*, 63).

87. Phillips, "Marina/Malinche," 107.

88. Rebolledo and Rivero, *Infinite Divisions*, 192. For other sources citing versions of the La Llorona legend in addition to those cited above, see Fernandez, "Tales Our Mothers Told Us"; Agogino et al., "Doña Marina and the Legend of La Llorona"; Palacios, "La Llorona Loca."

89. See Johnston, "Corinthian Medea and the Cult of Hera Akraia," for a detailed analysis of how Medea (and tangentially Lilith and La Llorona) represents a reproductive demon.

90. Ibid., 57–58.

91. Bernardino de Sahagún, *Florentine Codex*, book 1, 3–4. For slightly different wording, see the second edition (1970), 11. See also Barakat, "Aztec Motifs in 'La Llorona,' " 290.

92. Bernardino de Sahagún, *Conquest of New Spain*, 32.

93. Rebolledo and Rivero, *Infinite Divisions*, 194.

94. Castañeda Shular et al., *Literatura chicana*, 97.

95. Hadden, "La Llorona."

96. Casteñeda Shular et al., *Literatura chicana*, 100–101.

97. Hadden, "La Llorona."

98. Apart from and contrary to our limited modern conception of Medea as a deranged mother, "Medea was represented by the Greeks as a complex figure fraught with conflicting desires and exhibiting an extraordinary range of behavior" (Johnston, "Introduction," 6). She was a ruler of a state, founder of a city, and possessed magic powers, among other abilities, and her mythic character was developed in various Mediterranean and Middle Eastern locations. Many versions of the Corinthian story of Medea and Jason existed before Euripides wrote his famous play. In earlier versions of the story, Medea does not murder her children. One version indicates that the Corinthians, angered that Medea caused the deaths of King Creon and his daughter, stoned to death all fourteen of her children. In still another version, the Corinthians kill the children and thereafter must expiate their crime through an annual atonement ritual that requires seven girls and seven boys to spend a year in the temple where the murders were committed. Another version describes how the goddess Hera promised immortality for Medea's children if she laid them on Hera's altar, which she did and then fled in a chariot drawn by winged serpents. Robert Graves indicates that Euripides was paid by the Corinthians to absolve them of their guilt in murdering the children by writing a play that makes Medea responsible for killing two of her children while the others perished in the fire she caused (*The Greek Myths*, 254–56). Some sources say that Euripides invented this aspect of the story; however, it probably "developed out of a folkloric paradigm that was widespread both in ancient Greece and in other ancient Mediterranean countries—the paradigm of the reproductive demon" (Johnston, "Corinthian Medea and the Cult of Hera Akraia," 45). Still other versions

state that Medea killed the children accidentally or that Creon's kinsman killed the children in revenge for Creon's death and then circulated a rumor that Medea had murdered them (Classics Technology Center, "Medea," http://ablemedia.com/ctcweb/netshots/medea.htm, accessed July 1, 2002).

In early Hebrew writings, Lilith was Adam's first wife, who refused to lay beneath him and submit to his will. She fled to the Red Sea where she consorted with other like-minded spirits and gave birth to one hundred children daily. When she refused to return to Adam, God arranged for one hundred of her children to perish daily (Graves and Patai, eds., *Hebrew Myths*, 65–69).

99. Medea was an earlier goddess of the Corinthians displaced by Hera, with whom Medea shared aspects (Johnston, "Corinthian Medea and the Cult of Hera Akraia," 46). Graves suggests that "Zeus's love for Medea, like Hera's for Jason . . . suggests 'Zeus' and 'Hera' were titles of the Corinthian King and Queen," in other words establishing Jason and Medea as god and goddess (*The Greek Myths*, 256). While Euripides' play ends with Medea fleeing on a winged chariot, Robinson Jeffers's popular American rewrite removes any indication of Medea's association with divinity.

Lilith was most likely a fertility goddess of Greek and Sumerian origin (Graves and Patai, *The Hebrew Myths*, 12). She was transformed from goddess to demon when historical forces threatened the Israeli state. Initially, most Israelites were followers of the carefree Canaanite cult in which goddesses ruled and gods acted as their consorts. When the state was threatened by its neighbors a minority succeeded in elevating an authoritarian monotheism and declaiming the goddess-worship practiced in the sacred groves of Canaan. As with other goddesses, Lilith was exorcised from the Book of Genesis in order to emphasize the new precepts of a patriarchal, warring religious order (Graves and Patai, *The Hebrew Myths*, 14). This rewriting of history is similar to that practiced by the Mexica kings as noted earlier.

100. Mirandé and Enríquez, *La Chicana*, 33.

101. Anzaldúa, "Doing Gigs," 220.

102. Ibid., 229.

103. On her literary use of La Llorona, Anzaldúa says: "In fact she appears in three different projects. First, I have a children's bilingual story, the second in the *Prietita* series; it's called *Prietita Encounters La Llorona*. Instead of presenting the traditional Llorona story I'm rewriting her in a different light. Second, in *La Prieta*, the novela/cuentos collection, a lot of the stories use la Llorona. For example in "She Ate Horses" Llorona appears as a woman with a horse's head. And third, in *Lloronas, mujeres que lean y escriben* (the working title of a book intended as a sequel to *Borderlands*) I use the cultural figure of the serpent woman, la Llorona, through all the chapters, through all the theoretical writing" ("Doing Gigs," 229). See also Anzaldúa's interview with Donna Perry.

104. See plate 6, *Diosa del Maíz y La Llorona*, in Herrera-Sobek, ed., *Santa Barraza*.

105. See plate 34 in ibid.

106. Barraza, "Santa C. Barraza," 8–9.

107. See plate 13 in Herrera-Sobek, ed., *Santa Barraza*.

108. See plate 12 in ibid.

109. Barraza, "Santa C. Barraza," 49.

110. Anzaldúa, *Prietita and the Ghost Woman / Prietita y La Llorona*.

111. Nava. "La Llorona (The Weeping Woman)—Parts 1 and 2."

112. Ibid.

113. *Realidades*, "Got Latino?" Producer, Tom McMahon. *American Family* Series for KCET. PBS. Air date 2/6/02.

114. Virginia Urias, oral history.

115. Cisneros, *Woman Hollering Creek*, 116–29.

116. Poole, *Our Lady of Guadalupe*, 5, 10.

117. Reuters News Service, "Abbot's Words Infuriate the Public," 1996.

118. Poole, *Our Lady of Guadalupe*, 4.

119. Peterson, "The Virgin of Guadalupe," 40.

120. However, Peterson notes that although Hidalgo, "a creole priest who initially envisioned an autonomous creole kingdom," used Guadalupe as a liberatory symbol, "in a calculated move to attract a wider following," it was his successor Father José María Morelos, a mestizo, whose visionary land reform program first associated Guadalupe with democratic national concepts that addressed the economic and social inequities of the indigenous peoples. And only following the 1910 revolution that introduced "profound social and agrarian reforms did Guadalupe's image become a viable symbol of freedom for all classes" (45).

121. Peterson, "The Virgin of Guadalupe," 39.

122. Ruiz and Galán, *Chicano!;* Pesquera and Segura, "There Is No Going Back," 97–98.

123. Rebolledo and Rivero, *Infinite Divisions,* 191.

124. Chabram-Dernersesian, "I Throw Punches for My Race, But I Don't Want to Be a Man," 91.

125. Matter, "Sacred New Images."

126. Ibid.

127. Harlan, "A Conversation with Ester Hernández."

128. Alarcón, "Chicana's Feminist Literature," 39. Surveying Chicana/o writing, largely poetry of the 1970s and early 1980s, Alarcón notes that there is a "telling absence of poems by women to the Virgin of Guadalupe, while poems by men to her are plentiful" (187).

129. Rebolledo, *Women Singing in the Snow,* 53.

130. Debra Blake et al., "An Interview with Denise Chávez," 19.

131. Warren. "Some Like a Virgin, Some Don't."

132. Rodríguez and Gonzales, "The Body of the Sacred Feminine."

133. Elaine Wolff, "Virgen Matricides," *San Antonio Current*, December 26, 2006. http://www.anna-marielopez.com/interview/reviews.html. Accessed January 24, 2007.

CHAPTER TWO: CHICANA FEMINISM

1. Moraga, *The Last Generation*, 75–76.

2. Ibid., 76.

3. Anzaldúa, "Doing Gigs," 219, 220.

4. Anzaldúa distances herself from the essentializing and universalizing associations: "Some women writers when using these figures may tend to essentialize, but from the beginning I've been aware of the dangers in attributing innate qualities to women—for example the idea that it's genetic for women to be nurturing. I don't believe those things" ("Doing Gigs," 221–22).

5. Sandoval, "U.S. Third World Feminism," 1.

6. Original emphasis; Moraga, *Loving in the War Years*, 52.

7. Thanks to Jenny Cooley for suggesting that Mexican women writers portray a sense of history in the formation of their identity more than many U.S. women writers do. While this point is disputable, I believe that writings by U.S. women of color and ethnic-identified women writers often draw on cultural heritages and histories more than do works by white writers.

8. Ahern, ed., *A Rosario Castellanos Reader*, 81. For the original in Spanish and other translations, see Castellanos, *El rescate del mundo*; Casteñeda Shular et al., *Literatura chicana*, 292–93; and Palley, ed., *Meditation on the Threshold*, 52–53.

9. Cited in Alarcón, "Cognitive," 192. Alarcón translates "mosquitas muertas" as "wallflowers." The reference implies inaction and an inability to cause irritation. Another possible translation is more akin to "sleeping mosquitos," that is, beings who have the potential to sting but are lying dormant.

10. For example, the figure of Nacha, the indigenous cook in Laura Esquivel's book *Como agua para chocolate* (*Like Water for Chocolate*), functions similar to a curandera (folk healer) to Tita, the main character, and as such can be equated with indigenous beliefs and practices. Yet the book and the subsequent film generated debate among U.S. feminists as to whether it depicts an empowering feminist scenario or reinscribes traditional gender roles and sexist attitudes and sexualities.

11. Castillo, *Talking Back*, 29–30.

12. See Castellanos, *Mujer que sabe latín . . .* ; cited in and translated by Palley, *Meditation on the Threshold*, 21.

13. One of the earliest Chicana feminist writers to be published, Estela Por-

tillo Trambley, wrote the play *Sor Juana*, roughly based on the life of the Mexican scholar/writer. See *Sor Juana and Other Plays*.

14. This condition is not specific to Mexican women. Debra Castillo states that "Latin American women do not write. . . . Latin American women certainly do not write narrative. What little they do write—poetry, mostly—deserves oblivion. What narrative they produce, straightforward neorealist domestic fiction, does not stand up to comparison with the work of the great male writers of the Boom and after and is mercifully relegated to a footnote. The occasional exceptions—Western-trained and European-oriented women, such as . . . the Mexicans Elena Garro, Margo Glantz, Barbara Jacobs, and Elena Poniatowska (whose non-Hispanic-sounding last names are almost too suggestive)—neatly demonstrate the point, but they represent something of a conundrum in traditional literary histories" (26–27).

15. The 1972 anthology *Literatura chicana: Texto y contexto*, edited by Antonia Casteñeda Shular et al., features selections from various Mexican writers. One poem by Sor Juana Inés de la Cruz, a one-paragraph description of tortilla making by Elena Poniatowska, and one poem by Rosario Castellanos are the only selections by Mexican women to be included, compared with numerous selections by Mexican male writers. At that time and even now, these three are the most highly regarded of Mexican women writers, yet not all their works have been translated into English. Securing translations of the works of younger or lesser-known women writers is almost impossible.

16. Alma Gómez et al., "By Word of Mouth/De Boca en Boca," viii.

17. Castañeda Shular et al., *Literatura chicana*, xxvii.

18. Castillo, *Massacre of the Dreamers*, 214.

19. Ibid. Castillo herself appeared on a panel sponsored by the Mexican Fine Arts Center Museum in Chicago on March 16, 1994, which included Sandra Cisneros and Elena Poniatowska; each author read from her work and responded to questions from the audience.

20. Alarcón, "Cognitive Desires," 192.

21. For reviews of these positions, see Abu-Lughod, "Writing against Culture": Conkey with Williams, "Original Narratives"; di Leonardo, "Introduction"; and Meskell, "Goddesses, Gimbutas, and 'New Age' Archaeology."

22. In *Odd Girls and Twilight Lovers*, Lillian Faderman cites Moraga on this point. Faderman writes: "As Chicana author Cherrie Moraga wrote, Third World lesbians became fed up with white lesbian-feminist organizations that would claim: 'Well, we're open to all women. Why don't [lesbians of color] come?' but would refuse to examine how the very nature and structure of the group took for granted race and class" (243).

23. Vance, "Epilogue," 434.

24. The writings Moraga read at the conference, which are included in *Pleasure and Danger*, are "La Dulce Culpa," "What Is Left," "Loving in the War

Years," "Passage," and "The Slow Dance" (417–22). The essay published in *Powers of Desire* was cowritten with Amber Hollibaugh and titled "What We're Rollin Around in Bed With" (394–405).

25. It is important to note that Moraga was one of a few Chicanas actively participating in the movement and claiming a feminist identity. In addition to critiquing the shortcomings of second wave feminism, she also was critical of "feminist-oriented" Chicana writings that discounted the feminist movement in order to "stay safely within the boundaries of Chicano—male-defined and often anti-feminist—values." She credits the "research and writings of Norma Alarcón, Martha Cotera, Gloria Anzaldúa and Adelaida Del Castillo" and acknowledges the contributions of unnamed Latinas who spoke up "in isolation, ten and fifteen years ago, without a movement to support them" (*Loving in the War Years* 105, 107–8).

Pesquera and Segura also point out that Chicanas have been narrowly typecast by the second wave movement. They note that Chicanas were dismissed as a feminist force and relegated to the "margins of social inquiry" based on an article published in a well-known feminist anthology reporting the position of a group of Chicanas at a 1969 conference as " . . . the Chicana woman does not want to be liberated" (95–98). For a review of Chicana feminist positions and writings see Pesquera and Segura, "There Is No Going Back: Chicanas and Feminism." See also Alma M. García, ed., *Chicana Feminist Thought*.

26. Moraga, *Loving in the War Years*, 128.

27. King, *Theory in Its Feminist Travels*, 2–4.

28. DuBois et al., "Politics and Culture in Women's History," 30.

29. Ibid., 46.

30. Taylor and Rupp define lesbian feminism as "a variety of beliefs and practices based on the core assumption that a connection exists between an erotic and/or emotional commitment to women and political resistance to patriarchal domination" ("Women's Culture and Lesbian Feminist Activism," 33).

31. Ibid., 50.

32. Ibid., 50–51.

33. Felski, *Beyond Feminist Aesthetics*, 166.

34. Ibid., 168.

35. Ibid., 169–70.

36. Oral histories of Gonzales, Urias, and Vásquez.

37. Pesquera and Segura, "There Is No Going Back," 103, 106–7.

38. Conference presentations were open to anyone who joined the organization.

39. Subsequently published in 1993 in *Chicana Critical Issues*, ed. Castro et al.

40. For depictions of violence as an element of female sexual passion, see Moraga, "La Dulce Culpa" (*Loving*, 14–15) and "La ofrenda" (*Last Generation*, 77–86); for violence as an element of social change, see Moraga, "En busca de

la fuerza feminina" (*Last Generation*, 69–86); for violence as an element of female spirituality, see Anzaldúa, "*La herencia de Coatlicue*/The Coatlicue State" (*Borderlands*, 41–51). Villanueva's *The Ultraviolet Sky* and Castillo's *Sapogonia* examine male violence in erotic relationships as destructive.

41. Sandoval provides an excellent analysis of four different feminist positions and theorizes that U.S. Third World feminists selectively engage or disengage among the four forms, creating a fifth or "differential" mode ("U.S. Third World Feminism," 12).

42. Ibid., 11.

43. Alarcón, "The Theoretical Subjects," 365–66.

44. Gillespie, *The Aztec Kings*, 24.

45. Anzaldúa, *Borderlands*, 82–83.

46. Allen, "Who Is Your Mother?" 19.

47. Alarcón, "Chicana Feminism," 251. In "Who Is Your Mother?" Allen cites the power of the Iroquois matrons described in the tribe's constitution and the "feminist revolt" in 1600 that proved this power. She notes that "the price the feminist community must pay because it is not aware of the presence of gynarchical societies on this continent is unnecessary confusion, division and lost time" (17–18).

48. Irigaray, *Je, Tu, Nous*, 17. See also Allen for a similar argument.

In using Irigaray's concepts, I refer to two different works, *Je, Tu, Nous*, which touches briefly on some of her major ideas, and *Sexes and Genealogies*, a collection of speeches which elaborate those ideas more fully. Although Irigaray's writings consider woman as universal, the historical, cultural, racial, sexual, and class situatedness of my study and its focus as an "ethnography of the particular" (Abu-Lughod "Writing against Culture," 153) aim to prevent generalizations and universalizations. It is my belief that socially useful understandings can be gained only through considering specificities.

Irigaray's theorizing of gender differences is controversial, characterized by some critics, wrongly I think, as essentialistic. Her work highlights the tensions in contemporary feminist thought which, on the one hand, emphasize neutralization of laws and language that discriminate against women, and on the other, emphasize difference by biology (for example, in the recognition that medical studies of AIDS and cancer must be gender specific). While I think Irigaray's ideas are based on biological genealogy, it seems to me she is more concerned with a conceptual genealogy that relies on discourse—language and the law. Ultimately, the question that remains is whether the changes in language and law she proposes, to reflect rather than neutralize gender differences, will affect any changes in the balance of power and the material conditions of women's lives. See also Diana Fuss, "Luce Irigaray's Language of the Essence," in *Essentially Speaking* (55–72), and Jane Gallop's "Quand nos lèvres s'écrcivent."

49. Irigaray, *Sexes and Genealogies*, 62, 64.

50. Original emphasis; ibid., 67.

51. Alarcón, "Chicana Feminism," 250.

52. Fregoso and Chabram discuss the "predicament of double positioning" that Chicanas respond to, the male-dominated Chicano movement and mainstream critical theory ("Introduction," 206). While I believe these are two primary positionings, I expand them to include multiple positionings that Chicana writings refigure.

The recuperation of the goddesses directly confronts the Catholic Church's historical and continuing denigration of the "pagan" and "savage" pantheistic indigenous religious beliefs. The Church's teachings in this respect persist today, as evidenced by several of the women I interviewed who took pains to distance themselves from indigenous beliefs and practices (although admitting pride in their indigenous heritage) and to assure me that "they," the "Indians," preferred La Virgen de Guadalupe over their own indigenous deities. (Oral histories of Irma Vásquez and Virginia Urias.)

53. Fischer, "Ethnicity and the Post-Modern Arts of Memory," 197.

54. Moraga, Loving in the War Years, 130.

55. Madsen, "A God of One's Own," 481–82.

56. Ibid., 482.

57. Anzaldúa, Borderlands, 25–39, 41–51.

58. Schüssler Fiorenza, "Feminist Spirituality, Christian Identity, and Catholic Vision," 142.

59. Anzaldúa, Borderlands, 37–38.

60. Moraga, Loving in the War Years, 132.

61. Ruether, "Catholicism, Women, Body and Sexuality," 229.

62. Ibid., 228. Ruether notes that in 1977 the Catholic Theological Society of America published a study of human sexuality and proposed "an alternative ethic" regarding sexuality issues including homosexuality. The report recommended a move from a "legalistic to a relational sexual ethic" in which "the goal is to move towards relationships which are faithful, loving, mutual and life-enhancing, and away from relationships which are violent, unfaithful, deceitful, manipulative and exploitative." It also suggested that homosexuality be considered a "variant type of sexual orientation that occurs naturally in ten to twelve percent of the population" (229). As a dissenting view this report is significant; however, official policy remains the same. In regard to lesbians and gay males, pastors are instructed to counsel them to "convert" to heterosexuality (Ratzinger and Bouone, "Letter to the Bishops of the Catholic Church in the Pastoral Care of Homosexual Persons," 1–10). In 2004 Cardinal Ratzinger was selected to succeed Pope John Paul II. Ratzinger took the name Pope Benedict XVI.

63. Expanding on Taylor and Rupp's definition of lesbian feminism, I use "Chicana politics" to signify an awareness of intersecting oppressions and op-

position to racism and classism as well as sexism and heterosexism, regardless of one's sexual identity position.

64. Trujillo, "Chicana Lesbians," 187.

65. Moraga, *Loving in the War Years*, 99.

66. Ibid., 52. Moraga explains that the concept of "vendida" is linked to Malintzin Tenepal's (Malinche's) perceived betrayal of her race to the white man, and that Mexican American women, by association, are suspected of betrayal if they don't put the male first (*Loving*, 99, 103). Chicanas who are self-determining often are stigmatized as lesbians, Malinchistas, who are "corrupted by foreign influences" (113). She argues that Chicana and Mexicana lesbians bear the "brunt of this betrayal" because by "taking control of [their] own sexual identity and destiny" they fail to acquiesce to the men of their culture, therefore they must be "serving the white man" (112). "The choice is never seen as her own. Homosexuality is his disease with which he sinisterly infects Third World people, men and women alike" (114). See also Romo-Carmona, "Introduction," xx–xxix.

67. Trujillo, *Chicana Lesbians*, 192.

68. Anzaldúa, *Borderlands*, 27–28.

69. Morton, "The Goddess as Metaphoric Image," 116.

70. Butler, "Variations on Sex and Gender," 130.

71. Anzaldúa, *Borderlands*, 51.

72. Irigaray, *Sexes and Genealogies*, 71.

73. Castillo, *Massacre of the Dreamers*, 136.

74. In Robelo, *Diccionario de mitología Nahuatl*, Quetzalpetlatl is described as either the wife or sister of Quetzalcoatl, god of the sun, depending on the source (275). Little else is known about her.

75. Villanueva, *The Ultraviolet Sky*, 17.

76. Ibid., 221.

77. See Sullivan, "Tlazolteotl-Ixcuina," for more on the aspects of the mother earth goddess.

78. This characterization, found in Mesoamerican figurine imagery of women birthing standing up and of pregnant women as warriors, also defies anthropological constructs of originary women as passive reproducers, as noted by Conkey in her discussion of origins-based archaeology, which has influenced popular notions of human origin ("Original Narratives," 123–24).

79. Kristeva notes that only two discourses exist for the concept of "becoming-a-mother," science and Christianity, neither of which provides for mother as a speaking subject (*Desire in Language*, 237).

80. Villanueva, *The Ultraviolet Sky*, 23.

81. Gillespie writes that "gender ambiguity is an important aspect of the Aztec mother earth deity and pertains as well to their other major gods." Citing León-Portilla she explains that "what was at issue was the recognition that the

power of creation derived from the union of the two opposing genders" (*The Aztec Kings*, 61).

82. Castillo, *Sapogonia*, 150.

83. The novel leaves ambiguous whether Máximo actually murders the woman or whether he dreams it, and only in the epilogue does the reader discover that the woman is not Pastora.

84. Traub, "Jewels, Statues and Corpses," 121–22. See also "The Story of Pygmalion" in Ovid's *Metamorphoses* for an earlier depiction of the construction of an idealized virginal statue-cum-woman.

85. Castillo, *Sapogonia*, 180.

86. Ibid.,13.

87. Original emphasis; ibid., 1.

88. Castillo, *Sapogonia*, 349.

89. In *Mothering*, Glenn et al. write that "the colonizer's attempt to undercut or disrupt traditional institutions, however, motivate the colonized to defend and recreate their ways of life. The everyday activities of mothers in maintaining tradition and in keeping kin ties alive can be seen as resistance" (18).

90. Moraga, *The Last Generation*, 74.

91. Ibid.

92. Ibid.

93. Alarcón "Chicana Feminism," 251.

94. Collins, *Black Feminist Thought*, 5. Collins defines this concept as "the tension between the suppression of Black women's ideas and our intellectual activism in the face of that suppression" (5–6). I expand on this term to include material oppressions as well as intellectual suppressions.

95. Moraga, *The Last Generation*, 71.

96. Anzaldúa argues that the imposition of Western rational thought upon indigenous peoples denigrated and muted their spirituality (58–59). Similarly, Irigaray argues, although from an ahistorical and universalized position, that the "transfer of the transmission of maternal-female power from the daughter to the son" resulted in changes in the "style and quality of discourse" and a "censuring of women's speech" (*Je, Tu, Nous*, 17). Ronald Takaki has argued, like Anzaldúa, that American Protestantism emphasizes a dichotomy of reason and passion: "the bodies half-dead; genitals dissociated from heart; heart severed from head; head dissociated from genitals" (*Iron Cages*, 10).

97. Anzaldúa, *Borderlands*, 72.

98. Ibid., 73, 49.

99. Watson, "Unspeakable Differences," 140.

100. Anzaldúa, *Borderlands*, 81.

101. Ibid., 104.

102. McDonnell and Fineman, "Mexico Poised to OK Dual Nationality Law," 1996.

103. Cisneros, "Little Miracles, Kept Promises," 127.

104. For elaborations of a palimpsestic paradigm, see Cypess, *La Malinche in Mexican Literature*; and Alarcón, "The Aztec Palimpsest."

105. Cisneros, "Little Miracles, Kept Promises," 128.

106. Ibid.

107. Ibid., 125; and "Guadalupe the Sex Goddess," 46.

108. Moraga, *Last Generation*, 144.

109. In the poem, Moraga envisions La Virgen as a "pintora" as if referring to Hernández's work.

110. As noted in chapter 1, Hernández did not intend this version of Guadalupe as a sexual image, and the second printing of *Chicana Lesbians* featured a different image on the cover.

111. Cisneros, "Guadalupe the Sex Goddess," 49.

112. The goddesses as envisioned by the Mexica male elite class also may not have been accessible to or accepted by the Mexica commoners.

CHAPTER THREE: LAS HISTORIAS

1. See J. Rodríguez, *Our Lady of Guadalupe*, chapter 2.

2. Vicki Rivera Reyes is a pseudonym.

3. For other studies, see Rodríguez, *Our Lady of Guadalupe*; Isasi-Díaz and Tarango, *Hispanic Women*; and Guerrero, *A Chicano Theology*.

4. Rodríguez, *Our Lady of Guadalupe*, 120.

5. Ibid., xxi.

6. Anzaldúa writes, "La Virgen de Guadalupe is a symbol of ethnic identity" (*Borderlands*, 30). In *The Significance of Nuestra Señora Guadalupe and La Raza Cósmica in the Development of a Chicano Theory of Liberation* (Ann Arbor, Mich.: University Microfilm International, 1984, 124), Andrés Gonzales Guerrero Jr. writes, "*Desde entonces para el mexicano ser Guadalupano es algo esencial*/Since then for the Mexican, to be a Guadalupano is something essential" (cited in *Borderlands*, 29). See also Wolf, "The Virgin of Guadalupe," and Limón, "*La Llorona*, The Third Legend of Greater Mexico."

7. In March 1997, the Mexican community church in Muscatine was destroyed in a fire believed to be arson-related. Siqueiros says some community members suspect the act was a hate crime. In addition, rather than rebuilding the church in this neighborhood, the Catholic archdiocese encouraged the community to merge with another church in a nearby white neighborhood. Siqueiros says the community wanted to fight for its own church because it would be the only Catholic church in the city that maintained Mexican traditions such as a Spanish-language mass and celebrations for La Virgen de Guadalupe on her feast day (telephone conversation, March 24, 1997). Ultimately, the Mexi-

can community was denied a Spanish parish and La Misión de Guadalupe merged with Sts. Mary and Mathias Catholic Church. One Spanish-language mass is held on Sundays. Interestingly, four Spanish-named churches, founded by other denominations, are now located in Muscatine.

8. Siqueiros indicates that much of the racist behavior directed toward the Mexican community comes from the police force, which frequently patrols the neighborhood, stopping residents for minor infractions such as not wearing seat belts. In addition, she says the police force has targeted the Mexican neighborhood as gang-infested by issuing a bulletin to parents of school children that describes the type of clothing gang members wear, clothing that is also associated with Mexican youth culture and ethnicity, e.g., baggy pants and the colors of the Mexican flag.

9. Rodríguez explains that "popular religiosity is a hybrid with a life of its own: it continues to exist because for the poor and marginalized it is a source of power, dignity and acceptance not found in the institutional church" (*Our Lady of Guadalupe*, 144). See also Shorris, *Latinos*, 372–77; and Acuña, *Occupied America*. In *The Politics of Chicano Liberation* (New York: Pathfinder Press, 1977), Olga Rodríguez writes, "Although more than half of the Catholics in the Southwest are Chicanos, the Catholic church hierarchy has continuously insulted its Chicano membership by its racist practices" (cited in Castillo, *Massacre of the Dreamers*, 89).

10. Rodríguez, *Our Lady of Guadalupe*, 145.

11. Ibid., xix.

12. Limón describes the 1965 farmworkers' strike in Delano, California, as the initiatory moment when La Virgen de Guadalupe was used publicly as a symbol of popular resistance in the United States ("*La Llorona*," 64).

13. Geertz, "Art as a Cultural Symbol," 1473–99.

14. James S. Griffith describes how front-yard shrines in Tucson are "public sites" for neighborhood or community use. "Once a shrine is established in a front yard, neighbors with a strong devotion to that particular saint may well come by occasionally to pray in front of the shrine. In this way, the shrine starts to become a public site for prayer as well as a private statement of faith and obligation" (*Hecho a Mano*, 31). For articles discussing folk art, see Ybarra-Frausto, "Arte Chicano: Images of a Community"; Hattersley-Drayton, Bishop, and Ybarra-Frausto, eds., *Inside Out;* Turner, "Mexican American Home Altars."

15. Cantú, "La Virgen de Guadalupe," 15–20.

16. Griffith, *Hecho a Mano*, 19. A short distance outside Tucson, the San Xavier del Bac mission church contains a painting of La Virgen de Guadalupe believed to be more than one hundred years old, which reinforces that La Virgen came to the United States long before the recent waves of immigrants.

17. See Melion and Küchler, *Images of Memory*, 4.

18. "Cultural Identity and Cinematic Representation," 70. Hall makes this statement about the effects of the photographic work of Jamaican-born Armet Francis.

19. Martínez, "The Undocumented Virgin," 99, 102, 104–5.

20. Nora, "Between Memory and History," 12. Ironically, however, the basilica of La Virgen de Guadalupe as *lieux de mémoire* also entails forgetting Guadalupe's history in North and South America as a symbol of the conqueror's religion, a strategy that first contributed to the conversion and pacification of indigenous peoples and the erasure of their gods and later was used as a tool of upper-class criollos' goals for Mexican independence from Spain (see Poole, *Our Lady of Guadalupe*, and Peterson, "The Virgin of Guadalupe").

21. Turner, "The Cultural Semiotics of Religious Icons," 317–18.

22. Ibid., 342.

23. Turner discusses universal and local appeal in terms of La Virgin de San Juan de los Lagos (340–41). She lists other incarnations as the Virgin of Sorrows, the Virgin of the Assumption, the Virgin of the Annunciation, Mary, Queen of Heaven, and the Virgin of the Rosary (340).

24. Ibid., 341.

25. The Yaqui were indigenous to northern Mexico. They were never conquered by the Spaniards and fought mightily to keep their lands from the Mexican government and the revolutionaries during the Mexican Revolution. To escape attempted genocide by the Mexican government, many Yaquis fled to the United States. They continue to practice their cultural traditions in the town of Pascua, Arizona, where Carlos was accepted as a member.

26. Turner notes that the Texas sculpture is slightly smaller than the original icon. In addition, three small roses are embroidered on the front of the Texas icon's garment, differentiating it from the one large rose on the Mexican icon's dress ("The Cultural Semiotics of Religious Icons," 338).

27. Ibid., 321, 325.

28. Sandra Cisneros's short story "Little Miracles, Kept Promises" includes the petition of Teresa Galindo, who went to see La Virgin de San Juan in Texas twice with other female family members. In her petition letter, Teresa acknowledges that the women "all needed [La Virgen] to listen to us" (122).

29. Turner, "The Cultural Semiotics of Religious Icons," 319–20.

30. In "Guadalupe, Subversive Virgin," Randall recalls the subversions of the women she encountered as a midwife in Mexico City.

31. As Limón writes, citing Victor and Edith Turner's analysis, both the Mexican Catholic Church and the Partido Revolucionario Institucional (PRI), the political party that ruled Mexico for forty years, supported pilgrimages to the basilica of La Virgen de Guadalupe "to produce a false, pacifying maternal sense of 'national unity' for those who are clearly marginalized" ("*La Llorona,*" 66). In

the United States, the Church's official sanctioning of La Virgen may contribute to a similar pacifying effect.

32. Denise Chávez takes up the issue of Chicanas and Mexicanas as "servers" in several of her works. See her novel *The Face of an Angel*, and her performance piece *Women in the State of Grace: Part I: The Servers and Part II: The Served*, published as "Novena narrativas y ofrendas nuevomexicanas."

33. For studies on the exploitation of Chicana/Mexicana labor, see Martínez and McCaughan, "Chicanas and Mexicanas within a Transnational Working Class"; Arguelles, "Undocumented Female Labor in the United States Southwest"; Ruiz, "A Promise Fulfilled"; Segura, "Chicanas and Triple Oppression in the Labor Force"; Peña, "Between the Lines."

34. In *La Chicana*, Mirandé and Enríquez note that "Aztec" women were regulated by a rigid social structure and a strict moral code (15). "The highest womanly virtues in Aztec society were virginity and fidelity—virginity until marriage and thereafter fidelity to one's husband, ending only with death." Adultery was punished by public stoning until death (21). Gender roles and gender performances also were strictly regulated; women and men who were caught cross-dressing were executed (Klein, "Rethinking Cihuacoatl," 242). Ana Castillo analyzes the codes found in the mixture of North African Arab culture and Muslim religion that influenced Spanish Catholicism during eight hundred years of Islamic domination over Spain. Women are considered man's property and his children are heirs to his property. Religion justifies the economic perspective of women as property by legislating monogamy as sacred through the figure of the Virgin Mother, who "reinforce[s] the moral standard of female chastity before marriage" (Castillo, *Massacre of the Dreamers*, 70, 78).

35. Espín notes that the Catholic standards of honorability versus promiscuity "fell in a disproportionately harsh way on native and Mestizo women, who were less likely to be virgins because of the social and economic conditions in which they lived" ("Cultural and Historical Influences on Sexuality in Hispanic/Latin Women," 151).

36. Ibid., 154–55. In *Latinos*, Shorris writes that "the virgin birth comes to symbolize even more the mystery of faith, the victory of the metaphysical over the material world, a concept to which Latinos cling like no other people on earth" (364). In "The History of Chicanas," Sánchez writes that "within traditional families, sexual freedom for women, even working women continues to be taboo in the Chicano community" (24).

37. Espín, "Cultural and Historical Influences on Sexuality in Hispanic/Latin Women," 152, 160. For other sources that discuss the regulation of Chicana sexuality, see Garcia-Bahne, "La Chicana and the Chicano Family," and Mirandé and Enríquez, *La Chicana*.

38. Oral histories of Loya, Rivera Reyes, Ozuna, Siqueiros.

39. Smith, *Subjectivity, Identity, and the Body*, 9–11.

40. Trujillo, "Chicana Lesbians," 186. In her autobiographical essay "Guadalupe the Sex Goddess," Sandra Cisneros writes that she was afraid to examine her own body until, as a graduate student, she was given a mirror by a nurse at an Emma Goldman Clinic who encouraged her to look at her "sex" (*Goddess of the Americas*, 47).

41. Espín, "Cultural and Historical Influences on Sexuality in Hispanic/Latin Women," 156.

42. Brown, Oliver, and Klor de Alva, *Sociocultural and Service Issues in Working with Hispanic American Clients*, 73.

43. See also Sidonie Smith's discussion of female sexuality and textuality in Isak Dinesen's short story "The Blank Page" (*Subjectivity*, 2–4).

44. José Limón has analyzed gendered moral codes at the scene of the dance in "The Devil Dances" (*Dancing with the Devil*, 168–86).

45. Castillo, *Massacre of the Dreamers*, 50.

46. Anzaldúa, *Borderlands*, 17.

47. Castillo, *Massacre of the Dreamers*, 186.

48. Segura, *Familism and Employment among Chicanas and Mexican Immigrant Women*, 219.
Segura found that Chicano and Mexicano husbands support their wives' decisions to work outside the home "*so long as* this employment does not challenge the patriarchal structure of the family. In other words, so long as the Mexicanas 1) articulate high attachment to motherhood *and* family caretaker roles, 2) frame their employment in terms of family economic goals, 3) do not ask men to do equal amounts of housework or childcare, they encounter little resistance from husbands or other male family members" (225; emphases in original).

49. Paz writes that "masculine homosexuality is regarded with a certain indulgence insofar as the active agent is concerned. The passive agent is an abject, degraded being. Masculine homosexuality is tolerated, then, on condition that it consists in violating a passive agent" (*The Labyrinth of Solitude*, 40). See also Almaguer, "Chicano Men."

50. Castillo, *Massacre of the Dreamers*, 134.

51. Romo-Carmona, "Introduction," xxvi–xxvii. See also Cherríe Moraga's *Waiting in the Wings* for a slightly different perspective on queer motherhood.

52. Espín writes that older women, such as grandmothers, have a great deal of status and power within their families and are more respected in Mexican/Chicano culture than their European American counterparts. In addition, a number of women pursue alternative subjectivities, such as curanderas (healers), espiritistas (spiritualists) and santeras (holy women), who are valued within the culture for their healing abilities (156).

53. See Deutsch. *No Separate Refuge*; Lecompte, "The Independent Women of

Hispanic New Mexico, 1821–1846"; Gonzalez, "The Widowed Women of Santa Fe"; and Portal, *Las mujeres de la tierra del sol.*

54. See Mirandé and Enríquez, *La Chicana;* Melville, ed., *Mexicanas at Work in the United States;* Durón, "Mexican Women and Labor Conflict in Los Angeles"; Gonzalez, "The Chicana in Southwest Labor History, 1900–1975," 26–61; Mora, "The Tolteca Strike," 111–17; Ruiz, *Cannery Women, Cannery Lives;* Zavella, "The Politics of Race and Gender," 202–24; Kingsolver, *Holding the Line;* Pardo, "Mexican American Women Grassroots Community Activists"; Rose, "Traditional and Nontraditional Patterns of Female Activism in the United Farm Workers of America"; Lucas, *Forged under the Sun.* See also the films *Milagro Beanfield War* and *Salt of the Earth.*

55. Zinn, "Political Familism," 24. Analyzing the Chicano civil rights movement, Zinn concluded that "political familism itself does not transcend sex role subordination. But within the varied expressions and manifestations of El Movimiento are changes in sex role relationships and family structure, as well as the seeds of new roles for the women and men of La Raza" (24). For documentation of this occurrence, see Buss, *Forged under the Sun;* Kingsolver, *Holding the Line;* and the film and published screenplay *Salt of the Earth.*

56. Original emphasis; Irigaray, *Sexes,* 72.

57. Smith, *Subjectivity, Identity, and the Body.* 4. Smith cites bell hooks as the originator of the phrase "experientially based." See hooks, *Yearning,* 38.

58. The Tucson YWCA newsletter reported: "The Mensajeras de Salud spoke to 1,669 women about breast and cervical cancer risks, symptoms and screening" in the first year of their existence, 1994–1995 (*YWCA Focus,* "Mensajeras Provided 1,669 Women with Lifesaving Information").

59. Lucas, *Forged under the Sun,* 293.

60. Rodríguez, *Our Lady of Guadalupe,* xxi.

61. Turner, "The Cultural Semiotics of Religious Icons," 329.

62. In *Women Singing in the Snow,* Rebolledo cites Elizabeth Johnson to explain how La Virgen acts as a mediator between humans and Jesus/God: "She intercedes on behalf of humans before God and Christ her son—so she is a transmitter (or translator, if you will) through which and not to which Catholics pray, 'since love and honor paid to Mary is always an expression of thanksgiving and adoration to her son' (Johnson, 247)" (52). However, Rebolledo also notes that "many women feel the Virgin has much more power than the 'official' ascendancy given to her by the church. . . . that it is not just through him that she derives her power, but that from the respect he has for her, she only has to look at him for him to obey her commands" (53).

63. St. Teresa de Ávila, a nun of the Discalced Carmelite Order, lived and wrote in Spain during the sixteenth century. Her most famous works are *Interior Castle* and *The Life of Teresa of Jesus.*

64. Despite Ozuna's level of educational achievement, I include her as a semiprofessional because she was unable to find a permanent, full-time position as an educator. She relied on substitute teaching and often worked in temporary "pink-collar" positions. As a single parent her economic status was so precarious that she could not afford a telephone or a car.

65. Ozuna explained that, according to her birth certificate, her name is spelled Mary Madeline because the nurse who wrote it out could not spell "Magdalena."

CHAPTER FOUR: CULTURAL ANXIETIES AND TRUTHS

1. Oring, "Folk Narratives," 125.

2. Ibid., 126.

3. Foucault, *Discipline and Punish*, 226.

4. Ibid., 214.

5. Limón, "*La Llorona*," 60.

6. See Montejano, *Anglos and Mexicans in the Making of Texas, 1836–1986.*

7. When asked by Limón why La Llorona killed her children, one woman replied, "'*Pos, su* husband *la dejó por una vieja.*' (Well, her husband left her for 'another woman')" and another woman immediately commented "'*¡Qué cabrón!*' . . . Roughly equivalent to but not synonymous with, 'that bastard!' " ("*La Llorona*," 75).

8. See Anzaldúa's discussion of internalized racism in *Borderlands*, 45.

9. Rebolledo, *Women Singing in the Snow*, 78.

10. Hawes, "La Llorona in Juvenile Hall," 168–70.

11. Ibid., 170.

12. Oring, "Folk Narratives," 126.

13. In "Victimization or Oppression?" Mahoney discusses the pitfalls of the feminist rhetoric on "staying" and "leaving" abusive relationships. Particularly, she refutes the idea that women who "stay" lack agency and thus "fail" to leave, arguing instead that women "stay" for good reasons and continue to resist.

14. Pérez, "Words, Worlds in Our Heads," 51, 63.

15. *Weeping Woman*, 2. For a similar theme, see Rudolfo Anaya's *Bless Me, Ultima.*

16. Miller and Taube, *The Gods and Symbols of Ancient Mexico and the Maya*, 70.

17. Villanueva, *Weeping Woman*, 2. The black shawl also connects La Llorona to the goddess Quetzalpetlatl, the little-known sister of Quetzalcoatl, whom Villanueva featured in her novel *The Ultraviolet Sky.*

18. Casteñeda Shular et al., *Literatura chicana*, 97.

19. Stiffarm, "The Demography of Indigenous North America," and Frye, *Indians into Mexicans.*

20. Villanueva, *Weeping Woman*, 3.

21. Ibid., 3–4.

22. Ibid., 6.

23. Russo discusses how the feminist movement has attempted to gloss over female abuse of children. See *Taking Back Our Lives*, 16–17.

24. Villanueva, *Weeping Woman*, 138. Further references to "El Alma/The Soul" appear parenthetically in the text.

25. Ibid., 159. Villanueva may be referring to National Endowment for the Arts awards several Chicana writers have received and the MacArthur Fellowship (often referred to as a "genius grant") that was awarded to Sandra Cisneros in 1995.

26. Fregoso and Chabram, "Introduction," 205–6.

27. In *Sapogonia*, Ana Castillo refers to Pastora's Yaqui ancestry.

28. Many of the stories in the *Weeping Woman* collection repeat the frustrating plot elements found in Villanueva's first novel, *The Ultraviolet Sky*. The female characters drink a lot of wine and have a lot of sex, and the male characters are stereotypical abusers. However, the Luna series avoids these pitfalls for the most part although at times it gets mired in 1970s second wave feminism.

29. Cihuacoatl and Coatlicue are often considered manifestations of each other and the names are used interchangeably.

30. Moraga, *The Hungry Woman*, x.

31. Bierhorst, ed., *The Hungry Woman*, 23. In the introduction to his collection of indigenous myths, Bierhorst discusses the interrelationships between indigenous goddesses, La Virgin de Guadalupe, and La Llorona. He notes that few contemporary Mexicans know the stories of the male gods, but the indigenous religion survives in the figure of a woman, "therefore, whether as Tonantzin or as la llorona, [a female figure] takes modern Mexico back to its roots" (12).

32. Gillespie, *The Aztec Kings*, xli.

33. Parker et al., "Introduction," 6–7.

34. De Lauretis, "Sexual Indifference and Lesbian Representation," 161.

35. Moraga, *The Hungry Woman*, 6.

36. Moraga, *The Last Generation*, 147.

37. Ibid., 150.

38. Bhabha, "Introduction," 1.

39. Moraga, *The Hungry Woman*, 6.

40. Ibid., 24.

41. Miller and Taube, *The Gods and Symbols of Ancient Mexico and the Maya*, 70, 160.

42. See Mahoney, "Victimization or Oppression?" 59–72.

43. Moraga, *The Hungry Woman*, x.

44. Ibid., 22.

45. Parker et al., "Introduction," 6. See also Sedgwick, *Between Men.*

46. Moraga, *The Hungry Woman*, 31.

47. Ibid., 31, 33.

48. Ibid., 72.

49. Ibid., 86.

50. Graves, *The Greek Myths*, 254.

51. McDonald, "Medea as Politician and Diva," 300.

52. Moraga, *The Hungry Woman*, 91–92.

53. Ibid., 92.

54. See Nash, "The Aztecs and the Ideology of Male Dominance"; and Klein, "Rethinking Cihuacoatl."

55. Moraga, *The Last Generation*, 74.

56. Moraga, *The Hungry Woman*, 92.

57. Ibid., 97–98.

58. Ibid., 99.

59. Ibid., 27.

CHAPTER FIVE: READING DYNAMICS OF POWER

1. Melendez, "The Oral Tradition and the Study of American Literature," 75–76.

2. Krupat, *For Those Who Come After*, 23–24.

3. Rebolledo, *Women Singing in the Snow*, 14.

4. Boyce Davies, "Collaborations and the Ordering Imperative in Life Story Production," 7.

5. Hankiss, "Ontologies of the Self," 204.

6. Evelyn Gonzales, oral history.

7. Behar, "Rage and Redemption," 225.

8. Beverley, "The Margin at the Center," 94–95.

9. Thanks to Laretta Hendersen for bringing this to my attention and elaborating the similarities and differences of slave narrative conventions in regard to this text. Personal conversation, University of Iowa, July 1998. See Toni Morrison's "The Site of Memory."

10. See Portelli, "Oral History as Genre," 37–38.

11. Blake, "Unsettling Identities," 76–79.

12. Anzaldúa, *Borderlands*, 30.

13. Ibid., 75.

14. Sections of the following analysis were published in my "Reading Dynamics of Power through Mexican-Origin Women's Oral Histories."

15. I rely on Sandra Harding's definitions of method and methodology in the introduction to *Feminism and Methodology*, while recognizing the interrelated-

ness of the terms and their often interchangeable usage. See also Cancian, "Feminist Science."

16. Andersen, "Studying across Difference," 51.

17. Ibid., 41.

18. Ibid., 41–51.

19. See Wolf, "Situating Feminist Dilemmas in Fieldwork," 2, which theorizes three dimensions of power resulting from fieldwork. In the analysis that follows, I use Wolf's three dimensions to analyze the effects of my oral history gathering and publishing practices.

20. The oral history gathering process took place from 1995 to 1997.

21. I credit Kelly Ervin with introducing me to the concept of earned acceptance through association; personal conversation, June 1998. See Edwards's discussion of her attempts to access Afro-Caribbean women in England, "Connecting Methodology and Epistemology."

22. Andersen, "Studying across Difference."

23. Personal conversation with José Limón, July 12, 1995. See Limón's self-reflection as a "native" ethnographer in *Dancing with the Devil*.

24. Zavella, "Recording Chicana Life Histories," 17.

25. Griffen notes that when a Navajo woman revealed to her, a white woman, that she had had an abortion, a taboo among the Navajo, the Navajo woman was enough outside the culture and Griffen had been accepted as enough of an insider to allow the story to be shared ("Inside and Outside," 31).

26. Andersen, "Studying across Difference," 52.

27. Jameson, "May and Me," 7.

28. Tixier y Vigil and Elsasser, "The Effects of Ethnicity of the Interviewer on Conversation," 162.

29. Personal conversations with Yolanda Flores-Nieman and Elisa Facio, October 1997, at Washington State University.

30. Stacey, "Can There Be a Feminist Ethnography?" 113.

31. See Patai, "Is Ethical Research Possible?" 142.

32. I thank the anonymous audience member who reminded me of this following a conference presentation where I played excerpts of several of the taped interviews.

33. In questioning whether ethical research is possible, Patai writes that "collecting personal narratives, when done with professional and publishing goals in mind, is invariably in part an economic matter." She also acknowledges that this characterization is "muddied by the fact that the researcher typically plays the role not only of capitalist but also of laborer" because "transformation of 'raw material,' [is] a transformation accomplished through the researcher's labor of turning spoken words into written ones, editing, translating if necessary, or studying and analyzing the stories or data. One sort of discourse be-

comes another, and it is the transformer who derives the greatest benefit from the enterprise" ("Is Ethical Research Possible?" 146).

34. See Wolf, "Situating Feminist Dilemmas," 4.

35. For more analysis of the colonizing effects of white editors, see Deloria's introduction to *Black Elk Speaks* and Fisher's introduction to *Cogewea*.

36. See especially Wolf's "Situating Feminist Dilemmas in Fieldwork"; the essays in Gluck et al., eds., *Women's Words*; and Behar's *Translated Woman*.

37. Smith, *Decolonizing Methodologies*, 9–19.

38. Ibid., 187. At least one Native American researcher is studying whether and how the Maori research system may be applied to research by and for Native Americans, although her findings have yet to be published (personal conversation with Julie Peltier, August 2005).

39. Mary Ozuna, oral history.

40. Oral histories of Minerva Godoy, Ventura Loya, Cindy Siqueiros, and Irma Vásquez.

41. Here I'm thinking of the Spanish-language works of Tomás Rivera, Rolando Hinojosa, Miguel Méndez, Angela de Hoyos, and Bernice Zamora, among others.

42. Some Chicana writers prefer to publish their works with small, nonprofit presses that support feminist, antiracist, anticolonialist, and gay, lesbian, bisexual, and transgendered issues. For example, Cherríe Moraga has published all of her works with three nonprofit presses: Kitchen Table: Women of Color Press in New York, South End Press in Boston, and West End Press in Albuquerque. Gloria Anzaldúa published her works with Aunt Lute Books in San Francisco.

43. Acuña, *The Chicano Movement and Its Legacy Today*.

44. Castillo, *Massacre of the Dreamers*, 9. Castillo borrows the term "concientización" from Paolo Freire's *Pedagogy of the Oppressed*. She uses the Spanish term for consciousness raising to differentiate Chicana feminism from white, middle-class feminism.

45. Castillo, *Massacre of the Dreamers*, 38.

46. See in particular writings by Latina Anónima and Norma Cantú.

47. Anzaldúa, *Borderlands/La Frontera*, 38. She also writes, "To this day I'm not sure how I found the strength to leave the source, the mother, disengage from my family" (38).

48. Castillo, *Massacre of the Dreamers*, 63.

49. Oral histories of Loya, Siqueiros, Urias, Vásquez.

50. See Frye, *Indians into Mexicans*.

51. See Stiffarm, "The Demography of Native America."

52. Fregoso and Chabram, "Introduction," 208.

53. See Lincoln, *Discourse and the Construction of Society*.

54. Alarcón, "The Aztec Palimpsest," 34.

55. See the collection of essays by the Latina Feminist Group in *Telling to Live*. For articles on Chicana/o professional and theoretical marginalization within the academy in the late twentieth century, see Alarcón, "Cognitive Desires"; Sandoval, "U.S. Third World Feminism"; Castillo, acknowledgments section in *Massacre of the Dreamers*; Sierra, "The University Setting Reinforces Inequality"; and Fregoso and Chabram, "Chicana/o Cultural Representations." See also the program handout from the 1999 NACCS Conference at San Antonio, "Students Arrested at U.C. Berkeley over the Future of Ethnic Studies." See also *Noticias de NACS: The National Association for Chicano Studies* 11.1 (November 1992) and subsequent issues discussing Acuñas's denial-of-tenure court case (Rodolfo) *Acuña v. The Board of Regents, University of California*, and the controversy surrounding the removal of the director of Chicano/a studies, Yolanda Broyles-González, at the University of California, Santa Barbara in 1995. The tenuousness of Chicano/a faculty positions and Chicano/a studies programs was also evidenced by the actions of the president of the University of Texas, Arlington, on July 26, 1996, which included relieving José Angel Gutierrez of duties as director of the Center for Mexican American Studies (CMAS), the firing of two staff members, and the transfer of the center's activities to the School of Urban and Public Affairs (Rodríguez, "CMAS—Need Your Help"). See also the television documentary *Shattering the Silences: Minority Professors Break into the Ivory Tower* broadcast on PBS on January 24, 1997, and the explanatory Web site (http://www.pbs.org/shattering/).

56. "Doing Gigs," 231.

57. Ibid., 230.

58. For discussions of the ethnographic elements of Chicana fictional and scholarly writings, see Quintana, *Home Girls*, 34, 51; and Chabram, "Chicano/a Studies as Oppositional Ethnography," 232–44.

59. Behar, "Writing in My Father's Name," 72.

CONCLUSION

1. Saragoza, "Recent Chicano Historiography," 82.

2. Fregoso and Chabram, "Introduction," 211.

3. Evelyn Gonzales, oral history.

4. Hall, "The Spectacle of the 'Other,' " 270.

5. I use Gayatri Spivak's term "encounter" to signify that Third World women frequently experience male and colonial violence and "counter" or resist with their bodies. See her translation and introduction to Mahasweta Devi's story "Drapaudi" in *In Other Worlds*.

6. I refer to works such as *La Maravilla*, by Alfredo Vea Jr.; *The Humming-*

bird's Daughter, by Luis Alberto Urrea; *Erased Faces*, by Graciela Limón; and *The Flower and the Skull*, by Kathleen Alcalá. Several of Ana Castillo's works also mention Yaqui and Pueblo characters, histories, and folklore, although these identities are not developed throughout her works as are those in the aforementioned novels. See *Sapagonia, So Far from God*, and *Watercolor Women, Opaque Men*.

❀ REFERENCES

ORAL HISTORIES

Godoy, Minerva. Muscatine, Iowa, 1995.
Gonzales, Evelyn. Tucson, Arizona, 1995–96.
Harada, Aurora. San Antonio, Texas, 1995–97.
Loya, Ventura. Muscatine, Iowa, 1995–97.
Ozuna, Mary. San Antonio, Texas, 1995–97.
Rivera Reyes, Vicki. San Antonio, Texas, 1995.
Siqueiros, Cindy. Muscatine, Iowa, 1995–97.
Urias, Virginia. Tucson, Arizona, 1995–96.
Vásquez, Irma. Tucson, Arizona, 1995.

PUBLISHED SOURCES

Abu-Lughod, Lila. "The Romance of Resistance: Tracing Transformations of Power through Bedouin Women." *American Ethnologist* 17 (1990): 41–55.
———. "Writing against Culture." In *Recapturing Anthropology: Working in the Present*, edited by Richard G. Fox, 137–62. Santa Fe, N.M.: School of American Research Press, 1991.
———. *Writing Women's Worlds: Bedouin Stories.* Berkeley: University of California Press, 1993.
Acuña, Rodolfo. *Occupied America: A History of Chicanos.* New York: Harper-Collins, 1988.
———. *The Chicano Movement and Its Legacy Today.* Videocassette. Albuquerque: University of New Mexico, Center for Regional Studies Southwestern Collection, 1999.
Agogino, George A., Dominique E. Stevens, and Lynda Carlotta. "Doña Marina and the Legend of La Llorona." *Anthropological Journal of Canada* 11.1 (1973): 27–29.

Ahern, Maureen, ed. *A Rosario Castellanos Reader*. Austin: University of Texas Press, 1988.

Alarcón, Daniel Cooper. "The Aztec Palimpsest: Toward a New Understanding of Aztlán, Cultural Identity, and History." *Aztlán: A Journal of Chicano Studies* 19.2 (1988–90): 33–68.

Alarcón, Norma. "Chicana Feminism: In the Tracks of 'The' Native Woman." *Cultural Studies* 4.3 (1990): 248–54.

——. "Chicana's Feminist Literature: A Re-Vision Through Malintzin / or Malintzin: Putting Flesh Back on the Object." In *This Bridge Called My Back*, edited by Cherríe Moraga and Gloria Anzaldúa. New York: Kitchen Table: Women of Color Press, 1983. 182–90.

——. "Cognitive Desires: An Allegory of/for Chicana Critics." In *Chicana (W)rites on Word and Film*, edited by María Herrera-Sobek and Helena María Viramontes. Berkeley: Third Woman Press, 1995. 185–200.

——. "The Theoretical Subject(s) of *This Bridge Called My Back* and Anglo-American Feminism." In *Making Face, Making Soul: Haciendo Caras: Creative and Critical Perspectives by Feminists of Color*, edited by Gloria Anzaldúa. San Francisco: Aunt Lute Books, 1990. 356–69.

——. "Traddutora, Traditora: A Paradigmatic Figure of Chicana Feminism." *Cultural Critique* 13 (1989): 57–87.

Allen, Paula Gunn. "Who Is Your Mother? Red Roots of White Feminism." In *The Graywolf Annual Five: Multi-Cultural Literacy*, edited by Rick Simonson and Scott Walker. Saint Paul, Minn.: Graywolf Press, 1988. 13–27

Almaguer, Tomás. "Chicano Men: A Cartography of Homosexual Identity and Behavior." *differences: A Journal of Feminist Cultural Studies* 3.2 (1991): 75–100.

Anaya, Rudolfo. *Bless Me, Ultima*. Berkeley: TQS Publications, 1972.

Anaya, Rudolfo, and Francisco Lomelí, eds. *Aztlán: Essays on the Chicano Homeland*. Albuquerque: University of New Mexico Press, 1991 (1989).

Andersen, Margaret L. "Studying across Difference: Race, Class, and Gender in Qualitative Research." In *Race and Ethnicity in Research Methods*, edited by John H. Stanfield II and Rutledge M. Dennis. Newbury Park, Calif.: Sage Publications, 1993. 39–52.

Anzaldúa, Gloria. *Borderlands / La Frontera: The New Mestiza*. San Francisco: Aunt Lute Books, 1987.

——. "Doing Gigs: Speaking, Writing, and Change." An Interview with Debbie Blake and Carmen Ábrego. In *Interviews / Entrevistas: Gloria E. Anzaldúa*, edited by AnaLouise Keating. New York: Routledge, 2000. 211–33.

——. *Prietita Meets the Ghost Woman / Prietita y La Llorona*. San Francisco: Children's Book Press, 1995.

Arugelles, Lourdes, and Anne M. Rivero. "Gender/Sexual Orientation, Violence, and Transnational Migration: Conversations with Some Latinas We Think We Know." *Urban Anthropology* 22.3 / 4 (1993): 259.

——. "Undocumented Female Labor in the United States Southwest: An Essay on Migration, Consciousness, Oppression and Struggle." In *Between Borders: Essays on Mexicana/Chicana History*, edited by Adelaida R. Del Castillo. Encino, Calif.: Floricanto Press, 1990. 299–312.

Barakat, Robert A. "Aztec Motifs in La Llorona." *Southern Folklore Quarterly* 29.4 (1965): 288–96.

Barraza, Santa C. "Santa C. Barraza: An Autobiography." In *Santa Barraza: Artist of the Borderlands*, edited by María Herrera-Sobek. College Station: Texas A&M University Press, 2001. 3–49.

Behar, Ruth. "Rage and Redemption: Reading the Life Story of a Mexican Marketing Woman." *Feminist Studies* 16 (1990): 223–58.

——. *Translated Woman: Crossing the Border with Esperanza's Story*. Boston: Beacon, 1993.

Benmayor, Rina. "Testimony, Action Research, and Empowerment: Puerto Rican Women and Popular Education." In *Women's Words: The Feminist Practice of Oral History*, edited by Sherna Berger Gluck and Daphne Patai. New York: Routledge, 1991. 159–74.

Beverley, John. "The Margin at the Center: On *Testimonio* (Testimonial Narrative)." In *De/Colonizing the Self: The Politics of Gender in Women's Autobiography*, edited by Sidonie Smith and Julia Watson. Minneapolis: University of Minnesota Press, 1992. 91–113.

Bhabha, Homi. "Introduction: Narrating the Nation." In *Nation and Narration*, edited by Homi Bhabha. New York: Routledge, 1991.

——. "Signs Taken for Wonders: Questions of Ambivalence and Authority under a Tree outside Delhi, May 1817." *Critical Inquiry* 12.1 (1985): 144–65.

Bierhorst, John, ed. *The Hungry Woman: Myths and Legends of the Aztecs*. New York: Quill, 1984.

Blake, Debra J. "Reading Dynamics of Power through Mexican-Origin Women's Oral Histories." *Frontiers: A Journal of Women's Studies* 19.3 (1998): 24–41.

——. "Unsettling Identities: Transitive Subjectivity in Cherríe Moraga's *Loving in the War Years*." *a/b: Auto/Biography* 12.1 (June 1997): 71–89.

——. " 'Why Don't They Just Leave?' Theorizing Complexity of Agency, Resistance, and Oppression in U.S. Mexicanas' Oral Histories of Domestic Abuse." *Latino/a Studies* (forthcoming).

——. Unpublished interview with Ana Castillo. Iowa City, Iowa. 1994.

Blake, Debra J., with Doug Anderson and Rosalva Ray. "An Interview with Denise Chávez." *Iowa Journal of Cultural Studies* (Spring 1994): 13–20.

Boyce Davies, Carol. "Collaborations and the Ordering Imperative in Life Story

Production." In *De/Colonizing the Subject: The Politics of Gender in Women's Autobiography*, edited by Sidonie Smith and Julia Watson. Minneapolis: University of Minnesota Press, 1992. 3–19.

Brady, Mary Pat. *Extinct Land, Temporal Geographies: Chicana Literature and the Urgency of Space*. Durham, N.C.: Duke University Press, 2002.

Brown, Lester B., John Oliver, and J. Jorge Klor de Alva. *Sociocultural and Service Issues in Working with Hispanic American Clients*. Albany, N.Y.: Professional Development Program, Continuing Education Program/School of Social Welfare, Nelson A. Rockefeller College of Public Affairs and Policy, State University of New York at Albany, 1985.

Burgos-Debray, Elisabeth. "Introduction." *I, Rigoberta Menchú*, edited by Elisabeth Burgos-Debray. Translated by Ann Wright. London: Verso, 1984. xi–xxi.

Buss, Fran Leeper, ed. *Forged under the Sun / Forjada bajo el sol: The Life History of María Elena Lucas*. Ann Arbor: University of Michigan Press, 1993.

——. *La Partera: The Story of a Midwife*. Ann Arbor: University of Michigan Press, 1980.

——. "Work and Family: Low Income and Minority Women Talk about Their Lives." Tucson: University of Arizona Special Collections Library; Boston: The Arthur and Elizabeth Schlesinger Library of the History of Women in America, Radcliffe Institute for Advanced Studies, Harvard University, 1993.

Butler, Judith. "Imitation and Gender Insubordination." In *Inside/Out: Lesbian Theories, Gay Theories*, edited by Diana Fuss. New York: Routledge, 1981. 13–31.

——. "Variations on Sex and Gender: Beauvoir, Wittig, and Foucault." In *Feminism as Critique: On the Politics of Gender*, edited by Seyla Benhabib and Drucilla Cornell. Minneapolis: University of Minnesota Press, 1987. 128–42.

Cancian, Francesca M. "Feminist Science: Methodologies that Challenge Inequality." *Gender and Society* 6.4 (1992): 623–43.

Candelaria, Cordelia. "Letting La Llorona Go, or Re/reading History's Tender Mercies." *Heresies: A Feminist Publication on Art and Politics* 7.3 (1993): 111–15.

Cantú, Norma. "La Virgen de Guadalupe: Symbol of Faith and Devotion." In *Familia, Fe, y Fiestas / Family, Faith, and Fiestas: Mexican American Celebrations of the Holiday Season*, edited by Amy Kitchener. Fresno, Calif.: Arte Américas and the Fresno Arts Council, 1996. 15–20.

Castañeda, Antonia I. "History and the Politics of Violence against Women." In *Living Chicana Theory*, edited by Carla Trujillo. Berkeley, Calif.: Third Woman Press, 1998. 310–19.

Castañeda Shular, Antonia, Tomás Ybarra-Frausto, and Joseph Sommers, eds.

Literatura chicana: Texto y contexto. Englewood Cliffs, N.J.: Prentice Hall, 1972.

Castellanos, Rosario. *Balún-Canán*. Mexico City: Fondo de Cultura Económica, 1957.

——. *Book of Lamentations*. Translated by Esther Allen. New York: Penguin, 1998.

——. *City of Kings*. Trans. Robert S. Rudder and Gloria Chacón de Arjona. Pittsburgh: Latin American Literary Review Press, 1993.

——. *Ciudad Real*. Mexico City: Universidad Veracruzana, 1960.

——. *Mujer que sabe latín*. . . . Mexico City: Secretaría de Educación Pública (SepSetentasDiana), 1979 (1973).

——. *The Nine Guardians: A Novel*. Translated by Irene Nicholson. New York: Vanguard Press, 1960.

——. *Oficio de tinieblas*. Mexico City: Joaquín Mortiz, 1962.

——. *El rescate del mundo*. Mexico City: Ediciones de América, 1952.

Castillo, Ana, ed. *The Goddess of the Americas / La Diosa de las Américas: Writings on the Virgin of Guadalupe*. New York: Riverhead Books, 1996.

——. "Introduction: Goddess of the Americas." In *The Goddess of the Americas / Diosa de las Américas: Writings on the Virgin of Guadalupe*, xv–xxiii.

——. *Massacre of the Dreamers: Essays on Xicanisma*. Albuquerque: University of New Mexico Press, 1994.

——. *Sapogonia*. New York: Anchor Doubleday, 1994 (1990).

——. *So Far from God*. New York: Norton, 1993.

——. *Watercolor Women, Opaque Men*. Willimantic, Conn.: Curbstone, 2005.

Castillo, Debra. *Talking Back: Toward a Latin American Feminist Criticism*. Ithaca, N.Y.: Cornell University Press, 1992.

Chabram, Angie. "Chicano/a Studies as Oppositional Ethnography." *Cultural Studies* 4.3 (1990): 228–47.

Chabram-Dernersesian, Angie. "I Throw Punches for My Race, but I Don't Want to Be a Man: Writing Us—Chica-nos (Girl, Us) / Chicanas—into the Movement Script." In *Cultural Studies*, edited by Cary Nelson, Lawrence Grossberg, and Paula Treichler. New York: Routledge, 1992. 81–95.

Chávez, Denise. *Face of an Angel*. New York: Farrar, Straus and Giroux, 1994.

——. *Novena Narrativas y Ofrendas Nuevomexicanas*. In *The Goddess of the Americas / La Diosa de las Américas: Writings on the Virgin of Guadalupe*, edited by Ana Castillo. New York: Riverhead Books, 1996. 153–69.

Christ, Carol P. *Womanspirit Rising: A Feminist Reader in Religion*. New York: Harper and Row, 1979.

Cisneros, Sandra. "Guadalupe the Sex Goddess." In *Goddess of the Americas / La Diosa de las Américas: Writings on the Virgin of Guadalupe*, edited by Ana Castillo. New York: Riverhead Books, 1996. 46–51.

——. *The House on Mango Street*. New York: Vintage, 1989.

——. "Little Miracles, Kept Promises." In *Woman Hollering Creek and Other Stories*. New York: Random House, 1991.

——. "Woman Hollering Creek." In *Woman Hollering Creek and Other Stories*.

Clauss, James J., and Sarah Iles Johnston, eds. *Medea: Essays on Medea in Myth, Literature, Philosophy, and Art*. Princeton, N.J.: Princeton University Press, 1997.

Cockcroft, Eva Sperling, and Holly Barnet-Sánchez, eds. *Signs from the Heart: California Chicano Murals*. Albuquerque: Social and Public Art Resource Center and University of New Mexico, 1993.

Collins, Patricia Hill. *Black Feminist Thought: Knowledge, Consciousness, and the Politics of Empowerment*. New York: Routledge, 1991.

Conkey, Margaret, with Sarah H. Williams. "Original Narratives: The Political Economy of Gender in Archaeology." In *Gender at the Crossroads of Knowledge: Feminist Anthropology in the Postmodern Era*, edited by Micaela di Leonardo. Berkeley: University of California Press, 1991. 102–39.

Cypess, Sandra Messinger. *La Malinche in Mexican Literature: From History to Myth*. Austin: University of Texas Press, 1991.

Davis, Marilyn P. *Mexican Voices/American Dreams: An Oral History of Mexican Immigration*. New York: H. Holt, 1990.

Davis, Natalie Zemon, and Randoph Starn. "Introduction: Special Issue, Memory and Countermemory." *Representations* 26 (1989): 1–6.

de Lauretis, Teresa. "Sexual Indifference and Lesbian Representation." *Theater Journal* 40.2 (1988): 151–77.

Deloria, Vine Jr. "Introduction." In *Black Elk Speaks*, by Black Elk. Lincoln: University of Nebraska Press, 1988.

Deutsch, Sarah Jan. *No Separate Refuge: Culture, Class, and Gender on an Anglo-Hispanic Frontier in the American Southwest, 1880–1940*. New York: Oxford University Press, 1987.

Díaz del Castillo, Bernal. *The Conquest of New Spain*. Translated by J. M. Cohen. Middlesex, England: Penguin Books, 1978.

di Leonardo, Micaela. "Introduction: Gender, Culture, and Political Economy: Feminist Anthropology in Historical Perspective." In *Gender at the Crossroads of Knowledge: Feminist Anthropology in the Postmodern Era*, edited by Micaela di Leonardo. Berkeley: University of California Press, 1991. 1–48.

DuBois, Ellen, Mari Jo Buhle, Temma Kaplan, Gerda Lerner, and Carroll Smith-Rosenberg. "Politics and Culture in Women's History: A Symposium." *Feminist Studies* 6.1 (1980): 27–64.

Durón, Clementina. "Mexican Women and Labor Conflict in Los Angeles: The ILGWU Dressmakers' Strike of 1933." *Aztlán* 15.1 (1984): 145–61.

Echols, Alice. "Cultural Feminism: Feminist Capitalism and the Anti-Pornography Movement." *Social Text* 3 (1983): 34–53.

——. *Daring to Be Bad: Radical Feminism in America, 1967–1975*. Minneapolis: University of Minnesota Press, 1989.

——. "The New Feminism of Yin and Yang." In *Powers of Desire: The Politics of Sexuality*, edited by Ann Snitow, Christine Stansell, and Sharon Thompson. New York: Monthly Review Press, 1983. 439–58.

——. "The Taming of the Id: Feminist Sexual Politics, 1968–83." In *Pleasure and Danger: Exploring Female Sexuality*, edited by Carole S. Vance. London: Pandora Press, 1992 (1984). 50–72.

Edwards, Rosalind. "Connecting Methodology and Epistemology: A White Woman Interviewing Black Women." *Women's Studies International Forum* 13.5 (1990): 477–90.

Elsasser, Nan, Kyle MacKenzie, and Yvonne Tixier y Vigil, eds. *Las Mujeres: Conversations from a Hispanic Community*. Old Westbury, N.Y.: Feminist Press; New York: McGraw-Hill, 1979.

Espín, Oliva M. "Cultural and Historical Influences on Sexuality in Hispanic/Latin Women: Implications for Psychotherapy." In *Pleasure and Danger: Exploring Female Sexuality*, edited by Carole S. Vance. London: Pandora Press, 1989 (1984). 149–64.

Esquivel, Laura. *Como agua para chocolate*. New York: Doubleday, 1993.

Eysturoy, Annie O. *Daughters of Self-Creation: The Contemporary Chicana Novel*. Albuquerque: University of New Mexico Press, 1996.

Faderman, Lillian. *Odd Girls and Twilight Lovers: A History of Lesbian Life in Twentieth-Century America*. New York: Columbia University Press, 1991.

Felski, Rita. *Beyond Feminist Aesthetics: Feminist Literature and Social Change*. Cambridge, Mass.: Harvard University Press, 1989.

Fernandez, Sandy M. "Tales Our Mothers Told Us." *Hispanic*, November 1993, 56–58.

Fernández-Kelly, María Patricia. *For We Are Sold, I and My People: Women and Industry in Mexico's Frontier*. Albany: State University of New York Press, 1983.

Fischer, Michael M. J. "Ethnicity and the Post-Modern Arts of Memory." In *Writing Culture: The Poetics and Politics of Ethnography*, edited by James Clifford and George E. Marcus. Berkeley: University of California Press, 1986. 194–233.

Fisher, Dexter. "Introduction." In *Cogewea: The Half-Blood*, by Hum-ishu-ma/Mourning Dove. Lincoln: University of Nebraska Press, 1981.

Foucault, Michel. *Discipline and Punish: The Birth of the Prison*. New York: Random House, 1977.

Foundation for the Advancement of Mesoamerican Studies, Inc. FAMSI home page. http://www.famsi.org/. Accessed September 27, 2007.

Fregoso, Rosa Linda, and Angie Chabram. "Introduction: Chicana/o Cultural Representations: Reframing Alternative Critical Discourses." *Cultural Studies* 4 (1990): 203–12.

Freire, Paulo. *Pedagogy of the Oppressed*. Trans. Myra Bergman Ramos. New York Continuum, 1993 (1970).

Frye, David. *Indians into Mexicans: History and Identity in a Mexican Town.* Austin: University of Texas Press, 1996.

Fuss, Diana. *Essentially Speaking: Feminism, Nature, and Difference.* New York: Routledge, 1989.

———. "Inside/Out." In *Inside/Out: Lesbian Theories, Gay Theories,* edited by Diana Fuss. New York: Routledge, 1991. 1–10.

Gallop, Jane. "Quand nos lèvres s'écrivent: Irigaray's Body Politic." *Romantic Review* 74.1 (1983): 77–83.

García, Alma M. *Chicana Feminist Thought: The Basic Historical Writings.* New York: Routledge, 1997.

———. *Narratives of Mexican American Women: Emergent Identities of the Second Generation.* Walnut Creek, Calif.: AltaMira Press, 2004.

Garcia-Bahne, Betty. "La Chicana and the Chicano Family." In *Essays on La Mujer,* edited by Rosaura Sánchez and Rosa Martinez Cruz. Los Angeles: Chicano Studies Center Publications, University of California, Los Angeles, 1977. 30–47.

Garro, Elena. *Los recuerdos del porvenir.* Mexico: J. M. Ortiz, 1963.

———. *Recollections of Things to Come.* Trans. Ruth L. C. Simms. Austin: University of Texas Press, 1969.

Gaspar de Alba, Alicia. *La Llorona on the Longfellow Bridge: Poetry y otra movidas, 1985–2001.* Houston: Arte Público Press, 2003.

Geertz, Clifford. "Art as a Cultural System." *Modern Language Notes* 91.6 (1976): 1473–99.

Gillespie, Susan D. *The Aztec Kings: The Construction of Rulership in Mexica History.* Tucson: University of Arizona Press, 1989.

Glenn, Evelyn Nakano. "Social Constructions of Mothering: A Thematic Overview." In *Mothering: Ideology, Experience, and Agency,* edited by Evelyn Nakano Glenn, Grace Chang, and Linda Rennie Forcey. New York: Routledge, 1994. 1–29.

Gluck, Sherna Berger, and Daphne Patai, eds. *Women's Words: The Feminist Practice of Oral History.* New York: Routledge, 1991.

Gómez, Alma, Cherríe Moraga, and Mariana Romo-Carmona, with Myrtha Chabrán. "By Word of Mouth / De Boca en Boca." In *Cuentos: Stories by Latinas,* edited by Gómez, Moraga, and Romo-Carmona. New York: Kitchen Table: Women of Color Press, 1983. vii–xviii.

Gonzalez, Deena J. "The Widowed Women of Santa Fe: Assessments on the Lives of an Unmarried Population, 1850–1880." In *Unequal Sisters: A Multicultural Reader in U.S. Women's History,* edited by Ellen Carol DuBois and Vicki Ruiz. New York: Routledge, 1994.

Gonzalez, Rosalinda M. "The Chicana in Southwest Labor History, 1900–1975." *Critical Perspectives of Third World America* 2.1 (1984): 26–61.

Gordon, Deborah, Trinh T. Minh-ha, Lisa Bloom, Donna Haraway, and Aihwa Ong. "Panel Discussion 2." *Inscriptions* 3 / 4 (1988): 94–104.

Graves, Robert. *The Greek Myths: Volume Two.* Baltimore: Penguin, 1973.

Graves, Robert, and Raphael Patai, eds., *Hebrew Myths: The Book of Genesis.* New York: McGraw-Hill, 1966. 65–69.

Griffen, Joyce. "Inside and Outside: The Moebius Strip of Oral History." In *Insider/Outsider Relations with Informants,* edited by Elizabeth Jameson. Working Paper no. 13. Tucson: Southwest Institute for Research on Women, University of Arizona, 1982. 26–37.

Griffith, James S. *Hecho a mano: The Traditional Arts of Tucson's Mexican American Community.* Tucson: University of Arizona Press, 2000.

Guerrero, Andrés. *A Chicano Theology.* Maryknoll, N.Y.: Orbis Books, 1987.

——. *The Significance of Nuestra Señora Guadalupe and La Raza Cósmica in the Development of a Chicano Theology of Liberation.* Ann Arbor: University Microfilms International, 1984.

Hadden, Gerry. "Weeping Woman." Transcript. *Morning Edition.* National Public Radio. KNCM, Appleton, Minn. http://www.npr.org. Accessed December 28, 2001.

Halbwachs, Maurice. *The Collective Memory.* Trans. Francis J. Ditter Jr. and Vida Yazdi Ditter. New York: Harper and Row, 1980.

——. *On Collective Memory.* Trans. Lewis A. Coser. Chicago: University of Chicago Press, 1992.

Hall, Stuart. "Cultural Identity and Cinematic Representation." *Framework* 36 (1989): 68–81.

——. "The Spectacle of the 'Other.'" In *Representation: Cultural Representations and Signifying Practices,* edited by Stuart Hall. Thousand Oaks, Calif.: Sage, 1997. 223–79.

Hankiss, Agnes. "Ontologies of the Self: On the Mythological Rearranging of One's Life-History." In *Biography and Society: The Life History Approach in the Social Sciences,* edited by Daniel Bertraux. Beverley Hills, Calif.: Sage, 1981. 203–9.

Harding, Sandra. *Feminism and Methodology: Social Science Issues.* Bloomington: Indiana University Press, 1987.

Harlan, Theresa. "A Conversation with Ester Hernández." In *The Art of Provocation: Ester Hernández: A Retrospective.* CN Gorman Museum, Native American Studies, University of California, Davis, October 10–November 17, 1995.

Hastrup, Kirsten, ed. *Other Histories.* New York: Routledge, 1992.

Hattersley-Drayton, Karana, Joyce Bishop, and Tomás Ybarra-Frausto, eds. *Inside Out: Perspectives on Mexican and Mexican-American Folk Art.* San Francisco: Mexican Museum, 1989.

Hawes, Bess Lomax. "La Llorona in Juvenile Hall." *Western Folklore* 27 (1968): 155–70.

Herrera-Sobek, María, ed. *Santa Barraza: Artist of the Borderlands*. College Station: Texas A&M University Press, 2001.

hooks, bell. *Feminist Theory: From Margin to Center*. Boston: South End Press, 1984.

——. *Yearning: Race, Gender, and Cultural Politics*. Boston: South End Press, 1990.

Irigaray, Luce. *Je, Tu, Nous: Toward a Culture of Difference*. Trans. Alison Martin. New York: Routledge, 1993.

——. *Sexes and Genealogies*. Trans. Gillian C. Gill. New York: Columbia University Press, 1993.

Isasi-Díaz, Ada María, and Yolanda Tarango. *Hispanic Women: A Prophetic Voice of the Church*. San Francisco: Harper and Row, 1988.

Jaimes, M. Annette, ed. *The State of Native America*. Boston: South End Press, 1992.

Jameson, Elizabeth. "May and Me: Relationships with Informants and the Community." In *Insider/Outsider Relationships with Informants*, ed. Elizabeth Jameson. Working Paper No. 13. Tucson: Southwest Institute for Research on Women, University of Arizona, 1982. 3–13.

Johnston, Sarah Iles. "Corinthian Medea and the Cult of Hera Akraia." In *Medea: Essays on Medea in Myth, Literature, Philosophy, and Art*, edited by James J. Clauss and Sarah Iles Johnston. Princeton, N.J.: Princeton University Press, 1997. 44–70.

——. "Introduction." *Medea: Essays on Medea in Myth, Literature, Philosophy, and Art*, edited by James J. Clauss and Sarah Iles Johnston. Princeton, N.J.: Princeton University Press, 1997. 1–17.

Karttunen, Frances. "Rethinking Malinche." In *Indian Women of Early Mexico*, edited by Susan Schroeder, Stephanie Wood, and Robert Haskett. Norman: University of Oklahoma Press, 1997. 291–312.

King, Katie. *Theory in Its Feminist Travels: Conversations in U.S. Women's Movements*. Bloomington: Indiana University Press, 1994.

Kingsolver, Barbara. *Holding the Line: Women in the Great Arizona Mine Strike of 1983*. Ithaca, N.Y.: ILR Press, 1989.

Klein, Cecelia F. "Rethinking Cihuacoatl: Aztec Political Imagery of the Conquered Woman." In *Smoke and Mist: Studies in Memory of Thelma D. Sullivan*, edited by J. Kathryn Josserand and Karen Dakin. Oxford: BAR., 1988. 237–77.

Kristeva, Julia. *Desire in Language: A Semiotic Approach to Art and Literature*. Trans. Thomas Gora, Alice Jardine, and Leon Roudiez. New York: Columbia University Press, 1980.

——. "Women's Time." *Signs* 7.1 (1981): 13–35.

Krupat, Arnold. *For Those Who Come After: A Study of Native American Autobiography*. Berkeley: University of California Press, 1985.

Küchler, Susanne, and Walter Melion, eds. *Images of Memory: On Remembering and Representation*. Washington: Smithsonian Institution Press, 1991.

Latina Feminist Group. *Telling to Live: Latina Feminist Testimonios*. Durham, N.C.: Duke University Press, 2001.

Lecompte, Janet. "The Independent Women of Hispanic New Mexico, 1821–1846." *Western Historical Quarterly* 12.1 (1981): 17–35.

LeGoff, Jacques. *History and Memory*. Trans. Steven Rendall and Elizabeth Clamen. New York: Columbia University Press, 1992.

Limón, José E. *Dancing with the Devil: Society and Cultural Poetics in Mexican-American South Texas*. Madison: University of Wisconsin Press, 1994.

——. "*La Llorona*, the Third Legend of Greater Mexico: Cultural Symbols, Women, and the Political Unconscious." *Renato Rosaldo Lecture Series* 2 (1984–85): 3–93.

Lincoln, Bruce. *Discourse and the Construction of Society: Comparative Studies of Myth, Ritual, and Classification*. New York: Oxford University Press, 1989.

Lipsitz, George. *Time Passages: Collective Memory and American Popular Culture*. Minneapolis: University of Minnesota Press, 1990.

Lucas, María Elena. *Forged under the Sun / Forjada bajo el sol: The Life of María Elena Lucas*. Ed. Fran Leeper Buss. Ann Arbor: University of Michigan Press, 1993.

Madsen, Catherine. "A God of One's Own: Recent Work by and about Women in Religion." *Signs* 19.2 (Winter 1994): 480–98.

Mahoney, Martha. "Victimization or Oppression? Women's Lives, Violence, and Agency." In *The Public Nature of Private Violence: The Discovery of Domestic Abuse*, edited by Martha Alberson and Roxanne Mykitiuk. New York: Routledge, 1994. 59–92.

Marin, Cheech. Introduction. *Chicano Visions: American Painters on the Verge*, edited by Cheech Marin. Boston: Bulfinch Press, 2002. 7–8.

Martin, Patricia Preciado, ed. *Songs My Mother Sang to Me: An Oral History of Mexican American Women*. Tucson: University of Arizona Press, 1992.

Martínez, Demetria. "Hail Mary." In *Three Times a Woman: Chicana Poetry*, by Alicia Gaspar de Alba, María Herrera-Sobek, and Demetria Martínez. Tempe, Ariz.: Bilingual Review Press, 1989.

Martínez, Elizabeth, ed. *500 años del pueblo chicano / 500 Years of Chicano History in Pictures*. Albuquerque, N.M.: Southwest Organizing Project, 1991.

Martínez, Elizabeth, and Ed McCaughan. "Chicanas and Mexicanas within a Transnational Working Class." In *Between Borders: Essays on Mexicana / Chicana History*, edited by Adelaida R. Del Castillo. Encino, Calif.: Floricanto Press, 1990. 31–60.

Martínez, Rubén. "The Undocumented Virgin." In *The Goddess of the Americas /*

La Diosa de las Américas: Writings on the Virgin of Guadalupe, edited by Ana Castillo. New York: Riverhead Books, 1996. 98–112.

Matter, Kathy. "Sacred New Images: Lessons of a Latina Artist: Question all Stereotypes, including Those of Your People." *Journal and Courier* (Lafayette, Ind.), September 28, 1995, B1.

McCracken, Ellen. *New Latina Narrative: The Feminine Space of Postmodern Ethnicity*. Tucson: University of Arizona Press, 1999.

McDonald, Marianne. "Medea as Politician and Diva: Riding the Dragon into the Future." In *Medea: Essays on Medea in Myth, Literature, Philosophy, and Art*, edited by James J. Clauss and Sarah Iles Johnston. Princeton, N.J.: Princeton University Press, 1997. 297–323.

McDonnell, Patrick J., and Mark Fineman. "Mexico Poised to OK Dual Nationality Law." *Los Angeles Times*, December 17, 1996.

Meléndez, Theresa. "The Oral Tradition and the Study of American Literature." In *Redefining American Literary History*, edited by A. LaVonne Brown Ruoff and Jerry W. Ward Jr. New York: Modern Language Association, 1990. 75–76.

Melion, Walter, and Susanne Küchler. "Introduction: Memory, Cognition, and Image Production." In *Images of Memory*, edited by Susanne Küchler and Walter Melion. Washington: Smithsonian Institution Press, 1991. 1–46.

Melville, Margarita B., ed. *Mexicanas at Work in the United States*. Houston: Mexican American Studies Program, University of Houston, 1988.

Menchaca, Martha. *Recovering History, Constructing Race: The Indian, Black, and White Roots of Mexican Americans*. Austin: University of Texas Press, 2001.

Menchú, Rigoberta. *I, Rigoberta Menchú: An Indian Woman in Guatemala*. Ed. Elisabeth Burgos-Debray. Trans. Ann Wright. London: Verso, 1984.

Meskell, Lynn. "Goddesses, Gimbutas, and 'New Age' Archaeology." *Antiquity* 68 (1995): 74–86.

Meyer, Michael, and William L. Sherman. *The Course of Mexican History*. New York: Oxford University Press, 1995.

Miller, Elaine K., ed. *Mexican Folk Narrative from the Los Angeles Area*. Austin: University of Texas Press, 1973.

Miller, Mary, and Karl Taube. *The Gods and Symbols of Ancient Mexico and the Maya: An Illustrated Dictionary of Mesoamerican Religion*. New York: Thames and Hudson, 1993.

Mirandé, Alfredo, and Evangelina Enríquez. *La Chicana: The Mexican American Woman*. Chicago: University of Chicago Press, 1979.

Molina, Ida, and Oleg Zinam. "The Historical Role of a Woman in the Chicanos' Search for Ethnic Identity: The Case of Doña Marina." *Quarterly Journal of Ideology* 14.1 (1990): 39–53.

Montejano, David. *Anglos and Mexicans in the Making of Texas, 1836–1986*. Austin: University of Texas Press, 1987.

Mora, Magdalena. "The Tolteca Strike: Mexican Women and the Struggle for Union Representation." In *Mexican Immigrant Workers in the U.S.*, edited by Antonio Ríos-Bustamante. Los Angeles: Chicano Studies Research Center Publications, University of California, 1981. 111–17.

Moraga, Cherríe. *The Hungry Woman*. Albuquerque: West End Press. 2001.

——. *The Hungry Woman: A Mexican Medea*. In *The Hungry Woman*, 6–99.

——. *The Last Generation: Prose and Poetry*. Boston: South End Press, 1993.

——. "A Long Line of Vendidas." In *Loving in the War Years*, 90–144.

——. *Loving in the War Years*. Boston: South End Press, 1983.

——. *Waiting in the Wings: Portrait of a Queer Motherhood*. Ithaca, N.Y.: Firebrand Books, 1997.

Moraga, Cherríe, and Gloria Anzaldúa, eds. *This Bridge Called My Back*. New York: Kitchen Table: Women of Color Press, 1983 (1981).

Morrison, Toni. *Beloved: A Novel*. New York: Alfred A. Knopf, 1987.

——. "The Site of Memory." In *Inventing the Truth: The Art and Craft of Memoir*, edited by William Zinsser. Boston: Houghton Mifflin, 1998. 202–4.

Morton, Nelle. "The Goddess as Metaphoric Image." In *Weaving the Visions: New Patterns in Feminist Spirituality*, edited by Judith Plaskow and Carol P. Christ. San Francisco: HarperSanFrancisco, 1989. 111–18.

Mujeres Activas en Letras y Cambio Social (MALCS). "MALCS Declaration." In *Chicana Critical Issues*, edited by Rafaela Castro, Norma Alarcón, Emma Pérez, Beatriz Pesquera, Adaljiza Sosa Riddell, and Patricia Zavella. Berkeley, Calif.: Third Woman Press, 1983.

Nash, June. "The Aztecs and the Ideology of Male Dominance." *Signs* 4.2 (1978): 349–62.

Nava, Gregory. "La Llorona (The Weeping Woman)—Parts 1 and 2." *American Family*. El Norte Productions, KCET. (PBS). Air dates February 6 and 13, 2002.

Nicholson, H. B. "The New Tenochtitlan Templo Mayor Coyolxauhqui-Chantico Monument." *Indiana* (Berlin, Germany) 10 (1985): 77–98.

——. "Religion in Pre-Hispanic Central Mexico." In *The Handbook of Middle American Indians*, edited by Gordon F. Ekholm and Ignacio Bernal. Vol. 10 of *Archaeology of Northern Mesoamerica, Part I*. Austin: University of Texas Press, 1971. 395–446.

Nora, Pierre. "Between Memory and History: Les Lieux de Mémoire." *Representations* 26 (1989): 7–25.

Oring, Elliott. "Folk Narratives." In *Folklore Groups and Folklore Genres: An Introduction*, edited by Elliott Oring. Logan: Utah State University Press, 1986. 121–45.

Otero, Michelle. *Malinche's Daughter*. South Bend, Ind.: Momotombo Press, 2006.

Padilla, Genaro. *My History, Not Yours: The Formation of Mexican American Autobiography*. Madison: University of Wisconsin Press, 1993.

Palacios, Monica. "La Llorona Loca: The Other Side." In *Chicana Lesbians: The Girls Our Mothers Warned Us About*, edited by Carla Trujillo. Berkeley, Calif.: Third Woman Press, 1991. 49–51.

Palley, Julian, ed. *Meditation on the Threshold: Rosario Castellanos*. Tempe, Ariz.: Bilingual Press / Editorial Bilingüe, 1988.

Pardo, Mary. "Mexican American Women Grassroots Community Activists: 'Mothers of East Los Angeles.'" *Frontiers* 11.1 (1990): 1–7.

Paredes, Américo. "Mexican Legendry and the Rise of the Mestizo." In *American Folk Legend: A Symposium*, edited by Wayland D. Hand. Berkeley: University of California Press, 1971. 97–107.

Parker, Andrew, Mary Russo, Doris Sommer, and Patricia Yaeger. "Introduction: Nationalisms and Sexualities." In *Nationalisms and Sexualities*, edited by Mary Russo Andrew Parker, Doris Sommer, and Patricia Yaeger. New York: Routledge, 1992. 1–18.

Patai, Daphne. "Is Ethical Research Possible?" In *Women's Words: The Feminist Practice of Oral History*, edited by Sherna Berger Gluck and Daphne Patai. New York: Routledge, 1991. 137–53.

Paz, Octavio. *The Labyrinth of Solitude: Life and Thought in Mexico*. Trans. Lysander Kemp. New York: Grove Press, 1962.

Peña, Devon. "Between the Lines: A New Perspective on the Industrial Sociology of Women Workers in Transnational Labor Processes." In *Chicana Voices: Intersections of Class, Race, and Gender*, edited by Teresa Córdova. Albuquerque: University of New Mexico Press, 1990. 77–95.

Pérez, Domino Renee. "Words, Worlds in Our Heads: Reclaiming La Llorona's Aztecan Antecedents in Gloria Anzaldúa's 'My Black Angelos.'" *Studies in American Indian Literature*. 15.3 / 4 (2003): 51–63.

Perry, Donna. "Gloria Anzaldúa." In *Backtalk: Women Writers Speak Out*, edited by Donna Perry. New Brunswick, N.J.: Rutgers University Press, 1993. 18–42.

Pesquera, Beatriz M., and Denise A. Segura. "There Is No Going Back: Chicanas and Feminism." In *Chicana Critical Issues*, edited by Norma Alarcón. Berkeley, Calif.: Third Woman Press, 1993. 95–115.

Peterson, Jeanette Favrot. "The Virgin of Guadalupe: Symbol of Conquest or Liberation." *Art Journal* 51 (1992): 39–47.

Phillips, Rachel. "Marina/Malinche: Masks and Shadows." In *Women in Hispanic Literature: Icons and Fallen Idols*, edited by Beth Miller. Berkeley: University of California Press, 1983. 97–114.

Plaskow, Judith, and Carol P. Christ, eds. *Weaving the Visions: New Patterns in Feminist Spirituality*. San Francisco: HarperSanFrancisco, 1989.

Poniatowska, Elena. *Hasta no verte, Jesús mío*. Mexico City: Era, 1969.

——. *Here's to You, Jesusa!* Trans. Deanna Heikkinen. New York: Penguin, 2002.

——. *Massacre in Mexico*. Trans. Helen R. Lane. New York: Viking Press, 1975.

——. *La noche de Tlatelolco: Testimonios de historia oral*. Mexico City: Era, 1971.

Poole, Stafford. *Our Lady of Guadalupe: The Origins and Sources of a Mexican National Symbol, 1531–1797*. Tucson: University of Arizona Press, 1996.

Portal, Cecilia. *Las mujeres de la tierra del sol / Women from the Land of the Sun: An Oral History and Photo Documentation Recording the Lives of New Mexico's Hispanas*. Albuquerque: Center for Southwest Research, University of New Mexico, 1994.

Portelli, Alessandro. "Oral History as Genre." In *Narrative and Genre*, edited by Mary Chamberlain and Paul Thompson. London: Routledge, 1998.

Portillo Trambley, Estela. *Blacklight*. In *Sor Juana and Other Plays*. Tempe, Ariz.: Bilingual Press, 1983. 101–37.

——. *Sor Juana*. In *Sor Juana and Other Plays*. 143–95.

Pratt, Mary Louise. "Yo Soy La Malinche: Chicana Writers and the Poetics of Ethnonationalism." *Callaloo* 16.4 (1993): 859–73.

Quintana, Alvina E. *Home Girls: Chicana Literary Voices*. Philadelphia: Temple University Press, 1996.

Ramos Escandon, Carmen. "Alternative Sources to Women's History: Literature." In *Between Borders: Essays on Chicana/Mexicana History*, edited by Adelaida R. Del Castillo. Encino, Calif.: Floricanto Press, 1990. 201–12.

Randall, Margaret F. "Guadalupe, Subversive Virgin." In *Goddess of the Americas / La Diosa de las Américas: Writings on the Virgin of Guadalupe*, edited by Ana Castillo. New York: Riverhead Books, 1996. 113–23.

Ratzinger, Joseph Cardinal, and Alberto Bouone. "Letter to the Bishops of the Catholic Church in the Pastoral Care of Homosexual Persons." In *The Vatican and Homosexuality*, edited by Jeannine Gramick and Pat Furey. New York: Crossroad Publishing, 1988. 1–10.

Realidades. "Got Latino?" *American Family* series for KCET (PBS). Airdate February 6, 2002.

Rebolledo, Tey Diana. *Women Singing in the Snow: A Cultural Analysis of Chicana Literature*. Tucson: University of Arizona Press, 1995.

Rebolledo Tey Diana, and Eliana S. Rivero, eds. *Infinite Divisions: An Anthology of Chicana Literature*. Tucson: University of Arizona Press, 1993.

Reuters News Service. "Abbots' Words Infuriate the Public." Mexico City, 1996.

Riessman, Catherine Kohler. "When Gender Is Not Enough: Women Interviewing Women." *Gender and Society* 1.2 (1987): 172–207.

Robelo, Cecilio A. *Diccionario de mitología Nahuatl*. Mexico City: Ediciones Fuente Cultural, 1951.

Roberts, Mary Nooter, and Allen F. Roberts. *Memory: Luba Art and the Making of History*. New York: Museum for African Art, 1996.

Rodríguez, Jeanette. *Our Lady of Guadalupe: Faith and Empowerment among Mexican-American Women*. Austin: University of Texas Press, 1994.

Rodríguez, Richard. *Days of Obligation: An Argument with My Mexican Father.* New York: Penguin, 1992.

Rodríguez, Roberto, and Patrisia Gonzales. "The Body of the Sacred Feminine." *Column of the Americas.* Universal Press Syndicate. April 20, 2001. XCol umnOl.com. Archived at http://www.uexpress.com.

———. "Teachers Suffer Consequences for Challenging Traditional History." *Latino Spectrum.* San Francisco: Chronicle Features, March 14, 1997. http://www.azteca.net/aztec/mecha/latspec.html.

Rodríguez, Roy. "CMAS—Need Your Help." August 20, 1996. Online posting. Posted on Midwest Consortium for Latino Research (MCLR-L@msu.edu) on August 26, 1996.

Romo-Carmona, Mariana. "Introduction." In *Compañeras: Latina Lesbians: An Anthology,* edited by Juanita Ramos. New York: Routledge, 1994. xx–xxix.

Romo, Tere. "Mestiza Aesthetics and Chicana Painterly Visions." In *Chicano Visions: American Painters on the Verge,* edited by Cheech Marin. Boston: Bulfinch Press, 2002. 23–31.

Rose, Margaret. "Traditional and Nontraditional Patterns of Female Activism in the United Farm Workers of America, 1962–1980." *Frontiers* 11.1 (1990): 26–32.

Rousso, Henry. *The Vichy Syndrome: History and Memory in France since 1944.* Trans. Arthur Goldhammer. Cambridge, Mass.: Harvard University Press, 1991.

Ruether, Rosemary Radford. "Catholicism, Women, Body, and Sexuality: A Response." In *Women, Religion, and Sexuality: Studies on the Impact of Religious Teachings on Women,* edited by Jeanne Becher. Philadelphia: Trinity Press International, 1990. 221–32.

Ruiz, José Luis, and Hector Galán. *Chicano! The History of the Mexican American Civil Rights Movement* [video recording]. Produced by National Latino Communications Center and Galán Productions, Inc., in cooperation with KCET, Los Angeles. Distributed by NLCC Educational Media, 1996.

Ruiz, Vicki. *Cannery Women, Cannery Lives: Mexican Women, Unionization, and the California Food Processing Industry, 1930–1950.* Albuquerque: University of New Mexico Press, 1987.

———. "A Promise Fulfilled: Mexican Cannery Workers in Southern California." In *Between Borders: Essays on Mexicana/Chicana History,* edited by Adelaida R. Del Castillo. Encino, Calif.: Floricanto Press, 1990. 281–98.

Russo, Ann. *Taking Back Our Lives: A Call to Action for the Feminist Movement.* New York: Routledge, 2001.

Sahagún, Fray Bernardino de. *Conquest of New Spain: 1585 Revision.* Trans. Howard S. Cline. Salt Lake City: University of Utah Press, 1989.

———. *Florentine Codex: General History of the Things of New Spain.* Trans. Arthur Anderson and Charles Dibble. Santa Fe, N.M.: School of American Research, 1950.

Said, Edward. "The Public Role of Writers and Intellectuals." In *The Public Intellectual*, edited by Helen Small. Oxford: Blackwell, 2002. 19–39.

Salazar, Claudia. "A Third World Woman's Text: Between the Politics of Criticism and Cultural Politics." In *Women's Words: The Feminist Practice of Oral History*, edited by Sherna Berger Gluck and Daphne Patai. New York: Routledge, 1991. 93–106.

Saldívar, Ramón. *Chicano Narrative: The Dialectics of Difference*. Madison: University of Wisconsin Press, 1990.

Sánchez, Marta Ester. *Contemporary Chicana Poetry: A Critical Approach to an Emerging Literature*. Berkeley: University of California Press, 1985.

Sánchez, Rosaura. "The History of Chicanas: Proposal for a Materialist Perspective." In *Between Borders: Essays on Mexicana/Chicana History*, edited by Adelaida R. Del Castillo. Encino, Calif.: Floricanto Press, 1990.

Sandoval, Chela. "U.S. Third World Feminism: The Theory and Method of Oppositional Consciousness in the Postmodern World." *Genders* 10 (1991): 1–24.

Saragoza, Alex M. "Recent Chicano Historiography: An Interpretive Essay." *Aztlán* 19.1 (1988–90): 1–52.

Schüssler Fiorenza, Elisabeth. "Feminist Spirituality, Christian Identity, and Catholic Vision." In *Womanspirit Rising: A Feminist Reader in Religion*, edited by Carol P. Christ and Judith Plaskow. San Francisco: Harper and Row, 1979. 136–48.

Scott, James C. *Domination and the Arts of Resistance: Hidden Transcripts*. New Haven, Conn.: Yale University Press, 1990.

——. *Weapons of the Weak: Everyday Forms of Peasant Resistance*. New Haven, Conn.: Yale University Press, 1985.

Scott, Jim. "Everyday Forms of Peasant Resistance." *Journal of Peasant Studies* 13.2 (1986): 5–35.

Sedgwick, Eve Kosofsky. *Between Men: English Literature and Male Homosocial Desire*. New York: Columbia University Press, 1985.

——. *Epistemology of the Closet*. Berkeley: University of California Press, 1990.

Segura, Denise A. "Chicanas and Triple Oppression in the Labor Force." In *Chicana Voices: Intersections of Class, Race, and Gender*, edited by Teresa Córdova. Albuquerque: University of New Mexico Press, 1990. 47–65.

——, ed. *Familism and Employment among Chicanas and Mexican Immigrant Women*. Houston: Mexican American Studies Program, University of Houston, 1988.

Shorris, Earl. *Latinos: A Biography of the People*. New York: W. W. Norton, 1992.

Sierra, Christine Marie. "The University Setting Reinforces Inequality." In *Chicana Voices: Intersections of Class, Race and Gender*, edited by Teresa Córdova. Albuquerque: University of New Mexico Press, 1993. 5–7.

Smith, Linda Tuhiwai. *Decolonizing Methodologies: Research and Indigenous Peoples*. London: Zed Books, 1999.

Smith, Sidonie. *Subjectivity, Identity, and the Body: Women's Autobiographical Practices in the Twentieth Century.* Bloomington: Indiana University Press, 1993.

Snitow, Ann Barr, Christine Stansell, and Sharon Thompson, eds. *Powers of Desire: The Politics of Sexuality.* London: Virago, 1984 (1983).

Spivak, Gayatri Chakravorti. *In Other Worlds: Essays in Cultural Politics.* New York: Routledge, 1988.

Stacey, Judith. "Can There Be a Feminist Ethnography?" In *Women's Words: The Feminist Practice of Oral History,* edited by Sherna Berger Gluck and Daphne Patai. New York: Routledge, 1991. 111–19.

Stiffarm, Lenore A., with Phil Lane Jr. "The Demography of Native America: A Question of American Indian Survival." In *The State of Native America,* edited by M. Annette Jaimes. Boston: South End Press, 1992. 23–54.

Sullivan, Thelma D. "Tlazolteotl-Ixcuina: The Great Spinner and Weaver." In *Art and Iconography in the Late Post-Classic Period of Central Mexico,* edited by Elizabeth Hill Boone. Washington: Dumbarton Oaks, 1982. 7–35.

Tafolla, Carmen. "La Malinche." *Canto al pueblo.* San Antonio: Penca Books, 1978.

Takaki, Ronald. *Iron Cages: Race and Culture in Nineteenth-Century America.* New York: Alfred A. Knopf, 1979.

Taylor, Verta, and Leila Rupp. "Women's Culture and Lesbian Feminist Activism: A Reconsideration of Cultural Feminism." *Signs* 19.1 (1993): 32–61.

Tegel, Simon. "Pope Gives Mexico Its Own Aztec Saint." *The Scotsman,* August 1, 2002. http://news.scotsman.com/topics.cfm?tid=297&id=829842002. Accessed August 12, 2004.

Terdiman, Richard. "Deconstructing Memory: On Representing the Past and Theorizing Culture in France since the Revolution." *Diacritics* 15.4 (1985): 13–36.

Teresa de Ávila. *The Interior Castle.* New York: Paulist Press, 1979.

——. *The Life of Teresa of Jesus.* Trans. E. Allison Peers. Garden City, N.Y.: Image Books, 1960.

Teski, Marea C., and Jacob J. Climo, eds. *The Labyrinth of Memory: Ethnographic Journeys.* Westport, Conn.: Bergin and Garvey, 1995.

Tixier y Vigil, Yvonne, and Nan Elsasser. "The Effects of Ethnicity of the Interviewer on Conversation: A Study of Chicana Women." In *Sociology of the Language of American Women,* edited by Betty L. DuBois and Isabel Crouch. San Antonio, Texas: Trinity University Press, 1976. 161–69.

Todorov, Tzvetan. *The Conquest of America: The Question of the Other.* Trans. Richard Howard. New York: Harper and Row, 1984.

Traub, Valerie. "Jewels, Statues, and Corpses: Containment of Female Erotic Power in Shakespeare's Plays." In *Shakespeare and Gender: A History,* edited by Deborah Barker and Ivo Kamps. London: Verso, 1995. 120–41.

Trujillo, Carla. "Chicana Lesbians: Fear and Loathing in the Chicano Community." In *Chicana Lesbians: The Girls Our Mothers Warned Us About*, edited by Carla Trujillo. Berkeley, Calif.: Third Woman Press, 1991. 186–94.

Turner, Kay F. "The Cultural Semiotics of Religious Icons: La Virgen de San Juan de los Lagos." *Semiotica* 47.1/4 (1983): 317–61.

———. "Mexican American Home Altars: Towards Their Interpretation." Special Issue: Mexican Folklore and Folk Art in the United States, ed. Teresa McKenna. *Aztlán: International Journal of Chicano Studies Research* 13 (1982). 309–26.

Umpierre, Luz María. "Interview with Cherríe Moraga." *The Americas Review: A Review of the Hispanic Literature and Art of the USA* 14.2 (1986): 54–67.

Valdez, Luis. "Los Vendidos." *Actos*. Fresno, Calif.: Cucaracha Press, 1971. 35–49.

Vance, Carole S., ed. *Pleasure and Danger: Exploring Female Sexuality*. London: Pandora Press, 1992 (1984).

———. "Epilogue." In *Pleasure and Danger: Exploring Female Sexuality*. 431–46.

Villanueva, Alma Luz. *The Ultraviolet Sky*. Tempe, Ariz.: Bilingual Press, 1988.

———. *Weeping Woman: La Llorona and Other Stories*. Tempe, Ariz.: Bilingual Press, 1994.

Viramontes, Helena María. *Under the Feet of Jesus*. New York: Dutton, 1995.

Warren, Nancy. "Some Like a Virgin, Some Don't: Alma Lopez Generates Controversy in New Mexico." *San Francisco Gate*, April 24, 2001. http://www.sfgate.com/cgi-bin/article.cgi?file=/gate/archive/2001/04/27/queer.DTL. Accessed May 16, 2004.

Watson, Julia. "Unspeakable Differences: The Politics of Gender in Lesbian and Heterosexual Autobiographies." In *De/Colonizing the Subject: The Politics of Gender in Women's Autobiography*, edited by Sidonie Smith and Julia Watson. Minneapolis: University of Minnesota Press, 1992. 139–68.

Wolf, Diane L. "Situating Feminist Dilemmas in Fieldwork." In *Feminist Dilemmas in Fieldwork*, edited by Diane L. Wolf. Boulder, Colo.: Westview Press, 1996. 1–55.

Wolf, Eric R. "The Virgin of Guadalupe: A Mexican National Symbol." *American Journal of Folklore* 71 (1958): 34–39.

Wolff, Elaine. "Virgen Matricides." *San Antonio Current*, December 26, 2006.

Xochimeh, Tlahtoki. "An Overlooked Paradox: A Brief Analysis of Aztekism in Some Major Chicana/o Studies Texts." National Association of Chicana and Chicano Studies Conference. San Jose, Calif., April 6, 2007.

Yarbro-Bejarano, Yvonne. "Chicana Literature from a Chicana Feminist Perspective." In *Chicana Creativity and Criticism: Charting New Frontiers in American Literature*, edited by María Herrera-Sobek and Helena María Viramontes. Houston: Arte Público Press, 1988. 139–45.

Yates, Frances. *The Art of Memory*. Chicago: University of Chicago Press, 1966.

Ybarra-Frausto, Tomás. "Arte Chicano: Images of a Community." In *Signs from the Heart: California Chicano Murals*, edited by Eva Sperling Cockcroft and Holly Barnet-Sánchez. Albuquerque: University of New Mexico Press, 1993. 55–67.

YWCA *Focus* (Tucson, Arizona). "Mensajeras Provided 1,669 Women with Life-saving Information." 5.4 (1995): 1–3.

Zavella, Patricia. "The Politics of Race and Gender: Organizing Chicana Cannery Workers in Northern California." In *Women and the Politics of Empowerment: Perspectives from the Workplace and the Community*, edited by Ann Bookman and Sandra Morgan. Philadelphia: Temple University Press, 1988. 202–24.

——. "Recording Chicana Life Histories: Refining the Insider's Perspective." In *Insider/Outsider Relationships with Informants*, ed. Elizabeth Jameson. Working Paper No. 13. Tucson: Southwest Institute for Research on Women, University of Arizona, 1982. 14–25.

——. *Women's Work and Chicano Families: Cannery Workers of the Santa Clara Valley*. Ithaca, N.Y.: Cornell University Press, 1987.

Zinn, Maxine Baca. "Chicanas: Power and Control in the Domestic Sphere." *De Colores* 2.3 (1976): 19–31.

——. "Field Research in Minority Communities: Ethical, Methodological, and Political Observations by an Insider." *Social Problems* 27.2 (1979): 209–19.

——. "Political Familism: Toward Sex Role Equality in Chicano Families." *Aztlán: International Journal of Chicano Studies Research* 6.1 (1975). 13–26.

autobiography, 116, 126, 185–89, 202, 223 n. 4. *See also* oral histories

Avon Corporation, 80, 199

Aztec (term), 8–9, 25, 72, 208, 220, 224 n. 10. *See also* indigenous peoples; Mexica people

Aztec Kings, The (Gillespie), 14–17, 28, 34, 225 n. 6, 238 n. 81

Aztlan, 9; in Moraga's work, 173–83

Baldwin, James, 169

Balún-Canán (Castellanos), 73

Barnett-Sánchez, Holly, 26

Barraza, Santa, 25, 34, 43, 50–51

Behar, Ruth, 213–14

Beloved (Morrison), 48

Benmayor, Rina, 200

Bernadino de Sahagún, Fray, 47

betrayal: as historical theme for Chicanas and U.S. Mexicanas, 16, 228 n. 55; La Malinche's association with, 18, 22, 35, 37, 39–41, 43, 116, 119, 132, 174, 238 n. 66; sexual, by men, 44–46, 48, 52, 130–31, 151–52, 154; sexual, by women, 155, 243 n. 34

Beverley, John, 187

Bhabha, Homi, 176

Bierhorst, John, 247 n. 31

birth control, 5, 88, 104, 115, 118, 133–34

"Blank Page, The" (Dinesen), 244 n. 43

Book of Lamentations (Castellanos), 73

borderlands, 44, 97–98, 140, 146, 186, 212

Borderlands / La Frontera (Anzaldúa): 65, 86, 97–98, 189, 231 n. 103

Boyce Davies, Carole, 186

Broyles-González, Yolanda, 251 n. 55

Butler, Judith, 90

cancer prevention and support efforts, 5, 80–81, 126–27, 129–33, 191, 196, 199, 211, 215

Candelaria, Cordelia, 45

Castellanos, Rosario, 72–74, 234 n. 15

Castells, Jordi, 229 n. 80

Castillo, Ana: on Chicana identity, 204; as Chicana writer, 2, 247 n. 27; Coatlicue in work by, 93; goddesses (indigenous, Mexica) in work by 13, 27, 71–72, 86, 93–95, 207; indigenous identity in work by, 94; machismo in work by, 93; on "mandate of motherhood," 121–23; *Massacre of the Dreamers*, 13, 75, 204; on Mexican feminists, 75; *Sapogonia*, 93–95, 247 n. 27; on sexuality, 91, 243 n. 34; spirituality in work by 93–95; on La Virgen de Guadalupe, 65–66

Castillo, Debra, 73, 234 n. 14

Catholic Church: author's upbringing in, 191, 193, 199; discourse of, 17–18, 101; feminists' rejection of, 86–88, 168–69, 205; Immaculate Conception, 57, 65, 104, 108–9, 111, 115–16; indigenous Mexican religions and, united through La Virgen de Guadalupe, 16, 99, 100–114; in Mexico, 72, 102; in Muscatine, Iowa, 104, 241 n. 7; patriarchal ideology of, 5–7, 20, 45, 47, 59, 66, 80, 85, 87, 101, 115, 138–39, 169, 217, 237 n. 52; popular religiosity vs., 104–12, 241 n. 9; racism of, 20, 241 n. 9; saints, 108, 113, 139–40; on sexuality, 87–88, 115–18, 121, 123–24, 130, 157, 217, 237 n. 62; Spanish imperialism's emphasis on conversion to, 17–18, 55–56, 109–10, 207, 242 n. 20; spirituality outside of, 68, 90, 168–69, 237 n. 52; uses of La Virgen de Guadalupe by, 58–59, 64–65, 100, 114–16, 125–26, 207; U.S.

Mexicanas' affiliation with, 59, 101, 103–4, 106, 125, 133–34, 206, 211

Catholic Theological Society of America, 237 n. 62

Centro Cultural Aztlan (San Antonio), 68, 217

Centzon Huitznahua (Four Hundred Southerners), 30, 32

Chabram-Dernersesian, Angie, 172, 208, 216, 237 n. 52; "mujer valiente" concept of, 60, 64

Chalchiuhtlicue (She of the Jade Skirt), 30, 46–47, 162, 173

change (social): efforts and strategies, 161, 202, 205, 210, 212

Chávez, César, 22, 59

Chávez, Denise, 65, 243 n. 32.

Chicana (term), 4, 68, 202, 204

Chicana (documentary), 226 n. 15

Chicana feminism: artists and writers and, 2, 4, 6–7, 70–76; Catholic Church and, 86–88, 168–69, 205; continuum of, 6, 69, 79–82, 205, 209–10, 216; cultural refiguring and, 26, 64–65, 68; goddesses (indigenous, Mexica) and, 13–14, 17, 25; politics of location and, 201–21; second-wave, 72, 76; spirituality and, 84–90; Third World feminism and, 4, 71, 76, 81–82, 87, 211; as transformative, 84–85, 218–19; U.S. Mexicanas' identification as feminist, 7, 80–81, 83–84, 200, 211, 221; La Virgen de Guadalupe and, 64; *See also* resistance

Chicana Lesbians (Trujillo), 64, 100

Chicana/o civil rights movement: Chicanas as marginalized in, 19–20, 23, 41, 59–60, 85, 235 n. 25, 245 n. 55; description of, 4; images associated with, 24–26, 50, 59, 105, 227 n. 33; inspiration provided by, 64, 205; "Mexican" not used in, 204. *See also* Chicano nationalism

Chicana/o studies programs, 19, 203, 205, 208–9, 213

Chicana professional intellectuals (writers and artists): 1, 8; in academia, 4, 81–82, 200–202, 205–6, 209, 212–16; "Chicano Visions" exhibit protest and, 20; feminism of, 2, 4, 7, 13–14, 17, 20, 24–25, 27, 64–65, 68, 70–76, 81–82, 85, 201–21; goddesses (indigenous, Mexica) refiguring by, 4, 10, 16–17, 23–27, 34, 42, 49, 65–101, 125, 145, 161–84, 202, 206, 208, 210–15, 218, 220–21; historias in works by, 188–89; identity of, 4, 5, 24, 42, 81, 125, 202, 204, 206, 220–21; lesbianism and, 88, 92, 99–100, 174–75, 204–6, 209; La Llorona's refiguring by, 10, 25–26, 48–55, 67, 69, 89, 145, 216–18; La Malinche's refiguring by, 10, 15, 17–18, 25–26, 42–45, 69, 89, 95, 182, 184, 218; marginalization of, 75, 78, 81–82, 186, 203, 209, 235 n. 25; Mexican women writers vs., 74–75; multiple, simultaneous oppressions experienced by, 71, 77, 82, 85, 89, 237 n. 63; politics of, defined, 4, 237 n. 63; Spanish not first language of many, 74; as a term, 4, 68, 202, 204; themes in works by, 5–7, 13–14, 68–69, 73–74, 201–2, 205–6, 209–10, 221; U.S. Mexicanas as unfamiliar with, 3, 202–3; La Virgen de Guadalupe's refiguring by, 18, 23, 25–26, 59–69, 89, 97–100, 102, 135, 202, 212, 216–17. *See also* entries for specific intellectuals

Chicano (term), 19

"Chicano Art: Past, Present, Future" (panel discussion), 20

Chicano nationalism, 5, 23, 208; critique of, in Moraga's *Hungry Woman*, 174–75, 178–82. *See also* Chicana/o civil rights movement

Chicano School of Painting, 226 n. 18

Chicano! The History of the Mexican American Civil Rights Movement (documentary), 19–20

"Chicano Visions: American Painters on the Verge" (art exhibit), 19–20

Chichimeca people, 28

childbirth: goddesses of, 29–30; mothers in, likened to warriors, 29–30, 46, 61, 91, 160; virgin, 65, 104, 108–9, 111–12, 115–16. *See also* reproduction; reproductive demons

Chinampaneca, 29

Chingada, La, 41–42, 90, 116. *See also* Malintzin Tenepal; Paz, Octavio.

Christ, Carol P., 87

Chrystos, 76

Cihuacoatl (Serpent Woman), 27–30, 47, 83, 160; in Anzaldúa's work, 89–90, 97; avatars of, 33, 89, 97, 247 n. 29; in Cisneros's work, 99; as La Llorona, 46, 181; in Moraga's works, 173–76, 181–82; relationship of, to Coatlicue and Coyolxauhqui, 33; in Villanueva's work, 161–62, 164, 173

Cihuatateo, 46–47, 50, 179, 181, 184

Cihuatateo con Coyolxauhqui y la Guadalapana (Barraza), 50

Cisneros, Sandra: as Chicana writer, 2–3, 56, 167, 172, 202, 247 n. 25; goddesses (indigenous, Mexica) in works by, 72, 98–99, 244 n. 40; "Guadalupe the Sex Goddess," 99,

100, 244 n. 40; *The House on Mango Street*, 3, 202; "Little Miracles, Kept Promises," 56, 98–99, 212; La Llorona legend in work by, 49; La Malinche in work by, 98; on sexuality and spirituality, 99–100; La Virgen de Guadalupe in work by, 65, 98–100, 212; *Woman Hollering Creek and Other Stories*, 49, 98–99, 167

City of Kings (Castellanos), 73

Ciudad Real (Castellanos), 73

civil rights movement. *See* Chicana/o civil rights movement

class (social): of Chicana intellectuals, 4, 73–74, 205–6, 208; as factor in Chicana and U.S. Mexicana representational strategies, 6, 8, 204–5, 209–11, 213–16, 221; as factor in fieldwork, 10–11, 190–91; as factor in relevance of La Virgen de Guadalupe, 7, 10, 17, 26, 59–60, 69, 199, 201–2, 206–7, 210, 216–18, 237 n. 52; honor concept and, 115; in La Llorona legend, 45, 152–54; in Mexica history, 33–34; in Mexico, 72–74, 114, 242 n. 20; of those not represented in this work, 8; of U.S. Mexicanas, 2–3, 8, 82, 101, 201–5; in Villanueva's works, 168. *See also* middle class; working class

classism: between Chicanas and Mexican women writers, 75; faced by U.S. Mexicanas, 133; of Mexican government, 72; opposition to, 4, 71, 73, 81, 85, 89, 237 n. 63

Coatepec (Serpent Mountain), 30, 31

Coatlalopeuh, 97

Coatlicue (Serpent Skirt), 27–28, 83, 95; Alma López's depiction of, 54–55; in Anzaldúa's *Borderlands / La Frontera*, 86, 89–90, 97; avatars of, 247 n. 29; Barraza's depiction of, 25, 34; in Castillo's *Sapogonia*, 93; in Cisneros's work, 99; Mexica narrative of, 30–31; in Moraga's works, 174–75, 179–81; relationship of, to Cihuacoatl, Coyolxauhqui, and Huitzilopochtli, 30–33; stone sculpture of, 30–33; U.S. Mexicanas' lack of familiarity with, 207

Cockcroft, Eva Sperling, 26

codices: defined, 28; in Esquivel's *Malinche*, 44, 229 n. 80; Gillespie on, 225 n. 6; on La Malinche, 37–39, 140, 228 n. 54; of Mexica goddesses, 24, 175; in Moraga's *Hungry Woman*, 177

colonialism: internal, 169–70, 175–76, 218; opposition to, 4

community (family): Chicanas' distance from, of origin, 205–6, 213–14; construction of, through Guadalupe worship, 105–6; lesbians and, 80, 88–89, 123, 183, 205–6; political activity for, 95–96, 134–35, 202, 205, 209, 211, 215; popular memory and, 22, 212; as regulating women's sexuality, 120–21, 158–59; testimonios about issues in, 187–89; value of, to U.S. Mexicanas, 121, 158–59, 209; "woman's culture" as offering support to, 82, 213

Compañeras (Romo-Carmona), 123

condoms, 5, 133–34

Conkey, Margaret, 238 n. 78

Cooley, Jenny, 233 n. 7

Córdova, Alicia, 195

Córdova, Nadine, 21

Córdova, Patsy, 21

Corinthians, 230 n. 98, 231 n. 99

corridos, 22, 188, 226 n. 26

Cortés, Hernán: indigenous groups siding with, 9, 17, 34, 43; in legends, 47–48, 132; Malintzin Tenepal and, 15–16, 35, 37–41, 43, 45, 152, 228 n. 54, 229 n. 62; son of, with Malintzin Tenepal, 16, 37, 40, 42–43, 48, 152, 174, 178; in visual texts, 38, 43; in written texts, 44, 174, 178

Cortés, Martín, 16, 37, 40, 42–43, 48, 152, 174, 178

Cotera, Martha, 235 n. 25

Cott, Nancy, 78

counterdiscourse(s): class differences in, 208–9; in feminist movement, 79; goddess imagery as, 71; memory as, 14, 16, 20, 27, 212; oral histories as, 189; about La Virgen de Guadalupe, 58–68; about virginity, 119; woman of discord as, 20–21, 189

counterhistory, 21

countermemory, 22–23

Coyolxauhqui (Painted with Bells), 27, 61; in Alma López's artworks, 54–55, 66, 67–68; Anzaldúa on, 70–71, 89–90, 97; avatars of, 28, 83, 160; in Barraza's artworks, 50, 207; in Cisneros's work, 99; on Maestrapeace mural, 25, 34–36; Mexica narrative of, 30–31; as moon goddess, 51, 66, 70, 163–64, 167, 176, 182; in Moraga's work, 70, 95–97, 174–76, 180–82; relationship of, to Cihuacoatl, Coatlicue, and Huitzilopochtli, 30–33; re-membered, 25, 95–96; sculptures of, 25, 31–33, 35, 207

Coyolxauhqui Returns Disguised as Our Lady of Guadalupe. . . (Alma López), 66–68

criollos, 17–18, 152, 225 n. 13; La Malinche and, 40–41; La Virgen de Guadalupe and, 59, 227 n. 29, 242 n. 20
Cuauhtemoc, 42–43
Cuba, 183
cuentos, 188
Cuentos: Stories by Latinas (anthology), 74
Culhuacan people (Tolteca), 9, 24, 29, 72, 225 n. 6
cultural refiguring: altering dominant representations, 24; defined, 5–6, 24; differences in strategies of, between Chicana intellectuals and U.S. Mexicanas, 209–15, 221; of female sexuality, 10, 42, 44–45, 49–50, 55, 61, 64–66, 68, 217; of history, 13–17, 20–21, 25–27, 42, 44, 68–69, 206, 218; of La Llorona by Chicana intellectuals, 10, 25–26, 48–55, 67, 69, 89, 145, 216–18; of La Malinche by Chicana intellectuals, 10, 17–18, 25–26, 42–45, 69, 89, 95, 182, 184, 218; memory and, 24; of Mexica goddesses by Chicana intellectuals, 10, 17, 23–26, 34, 65–71, 75–76, 82–83, 86, 89, 125, 145, 161–84, 202, 206, 208, 210–11, 213, 216, 218, 220; through Mexican female cultural symbols, 6, 10–11, 16–17, 23–27, 42–45, 49–55, 59–72, 89–101, 144–84, 208–11, 215–18; of patriarchy, 16, 45, 60–64; question of U.S. Mexicanas' interest in, 201; as "trans-coding," 14, 218; by U. S. Mexicanas, 16, 20–21, 26, 45, 68–69, 189, 201–2; by U.S. Mexicanas through volunteer work and interpersonal relations, 5–7, 10, 16, 114, 126, 209, 211, 215; of La Virgen de Guadalupe by Chicana intellectuals, 18, 23, 25–26, 59–69, 89, 97–100, 102, 135, 202, 212, 216–17; of La Virgen de Guadalupe by U.S. Mexicanas, 26, 59, 69, 114, 126, 134–43; through visual texts, 16, 23–24, 34, 43–45, 50–55, 61–68, 136, 140–41, 217, 219; through written texts, 6, 16, 24, 42, 44–45, 49–51, 64–66, 145, 161–84, 212–14, 219. *See also* history: rewriting of
"Cultural Semiotics of Religious Icons, The" (Turner), 107–9
cultural symbols (Mexican female), 7; author's interest in, 193; Chicana intellectuals' representation of, 10, 23, 42–43, 215; Chicanas' favorite vs. U.S. Mexicanas' favorite, 206–8; images of, 23–24, 105; as inspiring resistance, 10, 17, 26–27, 45, 47–50, 60–61, 64, 69, 73, 88, 95–96, 103, 114, 125–26, 135, 137, 143–44, 167, 208, 218–19; official uses of, 26, 32, 41–42; refiguring through, 6, 10–11, 16–17, 23–27, 41–45, 49–55, 59–72, 89–101, 114, 126, 208–9, 215–19; as representing resistance to Spanish Conquest, 16, 47. *See also* goddesses; Llorona, La; Malintzin Tenepal; Virgen de Guadalupe, La
"Cyber Arte: Where Tradition Meets Technology" (art exhibit), 66
Cypess, Sandra Messinger, 18, 37, 40

Daring to Be Bad (Echols), 76–77
Davis, Angela, 76
Delano (Calif.), 59, 241 n. 12
Del Castillo, Adelaida, 235 n. 25
Denmark, 169–70, 173
Descartes, René, 171–72

Díaz del Castillo, Bernal, 40, 47, 228 n. 54, 229 n. 62
Diego, Juan. *See* Juan Diego
"differential consciousness" (Sandoval), 83–85
Dinesen, Isak, 244 n. 43
Discourse on Method (Descartes), 171–72
discourses: as an adjunct to force, 17–18; alternative religious, 86–101; Catholic, 17–18, 101; criollo, 17–18, 225 n. 13; of Mensajeras de Salud, 80–81; multipositional, 81, 83–84, 97, 204; national, 17–18; official dominant, 14, 17, 21–22, 32, 56, 58–59, 69, 101, 177–78; oppositional, 15, 21–22, 42, 73, 79–81, 84, 98, 101, 142, 159, 189; patriarchal, 18, 25–26; of power, 212; of woman of discord, 17, 20–21. *See also* counterdiscourse(s)
"Divine Women" (Irigaray), 85, 125
divinity: in Chicanas' selves, 64, 93–94, 97–98, 104, 171; single god representing, 34; as split from the mortal, 89; of women, 34, 65, 70, 84–85, 90, 95, 104–5, 113, 141, 212. *See also* goddesses; saints
divorce, 2, 115, 118, 122–23, 136, 158, 194
domestic abuse: author as survivor of, 199; as circumscribing women's lives, 1, 115; in oral histories by U.S. Mexicanas, 118–19, 122, 159–61, 187, 192–95, 211–12; refiguring of attitudes toward, by U.S. Mexicanas, 80, 127–29, 142, 211; as theme in Chicana writings, 2, 49, 98, 163, 167, 169–70; by women against women, 163–64. *See also* violence against women

"Doña Marina," 40–42. *See also* Malintzin Tenepal
duality (paired oppositions): in Anzaldúa's *Borderlands / La Frontera*, 97; in La Chingada depiction, 41–42; in cultural refiguring, 14, 25, 84, 162, 164, 170; among female cultural symbols, 48–49, 59, 219; in Mexica goddess powers, 15, 27, 29–30, 33–34, 46, 50, 82–83, 89–90, 170–71, 173–74, 219; of mind-body distinction, 87, 90, 100, 239 n. 96; in Villanueva's *Ultraviolet Sky*, 92; in virginity discourse, 119; of "woman's culture," 79–80, 83–84
DuBois, Ellen, 78
dystopia, 170, 175–176

Echols, Alice, 76–78, 83
education: of Chicana intellectuals, 75, 101, 205, 213; as difference between Chicanas and U.S. Mexicanas, 204–5, 208–11, 213–14, 216, 221; differences in, as factor in oral history fieldwork, 190, 199–200; about sex, 118; of U.S. Mexicanas, 4, 115, 141, 155, 202–3, 207–8, 211–12, 246 n. 64. *See also* academia
Elsasser, Nan, 193–94
Enríquez, Evangelina, 48, 243 n. 34
"Entering into the Serpent" (Anzaldúa), 86
Ervin, Kelly, 249 n. 21
Espín, Oliva, 115, 118, 244 n. 52
Esquivel, Laura, 44, 74
essentialism, 76–77, 82, 175, 216, 236 n. 48; in Villanueva's *Ultraviolet Sky*, 92, 172
Estés, Clarissa Pinkola, 100
Euripides, 48, 173–74, 179, 230 n. 98, 231 n. 99

European folktales, 45–48
Eve (biblical), 22, 87, 95, 174

Faderman, Lillian, 234 n. 22
Felski, Rita, 79
fem (journal), 217
feminism: association of, with term
   "Chicana," 4, 85; Catholic Church
   and, 86–88, 168–69, 205; first-
   wave, 78; history's refiguring by,
   13–17, 20–21, 27, 42, 44, 68–69,
   206, 218; incubation sites for, 79–
   83; lesbian, 78, 235 n. 30; among
   Mexican women writers, 73–74;
   oral history fieldwork and, 189–
   201; radical, 76–78; second-wave
   U.S., 7, 71–72, 76–77, 85, 101, 167,
   221, 235 n. 25, 247 n. 28; transformative, 84, 218–19; U.S. Mexicanas as not identifying with, 80–
   81, 83–84, 200, 211, 221; U.S.
   Third World, 4, 71, 76, 81–82, 87,
   211. *See also* Chicana feminism;
   gender oppression; resistance
Feminism and Methodology (Harding),
   248 n. 15
Ferguson, Ann, 80
Fischer, Michael, 85–86
500 años del pueblo chicano (textbook),
   21
Florentine Codex XII, 37–38
folklore, 22, 45–48, 185
force (physical): as inadequate without discourse, 17–18. *See also*
   domestic abuse; violence against
   women; wars
Forged Under the Sun (Lucas), 134–35,
   188
Foucault, Michel, 22, 147–48, 158,
   181
Four Hundred Southerners (Centzon
   Huitznahua), 30, 32

Franco, Ramona, 106
Fregoso, Rosa Linda, 172, 208, 216,
   237 n. 52
Fuentes, Carlos, 73–74, 202

Gamboa, Diane, 20
Garro, Elena, 72–73, 234 n. 14
Gaspar de Alba, Alicia, 53
Geertz, Clifford, 105
gender ambiguity of indigenous goddesses, 27, 29, 92, 238 n. 81
gender oppression (sexism), 7, 72, 75,
   96, 122, 179, 187, 219; as one of
   multiple, simultaneous oppressions, 71, 77, 82, 85, 89, 237 n. 63;
   opposition to, 45, 60, 64, 73, 76,
   79, 101, 134, 206, 209, 215, 238 n.
   63. *See also* heterosexism
gender roles: in Aztec society, 243 n.
   34; Chicana visual artists' refiguring of, 20, 136; institutions and
   ideologies limiting, for women, 1,
   5–7, 13, 18, 20, 24–25, 45, 47, 59,
   66, 73, 80, 82, 85, 87, 93, 101, 114–
   25, 138–39, 154, 169, 178, 217, 237
   n. 52, 244 n. 48; in La Llorona legend, 10, 154–56, 161; in Mexica history, 33–34; as theme in Chicana
   intellectuals' written texts, 5, 7, 19,
   23, 42, 92–93, 98, 101; as theme in
   U.S. Mexicanas' oral histories, 5,
   10, 18–19, 23, 101, 113, 154–56,
   205, 215. *See also* mothers; virgins
genealogy (female), 15, 84–85, 92,
   98–99, 101, 172; of woman of discord, 16, 18–19, 25, 71, 82, 160,
   173, 218
Gillespie, Susan, 14–17, 28, 34, 175,
   225 n. 6, 238 n. 81
Glantz, Margo, 234 n. 14
Glenn, Evelyn Nakano, 239 n. 89
goddesses (indigenous, Mexica):

associations with, 27, 32–34; Chicana intellectuals' refiguring of, 10, 17, 23–26, 34, 65–71, 75–76, 82–83, 86, 89, 125, 145, 161–84, 202, 206, 208, 210–11, 213, 216, 218, 220; devaluation of, 20, 28, 31–32, 34, 54, 85, 208; dual aspects of, 15, 27, 29–30, 33–34, 46, 50, 82–83, 89–90, 170–71, 173–74, 219; function in Mexica historical narratives of, 28; gender ambiguity of, 27, 29, 92, 238 n. 81; as having multiple aspects, 25, 28, 33, 82–83, 89, 97, 160, 247 n. 29; in La Llorona legend, 46; La Malinche and La Virgen de Guadalupe as structural equivalents of, 15, 43, 66, 68, 100, 102, 125; memory of, 24, 76, 84–85, 207–8, 210, 212, 221; as Mexican female cultural symbols, 6–7, 10, 26–69, 83; Mexican female writers' lack of references to, 72, 75; monstrous and dismembered, 25, 30–33, 35, 50, 54–55, 70, 95–96, 207; representations of, 13–14, 24, 26–69; use of, to justify Mexica wars, 9, 25, 32–33; U.S. Mexicanas' lack of knowledge about, 201, 206–10, 213, 216, 220; violence associated with, 82, 95–96. *See also* divinity; woman of discord; and entries for specific goddesses
Godoy, Minerva, 2, 102, 134, 142, 151–52, 211
gods (women as), 34, 65, 70, 84–85, 90, 95, 104–5, 113, 125, 135, 141, 212. *See also* divinity; goddesses
Gonzales, Evelyn, 2, 126–27, 130–32, 196, 198–99, 211; on La Llorona, 145–48; on La Virgen de Guadalupe, 102, 105, 107–10, 112–14, 136–37, 217

Gonzales Guerrero, Andrés, Jr., 240 n. 6
Gonzalez, Maya Christina, 51
"Got Milk" commercial, 53, 217
Graves, Robert, 230 n. 98, 231 n. 99
Great Britain, 78
Griffen, Joyce, 249 n. 25
Griffith, James S., 106, 241 n. 14
Grupo de Apoyo para Mujeres con Cancer, 126–27, 133
Guadalupe Cultural Arts Center (San Antonio), 213
"Guadalupe the Sex Goddess" (Cisneros), 99–100, 244 n. 40
Guatemala, 35, 52
Gutiérrez, José Angel, 251 n. 55

Hall, Stuart, 14, 26, 106, 218
Hankiss, Agnes, 186
Harada, Aurora, 2, 142, 187; on La Llorona, 152–56, 161; on La Virgen de Guadalupe, 102, 136–39, 211–12
Harding, Sandra, 248 n. 15
Harlan, Theresa, 64
Hasta no verte, Jesús mío (Poniatowska), 73
Hawes, Bess Lomax, 156–57
health. *See* cancer prevention and support efforts
Henderson, Laretta, 248 n. 9
Hera (Greek goddess), 179, 230 n. 98, 231 n. 99
"*Herencia de Coatlicue*: The Coatlicue State, La" (Anzaldúa), 86
Here's to You, Jesusa (Poniatowska), 73
Hernández, Ester, 20, 60, 64, 66, 68, 99–100
heterosexism, 7, 49, 71, 81, 85, 179–80, 205, 215, 219, 238 n. 63
Hidalgo, Miguel, 59, 225 n. 13
Hijas del Quinto Sol, 191

Hispanic (term), 3, 204

historias (term), 8

history: cultural, of Mexico, 72, 233 n. 7; exclusion of women from official, 13–14, 19–23, 72, 185–87; linear vs. cyclical versions of, 14–15, 28, 192; Malintzin Tenepal's silence in record of, 35, 43–44; memory as counterpart of, 21–28; in oral narratives, 8, 185–89; recovery of, 221; refiguring of, by feminists, 13–17, 20–21, 27, 42, 44, 68–69, 206, 218; rewriting of, 14, 17, 19, 26, 27, 41–42, 44, 49, 68–70, 97, 101, 175, 177, 180–81, 215, 218, 224 n. 7, 225 n. 6, 229 n. 62, 231 n. 99, 231 n. 103; story vs., 177–78; uses of, 16–17; U.S. Mexicanas' lack of familiarity with pre-conquest, 206–7, 220

homosexuality: Catholic Church on, 88, 123–24, 130, 237 n. 62; male, 123–24, 178, 194, 244 n. 49. *See also* lesbians

honor (Latin), 115, 119, 243 nn. 34–35

hooks, bell, 78, 245 n. 57

House on Mango Street, The (Cisneros), 3, 202

Huastec people, 227 n. 40

Huerta, Dolores, 18

Huitzilopochtli (Hummingbird on the Left), 9, 25; goddesses (indigenous, Mexica) and, 28–33, 35, 95–96, 160, 180–81; in Moraga's works, 95–96, 181; U.S. Mexicanas' lack of familiarity with, 207; woman of discord plot of, 29

human sacrifice. *See* sacrifice

"humilde," 139–40, 142

Hungry Woman, 46, 53, 174–75

Hungry Woman, The (Moraga), 49, 161, 173–84

identity: Chicana, 4–5, 24, 42, 81, 125, 202, 204, 206, 220–21; Chicano, 19–20; collective, 23; cultural, 26, 143; feminist, 79, 81, 204; indigenous, 7, 18, 72, 94, 109, 164; lesbian, 88, 92, 99–100, 174–75, 204–6, 209; loss of, through assimilation, 85–86, 94, 164; male, 179; male writers' robbing of women's, 41–42; memory and, 23–24, 84–85; mestiza, 7, 84; Mexican ("Mexicanidad"), 58, 69, 72, 81, 101, 103–6, 109–14, 140–41, 143, 164, 186, 202, 204, 207, 216, 220, 233 n. 7; multiple, 3, 97; national, 224 n. 7; "nested," 3; sexuality and, 80, 91; as theme in Chicana art, 66; as theme in Chicana writings, 2, 5, 7, 42, 89–91, 162, 204–6; as theme in U.S. Mexicanas' oral histories, 5, 101–43, 202; of U.S. Mexicanas, 3–4, 24, 80–81, 83–84, 103–24, 200, 202–7, 211, 221; writers' shaping of, 1

Immaculate Conception, 57, 65, 104, 108–9, 111, 115–16

immigrants: Catholicism among, 106; illiteracy among, 203; sexual attitudes among, 115, 130–31; transnational migration and, 160–61, 169–70, 173, 218–20; undocumented, 52–53, 94, 211; U.S. communities of, 81–82, 129

indigenous peoples: author's use of term, instead of "Aztec," 8–10; Catholic conversion as aspect of conquering, 17–18, 55–56, 109–10, 207, 242 n. 20; culture of, as negated by conquerors, 207–8, 220, 225 n. 6; depiction of, in written texts, 72–73, 173–84, 225 n. 6, 228 n. 54; as extinct, 162, 207;

fieldwork with, 189–201, 249 n. 21, 249 n. 33; La Llorona legend and, 45–48, 50; Malintzin Tenepal and, 37–39, 41–43, 48, 50, 219; marginalization of, 72; oral texts by, 185; reclaiming heritage of, 24, 35, 42, 44–45, 60, 68–69, 72, 98–99, 171–79, 208, 212, 220; religions associated with, 207, 237 n. 52; resistance to Spanish conquest by, 43, 48, 161, 175, 225n. 6; siding of some, with Spanish conquerors, 9, 17, 34, 43; spirituality of, 68, 90, 237 n. 52, 239 n. 96, 242 n. 20; as term, 8–10; variety of, 220; La Virgen de Guadalupe as representing, 56–58, 102, 109. *See also* entries for specific groups

individual (vs. collective) struggles, 2, 94, 186–89, 202, 211–12

infanticide in La Llorona/Medea legend, 45–50, 52–53, 145–52, 155, 161–62, 164, 179, 181–83

infidelity: female, 155, 243 n. 34; male, 44–46, 48, 52, 130–31, 151–52, 154; marriage and, 88, 115–19, 123–24, 139–41, 148–50

intellectuals. *See* Chicana professional intellectuals

intermarriage, 16, 37, 40, 42, 44, 48, 152. *See also* mestiza/o people

Irigaray, Luce, 84–85, 90, 105, 125, 236 n. 48, 239 n. 96

Iroquois people, 236 n. 47

Jacobs, Barbara, 234 n. 14
Jameson, Elizabeth, 193
Jaramillo, Juan, 37
Jeffers, Robinson, 231 n. 99
Jesus, 64–65, 108, 121, 127–28, 138–39, 245 n. 62
Johnson, Elizabeth, 245 n. 62

Johnston, Sarah Iles, 46–47
Juana Inés de la Cruz, 18, 73–74, 234 n. 15
Juan Diego, 55–56, 58, 102, 108–10, 135, 207
Juárez (Mexico), 53–55

Kali, 89
Kaplan, Temma, 78
Karankawa people, 44
King, Katie, 77
Klein, Cecelia F., 29–30, 33–34
Klor de Alva, J. Jorge, 118
knives and swords, 60, 62, 67, 160, 169, 180
Kristeva, Julia, 238 n. 79
Krupat, Arnold, 185

Labyrinth of Solitude, The (Paz), 41
Lacandon people, 220
land: in Castillo's *Sapogonia*, 94; grants of, 37; in Moraga's *Hungry Woman*, 174–83; promised, 29, 31; rights to, 59, 72, 151, 174, 189, 216; U.S.'s appropriation of Mexican, 74; woman as metaphor for, 41, 175–76
language: author's use of, 8–9; English, 98, 146, 192, 195–98; as factor in oral history research, 191–92, 195–98; as factor in oral texts' marginalization, 185; Mayan, 37; Nahuatl, 9, 37, 40; Spanish, 37, 74–75, 98, 133, 146, 189, 195–96, 198–99, 202. *See also* translation
langue vs. *parole* moments, 108–9
Laredo (Tex.), 151
Last Generation, The (Moraga), 70, 95–97, 175, 181
Latina Feminist Group, 200
Latina Letters conference, 191
"lengua, la," 35, 37. *See also* Malintzin Tenepal

León, Carmen, 50–51, 162
León-Portillo, Miguel, 238 n. 81
lesbians: association of, with term "Chicana," 4; Catholic Church on, 88; fear of revealing identity of, 80; as identity associated with writers in this book, 88, 92, 99–100, 174–75, 204–6, 209; images associated with, 64–65, 100; lesbian feminism and, 78, 235 n. 30; Moraga on, 175–76, 178, 180; mothers among, 123, 176; oppression of, 71, 123–24; in second-wave feminism, 76, 78; in Villanueva's work, 168
Lienzo de Tlaxcala codex, 37–39
lieux de mémoire, 107, 109–13, 242 n. 20
Lilith (Judaic), 48, 231 n. 98
Limón, José, 150, 192–93, 241 n. 12, 242 n. 31, 244 n. 44
Lipsitz, George, 22–23
Literatura chicana (Castañeda Shuler et. al.), 74, 234 n. 15
"Little Miracles, Kept Promises" (Cisneros), 56, 98–99, 212
Llorona, La (Wailing/Weeping Woman): ambiguity of, 144–45; Anzaldúa and, 48–49, 51, 161, 231 n. 103; appeal of, 145, 216, 242 n. 23; article in name of, 8; author's interest in, 193; cautionary uses of legend of, 45–49, 121, 144–45, 155–56, 217; Chicana intellectuals' refiguring of, 10, 25–26, 48–55, 67, 69, 89, 145, 216–18; Cihua-coatl as, 160–61, 164, 173–175, 179, 181; Cisneros and, 49; faceless gaze of, 157–58; infanticide and, 45–50, 52–53, 145–52, 155, 161–62, 164, 179, 181–83; legend of, 45–46, 145–51; "Llorona moments" and, 145, 154–61, 184; La Malinche

and, 45–51, 174; Medea as, 173–83; as Mexican female cultural symbol, 6, 10, 26; Moraga and, 49, 161, 173–84; as La Muerte, 46, 153–54; in oral histories by U.S. Mexicanas, 10, 17, 136, 144–45; representations of, 13–14, 25, 49–55, 212; seashell of, 50–51, 162–66, 168, 170–73; U.S. Mexicanas' interest in refiguring of, 201; Villanueva and, 49–51, 161–73, 179; as woman of discord, 16, 18, 116
"Llorona, La / Weeping Woman" (Villanueva), 161–66
Llorona Desperately Seeking Coyolx-auhqui, La (Alma López), 54–55
Llorona Desperately Seeking Coyolx-auhqui in Juárez, La (Alma López), 53–54
"Llorona moments," 145, 154–61, 184
Llorona on the Longfellow Bridge, La (Gaspar de Alba), 53
Lloronas: mujeres que lean y escriben (Anzaldúa), 231 n. 103
Llorona II, La / The Weeping Woman (Barraza), 50
location, politics of: of Chicana professional intellectuals, 4, 204–6, 213–14; differences in, between author and U.S. Mexicanas, 205; differences in, among Chicana intellectuals and U.S. Mexicanas, 202–14; diverse change efforts produced by differences in, 6, 202, 205, 209–214; "in between" location, 213; between researcher and subjects, 213–14; of U.S. Mexicanas, 202, 205
López, Alma, 53–55, 66–68, 212, 217
López, Anna-Marie, 68, 217
López, Yolanda, 60–64, 140–41, 212, 217

López de Gómara, Francisco, 40, 228
n. 54, 229 n. 62
Lorde, Audre, 76, 91
Los Angeles, 52, 156
Loving in the War Years (Moraga), 71,
96, 188–89
Loya, Ventura, 2, 118–21, 142, 194–
95, 198, 211–12; on La Llorona,
156–61; on La Malinche, 39; on La
Virgen de Guadalupe, 102, 113–14,
139
Lucas, Maria Elena, 134–35, 188

MacArthur Fellowship, 247 n. 25
machismo, 93, 96, 130–31
Madsen, Catherine, 86
Maestrapeace muralist group, 25, 35–
36, 213
maguey plants, 25, 34, 43, 50
Mahoney, Martha, 246 n. 13
MALCS (Mujeres Activas en Letras y
Cambio Social), 81
Malinche, El (Cortés), 39
Malinche, La. *See* Malintzin Tenepal
Malinche, La (Barraza), 43, 50
"Malinche, La" (Tafolla), 43
Malinche: A Novel (Esquivel), 44
Malinche in Mexican Literature, La
(Cypess), 37
"malinches," 41, 98
Malinche's Daughter (Otero), 44–45
"malinchismo," 41
"malinchista," 39, 41, 98, 238 n. 66
Malintzin Tenepal (La Malinche):
Chicana intellectuals' refiguring
of, 10, 15, 17–18, 25–26, 42–45,
69, 89–90, 95, 182, 184, 218;
Cortés and, 15–16, 35, 37–41, 43,
45, 152, 228 n. 54, 229 n. 62;
daughter of, by Jaramillo, 37; as
Doña Marina, 40–42; "hijo de la
malinche" (derogatory), 39; indigenous peoples' representations of,
37; as "la lengua," 35, 37; La Llorona legend and, 45–51, 174; as
Mexican Eve, 41, 174; as Mexican
female cultural symbol, 6–7, 10,
26, 45, 55; names given to, 35, 37,
40–42; Paz and, 41–42, 65; representations of, 13–14, 37, 43–45, 55,
87; son of, by Cortés, 16, 37, 40,
42–43, 48, 152, 174, 178; as traitor,
18, 22, 35, 37, 39–41, 43, 116, 119,
132, 174, 238 n. 66; as transgressive, 45; translating done by, 35,
37–39, 42–43, 140; U.S. Mexicanas on, 39–40, 118–19, 140–41,
201, 208; in virgin/whore opposition with La Virgen, 41–42; as
woman of discord (historical), 15–
16, 35, 37–40, 45, 69, 140–41, 144,
152
mandas (promises of service), 56,
110–13
Maori research, 200, 250 n. 38
*Margaret F. Stewart: Our Lady of Gua-
dalupe* (Y. López), 60–62, 140, 212
Marin, Cheech, 20
marriage: as an institution, 80; intermarriage, 16, 37, 40, 42, 44, 48,
152; sexuality outside of, 88, 115–
18, 123–24, 139–41, 148–50, 243 n.
34
Martínez, Rubén, 106
Mary (mother of Jesus), 64–65, 98,
102, 108–9, 126, 138, 156; La Virgen de San Juan de los Lagos and,
103, 110–13, 242 n. 23. *See also* Virgen de Guadalupe, La
Mary Magdalene, 141–42
Massacre in Mexico (Poniatowska), 73
Massacre of the Dreamers (Castillo), 13,
75, 204
masturbation, 130

Matlaciuatl, 162

Maya people, 37, 50, 72, 94

Medea (in Corinthian and Greek mythology) 45, 47–49, 173–78, 230–31 nn. 98–99

Medea (Euripides), 48, 173–74, 179, 230–31 nn. 98–99

Meléndez, Theresa, 185

memory: collective, 23, 26–27, 40, 68–69, 88, 97, 105; as a counter-discourse, 14, 16, 20, 27, 212; cultural, 92, 162–63, 207; as history's counterpart, 21–28; of indigenous goddesses, 24, 76, 84–85, 207–8, 210, 212, 221; racial, 91; repression of, 24, 72; sites of, 107, 109–13, 242 n. 20; transformation of, through art, 25–27, 68–69

men: absence of, in Yolanda López's images, 61, 64; as betrayers of women, 44–46, 48, 52, 130–31, 151–52, 154; fear of women's power by, 93; homosexuality among, 123–24, 178, 194, 244 n. 49; lesbians as threat to, 88; La Llorona legend and, 152–54; Malintzin Tenepal portrayed as having renounced indigenous, 41; memory and, 22–23; Mexican writers among, 41, 65, 73–74, 202, 244 n. 49; as Mexica rulers, 15, 42–43; women as antitheses of, 28. *See also* Chicano nationalism; gender roles; patriarchy

Menchú, Rigoberto, 35

Mensajeras de Salud (Messengers of Health), 80–81, 124, 129–33, 191, 196, 199, 211

"Mestiza Aesthetics and Chicana Painterly Visions" (Romo), 20

"mestiza consciousness" (Anzaldúa), 84

mestiza/o people, 7, 94; aesthetic of, 20; Anzaldúa on, 84, 97, 212; La Llorona depicted as, 48, 50; Malintzin Tenepal and Hernán Cortés's son as first of, 16, 37, 40, 42, 48; marginalization of, 20, 22; reclaiming heritage of, 45, 68–69, 98–99; in the United States, 75; "la virgen morena" as representing, 56, 102, 109. *See also* Chicana intellectuals; indigenous peoples; U.S. Mexicanas

Metamorphoses (Ovid), 239 n. 84

"Mexicanidad" (Mexicanness), 58, 69, 72, 81, 101, 103–6, 109–14, 140–41, 143, 164, 186, 202, 204, 207, 216, 220, 233 n. 7

Mexican Revolution, 22–23, 40, 59, 227 n. 33, 242 n. 25

Mexica people: cyclical conception of history and cosmology of, 14–15, 28; dominance of, in central plateau region, 16, 28; as faction of Chichimecas, 28; history of, 9, 14–17, 25, 28–29, 32–34, 42–43, 225 n. 6; human sacrifice during rule of, 25, 28, 30–33, 93; migrations of, 28–31; patriarchy among, 34, 43, 45, 54, 70, 89, 175; queens of, 15; symbols of, 42–43, 103–4, 180–81; temples of, 31; as a term in this work, 9; wars of, 9, 17, 25, 32–33, 40–41, 43, 95. *See also* Aztlan; goddesses; Tenochtitlan

Mexico: author's experience of, 193; dual citizenship in, 98; government repression in, 72–73, 172, 220; independence of, from Spain, 17, 40, 59; La Malinche as scapegoat in republican narratives in, 18; nationalism in, 40–41; racism in, 207; revolution in, 22–23, 40, 59,

Paz, Octavio, 41–42, 65, 73–74, 244 n. 49

Pérez, Domino Renee, 161

Pérez, Irene, 35

Pesquera, Beatriz M., 235 n. 25

Peterson, Jeanette Favrot, 58–59

petición (petition for help), 110–13, 138

"Plan Espiritual de Aztlán, El," 23

Plaskow, Judith, 87

Pleasure and Danger: Exploring Female Sexuality (anthology), 77

Poniatowska, Elena, 72–74, 234 nn. 14–15

Poole, Stafford, 58, 227 n. 29

"popular religiosity," 104–12, 241 n. 9

Portillo Trambley, Estela, 233 n. 13

Portrait of the Artist as the Virgin of Guadalupe (Y. López): 61, 63

Poteet (Tex.), 150–51

power: Chicanas' and U.S. Mexicanas' representations of, through female cultural symbols, 7, 16–17, 35, 42–45, 49, 60–64, 82, 183–84, 216–18; feminist spirituality as erotic, 87–88; relations of, in fieldwork, 10, 189–201; understanding of, by different feminisms, 71; women's efforts to achieve, 1–2, 5–7, 20–21, 81–82, 84–101, 159–61, 185–201, 210–16, 218–19. *See also* oppressions; resistance

Powers of Desire: The Politics of Sexuality (anthology), 77

Pratt, Mary Louise, 43

PRI (Mexican political party), 114

Prietita and the Ghost Woman / Prietita y La Llorona (Anzaldúa), 49, 51; by different name, 231 n. 103

professional intellectuals (defined), 4. *See also* Chicana professional intellectuals

prostitute. *See* puta

Protestant religions, 87, 239 n. 96

Puerto Ricans, 192, 200

pulque, 25

purification rituals, 46–47, 180

puta (prostitute), 90, 116, 120, 153–54, 163–64, 167

Quetzalcoatl, 9, 24, 91–92

Quetzalpetlatl (the Precious One), 91–92, 246 n. 17

race: affirmation of, 188, 204; contesting dominant narratives of, 20; as factor in oral history fieldwork, 190–91, 193–94; intersectionality of, 13, 204; La Llorona as mixed-race, 48; Malintzin Tenepal as symbol of syncretism of races, 40, 42; mestiza/os as mixture of races, 16; pleasure in raced bodies, 89; survived discrimination against, 61; U.S. Mexicanas identity, 81

racism: of Catholic Church, 20, 241 n. 9; charges of, against Chicana school teachers, 21; Chicana/o civil rights movement's opposition to, 4; Chicanas' and U.S. Mexicanas' exposure to, 1, 69, 75, 96, 104, 121, 133, 150–51, 153–54, 188, 193–94, 204, 212; denial of indigenous heritage due to, 207–8; against "Indians," 207–8; internalized, 153–54, 163–64; of Mexican government, 72; of Mexican women writers toward Chicana writers, 75; opposition to, as theme in Chicana writings, 1, 70, 75, 85, 163, 206, 215, 237 n. 63; overcoming, as theme in artwork, 60; of second-wave feminism, 76–77

Randall, Margaret F., 242 n. 30

rape. *See* violence against women

Rebolledo, Tey Diana, 64, 155, 186, 229 n. 86, 245 n. 62

refiguring. *See* cultural refiguring

regulation: cultural symbols' role in, 10, 48–49, 98, 145–51, 184; of women's lives, 1, 114–43, 181–82. *See also* La Llorona: cautionary uses of legend of; sexuality (female): efforts to control

re-membering, 25, 91, 95–96, 172

reproduction: continuous, 157; cycles in, 15, 46; formal education about, 118; as sole purpose of sex, 115, 117, 121, 123, 130. *See also* birth control; childbirth

reproductive demons, 46–47, 49, 155, 180, 184, 230 n. 98. *See also* Cihuatateo

resistance: to assimilation, 8, 69, 104–6, 111, 115, 121, 204; by Chicanas and U.S. Mexicanas to efforts to confine them, 1–2, 5–6, 18, 69, 71, 79–84, 125–43, 186–89, 216–19; to continuous reproduction, 157; genealogical precedents for, 14–16, 18–19, 42, 45, 68–69, 71, 82, 160; indigenous goddesses as inspiring women's, 10, 17, 27, 73, 88, 95–96, 144, 167, 208, 218–19; by indigenous groups to Mexica wars, 9, 17, 43; individual vs. collective, 2, 186–89, 202, 211–12; among lesbian feminists, 78; La Llorona as inspiring women's, 10, 17, 26–27, 45–55, 144–45, 155–56, 162–63, 183–84; La Malinche as inspiring women's, 10, 17, 26–27, 45, 49, 55, 140, 144, 208, 218–19; narrative strategies demonstrating, 94, 192; as recovery of the lost, 84–85; to Spanish conquest, 16, 43, 47–48, 161, 175,

225 n. 6; tattoos as, 64, 100; La Virgen de Guadalupe as inspiring, 10, 17, 55–69, 103, 114, 125–26, 134–44. *See also* cultural refiguring; feminism; woman of discord

"return of the repressed" (Rousso) 22, 68

Riessman, Catherine Kohler, 192

Rio Grande, 54, 218

Rio Verde, 157

Rivera Reyes, Vicki, 2, 110–14, 116–18, 224 n. 5; on La Llorona, 148–49, 161; on La Virgen de Guadalupe, 102, 104–5

Rodríguez, Jeanette, 103, 135, 241 n. 9

Rodríguez, Olga, 241 n. 9

Romo, Tere, 20

Romo-Carmona, Mariana, 123

Rousso, Henry: "return of the repressed" concept of, 22, 68

Ruether, Rosemary Radford, 88

Rupp, Leila, 78, 237 n. 63

Russo, Ann, 247 n. 23

sacrifice, 94; of goddesses in Mexica historical accounts, 28, 95; human, during Mexica rule, 25, 27–28, 30–33, 93; in La Llorona / La Malinche legend, 48, 179–80; mandas to La Virgen de Guadalupe and, 56, 110–13, 138; of woman of discord, 15–16, 19, 28

Said, Edward, 224 n. 7

saints, 108, 113, 139–40

Salinas, Raquel, 66

San Antonio (Tex.), 2, 68, 111, 151, 191, 213, 217

Sánchez, Rosaura, 243 n. 36

sanctuary movement, 94

Sandoval, Chela, 71; "differential consciousness" concept of, 83–85

Siqueiros, Cindy, 2, 102–4, 121–23, 194, 212
slaves: Malintzin Tenepal as slave, 37, 39–40, 43, 45, 228 nn. 54–55; in Morrison's *Beloved*, 48; narratives by, 187–88
Smith, Linda Tuhiwai, 200
Smith, Sidonie, 116, 126, 244 n. 43
snakes. *See* serpents
soldaderas, las, 22–23, 40, 184
Soto, Shirlene, 48–49
South Texas, 150–51, 153–54
Spain, 17, 40, 59
Spanish conquest: Catholic conversion as aspect of, 17–18, 55–56, 109–10, 207, 242 n. 20; destruction of Mexica history during, 31, 225 n. 6; documents from, on Malintzin Tenepal, 35, 37; indigenous groups siding with Spain during, 9, 17, 34, 43; intermarriage during, 16, 37, 40, 42, 44, 48, 152; La Llorona as warning of, 16, 47; Malintzen-related metaphors for, 41, 50; Mexica as ruling group at time of, 9; patriarchal legacy of, 45; resistance to, 16, 43, 47–48, 161, 175, 225 n. 6; in Villanueva's work, 162; violence of, 18. *See also* Cortés, Hernán
spirituality: representations of, by Chicana feminists, 10, 65–66, 68–76, 84–101, 105, 168–69, 212–14, 239 n. 96. *See also* Catholic Church; divinity; goddesses
Spivak, Gayatri, 251 n. 5
Stanton, Elizabeth Cady, 78
stereotypes: Mensajeras de Salud's breaking of, 80; in official histories, 14, 42; about La Virgen de Guadalupe, 60–61, 64–65. *See also* racism

swords and knives, 60, 62, 67, 160, 169, 180
symbols, 50, 59, 108; semiotics, 10, 107–9, 113–14, 135–37, 166. *See also* cultural symbols

Tabascan people, 37
Tableaux Vivant: Guadalupe Series (Y. López): 61, 63
Tafolla, Carmen, 43
Takaki, Ronald, 239 n. 96
Talking Back (D. Castillo), 73
Taller de Literatura Feminina Mexicana, 73
Tamoanchán, 177
Tarahumara people, 220
tattoos, 24, 50, 54, 64, 100, 105
Taube, Karl, 33
Taylor, Verta, 78, 237 n. 63
television, 19–20, 52–53
Telling to Live: Latina Feminist Testimonios (anthology), 200, 206
Templo Mayor, 31–32
Tenayuca, Emma, 18
Tenochca people, 9. *See also* Mexica
Tenochtitlan (Mexica capital), 9, 16, 29, 31, 43, 55, 109, 220
Teotihuacan, 9
Teotl (Barraza), 50
Tepeyac (Mexico), 56, 58, 98–99, 107, 109, 110, 113
Tepoztlán (Mexico), 70
Terdiman, Richard, 13, 26
Teresa de Ávila, 139–40
testimonio (testimony), 73, 98, 187–89, 200. *See also* oral histories
Texas Rangers, 226 n. 26
This Bridge Called My Back (Moraga and Anzaldúa), 71, 77
Time Passages (Lipsitz), 22
Tixier y Vigil, Yvonne, 193–94
Tizaapan, 29

Tlazolteotl, 89–90, 97, 227 n. 40

Toci. *See* Tonantzin

Todorov, Tzvetan, 37–38

Tolteca people (Culhuacan), 9, 24, 29, 72, 225 n. 6

Tomochiteco people, 220

Tonantzin (Toci/Tonan), 27–30, 33, 97, 207; La Virgen de Guadalupe as associated with, 16, 28, 34, 56, 58, 66, 68, 89–90, 98–100, 102

"Towards a Politics of Sexuality" (conference), 77

"trans-coding" (Hall), 14, 218

transgressions: woman of discord and, 15, 26, 218–19. *See also* resistance

translation: Malintzin Tenepal's, for Cortés, 35, 37–39, 42–43, 140; in transcribing oral histories, 5, 195–96, 249 n. 33; of women writers' works, 73–75, 234 n. 15

transnational migration, 109, 160, 170, 173, 218–19

Traub, Valerie, 93, 96

Trujillo, Carla, 64, 88, 118

Tucson, 241 n. 14; cancer prevention efforts in, 5, 80–81, 126–27, 129–33, 191, 196, 199, 211, 215; oral histories from, 2, 105–6, 191

Turner, Edith, 242 n. 31

Turner, Kay F., 107–9, 113, 135, 242 n. 26

Turner, Victor, 242 n. 31

Tzeltal people (Mayan), 220

Tzotzil people (Mayan), 220

Ultraviolet Sky, The (Villanueva), 91–94, 160, 164–65, 172, 247 n. 28

"Undocumented Virgin, The" (Martínez), 106

United Farm Workers, 134–35, 226 n. 26; symbols associated with, 50, 59, 105

United States: American Dream in, 153–54, 169; appropriation of Mexican land by, 74; first-wave feminism in, 78; immigration authorities in, 52; nationalism of, 175; U.S. Mexicanas' residency in, 3–4, 186, 196

universalizing. *See* essentialism

University of Minnesota, 20

Urias, Virginia, 2, 123–24, 131–33, 142, 188, 196, 198–99, 211, 237 n. 52; on La Llorona, 146–48; on La Virgen de Guadalupe, 102, 105–6, 127–29, 139

Urrea, Teresa, 18

U.S. Mexicanas: Catholic affiliation of, 59, 101, 103–4, 106, 125, 133–34, 206, 211; cultural refiguring by, 5–7, 10, 16, 20–21, 26, 45, 68–69, 102–61, 189, 201–2, 209, 211, 215; defined, 3–4; education of, 4, 115, 141, 155, 202–3, 207–8, 211–12, 246 n. 64; not identifying as "Chicana," 68, 202, 204; identity of, 3–4, 24, 68, 80–81, 83–84, 103–24, 200, 202–7, 211, 221; as labor activists, 18, 125, 134–35, 226 n. 13; knowledge of, about indigenous goddesses, 201, 206–10, 213, 216, 220; knowledge of, about Malintzin Tenepal, 39–40, 118–19, 140–41, 201, 208; "Llorona moments" experienced by, 145, 154–61, 184; La Llorona stories by, 10, 17, 136, 144–45; social class of, 2–3, 8, 202–5; La Virgen de Guadalupe embraced by, 7, 10, 60, 69, 199, 201–2, 206–7, 210, 216–18, 237 n. 52; La Virgen de Guadalupe's refiguring by, 26, 59, 69, 114,

images of, in this work 57, 62–63, 67; women's personal experiences with, 102–3, 107–10, 113, 126, 136–38, 211–12

Virgen de Guadalupe Defendiendo Los Derechos De Los Xicanos, La (Hernández), 60, 66

Virgen de San Juan de los Lagos, La, 103, 110–13, 242 n. 23

Virgin (Anna-Marie López), 68

virgins, 124–25, 243 nn. 34–35; concerns about not being, 115–19; mothers as, 65, 104, 108–9, 111, 114–16; refiguring of, 168; virgin/whore split, 90

visual texts (artworks): Chicana intellectuals' marginalization in exhibits of, 19–20; on Chicana/o civil rights movement, 23; cultural refiguring through, 16, 23–24, 34, 43–45, 50–55, 61–68, 136, 140–41, 217, 219; gods and goddesses in, 9, 16, 23–25; La Llorona images in, 50–55, 212; La Malinche images in, 38, 43–44, 140; Mexican female cultural symbols in, 10, 14; role of, in this book, 2; themes of, 1, 105, 212; La Virgen de Guadalupe images in, 25, 60–66, 68, 136, 212, 217. *See also* specific artists and works

voice: absence of Malintzin Tenepal's, from historical record, 35, 43; cultural refiguring as giving, to feminists, 49, 84–85, 97, 135–36; multiple voices in published oral histories, 5; representations of U.S. Mexicanas', in this study, 8, 197; of Teresa de Ávila, 139–40. *See also* oral texts; silence

volunteer work, 5–7, 10, 16, 114, 126, 202, 209, 211, 215

vulva, 97, 99–100

Wailing/Weeping Woman. *See* La Llorona

Waiting in the Wings: Portrait of a queer motherhood (Moraga), 244 n. 51

War of Independence, Mexican (1810), 17, 40, 59, 225 n. 13

wars: childbirth likened to, 29, 46, 61, 91, 160; Mexica, 9, 17, 25, 32–33, 40, 46, 61, 91, 95, 160. *See also* Mexican Revolution; Spanish conquest

water imagery, 45–46, 145–47, 151, 155, 157, 179; seashell of La Llorona, 50–51, 162–66, 168, 170–73

Weaving the Visions: New Patterns in Feminist Spirituality (anthology), 87

Weeping Woman (León), 50–51

Weeping Woman: La Llorona and Other Stories (Villanueva), 49–51, 161–73, 179

Weisman Art Museum, 20

Wicca, 168

Winter's Tale, A (Shakespeare), 93

Wolf, Diane L., 249 n. 19

"Woman Hollering Creek" (Cisneros), 49, 167

Woman Hollering Creek and Other Stories (Cisneros), 49, 98–99, 167

woman of discord: Chicana intellectuals as 16, 19, 86–88; in Chicana intellectuals' works, 86, 166, 180; description of, 15–16, 18–19; discourse of, 17, 19–21; as example for feminists, 68–69, 84; female cultural symbols as, 16, 28–29, 34, 45, 86, 161, 175, 184, 218; genealogy of, 16, 18–19, 25, 71, 82, 160, 173, 218; La Llorona and La Virgen de Guada-

woman of dischord (*continued*)
lupe as, 15–16, 18, 166; Malintzin
Tenepal as historical, 15–16, 35,
37–40, 69, 140–41, 144, 152; in
Mexica history, 14–16; structural
equivalents of, 15–16, 43, 66, 68,
100, 102, 125; power of, 15–16; plurality and opposition represented
by, 15–16, 83; as repeating cycle,
15–16; as transgressive women, 15,
26, 218–19; U.S. Mexicanas and
Chicanas as, 16, 18–19, 87–88
woman's culture: in Chicana intellectuals' works, 71, 82–83; debates of
second-wave feminism and, 72, 76;
Chicana and U.S. Mexicana sites
of, 78, 83; thinking in Villanueva,
167–68
women: as abusers, 163–64; as
exploited workers and labor activists, 18, 54, 75, 115, 125, 134–35, 151,
188–89, 226 n. 13; as gods, 34, 65,
70, 84–85, 90, 95, 104–5, 113, 125,
135, 141, 212; marginalization of,
19–20, 22, 40, 65, 69, 75, 78, 81–
82, 85, 223 n. 4, 234 n. 15; as metaphor for nations, 175–76; older, in
Mexican/Chicano culture, 244 n.
52; oral histories as associated
with, 185; real, depicted as La Virgen de Guadalupe, 60–64; risks
taken by, as oral history inter-
viewees, 191–92, 194–95; stories
about female relatives in Chicana
intellectuals' works, 186, 188–89;
La Virgen de Guadalupe as representing the ideal for, 18, 42, 48, 57,
59, 64–65, 95–96, 103–5, 113–29,
135, 139, 141, 216–17. *See also* Chicana professional intellectuals;

feminism; gender oppression; gender roles; goddesses; lesbians;
mothers; U.S. Mexicanas; violence
against women
Women in the State of Grace (Chávez),
65, 243 n. 32
working class: author's background
in, 190–91; Chicana professional
intellectuals' backgrounds in, 4, 73,
75, 205–6; defined, 2–3; U.S. Mexicanas as, 2–3, 8, 82, 101, 201–5;
La Virgen de Guadalupe's relevance to, 10, 17, 60, 102
written texts: cultural refiguring
through, 6, 16, 42, 44–45, 49–51,
64–66, 145, 161–84, 212–14, 219;
gods and goddesses in Chicana
intellectuals', 9, 70–76, 86–101,
161–84; Mexican vs. Chicana, 72–
76; oral histories' transformation
to, 4–5, 10–11, 195–98; oral texts'
marginalization by, 185–86; role
of, in this book, 2; as testimonios,
187–89, 200; themes of, 1–2, 5–7,
19, 23, 73, 86–93, 97, 168, 205–6,
209, 217–18; U.S. Mexicanas' lack
of familiarity with, by Chicanas, 3,
202. *See also* entries for specific
authors and titles

Xicanas (term), 68
Xicoténcatl (anonymous novel), 18
Xilotepec, 37
Xochimeh, Tlahtoki, 224 n. 10

Yaqui people, 92, 94, 109, 172–73,
220, 242 n. 25

Zapata, Emiliano, 59
Zavella, Patricia, 193
Zinn, Maxine Baca, 125

❀ DEBRA J. BLAKE

teaches in the departments of

Chicano studies and English at

the University of Minnesota.

Library of Congress Cataloging-in-Publication
Data
Blake, Debra J., 1955–
Chicana sexuality and gender : cultural
refiguring in literature, oral history, and art /
Debra J. Blake.
p. cm.
Includes bibliographical references and index.
ISBN 978-0-8223-4294-6 (cloth : alk. paper)
ISBN 978-0-8223-4310-3 (pbk. : alk. paper)
1. Mexican American women—Attitudes.
2. Mexican American women—Sexual behavior.
3. Mexican American women—Ethnic identity.
4. Mexican American women—Interviews.
5. Mexican American women authors—
Interviews. 6. Mexican American women
artists—Interviews. 7. Feminism—United
States. I. Title.
HQ1166.B53 2008
305.48′86872073—dc22